Ex Libris

W.T. Binford, Jr.

Millennialism:
The Two Major Views

Millennialism: The Two Major Views

*The Premillennial and Amillennial
Systems of Biblical Interpretation
Analyzed & Compared*

Third and Enlarged Edition

CHARLES L. FEINBERG, Th.D., Ph.D.
*Dean Emeritus and Professor of Semitics and Old Testament
Talbot Theological Seminary
La Mirada, California*

MOODY PRESS
CHICAGO

Copyright © 1936, 1954, 1961, 1980 by
THE MOODY BIBLE INSTITUTE
OF CHICAGO
Revised Edition

Original title: PREMILLENNIALISM OR AMILLENNIALISM?

Library of Congress Cataloging in Publication Data
Feinberg, Charles Lee.
    Millennialism, the two major views.

    First-2d ed. published under title:
Premillennialism or amillennialism?
    Bibliography: p.
    1. Millennialism.   I. Title.
BT891. F44   1980   236'.3
ISBN 0-8024-6815-2

Printed in the United States of America

TABLE OF CONTENTS

Foreword to the First Edition

Dr. Lewis Sperry Chafer
Late President, Dallas Theological Seminary

There has been a millennial question among Biblical interpreters ever since speculative theologians began to take liberty with the Scriptures, either by a "spiritualizing" system of interpretation or by an utter neglect of the plain teaching of the Bible. Of the three contentions—postmillennialism, amillennialism and premillennialism, or as the latter was known in the early centuries from the Greek designation, chiliasm—postmillennialism is dead. Whether the present insane, corrupt condition of the world killed the theory by the contradiction of its own developing character, or whether the more intensified study of prophetic truth in these latter times so magnified its inconsistencies that it died, future historians must determine.

To say that postmillennialism is dead, is not to imply that it does not occupy a large place in historical theology, nor that its theories are not found in theological works which were written in the days when eschatology was handed down practically without change from generation to generation and before the benefits which accrue to it from fresh analyses of Scripture were enjoyed. But it is dead in the sense that it offers no living voice in its own defense when the millennial question is under discussion.

Amillennialism can set up no claim of being an entirely new system in this agelong controversy; but until recent times it has been too feeble to be classified. Apparently it has gained much through a blood transfusion which cost postmillennialism its life. At no time, however, could this sustaining blood stream, either when giving life to postmillennialism or later to amillennialism, be said to be rich in the vitalizing elements of the Word of God.

Amillennialism has produced a very inadequate literature, partly due to its own limited scope. The theory is held principally by seminarians who delete from their courses of study nearly all that which belongs to a full-orbed eschatology, and which should include the whole field of prophecy with its revelatory testimony concerning the destiny of all things. It should be pointed out, however, that the teaching of seminarians of this class is not characterized alone by an emasculated eschatology which eliminates a large portion of the revealed program of God in all the ages. It fails also to meet the demands presented in the field of the Pauline doctrine of the true church; in the field of practical conduct in relation to doctrine, and the specific claims of God upon people of different dispensations; in the field of angelology which includes the most vital doctrines of demonology and Satanology; in the field of typology with its divinely wrought illustrations of living truth; and in the field of the present priestly ministry of Christ in heaven with its unique benefit to the believer.

During the last two generations, particularly, the unprecedented investigation and study of the prophetic Scriptures, in which many scholars of first rank have taken part, has resulted in illuminating contributions to the premillennial interpretation of the Scriptures. The fact also has been uncovered that this interpretation was the unquestioned belief of the prophets, apostles, and Early Church fathers. The teaching by some conservative scholars that chiliasm was a heresy of the first century has been effectually exploded. Modern critics who are not concerned with the truth or falsity of the Biblical testimony are united in including the New Testament writers with the "early Christians" who taught the premillennial view. Moreover, during this period of intensive study a great company of devout believers, loyal to the Word of God and devoted to the missionary evangelization of the world, have been happy to accept this teaching of the Scriptures as well as all other revealed truth.

Dr. Feinberg is peculiarly qualified to discuss the problems presented in this volume. He is a Hebrew, having been reared in a strictly orthodox Jewish home, and for many years received training in the Hebrew language and the Old Testament with rabbinical service in view. He therefore knows the Scripture grounds for the Jewish hope. Since his conversion to Christ he has completed an extensive discipline in Christian theology, majoring in a systematic theology which includes the divinely taught distinction between Israel and the Church. He not only recognizes that all Jewish promises and covenants are secured forever by the oath of Jehovah (including the predicted kingdom reign of Christ on earth, and the everlasting glory for Israel following in the new earth to come), but in the present age God has placed both Jew and Gentile on the same level of responsibility and privilege in order that from these two sources He might gather out a people whose destiny is heavenly and whose glory is that of the Lord Himself.

The material contained in this book was presented to me as professor of Systematic Theology in the Evangelical Theological College [now Dallas Theological Seminary] in part fulfillment of the requirements for the degree of Doctor of Theology. The author has so thoroughly clarified the subject and thereby met a great need at the present time in the theological world, that I have been constrained to suggest that it be published in book form, and the commendation of this work by me is a genuine pleasure.

Preface to the First Edition

When setting out to write on this subject, it was not our intention to add to the vast literature on the premillennial view. It was not even our purpose to refute at length the amillennial view, although such a refutation had never been attempted to our knowledge. Furthest, to be sure, was it from our mind to indulge those who are seeking for sensational discussions of the themes of prophetic truth. Indeed, our only aim was to satisfy our own thinking on the premillennial view. The question that occurred to us was, Can it really stand the test at all times and at all points? To our delight and satisfaction we feel we can bear witness that the position is an impregnable one, because it is the only one that is consistently true to the entire Word of God. If we seem to have made much of the millennium and comparatively little of the return of the Lord, let it be remembered that both views accept His return, although they differ as to those events that take place after His coming. We are confident that to the heart of the believer who is waiting daily for the coming of our Lord Jesus Christ, this discussion will come, not as a superfluous consideration on this important subject, but as a most welcome presentation of the truth. "Amen. Even so, come, Lord Jesus."

Charles L. Feinberg
Dallas, Texas

Foreword to the Second Edition

Alva J. McClain, Th.M., D.D., LL.D.
Former President, Grace Theological Seminary

The battles of theology too often have been fought not only in what Dr. Patton once called a "condition of low visibility," but also against opponents who are dead and whose literature has been relegated to the back shelves of the libraries or to the trash heap. This is especially true of the millennial controversy. And it is one of the chief excellencies of Professor Feinberg's book that it brings the battle up to date. This is especially true of the massive Appendix which the author has now added to his original edition of 1936. He tilts with no forgotten foes, but deals with current issues and, in the main, with living men.

The timely nature of this book can best be stated in the words of the late President Lewis Sperry Chafer: "Post-millennialism is dead . . . in the sense that it offers no living voice in its own defense when the millennial question is under discussion." The present inheritors of the postmillennial burden, having found that load too heavy to be borne successfully, have attempted to lighten the burden and shorten the line of battle by scuttling in its entirety the idea of a future Millennium. Hence the appropriate name of this eschatological system, "amillennialism," with which Dr. Feinberg deals in his book. If there has been any shifting of position since 1936, it appears that the proponents of the system, by their increasingly *anti*-millennial attitudes, have more clearly than ever provided ample justification for Dr. Feinberg's main thesis.

The author's approach and method is primarily biblical; that is, his appeal is to Scripture rather than to subsequent church Fathers and scholarly opinion, although the latter is not ignored. On the basis of the "more sure word of prophecy," he refutes the superficial charge that Premillennialism depends upon a single passage in Revelation, or even upon a series of carefully chosen proof-texts, and shows its foundation to be the entire eschatological scheme of the Old and New Testaments with their related doctrines. When one has finished this book, he will see more clearly that the difference between Premillennialism and its opponents is no mere hair-splitting controversy of speculative theologians, but a dividing of paths which logically leads to two different

] 13 [

systems of thought. Fortunately for the Church, not all the dissenters have followed the logic of their own positions.

Recognizing frankly at the outset that the basic difference arises out of differing methods of interpretation, Dr. Feinberg begins with a discussion of the principles of biblical interpretation. His exposition and defense of literal interpretation is sound and reasonable, presenting none of the usual vulnerabilities. Assuming the complete inspiration of all Scripture, he repudiates the two most common demands of modern biblical criticism; namely, that the interpreter must wait for the critic to determine the validity of any particular text of the Bible; and second, that progress in revelation involves error in at least earlier stages of the process. Yet he observes rightly that the acid of historical criticism has actually helped to settle the question of interpretation in favor of the premillennialist view. For the critics had no inhibitions regarding the millennial problem. Feeling no obligation whatever to accept the divine authority of Scripture in the settlement of such matters, they were generally willing to let the Bible say whatever it said. The admission of Davidson is especially frank: "There is no question as to the meaning of Old Testament prophecies," he writes. "Their meaning is the literal sense of their words." Then he adds a significant qualification, "The question is how far this meaning is now valid." On this latter point, Dr. Feinberg appeals to history as an irrefutable argument: "The only way to know how God will fulfill prophecy in the future, is to ascertain how He had done it in the past."

Following the introductory section, the book consists of three main parts. First, there is an analysis of the premillennial system of eschatology, in which the author makes a rapid survey of the whole field of Kingdom prophecy from Genesis to Revelation. The second part presents an analysis of the amillennial system as set forth in the writings of its modern exponents, chiefly those of Vos, Masselink, and Wyngaarden. The third main part of the book lays the two systems side by side for purposes of comparison and contrast. To this able and excellent treatment, Dr. Feinberg in his second edition has now added a very large and fully documented Appendix, in which he brings the discussion completely up to date. Here the arguments, attacks, and inconsistencies of recent amillennial authors are handled with great apologetical acuteness. And as to those who with myopic carelessness are now counseling the surrender of certain premillennial positions, Dr. Feinberg warns of the possibility of throwing out the baby with the bath.

An immense amount of ground is touched in the argument, yet the author never loses sight of the constructive and positive purpose of his work. "We shall be satisfied," he remarks, "if we shall have proved by the end of the study that the premillennial view is harmonious, self-consistent, and, above all, based upon the infallible authority of the Scriptures."

The author is to be commended especially for his general attitude toward those Premillennialists who may differ with him in minor points. In this he shows his confidence in the soundness of the general position taken, and also his lack of fear that his argument can be overthrown by any small skirmishes among friends.

The book has many excellencies. While scrupulously fair to the critics of the premillennial view which he defends, the author demolishes some of the straw men set up by them: such as, for example, that the premillennialist believes in two ways of salvation, and in three second comings. He also insists upon the literality of prophetic number without absolutely excluding a possible symbolic meaning. He reveals his independence as an interpreter of the Word in abandoning the popular meanings attached to certain texts. On this point, compare his very sensible interpretation of Daniel 12:4, which gives some due consideration to the context. In replying to the amillennial criticism of the so-called "postponement theory" of the kingdom, namely, that such a theory makes the Cross of Christ uncertain, Dr. Feinberg frankly acknowledges the problem and also rightly points out that the problem is not new but only a recurrence of the ancient one having to do with the divine sovereignty versus human responsibility. It is quite astonishing, in my opinion, that any competent theologian should ever have raised this problem as an argument against the premillennial position. Since it has been raised, the author deals with it patiently, effectively.

Looking at the matter from the theological standpoint, it sometimes appears that we live in a rather superficial era. Men are saying they accept Christianity but reject prophecy. This book shows clearly that no such final distinction can be drawn; for all of Christianity was at one time nothing but eschatology. The sole difference between the two at the present moment is that what is generally called Christianity is now *fulfilled* prophecy, the other, prophecy *unfilled*.

In conclusion, it should be said that Dr. Feinberg has drawn the issue sharply, with no attempt to blur or evade the vital problems. For this he deserves the commendation of all who believe in the merit of frank discussion, regardless of theological bias. And to many who have given careful thought to the prophetic Word, his work will deepen a growing conviction that between the position of Premillennialism and that of complete skepticism regarding the future there is no permanent resting place for the human mind.

His book is also concrete evidence that in some quarters at least the vast field of biblical eschatology is being given serious consideration, not merely as a somewhat troublesome problem to be explained as the addenda to a theological system, but rather a vital part of the Christian faith itself, representing the embodiment of all our Christian hopes and aspirations.

Preface to the Second Edition

Far beyond our expectation the Lord has graciously blessed the first edition of this work published in 1936. Although many extended articles and refutations have been written against it, nevertheless many have been the expressions of blessing and edification from various sources. The first edition has long been exhausted, and requests have come repeatedly for a reprinting of the material. It was felt that, rather than recast the original material in a second edition, it would serve a better purpose to incorporate the new material in an appendix, which has become almost as lengthy as a volume of its own.

No one can consider and study such lofty themes of Scripture without resultant blessing. Our heart has been repeatedly refreshed and challenged. It has been a constant joy to realize that the tried and tested position of the premillennial system is impregnable. Too many are trying small skirmishes in guerrilla warfare instead of an all-out frontal attack. The premillennial view withstands them with force.

Acknowledgements with thanks are herewith made to the following publishers for permission to quote from their publications:

Marshall, Morgan & Scott, Ltd.: *The Approaching Advent of Christ,* by Alexander Reese.

Staples Press, Ltd.: *The Israel Promises and Their Fulfillment,* by S. H. Wilkinson.

Oosterbaan & Le Cointre N. V.: *Premillennialism in America,* by W. H. Rutgers.

Interpretation: Dispensationalism and the Covenant of Grace, by J. E. Bear.

Dallas Theological Seminary: published and unpublished material as indicated in the bibliography of the appendix.

Earl Miller: *The Kingdom of God and the Kingdom of Heaven,* by E. Miller.

Loizeaux Brothers, Inc.: *Amillennialism,* by R. J. Reid.

Mennonite Publishing House: *The Fulfillment of Prophecy,* by C. K. Lehman.

Sunday School Times: "Israel and the Church in Prophecy," by W. M. Smith.

Baker Book House: *Millennial Studies,* by G. L. Murray.

Bible Truth Depot: *A Candid Examination of the Scofield Bible,* by A. Pieters.

The Presbyterian and Reformed Publishing Co.: *Prophecy and the Church*, by O. T. Allis.

Faber & Faber, Ltd.: *The Throne of David*, by A. G. Hebert.

Wm. B. Eerdmans Publishing Co.: *Systematic Theology* and *The Kingdom of God*, by L. Berkhof; *Christian Theology*, by P. B. Fitzwater; *The Basis of Millennial Faith*, by F. E. Hamilton; *The Millennium in the Church*, and *The Millennium*, by D. H. Kromminga; *Crucial Questions About the Kingdom of God*, by G. E. Ladd; *The Seed of Abraham*, by A. Pieters; *Introductory Lectures in Systematic Theology*, by H. C. Thiessen; and *Biblical Theology*, and *The Kingdom and the Church*, by G. Vos.

Deepest appreciation is extended to my dear wife for proofreading the entire work, and for constant inspiration and encouragement. Without her intelligent and sympathetic cooperation this work would not have come to fruition in the midst of multiplied duties of teaching and preaching.

If these pages will serve to set forth clearly and connectedly the blessed truth of the Word of God to the inquiring mind, and to draw out greater devotion to and service for our Lord Jesus Christ, the purpose of the writer will have been accomplished. *Ad majorem gloriam Dei!*

Charles Lee Feinberg

Hunt-Haven
Manhattan Beach, California

Foreword to the Third Edition

Herman A. Hoyt, Th.M., Th.D., LL.D.
President Emeritus, Grace Theological Seminary

It has been forty-four years since the first edition of this work came from the pen of Dr. Charles L. Feinberg. Twenty-six years have elapsed since the second and enlarged edition was issued. The need for such a volume in 1936 was acute. That need increased by 1954. Now, after twenty-six more years, the need has reached the point of extremity. A whole new breed of speculative theologians has appeared on the scene and a whole new approach to millennialism has developed all across the theological horizon. It is therefore providential and timely that the third edition of this publication now appears.

In this new edition Dr. Feinberg not only demonstrates that he is thoroughly familiar with the movement of thought and doctrine from earliest Christian times, but also that he is familiar with the latest developments in that field. The current interest in millennialism has resulted in a vast amount of new literature dealing with that subject. Dr. Feinberg has come to grips with that material and has displayed in his discussion the fallacious quality of the reasoning and the desperate extremes to which men are resorting to rid the Christian faith of any hope in a coming Millennium.

This work incorporates a smoothing of the text, the biblical support for the statements of fact, the clear refutation of unscriptural assertions, expanded explanations, and documentation that is almost endless. The reader of this volume cannot help but conclude that Dr. Feinberg is in full control of his topic. He exhibits historical knowledge bearing on the subject, theological insight into the intricacies of the doctrine, clear diagnosis of opposing theories, eschatological perception of the trends in operation, and best of all, an absolute loyalty to the inspiration and authority of the Word of God.

Even though Dr. Lewis Sperry Chafer affirmed in his foreword to the first edition forty-four years ago, "Postmillennialism is dead," and at that time it appeared to be so, quite evidently the corpse had not yet been buried. And so today there seems to be a slight movement in that eschatological corpse. Since there is such a close affinity between postmillennialism and amillennialism, that is to be explained by the fact that amillennialism, which originally gave birth to postmillennialism, is now also experiencing a resurgence. The resurgence of twenty years ago has now mounted to the proportions of a moving tide, and an increasing amount of fresh literature is coming forth from the press, designed especially to refute premillennialism.

That resurgence has not only expressed itself in the field of millennialism, but it has also spilled over into the field of tribulationism. And this should be expected. Biblical truth is a complete circle, and therefore it cannot be touched at any point without some other area of the scriptural circle also being affected. The basic assumptions of amillennialism therefore provide the groundwork for postmillennialism, and also for mid-tribulationism and post-tribulationism. The battle among premillennialists over the rapture of the church in relation to the Tribulation has thrown confusion into the camp. Well-meaning men in the camp of the premillennialists, caught in the tangled web of amillennial assumptions, are fighting desperately to hold their convictions in the pre-Tribulation rapture. Because that matter is so vitally and inextricably bound up with the whole eschatological scheme, Dr. Feinberg devotes pages to that theme.

It is of deep significance that Dr. Feinberg recognizes the sharp line of distinction between Israel and the church, and therefore, between the mediatorial kingdom and the church. The Scriptures provide that insight. And that can be discovered only by a careful exegetical examination of the Scriptures themselves. Once the distinction is comprehended, the great mass of the Scriptures unfolds in a pattern displaying remarkable harmony. But as Dr. Feinberg has pointed out over and over again, when that distinction is confused in the mind of the student of Scripture, he is confronted with endless problems in this dispensation of the church and with hopeless confusion concerning the future.

Amillennialism identifies the mediatorial kingdom with the church and of necessity is compelled to limit the period of its duration to the period of the sojourn of the church. That means that the period of redemption comes to its close when the church is caught away from the world. That means that that great body of Scripture delineating the salvation of Jews and Gentiles following the rapture must be ignored or reinterpreted. In this treatise, Dr. Feinberg points out the excesses of spiritualization and the juggling and rearrangements of Scripture to which amillennialists must resort to give some semblance of order to their system of eschatology. The resulting scheme, however, is beset with insuperable problems.

Pious affirmations as to the infallibility and authority of the Word of God provide a deceptive cloak for a method of interpretation that cleverly cheats the Scripture of its clear truth and introduces a system of doctrine that robs the believer of his hope. Dr. Feinberg recognizes that trend and as kindly as possible seeks to bring it to the attention of the reader. For this courageous and penetrating analysis of the amillennial system on the one hand and the accuracy and excellencies of the premillennial system as over against it, the writer is to be commended.

Having known Dr. Feinberg for almost forty years, having profited greatly from his writings and from his own personal ministry, it was an exceedingly profitable experience to read the manuscript constituting the third edition of this book. The frankness with which he has confronted the subject, the courage with which he has pointed out the errors of the amillennial system, and the breadth and beauty of the premillennial system as it has been unfolded from the Scriptures have given me new hope and courage to face the increasing number of enemies that confront believers in these last days. Within the premillennial system, which unfolds the message of the Bible from its opening words to its close, lies the hope of victory and the final exaltation of our Lord and Savior Jesus Christ. Therefore, I count it a privilege and a pleasure to write this foreword.

Preface to the Third Edition

Decades have come and gone since the material in this volume was first researched for a doctorate in theology. Subsequently, the entire subject has been reviewed again and again, and the work has seen both revision and updating. Happily, no basic position has been altered or abandoned, though the book has been reprinted a number of times. This latest edition has been the most thorough of all. Many requests have come for the reissuance of the book.

It is a genuine pleasure to thank Dr. Herman A. Hoyt, Th.D., LL.D., President Emeritus of Grace Theological Seminary, a true friend of many years and one who espouses knowledgeably the position of the worthies—Dr. Lewis Sperry Chafer, my mentor, and Dr. Alva J. McClain, his mentor and my close colleague in the work of the New Scofield Reference Bible—for his able and discerning introduction to this volume.

Thanks are due to Moody Press for its helpfulness at every stage of the publication of the book. Most difficult it is to express adequately my deep appreciation to my dear wife for her understanding, help, encouragement, and sacrifice during many months of labor on the manuscript in the midst of many duties of administration, teaching, radio preaching, and conference ministry in many areas of the globe.

The work is now commended to the Triune God for His glory and for blessing to the household of faith.

Charles Lee Feinberg
Dean Emeritus
Talbot Theological Seminary

La Mirada, California

Part One
INTRODUCTION

1
Preliminary Considerations

In the treatment of a subject such as ours, one finds it not only eminently worthwhile, but downright imperative to define terms at the very outset of the discussion. Webster defines premillennialism as that system that holds the doctrine that the second coming of Christ precedes the Millennium. The word *millennium* is found nowhere in Scripture. It is the Latin equivalent ("mille," a thousand, and "annus," a year) for the Greek *chilia ete* found in the twentieth chapter of the book of Revelation. Those holding the premillennial doctrine are interchangeably designated and referred to as millennialists, premillenarians, and chiliasts. Let it be noted here that the absence of the word *millennium* in the Scriptures militates no more forcefully or conclusively against the premillennial doctrine than does the absence of the word *trinity* against those who hold that the Godhead consists in three eternal Persons forming one Being.

By *amillennialism* is meant that view of the Scriptures that rejects the idea of any period of a thousand years either before or after the return of Christ. Although that system has a great deal in common with the now practically defunct postmillennial interpretation of prophecy, the two are not to be confused. It is interesting to note that just such a confusion is present in the article in the *International Standard Bible Encyclopedia* on "The Millennium" by Geerhardus Vos of Princeton, who is the acknowledged eschatological scholar in the amillennial camp. So in our discussion, although there will be many points of similarity to be seen between the postmillennial and amillennial positions, we shall confine ourselves to the premillennial and amillennial doctrines.

Later in our study we shall define more fully what is involved in our choice of the words "biblical interpretation" in the original title, but in passing we merely say that it is intended to convey to the reader the thought that this study is to be based for its source material upon the Bible alone and not upon secular or apocryphal literature. Why the necessity for such an explanation? The answer is to be found in the number of books that attempt to trace the roots of millennial doctrine in some perverted works extraneous to the Bible.

One writer was found who concluded such a discussion with the honest admission that a study of such sources yielded nothing to a biblical study of the question of the Millennium. So we intend to center our attention upon the Word of God as our first and last authority, which is as it should be with all doctrines held by those who adhere to the orthodox position on the Bible.

A discussion of this nature, however, would hardly be complete without a preliminary word on eschatology. The fact that for many centuries the study of eschatology suffered immeasurably from those who held and enthusiastically propagated extreme, false, and wild notions concerning the future, should not blind our eyes to the importance of eschatology. It is a matter of common agreement between both the church and the world that we are living in troublesome and perplexing times. It is not surprising to find that, although the greatest minds are engaged with the state of affairs in the world, they have been able to come to no final or satisfying conclusion as to either the cause of or the cure for present world conditions.

The rank and file are interested only insofar as their own lives are touched by those circumstances, and, sad to say, many untaught Christians are to be found in that group. The latter ask: "Why worry about conditions everywhere and those things that are future? If we live for Christ and testify for Him here and now, He will take care of the rest." Is it, then, merely a fancy on the part of some Christians to find out something not meant for them, when they seek to learn the things that lie ahead? We think not for several definite reasons.

It was the Dutch theologian J. J. Van Oosterzee who succinctly said: "All true Theology is at the same time Teleology, which must of itself lead to Eschatology."[1] From a cursory examination of the entire Word of God it will be found that there are seventeen books of the Old Testament strictly prophetic, besides the prophetic books of the New Testament and the many portions of eschatological import in other books. Further study will reveal that fully one quarter of the Bible is prophecy, which rightfully includes all that was predictive at the time of its utterance. With such a large place given to eschatology in the Word by the Spirit, it not only deserves but commands our faithful and prayerful study. It certainly was never in the purpose of God that such a large portion of His Word should be neglected.

But Christians in this age have more reason—if I may so put it—to be interested in prophecy and its themes than ever before, because it is one of the purposes for which the eternal Son sent the eternal Spirit into the world. The Scriptures reveal an eightfold ministry of the Holy Spirit in this present age. He restrains evil in the world; He is said to reprove the world of sin, righteousness, and judgment; it is through His agency that regeneration is effected; He dwells in every believer, who becomes a temple of the Holy Spirit by faith in Christ; it is His office to baptize all believers into the Body of Christ; the Holy Spirit of God seals every believer, Himself being the seal; the obedient and yielded believer is filled with the Spirit; and the Holy Spirit guides into truth.

It is with that last phase of the Spirit's ministry that we are here specifically interested. The apostle John in writing to believers reminds them that the anointing they have received of God abides in them, so that they have no need that man should instruct them. The anointing suffices to teach all things. Moreover, before His departure from this world the Lord Jesus in the upper room discourse recorded by John declared to His disciples that, although He had been with them for some time, there were yet many things that they could not bear at that time. But, they were told, when the Spirit of truth came into the world, He would guide into all truth and would show (lit., *disclose*) them "things to come." With the Spirit present and willing to teach us, we ought to be willing to listen to His instruction.

Eschatology is of inestimable value, furthermore, because of the testimony it yields to the omniscience and omnipotence of our God. When Isaiah was exhorting Israel in Babylon to see that their God was greater and mightier than the gods of Babylon, even though the Babylonians had taken Israel captive from their land, he pointed out among other things that the gods of heathen Babylon were totally incapable of showing and declaring future events to prove their claim to worship. But, on the other hand, the true God could say: "Before they spring forth I tell you of them" (Isa. 42:9). Again and again God is represented by the prophet as saying: "Yea, I have spoken it, I will also bring it to pass; I have purposed it, I will also do it" (Isa. 46:11).

Another reason for the significance attached to eschatology is that it is an indispensable concomitant of a normal Christian walk and service. As in former times, much is heard in religious circles these days of the great task of bringing in the kingdom that lies before the church. Such energy is misdirected and were better utilized along lines consonant with the eternal purposes of God in Christ Jesus for this present age. Others are laboring in the church to make the world a better place in which to live, to mitigate as far as possible the line of cleavage and separation between the church and the world. The result is a satanic social gospel and a situation in which the church is to be found in the world and the world in the church. Eschatology furnishes the answer to the question as to the work of the believer in this age. But there is more than that. A knowledge of prophecy, particularly of the imminent return of our Lord, is conducive to a proper Christian walk. Values are seen in their relative importance. There is not a dissipating of purpose and energy between the things of this world and those of heaven. A wise teacher once attributed the suffering and misery of man to the fact that he has one foot in the finite and one in the infinite, with the result that he is torn asunder, not by four horses as in olden times, but between two worlds. Many Christians are attempting to walk with Christ while they consort with the world. The cause is often to be found in their utter lack of knowledge of prophetic things, the knowledge of which would have a strong tendency, to say the least, to draw their eyes from the things of this world and fix them upon Christ and His future purposes.

Quite a substantial benefit that accrues to those who engage in the study of the prophetic word is that of comfort. When the believers in Thessalonica were mourning for their departed loved ones even as those who had no hope, the apostle Paul directed their attention to one eschatological event in the possibly near future. At another time when those same Christians were disturbed and perplexed as to the meaning of their trials and sufferings in the faith, Paul pointed out to them clearly and convincingly that their fears were unfounded and that they did well to rest in the security that God had provided for them in a coming day.

And it has ever been thus. Church history recounts time and again instances wherein groups, having separated themselves from the moral filth in practice and corruption in doctrine present in the state church, found comfort and consolation in the contemplation of the millennial hope, notwithstanding the fact that most of the time their conceptions were grossly materialistic and sensualistic. Some have thought that that situation counted as a decided disadvantage to the millennial doctrine and that by virtue of it that truth was rightly discountenanced. But the exact opposite is the case. How much real comfort to the Christian heart must there be in the pure doctrine, if even corruptions, exaggerations, and misconceptions of it brought solace to the hearts of those undergoing adversities and persecutions? Assuredly, he spoke wisely who said: "Only he who knows prophecy can dwell in the calm of eternity now."

Eschatology, in addition to the reasons given above, is important for the completeness of God's revelation. Prophecy is one means, among others, by which God reveals His purposes and will to man.

Poorer indeed would be the Word of God without the presence in it of eschatology. It is often overlooked that the reason for the lack of understanding of much of the didactic and hortatory portions of the Scriptures is to be found in the neglect of the prophetic portions, which are absolutely indispensable to the full-orbed truth of God. Canon Dyson Hague has shown in an excellent little pamphlet entitled *The Wonder of the Book* that, although some parts of the Bible are considered by many as relatively more important than others or doctrinally more valuable, the excision of the so-called minor portions would be as injurious and detrimental to the completeness of God's revelation as would be the destruction of the lobe of the ear or the very tip of the smallest finger to the perfection of the human body.[2] How much less complete then would be the Word of God without the prophetic portions, which occupy so much space in the canon?

But that is not all. Somehow there is in every heart, believer and unbeliever alike, an insatiable desire to know what the future holds. God's Word is not written to satisfy every such desire, be it intense or otherwise, but He does take His children aside—those children, mark you, whom He graciously counts as His friends—to reveal to them the completeness and ineffable wisdom of all His purposes.

Probably the most cogent reason for the significance of eschatological study is to be seen in the position or place of the present age. In his valuable work, *The Progress of Dogma,* James Orr shows with his usual ability and clarity that Christian doctrine has not only a chronological development, but a logical one as well.[3] For instance, it follows the accepted lines of systematic theology: first, bibliology (the fixing and defining of the canon of Scripture); then, theology proper (Arian, Nestorian, Eutychian, Monophysite, and Monothelite controversies); then, anthropology (Pelagian controversy); and so on. Such has been the case until now there are before the minds of men who are studying the Scriptures the great themes of predictive prophecy as never before. The prophet Daniel was told at the end of this prophecy to close up and seal the words until the time of the end (Dan. 12:9). The time of the end is, according to verse four of the same chapter, to be characterized by two features. Many will run to and fro, and knowledge will be increased.

Norman B. Harrison, voicing the opinion of many other interpreters of the prophecies of Daniel, understands the running to and fro to point to the tremendous increase in travel and communication, and the growth in knowledge to refer to the unprecedented multiplication of educational advantages and facilities. In his work on the return of the Lord, the author gives statistics to show the amazing strides in railroad, automobile, and airplane transportation during the past few decades. Further proof is adduced to set forth the phenomenal growth in the student bodies of the schools of higher learning throughout our land. A journal of education is quoted to point out that any book on physics, electricity, astrology, geography, history, philosophy, physiology, psychology, chemistry, biology, sociology, economics, industry, or commerce that was written a few years ago is hopelessly out of date.[4]

We are inclined to believe, however, that the prophet is not speaking of such things. The Hebrew equivalent for the verb "shall run to and fro" is *yeshottu,* which means "to peruse a book." Furthermore, the word for "knowledge" has the definite article (*hadda'ath*), which conveys the thought of a particular and defined knowledge. The interpretation of the passage would then be: The time of the end is to be characterized by a perusal of the contents of the prophecy of Daniel (other prophecies are not necessarily excluded, because they would aid in the interpretation and understanding of Daniel's prophecy), and the knowledge of the contents of Daniel will be increased. Such is the case today and is ample reason that, because we are in the time of the end, much emphasis should be placed upon eschatology.

Because many reasons can be brought forth in favor of the necessity and significance of prophetic study, one would expect that eschatology would hold a prime place in works of theology and in the curricula of theological seminaries. But, despite what we have said in regard to the increase in prophetic study in recent times, eschatology remains a much neglected field of theological study and research. If one were to scan the standard works of theology, he would be surprised to find the little attention that is given to eschatology. Since those works, moreover, constitute the textbooks of the regular theological courses in the seminaries, it is immediately evident how abridged and circumscribed is that phase of theology. Much time is spent and many pains are taken with the other great doctrines of the Scriptures, but the doctrine of future things is relatively an untouched and unexplored territory. Its treatment is usually limited to the fact of a life after death, the second advent of the Lord, the general resurrection, the final judgment, heaven, and hell. The situation gains more serious proportions when it is fully realized that prophecy forms a large part of the whole counsel of God and the Word that the faithful minister of Christ is enjoined and exhorted to preach.

At this stage of our discussion we would define the scope of our theme and our position relative to it. First, we wish to make it clear that we cannot accept the position taken by Eugene C. Caldwell in the "Christian Observer" of June 28, 1933. He contends that whereas there are definite elements of truth in the premillennial, postmillennial, and amillennial systems of interpretation, there are also points wherein they depart from the New Testament teaching on the question. Hence he prefers not to be classified with any one of those schools, but would rather hold to the scheme of eschatology laid down in the New Testament. There are two fundamental errors, as we see it, with such a position. First, all three views claim to have as their basis the teaching of the New Testament, just as Caldwell maintains he does. Second, when such a view of the Scriptures as the premillennial declares that it finds in the Word a teaching, clear and consistent, concerning the Millennium, and there is alongside of it another view of the Scriptures that purports to find no such teaching anywhere in the revelation of God, such diametrically opposite views fail to show any similarity in "elements of truth."

It is impossible to straddle an issue that has so much dissimilarity in the views taken with regard to it. In the final analysis the crux of the matter is this: the Bible either definitely teaches or unequivocally does not teach a Millennium, by which term is meant, according to Webster, the thousand-year era mentioned in the twentieth chapter of the book of Revelation, during which time righteousness will be triumphant with Christ personally reigning on earth with His saints. If the Bible does teach a Millennium, then we are compelled to admit that the premillennial view of biblical eschatology is the correct one. If, on the other hand, it can be demonstrated that the Word does not teach a

Millennium, then we are logically constrained to acknowledge that the truth is with the amillennialists.

We have been consistently referring to the fact that the premillenarian view is based on the interpretation of Scripture. That could be corroborated many times over by references to the beliefs of the early church. Every book that we have read on the question of the Millennium, whether it was favorable or unfavorable to the doctrine, whether it gave full force and value to the testimony or tried to dissipate its implications, admitted freely that the entire early church for the first three centuries was premillennial, almost to a man. Adolf Harnack, whose liberal views are a matter of common knowledge to all who are acquainted with theological literature, could by no stretch of the imagination be accused of premillennial leanings. He was recognized as the ablest patristic scholar of his time. His testimony, then, should and does carry weight, and it is this:

> In the history of Christianity three main forces are found to have acted as auxiliaries of the gospel. They have elicited the ardent enthusiasm of many whom the bare preaching of the gospel would never have made decided converts. These are (1) a belief in the speedy return of Christ and in His glorious reign on earth. . . . First in point of time came the faith in the nearness of Christ's second advent and the establishing of His reign of glory on the earth. Indeed it appears so early that it might be questioned whether it ought not to be regarded as an essential part of the Christian religion.[5]

But there are those, nevertheless, who would try to strip that and similar testimony of its force. They contend that premillennialism is merely an undesirable vestige and inheritance from ancient Judaism with its apocalyptic literature that unfortunately found its way into the early church, and that explains the Judaistic features of millenarianism. Others argue that the church throughout her orthodox development has ever and always condemned chiliasm as a heresy. The reason the doctrine was not denounced before it was, it is asserted, was due to the fact that the early church was drawn mainly from Jewish converts. After the influx of Gentile believers the Jewish elements gradually disappeared. To all such arguments we merely reply that it is inconsistent to the highest degree to go back and diligently search to ascertain the doctrine and belief of the early church on every other vital subject of the Christian faith and reject the early church's view of the Millennium.

But we do not expect to develop our theme along the historical line, adducing witness after witness and testimony after testimony to prove the premillennial view to be the biblical one. Nor do we expect to lay any stress upon the scholarship that has been drawn from many quarters in support of the doctrine throughout the centuries. To be sure, there are those who confidently declare that as far as actual scholarship—which in the last analysis, according to their mind, will settle the question some day once for all—is concerned, premillennialism will always remain a "negligible quantity." But honest research and study will prove beyond a peradventure of a doubt that the chiliastic position can boast, if it should be so minded, of great numbers of men both in Europe and in this country who are preeminent in "intellectual endowments, scholastic attainments, fervent piety, faithful service and intimate acquaintance with the Scriptures." A lack of real and honest scholarship has never been the lot of the millennial doctrine.

Our aim is not, furthermore, to show that all premillennialists see eye to eye in all the details involved in the subject. Amillennialists make much of the fact that their opponents disagree among themselves. But he must be unusually nearsighted who cannot see that the selfsame argument acts as a boomerang and operates with a telling force against the amillennial position. We shall be satisfied if we shall have proved by the end of the study that the premillennial view is harmonious, self-consistent, and above all, based upon the infallible authority of the Scriptures.

Before we close these preliminary considerations we would make plain all that is involved in the words "biblical interpretation" in the subtitle of this discussion. We have already noted that in one sense they are intended to convey the idea that this work is an interpretation of biblical material and not secular or apocryphal literature. But by those words we mean more than that. This study is intended to show that the premillennial view is based upon the whole teaching of the Bible and deserves to be recognized as a complete system of interpretation of the entire Word and not of a single passage or several passages in the Bible. If amillennialism is to stand, it must prove its right to our belief by a consistent and harmonious interpretation of the Scriptures in their totality. It is sad to see and harder to explain how amillennialists continue to insist that the premillenarian system is based upon one single passage of Scripture.

G. P. Mains in his work against premillennialism asks the reader to keep in mind during the course of the discussion that the literal doctrine of a Millennium is based upon "a short paragraph of three verses," which are found in a book confessedly of highly wrought symbolism and mystery." Such a basis he declares to be totally inadequate and insufficient for a "distinctive school of Christian belief."[6] Abraham Kuyper is also of those who hold that the premillennial doctrine is built upon Revelation 20. In the first place, by way of reply we can say that if God would choose, which in this case He did not, to give us a doctrine in one passage, He could easily do so. One portion of His Word is just as worthy of our faith as another. In the second place, the groundlessness of the statement made so often by amillennialists is easily brought to light, because it is well known that the Jews had a fully developed doctrine of the millennial age long before the book of Revelation, or any portion of the New Testament for that matter, was written.

But what do the millenarians say as to the basis of their doctrine? Surely they should know their own position. Everyone of them to a man declares unreservedly and unequivocally that he builds the doctrine on the entire Word of God. C. I. Scofield has pronounced the Kingdom to be the great theme of predictive prophecy. It is, according to George C. Needham, not gleaned from one proof-text or any group of them, but from the entire trend of Scripture revelation. One of the great French writers said of the doctrine of the Millennium that it is supported by "more ancient and formal texts than many other doctrines now universally accepted." We are driven to the conclusion, then, that chiliasts affirm: "Premillenarianism is . . . a method of interpretation from Genesis to Revelation. It proposes to discover all the Bible teaches on a given subject and to abide by the results."[7]

The position taken in this study is premillennial and dispensational. We are aware that many premillennialists would not agree with us on many points of detail in our interpretation, as well as the dispensational approach to the Scriptures and the futurist interpretation of the Revelation. But we have stated our stand, and the reader must decide whether the Scriptures bear it out or not.

NOTES

[1] J. J. Van Oosterzee, *Christian Dogmatics*, 2:581.

[2] C. D. Hague, "The Wonder of the Book" (Atlantic City, N.J.: The World Wide Revival Prayer Movement), nd.

[3] J. Orr, *The Progress of Dogma*, pp. 20-30

[4] N. B. Harrison, *His Sure Return*, pp. 47-48

[5] J. H. Brookes, *Till He Come*, p. 136

[6] G. P. Mains, *Premillennialism*, p. 41

[7] L. S. Chafer, *Must We Dismiss the Millennium?* p. 27. Cf. Ladd's correct conclusion: "The second coming of Jesus Christ [and the related prophetic themes] is an absolutely indispensable doctrine in the biblical teaching of redemption" (G. E. Ladd, *The Blessed Hope*, p. 6).

A consonant testimony is that of Walvoord: "It is not too much to say that millennialism is a determining factor in biblical interpretation of comparable importance to the doctrines of verbal inspiration, the deity of Christ, substitutionary atonement, and bodily resurrection. . . . It is of course true that to an individual a denial of the deity of Christ is more momentous and far-reaching than denial of premillennialism, but, as far as a system of interpretation is concerned, both are vital. The growing recognition of the importance of the millennial doctrine is one of the principal causes of resurgence of interest in this field." Again, "Instead of being simply a way of interpreting prophecy, millennialism now is seen to be a determining factor in any system of theology" (J. F. Walvoord, *The Millennial Kingdom,* pp. 16-17, 68).

2
Biblical Interpretation

Since it is admitted by both premillennialists and amillennialists that the root of their differences lies in the method of biblical interpretation, it is well to consider the whole question of interpretation. A primary distinction that must be made and borne in mind is that inspiration is one thing and interpretation is another. If that essential differentiation were kept to the fore, much of the theological literature on the subject of the Millennium would be more readable and more biblical.

Inspiration may be defined as that gracious influence of the Holy Spirit whereby He communicates truth to men and guarantees its inerrancy and infallibility in the original languages. That work is begun by God and carried out through specific men at definite times for special purposes. The human element enters into inspiration, but it is completely under the control of the Spirit of God.

Interpretation is an altogether different matter. The only point that it has in common with inspiration is its dependence upon the Holy Spirit, for he is no interpreter of the Bible who is not indwelt and guided by the Spirit of God (1 Cor. 2:14). Man, functioning in his natural state and capacities, does not grasp the things of the Spirit, because they are foolishness to him. They must be discerned by means of the Spirit. Apart from that, interpretation is in the human realm and is subject to human imperfections and errors. What must be remembered, however, is that interpretation does not require one to pass judgment, as many have taken in hand to do, as to what shall be found in this portion or that passage of Scripture. It is the task of interpretation to use materials already provided and to make them understandable to all.

Perhaps a still more important distinction exists between interpretation and application. It was that great biblical scholar Franz Delitzsch who said: "Interpretation is one; application is manifold."[1] In studying the Bible, as in studying any other book, the objective is to find out the exact meaning of the text at hand. After that has been ascertained, it can be applied to the life of an individual or a group. Much confusion has resulted from using the Scriptures practically wholly for application. For instance, it is true, and eminently so, that for every believing heart the eternal God is a refuge, and His arms can be depended upon to uphold and sustain. But Deuteronomy 33:27 has a specific meaning in the context that refers it directly to Israel. Such is the case with the Psalms and the prophecies. Isaiah 53 may be applied to all sinners, but its interpretation reveals that it is speaking of the confession of the nation Israel in a coming day. The gospels have suffered in that respect probably as much as any portion of the Word, with the result that the primary meaning is foreign to most people. True interpretation demands of the student to ascertain to the best of his ability with the help of the Spirit exactly what a text means and to whom it is addressed.

There are, moreover, certain definite and recognized principles of biblical interpretation. The first general principle of all sound hermeneutics is to interpret grammatically, which calls for attention to the meaning of words, the construction and form of sentences, and the distinguishing idioms of the language in question. A word is the vehicle of a thought, and the meaning of any passage must be determined by a study of the words and the relationships sustained in the sentence. There is no more basic rule in interpretation; without it there is confusion. But many times a word is modified or limited by the connection in which it appears and that necessitates a study of the context. Any text taken from its context is but a pretext.

Todd claims that even in the Psalms and Proverbs, where it is difficult at first sight to see the qualifying connection, there is nonetheless much value to be attached to the context of passages.[2] Certain words and phrases may have an altogether different meaning in various connections. For example, the word "law" in Romans may mean any one of several possibilities. In Romans 2:14 the first three uses of the word refer to the Mosaic law, whereas the last refers to natural or inherent law. The use of the word in 2:20, 23 points more specifically to the Ten Commandments of the Mosaic system. The meaning of "law" in 3:27 is rule, or principle. It would be most unwise, then, to demand that a word should always mean the same wherever found.

Sometimes not only the immediate context must be searched for a true interpretation, but the broad context or the whole book must be considered. Such an example is to be found with regard to Paul's use of the idea of works, and that of James. The former, undoubtedly, discredits them as means of attaining merit before God; the latter commends them only in believers as a manifestation to other believers and the world that saving faith is present. There are times, however, when even more than that is required. In such instances the most comprehensive rule of hermeneutics is applied; namely, the comparing of Scripture with Scripture. E. M. Milligan has well said: "The only safe and infallible rule for the interpretation of Scripture is the Scripture itself."[3] The best and safest interpreter of the Bible is the Bible itself.

Such was the thought in Paul's mind when he said through the Spirit that in regard to the things that the Holy Spirit teaches it is a matter of "comparing spiritual things with spiritual" (1 Cor. 2:13; cf. ASV and NASB). The logic of that principle is evident to one at all acquainted with the Word of God. All that God has to say on one particular theme is not to be found in one place alone. Different divisions and phases of the same truth are spread throughout the Scriptures. It is the part of interpretation to show how all those many parts form one beautiful and harmonious whole. Of course, no contradictions will be present in a true grasp of any of the doctrines of the Bible. Apparent contradictions will be reconciled, and the obscure and difficult parts will be made clear by the unambiguous places. Every added mention of a truth will contribute to the final and full-orbed understanding of the same.

Finally, before passing to a brief perusal of the principles of prophetic interpretation, we note two other principles of general interpretation that are particularly relevant to such a discussion as this wherein two conflicting and opposing views will be dealt with.

First, when certain difficulties are affirmed of a doctrine that claims to be biblical, one is only required to show that a solution of the alleged problem is possible. When certain passages are referred to that are said to contradict the premillennial doctrine, all that is necessary is to demonstrate that according to the rules of exegesis a harmonization is possible.

Second, sometimes even that cannot be fairly required. If any doctrine is shown on the basis of the laws of exegesis to be taught in the Bible, then to prove the doctrine false more is needed than the mere statement that the teaching brings to light even unanswerable problems. Otherwise, it could be demonstrated that the doctrines of salvation and redemption are false. The same method is used in rejecting and denying those doctrines that is employed in opposing premillennialism. In order to disprove the premillennial interpretation of Scripture, its opponents must show that its exegesis of the passages of Scripture involved is false and erroneous.

As to the question of the principles of prophetic interpretation, it must be recognized that prophecy is not something superimposed upon the message of the Bible, but is itself a method of revelation. Prophecy in its predictive role can be distinguished by certain distinct characteristics. First of all, it is a clear statement of a future event, wholly to be distinguished from the garbled and incomprehensible ambiguities of heathen oracles. Second, it must not only foretell an event, but the event itself must be without the realm of human view or insight. It cannot be deduced from former events. Third, the one who is predicting must recognize, in practically all cases, that his utterance is from God. (Balaam and Caiaphas, of course, were exceptions to that general rule.) Particular caution must be taken in interpreting prophecy that, notwithstanding the presence of figurative and symbolic language, the prophecies be not rendered devoid of meaning.

Robert Baker Girdlestone in his work on the grammar of prophecy, as also M. S. Terry in his volume on biblical hermeneutics, maintains that prophecy as a whole is more or less figurative.[4] That position is extreme, for particularly with regard to prophecies related to the kingdom—which occupy a large space in the prophetic message, as will be shown—the language of prophecy is relatively free from symbolic language and is not smothered into incomprehensibility by so much symbolic drapery.

Indeed, far too great liberties have been taken with prophetic truth; the like practice with regard to salvation truth would long have rendered it void as to the actual teaching of God's Word. Let that statement not be misunderstood, however, for some prophecy is conveyed by means of symbolic language. But whenever such is the case, the symbols are explained in the immediate context, in the book in which they occur, or elsewhere in the Word; no room is left to the imaginations of men to devise explanations.

There are several well-defined laws for the interpretation of prophecy. Scripture itself lays down the first and most essential. Peter states in his second letter, "No prophecy of the Scripture is of any private interpretation" (2 Pet. 1:20). That is not meant to affirm that no private individual can interpret prophecy. The idea intended by the apostle is that no prophecy of the Word is to be interpreted solely with reference to itself *(idias epiluseos ou ginetai)*, but all other portions of the prophetic revelation are to be taken into account and considered. Every prophecy is part of a wonderful scheme of revelation; for the true significance of any prophecy, the whole prophetic scheme must be kept in mind and the interrelationship between the parts in the plan as well.

A second rule in the interpretation of prophecy is that due attention must be paid to perspective. Certain events of the future are seen grouped together in one circumscribed area of vision, although they are really at different distances. That is particularly true of the predictions of the so-called major prophets, where many times prophecies concerning the Babylonian captivity, the events of the Day of the Lord, the return from Babylon, the worldwide dispersion of Israel, and their future regathering from all corners of the earth, are grouped together seemingly almost indiscriminately.

Another rule of prophetic interpretation is what is known as "foreshortening," which, according to Arthur T. Pierson, may assume any one of several forms.[5] Two or more events of a like character may be described by a common profile. An example is to be found in the prophecy of Rachel's mourning for her children. Scripture reveals that it applied to the Babylon captivity in the first instance and then to the slaughter of the innocents under Herod in the second. Furthermore, a common and important example of foreshortening is evident when future events are placed side by side whereas in the fulfillment of them there is a great gap. S. H. Kellogg maintains that the fact that two events are spoken of together or in close sequence is no proof that those events will take place simultaneously or even in immediate succession, unless the Scripture specifically affirms so.[6] Stanley Leathes confirms that statement when he declares that it is contrary to analysis of the prophetic Scriptures to suppose that because events are mentioned in immediate juxtaposition they must necessarily come to pass in immediate chronological order. Familiar examples of that law of prophecy are to be found in Isaiah 61:1-2; Daniel 9:26-27; and Luke 1:31-33.

Finally, in the interpretation of prophecy that has not yet been fulfilled, those prophecies that have been fulfilled are to form the pattern. The only way to know how God will fulfill prophecy in the future is to ascertain how He has done it in the past (Isa. 44:6-8; 45:11; 46:9-11; 48:3). All the prophecies of the suffering Messiah were literally fulfilled in the first advent of Christ. There is no reason to believe that the predictions of a glorified and reigning Messiah will be brought to pass in any other manner. Take, for example, the words of Gabriel in Luke 1 where he foretold the birth of Christ. According to the angel's words Mary literally conceived in her womb; literally brought forth a son; His name was literally called Jesus; He was literally great; and He was literally called the Son of the Highest. Will it not be as literally fulfilled that God will yet give to Christ the throne of His father David, that He will reign over the house of Jacob forever, and that of His glorious kingdom there shall be no end? (vv. 31-33).

Two definite systems, or methods, of interpretation underlie the premillennial and the amillennial approaches to the Scripture, the *spiritualizing and/or allegorizing* and the *literal,* and it is to those two methods that we now direct our attention.

At first glance, spiritualizing and/or allegorizing—the latter being more specifically confined to that interpretation where allegories are present—does not seem to be synonymous or interchangeable, but in general they are so regarded (for example, Nathaniel West) as opposed to the literal method of interpretation.[7] The allegorizing and spiritualizing method had its beginning with the rabbis and the Alexandrians and developed through the writings of the church Fathers, the scholastic theologians, and even the Protestant dogmatists who steadfastly maintained that the Old Testament in its literal sense is at times inadequate because of its imperfection, triviality, and conduciveness to moral error. Their remedy, then, was to twist the letter of the Word by means of allegories and spiritualizations into whatever conception was most amenable to their reasonings or their preconceived views.

Often the claim is advanced that the unity of the Bible is moral rather than literal, and, in addition, much of Old Testament prophecy was "crudely rudimental" and was soon to pass away before a permanent and fuller revelation in the New Testament. Geerhardus Vos argues that when the New Testament spiritualized the Messianic predictions of the Old, it brought the latter into conformity with the "content of the highest eternal hope."[8] The Jews, says he, in interpreting prophecy in a literal manner were giving away to "a considerable element of individual and collective eudaemonism."

In short, in all the arguments of the spiritualizers and allegorizers there is evident the conception that what really matters in prophecy is the inner thought; the words are, to use their own expressions, "nonessential details," "the rough rind of a sacred bulb," or "Oriental figure."[9] The result is that upon each individual interpreter devolves the colossal task of determining what is essential in prophecy and what is connected with the mere outward form of expression. When prophetic numbers are introduced into the discussion, they are stripped of their chronological exactness and are said to be symbols of a symbol or figures of a figure. In fact, they really do not count at all. Finally, it is maintained that the spiritualizing method of interpretation does not absolutely exclude the possibility of prophecy being literally fulfilled. Indeed, "The literal and spiritual fulfillment of prophecy are often contained in one single passage."[10]

In denying the legitimacy of the spiritualizing and allegorizing method it can be pointed out, first of all, that the allegory found in Galatians 4:24-31 militates in no sense against a literal interpretation of Scripture, nor does it form any sufficient basis for allegorization and spiritualization. The passage actually confirms the literal sense of the Scriptures, for Hagar and Sarah had a literal existence, and Mount Sinai and Jerusalem were literal places. Moreover, no interpretation can be at all satisfactory that does not allow words to have their natural meaning. Spiritualizers find it hard to explain—and not one has even successfully attempted it—if the Scriptures do not mean what they say, why they do not say what they mean. Is it not passing strange that the God who called light into existence with two words *(yehi 'or)* should not be able to say exactly what He means? A further condemnation of that method comes from G. H. Schodde, who tellingly points out that one of the characteristic features of the New Testament writers is their freedom from the use of the allegorical method of interpretation prevalent not only at that time, but even in later centuries among the early Christian exegetes.[11]

Just one word need be said with regard to numbers and their interpretation. When a grossly materialistic chiliasm became peculiarly distasteful to the church in the fourth and fifth centuries, the practice was begun of allegorizing and spiritualizing not only the thousand years but also all prophetic numbers. Instead of denoting time, those numbers were said to be mere signs of abstract ideas. It cannot be denied that numbers have symbolic value, but that is not admitting that they have no temporal significance. Prophetic numbers are symbolic just because and only because they are literal. The only reason four is a number symbolical of the earth is due to the fact that it is literal—four directions of the compass. It is true that the seven lampstands of Revelation 1 are symbolical of completeness, but that does not imply that there are six or five lampstands. There are literally seven, and the symbolic significance is derivable from the literalness of the number. In like manner, the thousand years may symbolize "potentiated ecumenicity,"[12] but does that make them five thousand or ten thousand years? Symbolical value may be attached to or derived from numbers solely because numbers have literal meaning.

That which clinches the argument is the fact that prophetic numbers have been literally fulfilled in the past. When the prophet Jeremiah foretold that Israel would be in Babylon seventy years, the fulfillment of the prophecy showed that God meant exactly seventy literal years. In that manner Daniel understood them when he studied Jeremiah's prophecy. Daniel's sixty-two weeks have also come to pass literally, and that in spite of the fact that his prophecy has symbols. Finally, one wonders if the spiritualizers stop to consider that such dissipating of the literal sense of Scripture, as is common in their interpretations of prophetic Scriptures, would eventually rob us of every doctrine in the Word of God.

The spiritualizing method has been applied to the Scriptures in varying degrees by different writers. M. J. Wyngaarden's work on the future of the Messianic kingdom in prophecy and fulfillment, is one of the most interesting books on the question of the Millennium. The book purports to be a study in the scope of spiritualization in Scripture; it is that as well as an attack on premillennialism. The book is of special interest for this study for two reasons: it appears to be one of the ablest attempts, if not the only one, to apply inductively the principle of spiritualization to prophecy with regard to all phases of the kingdom, and it shows at the same time to what conclusions the spiritualization of the Word, when consistently pursued, will lead. In the preface to his book the author confesses that he found comparatively few works dealing with his subject in contrast to the many books dealing with the scope of the many prophecies literally fulfilled.

Another concession made at the outset is that in regard to Old Testament prophecies it is quite remarkable how "exceedingly literal" are their fulfillments. That they are so literally fulfilled raises a problem in the mind of the author as to which prophecies ought to be spiritualized. It is difficult to see wherein the problem lies, but consider his position further.

The claim is then made that by an inductive study of the Scriptures, it can be conclusively demonstrated that every phase of the theocratic kingdom has been spiritualized by the Scriptures themselves. That is quite a claim. The purpose of the theocracy in the Old Testament is said to have been the foreshadowing of the present kingdom of grace and the future kingdom of glory, the latter to be realized in the new heavens and new earth. After attempting to establish the theory that the literal interpretation is inadequate and insufficient to explain all the prophecies, he advances his own definition of what he believes spiritualization to be. In essence, it is the comment of the Holy Spirit on elements of the kingdom wherein each item is given a spiritual significance. It is to be differentiated from allegorization, which is the work of man. Spiritualization is the interpretative work of the Holy Spirit Himself.

For the biblical spiritualization of any item, connected with the typical Old Testament kingdom, includes any special import, or broadened meaning, or figurative usage, or richer implication [quite a variety of possibilities here] that the Holy Spirit gives to this item, with a view toward realizing the fulfillment of the typical, Old Testament kingdom, church, both here and in eternity, hereafter.[13]

The author finds that the chief and fundamental difficulty with the premillennial position is its insistence on the literal interpretation of Scripture to such an extent that it fails to take note of the presence of a latent spiritualization in the Old Testament and an evident spiritualization in the New.

When the writer proceeds to the application of the foregoing principles, the results are most interesting. Even in the Old Testament, it is alleged, there is a latent spiritualization of Zion and Jerusalem. Such is the case when the prophet Isaiah declares: "But Zion said, The LORD hath forsaken me, and my Lord hath forgotten me" (Isa. 49:14). Spiritualized Zion is spoken of when the prophet foretells that the Lord will comfort Zion and all her waste places, making her wilderness like Eden and her desert like the garden of the Lord, wherein are to be found joy, gladness, thanksgiving, and the voice of melody (Isa. 51:3). The exhortation to Zion to put on her strength and to Jerusalem to put on her beautiful garments, is cited as another case of the same kind (Isa. 52:1). Wyngaarden sees in those references to Zion and Jerusalem latent spiritualization that relates them to the people of God whether they are in Jerusalem or not.

From that starting point, then, he proceeds to show the evident spiritualization in the New Testament, which makes Zion and Jerusalem mean Jewish and Gentile Christians. That is to be found in Hebrews 12:22 where the inspired writer says: "But ye are come unto mount Sion, and unto the city of the living God, the heavenly Jerusalem"; in Galatians 4:26 where Paul writes: "But Jerusalem which is above is free, which is the mother of us all"; and in Revelation 3:12 where the Word of the Spirit through the apostle John to the overcomer is: "I will write upon him the name of my God, and the name of the city of my God, which is new Jerusalem, which cometh down out of heaven from my God." Let that suffice to show how the theocratic kingdom is summarily dismissed from the realm of the literal. In evaluation of the view thus far, it should be stated that whenever the literal Jerusalem is not meant, as in the cases just noted, the Scriptures have a qualifying adjective or a qualifying statement in the context that would and should keep one from asserting that the literal Zion or Jerusalem is spiritualized. The quotations cited above by no means prove that Zion and Jerusalem are not actually the literal places bearing those names.

The Holy Land as the inheritance of the covenant people has its latent spiritualization in the Old Testament and its evident spiritualization in the New. Spiritualization is seen in Numbers 18:20 where the Lord tells Aaron that he will not have any inheritance in the land, because "I am thy part and thine inheritance among the children of Israel." Jeremiah voices the same conception in 10:16 among other places: "The portion of Jacob is not like them: for he is the former of all things; and Israel is the rod of his inheritance: The LORD of hosts is his name." The evident spiritualization is said to be found in Matthew 5:5: "Blessed are the meek: for they shall inherit the earth"; in Romans 4:13 "For the promise, that he should be the heir of the world, was not to Abraham, or to his seed, through the law, but through the righteousness of faith." And such confusion is meant to show the fallacy of the premillennial doctrine and undermine it! It is indeed sad.

But the writer goes on insistently to demonstrate that the kingdom itself shows a latent spiritualization in the Old Testament. In Exodus 19:5-6, God promises Israel, before offering them the law, that He would make them a peculiar treasure unto Himself above all the nations. He continues: "And ye shall be unto me a kingdom of priests, and an holy nation." In Isaiah 43:15 it is the same God who declares: "I am the LORD, your Holy One, the creator of Israel, your King." The evident spiritualization is said to be found in Christ's words to the disciples after the display of faith on the part of the centurion: "And I say unto you, That many shall come from the east and west, and shall sit down with Abraham, and Isaac, and Jacob, in the kingdom of heaven" (Matt. 8:11). That instance has exactly as much to commend itself as have the others.

Nothing daunted, the author goes on with the same principle in regard to the seed of Abraham as the covenant people and the heirs of the kingdom. Strange to say, however, no Scripture is distinctly quoted for the Old Testament latent spiritualization, although reference is made to *Lo-ammi* and *Lo-ruhamah* in Hosea. For the patent spiritualization, reference is made to Galatians 3:29, where Paul notes that all believers are the seed of Abraham and heirs of the promise; to Romans 4:12, where Abraham is said to be the father of circumcision to both believing Jews and Gentiles; and to Romans 9:7, where all Israel is not synonymous with the true Israel, which comes from the promised seed.

But that is not all. The covenant people as the Bride of the Lord find their place in the prophetic scheme. When Isaiah asked (50:1): "Where is the bill of your mother's divorcement, whom I have put away?" he was laying the ground for a full-grown spiritualization found in the words of Jesus in Matthew 9:15: "Can the children of the bridechamber mourn, as long as the bridegroom is with them?" and in the words of John the Baptist in John 3:29: "He that hath the bride is the bridegroom." The same process is applied to Israel as the covenant people and the recipients of the kingdom; to Israel's enemies exemplified by Edom; to the cultus, or sacrificial system, with particular reference to the ark, the Temple, and the sacrifices; to the priestly, royal, and prophetic types of the church; to the covenant of grace; to the Old Testament "sacraments" of circumcision and Passover; and to the Psalter as the praise book of the kingdom.[14]

Is it possible to conceive of a system, professedly logical and plausible, that would dissipate the force of the Scriptures any more than that one? Yet the author believes that even in Old Testament times those Old Testament Scriptures had to be understood as embodying latent and incipient spiritualization. How those portions *were* understood in Old Testament times, one need not be informed; it is a matter of common knowledge and open to the careful investigation of all. They were taken only and solely as literal.

The method of interpretation that underlies the premillenarian position is the literal. That fact is recognized by the opponents of the view, who claim that, if the literal sense must be taken in prophecy, the millenarian doctrine must stand as the correct view of the Scripture. Mains feels it is not possible so to do, because the Bible is an Oriental book full of pictures and symbols.[15] Charles Hodge maintains that the "torch of the literalist is an 'ignis fatuus,' leading those who follow it, they know not whither."[16] W. Masselink claims that to interpret the prophetic Word so that Jerusalem always means the city of that name and Israel always means the Jews, would be nothing more nor less than "to bring down heaven on earth and to transmute Christianity into the corrupt Judaism of the apostolic age."[17] If that method was proved wrong with regard to prophecies of Christ's first coming, it would be unmitigated folly, so he affirms, to attempt its application in connection with unfulfilled prophecies. M. S. Terry, however, not only states that the grammatico-historical sense is essentially the same as the literal, but also repeats the old hermeneutical principle that words are to be taken in their literal meaning unless such a procedure involves the Scriptures in a contradiction or absurdity. However, he claims that the principle in practice can become, in the last analysis, an appeal to every man's judgment.[18] How can that be safeguarded against? The solution lies in noting the general teaching of the book in question and then that of the whole Word, determining by the guidance of the Holy Spirit which meaning best harmonizes all the Scriptures. It is impossible to exclude all personal judgment, but it is best to reduce it to the lowest possible quantity.

The arguments that can be advanced for the literal method are several and convincing. First, most will admit that God intended His revelation in prophecy to be understood as much as other parts of the Word. In that case He must have embodied His ideas in exact and specific terms that would accurately convey the meaning He originally intended when interpreted according to the laws of grammar. Figures of speech are, to be sure, necessarily to be interpreted in the light of the context of the passage. Second, God often calls attention in His Word to the literal fulfillment of predictions that came to pass just as foretold. What a valuable testimony is the gospel of Matthew to that very thing. Third, the literal interpretation does not minimize the worth of the Old Testament revelation. Spiritualizers seem to think that because revelation came gradually, the later the prophecy or revealed matter, the more valuable it is. The face of a gradual revelation has no force in determining the method of interpretation. Any system that differentiates between later and former prophecies as to value, or between prophetic and didactic portions of Scripture as to worth, stands self-condemned as false and inadequate.

Furthermore, a proper interpretation of 2 Corinthians 3:6 does not detract in the slightest from the literal position. When Paul said: "The letter killeth, but the spirit giveth life," he was not authorizing the spiritualizing interpretation of Scripture. If the literal kills, then how is it that God gives His message in such a form? The meaning of the apostle evidently is that the mere acceptance of the letter without the work of the Holy Spirit related to it, leads to death. Moreover, the early Christians, it can be shown, interpreted the Scriptures literally, and consequently held the premillenarian doctrine. Finally, it is not true that premillennialists require every single passage to be interpreted literally without exception. They do hold, on the other hand, that if the language is symbolic, it is to be governed by the laws relating to symbols; if figurative, by the laws dealing with figues; if typical, by the laws connected with types; if literal, by the laws of nonfigurative speech. How is one to know which is metaphorical or symbolic or not? The Scriptures themselves furnish the key. In John 7:38 Christ is recorded to have said on the last great day of the feast that whoever believed in Him, out of his innermost being would flow rivers of living water. Then the Scripture immediately explains that reference is being made to the Holy Spirit, whose ministry in that manner had not yet begun, because Christ had not yet been glorified. There is, then, no mistaking the meaning of the verse. And if the Scriptures do not mean what they declare, they are valueless to us.

In closing this part of the discussion on the literal method of interpretation, one could quote many testimonies of eminent scholars in favor of that system of approach to the Scriptures. Only a few are given here. It was Bishop Hooker who held to the rule that when a literal meaning would stand, the furthest from it was usually the worst.[19] Sir Isaac Newton with great insight and foresight foretold that about the time of the end, certain men would rise who would devote their energies to prophetic studies and "insist upon their literal interpretation in the midst of much clamor and opposition."[20] Probably as valuable as testimony as any that could be offered was given by Horatius Bonar. When speaking of the results of having studied prophecy for fifty years, he concluded with the statement that, first of all, he had gained assurance as to the authority and inspiration of the Scriptures. Second, he felt more certain than ever that the literal interpretation of the Word is the best. Said he: " 'Literal, if possible,' is, I believe the only maxim that will carry you right through the Word of God from Genesis to Revelation."[21]

It might be asked, Why is time taken to compare both principles and methods of interpretation? Surely, interpretation is important for any study of any phase of theology. True, but it is particularly necessary in this study, for therein lies the crux of the entire matter. For it can be shown that the fact the early church was premillennial was traceable to its interpretation of the Word in a literal manner, whereas the cause of the departure from that view in later centuries of church history is directly attributable to a change in method of interpretation beginning with Origen in particular. Joseph Milner, the great English historian of the past century, was not astray in the least when he said: "No man, not altogether unsound and hypocritical, ever injured the church more than Origen did."[22] Authorities of former years who claim a change came with Origen are Mosheim, Giesler, Hagenbach, Chillingworth, and Gibbon. Recent writers who maintain the same are Blackstone, Chafer, Kellogg, Mains, Masselink, Silver, West, Peters, and a host of others. Mains agrees that it was through the "powerful teachings and influence" of Clement of Alexandria and Origen that the cause of chiliasm suffered eclipse in the established church. His praise of that accomplishment is somewhat dimmed, it appears, when he must admit that the interpretations of Origen and men of like method are so "fantastic and absurd as could well enter into the most childish imagination."[23] The impetus given to such interpretation of the Bible has gone on through the centuries and is manifest today. Its failure lies in the fact that it does not adequately deal with all the materials of revelation. The aim of this study is to show the consistency of the premillennial position as it is based on the literal sense of the Scriptures, and to demonstrate that by that method, and that alone, can the entire Word of God be brought into harmony.

It cannot be stated too often nor stressed too strongly that the basic and underlying difference between premillennialists and amillennialists is their respective principle of interpretation. C. K. Lehman has not overdrawn the case when he states: "Ultimately these differences [that is, in the matter of interpretation] affect evangelism and missions."[24] The results are indeed far-reaching, and they extend into every phase of theological study.

Premillennialists recognize that the foundation principle of amillennialism is the allegorizing or spiritualizing method. Homer Payne notes, "The cornerstone of amillennialism is its figurative approach to prophecy. By this it is not implied that all prophecy is given a non-literal sense but that the spiritualizing principle is allowed as valid wherever content and context appear to warrant its use. This is a basic tenet of the system and crucial to its maintenance."[25]

George Ladd correctly points out that, if the spiritualizers had their way consistently, then the second coming of Christ would have to be a spiritual coming instead of a literal one.[26] Is that not precisely the conclusion and predicament of the liberals?

Interestingly enough, amillennialists themselves are prepared to admit the danger of allegorizing. Lehman states, "Allegorizing or spiritualizing Scripture is an entirely erroneous method of interpretation. This method regards unfigurative language as figurative. Its only limitation is the imagination of the interpreter."[27] Louis Berkhof maintains, "The Alexandrian school, and especially Origen, its most brilliant representative, undermined Chiliasm by means of its allegorizing interpretation of Scripture."[28] He shows further how Augustine's view of the kingdom led unfortunately to the hierarchical conception of the Middle Ages.[29] W. H. Rutgers reveals the disastrous results of that principle. Says he, "The whole Alexandrian School is tinged with Platonic idealism which tended to disparage the temporal and spacial. Indeed, this allegorical method made unreal the historic facts of Christianity."[30] Yet he must acknowledge that "the principle laid down in his [Augustine's] theory of the millennium is that which coincides with the A-millennial view, indorsed by the Reformers and still held by those of Reformed persuasion today."[31]

How some amillennialists utilize the spiritualizing method can be seen from the position of Oswald T. Allis who not only employs allegorizing in the New Testament but uses it in the Old Testament as well. Because of the stringency of his theory, he has to take "in the days of these kings" of Daniel 2:44 as referring to all the kings of the four kingdoms, and his explanation is that it "is permissible because, while distinct, these four kingdoms were also in a sense one."[32] In what sense that is to be understood he does not satisfactorily explain, but he continues, "So we may say that it was in the period of those four empires as together representing Gentile world dominion but in the days of the last of the four that the kingdom of Messiah was set up."[33] Having permitted himself latitude to that extent, he has not prepared the reader for his position on Daniel 2 and 7 that "it is hazardous to connect them too closely. . . . It is nowhere stated in Dan. ii. that there are *ten* toes. This is only an inference from the fact that the image has the form of a man."[34] What other inference would be valid? And why such hesitancy in admitting the obvious?

Much has been made by Wyngaarden and others of the application of the spiritualizing method to the Old Testament quotations in the New Testament. The contention is that those are to be uniformly interpreted in the New Testament as spiritualizations of the Old Testament concepts. C. H. Toy tells us, on the other hand:

> We get as little light on the question, whether the Old Testament passages are cited as direct predictions, or authoritative divine utterances, respecting the persons, events, rules, or propositions, in connection with which

they are quoted; or whether these last are regarded only as illustrations of the Old Testament word. This question must be decided from the context in every case; and it is not till we have settled it from general considerations that we can determine definitely what the significance of the formula is.[35]

In each instance the nature and import of the quotation must be determined from the context. Thus it is that "the choice of a particular formula in the New Testament is determined, not according to any rigorous system of scientific use, but by the natural proprieties of the discourse."[36] Let one striking example suffice. In Romans 10:5-8 there is a quotation of Deuteronomy 30:11-14. In the Deuteronomy passage there is no question that the subject of discussion is the law of Moses. However, in the Romans passage there is equal certainty that Paul is quoting the Deuteronomy portion in a context where he is dealing with faith righteousness. The same concepts that Moses used to convey the truth of law righteousness, Paul employs to set forth faith righteousness by way of contrast. Can it be said then that the Romans passage is an interpretation, a spiritualization, an allegorization, or a fulfillment of the Old Testament quotation? It is none of those. Paul is using the Old Testament passage by way of illustration alone, as can be seen from the added material in it relative to the work of Christ in redemption, and the concluding words, "the word of faith, which we preach" (Rom. 10:8). We must ever beware of oversimplification.

The treatment of the Old Testament quotations in the New Testament leads naturally to the matter of the fulfillment of prophecy. In the case of the doctrine of the Millennium, the interpretive principle will be determining. What is the amillennial attitude toward the fulfillment of Old Testament predictions in the New Testament? Rutgers suggests that "prophecy must be interpreted in accordance with her genius."[37] Surely that is general enough and subjective enough. Lehman is more specific in telling us that the entire Old Testament was fulfilled in the New Testament. He holds:

The New Covenant is not one new disclosure to be followed by others; it is rather the consummate disclosure beyond which there remains no covenant to be made. . . . There is no promise either in the Old or New Testament of a second outpouring of the Holy Spirit; the Holy Spirit has come. There is no reference to any kingdom other than Christ's present spiritual and the Father's future eternal kingdoms. There is no reference to Christ's receiving kingly authority in the future; He is already enthroned and now possesses all authority in heaven and on earth. There is no prediction of a still more universal diffusion of the Gospel than that under the New Covenant. There is no promise of an era of salvation beyond that of the New Covenant; the ultimate that the prophets saw was the residue of men seeking the Lord and all the Gentiles upon whom God's name is called. When the Gospel is preached in all the world, the end shall come. There is no unfulfilled prophecies concerning Christ or Israel which are not comprehended under the New Covenant.[38]

When Lehman treats Daniel 9:24-27, he maintains, "The seventy weeks are found to be a continuous prophetic era which terminates with the great redemptive work of Christ, His enthronement, and the destruction of the great symbol of the Jewish state, the city of Jerusalem."[39] The reader can determine how much detailed and specific prophecy of the Old Testament such a view spiritualizes. But that is common to the amillennial position.

G. L. Murray tries to find a fulfillment in time of all Old Testament prophecies. For him Deuteronomy 28 was fulfilled in A.D. 70 (he says nothing of Deut. 30); the Davidic covenant was fulfilled in Solomon with the eternal aspects of it including Christ; and the alleged millennial prophecies of Isaiah 9 and 11, all symbolize heavenly bliss. In the case of Isaiah 11 the same symbolism is supposed to set forth the Lord's first coming, Gentile response to the gospel, and the final deliverance of creation from sin's curse.[40] That is quite a bit of spiritualizing for one chapter, but on what kind of basis?

Allis, whose basic thesis is that the prophecy of the Old Testament is fulfilled in the church of the New Testament, would have us believe that the quotation in Acts 1:20 of Psalm 69:25 and 109:8 is meant to be an "application of the Psalms to the circumstances and needs of the Church age which is about to begin."[41] Premillennialists do not deny fulfillments of Old Testament prophecy in the New Testament, but that is a far cry from the claim that the Old Testament is completely fulfilled and displaced by the New Testament revelation. After quoting Scofield on the Joel passage in Acts 2, Allis concludes: "This is an admission that Joel's words do concern the Church, and amounts to a confession that the Church is the subject of prophecy."[42]

Scofield, it is certain, confessed no such position. Peter is not citing a fulfillment of the Joel prophecy, for many features of the prophecy as quoted were not fulfilled on the day of Pentecost, but rather a partial fulfillment or preview of it, and that was not even latent in the prophecy when Joel penned it. Peter's quotation of Psalm 110:1 is a fulfillment of that prophecy, but it does not justify Allis's claiming that Christ "is now exercising that royal authority" and that the kingdom has now come. He himself must admit that Christ's enemies are not yet subdued under Him as the full prophecy in the Psalms requires.[43]

In commenting on 1 Peter 2:9-10, Allis asks: "What clearer proof do we need that the prophets foresaw and foretold the establishment of the Christian Church?"[44] It is surprising that Allis has not noted that Peter is referring here to no Old Testament prophecy whatever. Just as Israel had its Levitical priesthood and a national ideal to be a kingdom of priests and a holy nation (Exod. 19:6, which is to be fulfilled in the time of Messiah's visible coming as indicated in Zech. 3:1-10), so the church is constituted of God a chosen race and a royal priesthood. But there is no link of prophecy between these two facts. It is injected here only through an unfounded spiritualization. On John 19:37 he wants not only a past fulfillment, but a present fulfillment, and a future fulfillment. The past fulfillment in the death of Christ is delegated to Israel; the future fulfillment is also assigned to Israel (Rev. 1:7); but the present fulfillment concerns the church on the basis of John 12:32 and Matthew 16:18.[45]

Ladd appears at first to make such a broad concession, that the amillennial principle may have validity, when in discussing Hebrews 8:6-13 he states: "This passage alone proves that the Old Testament prophecies do indeed have a spiritual fulfillment in the Church, for the prophecy quoted in Hebrews is, in Jeremiah 31, addressed to the house of Israel and Judah."[46] Moreover, he indicates his agreement still further: "The present writer is ready to agree with the amillennialists that there is only one place to find a hermeneutic: in the New Testament."[47] That position has served to vitiate much of the force of Ladd's work.

The place to find a hermeneutic, a biblical hermeneutic, is in the Old Testament *and* the New Testament. Is it scientific induction to begin at the latter division of Scripture first? The Spirit of God can be depended upon to give us a revelation in orderly fashion from incompleteness to completeness; we need not fear that the latter portion will contradict the former. It is maintained and must be insisted on that the Bible can be read in order and interpreted according to proper literal principles without misgivings that the New Teatament will invalidate what is revealed in the Old Testament.

But Ladd himself is not committed to a spiritual interpretation or a spiritual fulfillment of the Old Testament in the New. He rightly indicates that "although the intellectual atmosphere of our times is against it, this literal fulfillment of biblical prophecy remains to an open mind a strong apologetic for the supernatural character of the Scriptures,"[48] and holds that "unless there is some reason intrinsic within the text itself which requires a symbolical interpretation, or unless there are other Scriptures which interpret a parallel prophecy in a symbolic sense, we are required to employ a natural, literal interpretation."[49] That is a canon of interpretation in all literature, biblical or otherwise.

Thus a spiritualizing or allegorizing principle of interpretation cannot properly be gleaned from the manner in which the New Testament deals with the Old Testament. With unusual insight and clarity S. H. Wilkinson has gone to the heart of the problem in discussing Acts 3:20-21. He contends:

> The whole body of Old Testament prophecy concerning Israel is involved in this New Testament statement. And the said New Testament statement endorses, confirms, establishes the utterances of all the Old Testament prophets and locates the fulfillment of them at the period of time when

the Lord Jesus shall return from heaven, viz. at the time of the complete restoration or re-establishment *(apokatastasis)* of all things.[50]

When the discussion comes to the broader consideration of the allegorizing versus the literal interpretation of Scripture, it is found that S. J. Case, both a liberal and a nonmillenarian, admits that Origen's method spiritualized the entire gamut of millennial hopes previously held by the church, in which procedure he has been generally followed by the opponents of chiliasm to this day.[51] He goes further in declaring that to seek to evade the literal features of the millennial hope is futile,[52] and justifies premillennialists in their opposition to the spiritualizers, who still retain the phrases of Scripture but change their original meaning.[53] Although Rutgers calls the literal principle of premillennial interpretation "rabbinical literalism,"[54] "exegetical nivelism," or the reducing of the Bible to one plane,[55] and the "fundamental error" of the premillenarians,[56] he manifests his own confusion in the matter by declaring, "Let it be understood that a belief in a literal fulfillment of the prophecies does not yet mean a literal interpretation. These two are not identical; a fact which Pre-s obviously and sadly fail to recognize."[57] His own suggestion is that "prophecy must be interpreted in accordance with her genius"—which is surely subjective enough.[58] Finally, he determines to call his own interpretation "not spiritualistic or allegoristic, but an interpretation of the Spirit of truth."[59]

F. E. Hamilton, in discussing the principle of interpretation, makes an admission: "Now we must frankly admit that a literal interpretation of the Old Testament prophecies gives us just such a picture of an earthly reign of the Messiah as the premillennialist pictures."[60] He concedes further: "At first sight, to one who accepts the Bible as the Word of God and the only infallible rule of faith and practice, the argument of the premillennialist seems unanswerable."[61] But he cannot allow the matter to rest thus, so he continues:

> However, a little deeper study of the implications of the position taken raises a doubt in one's mind in regard to the necessity of interpreting *all* Old Testament prophecies literally, and if it be admitted that even *one* prophecy is to be interpreted symbolically or spiritually, the whole principle of interpretation used by the premillennialists breaks down, and other principles of interpretation must be admitted possible.[62]

But that rule will have to work both ways. It must mean that once the amillennialists interpret any prophecy literally, then their position breaks down. They believe that Christ is coming again. That means they must have taken the many prophecies of His second coming literally. It is well known that liberals interpret the second coming in a spiritualizing manner as an ever-present one. Hamilton has laid down a rule that he will find difficult to adhere to.

Hamilton's complaint is that "a literal interpretation of the Old Testament prophecies brings them into *direct conflict with the New Testament prophecies* pertaining to the events preceding and following the Second Coming of Christ."[63] That is a serious charge if it could be proved true. He spends much time in his volume on the supposed discrepancy between the premillennial claim for procreation in the Millennium (on the basis of Isaiah 65:20, which he nowhere in his work interprets from his point of view), and the words of our Lord in Luke 20:27-36 that there will be neither marrying nor giving in marriage. Instead of charging premillennialists with bringing the Old Testament into conflict with the prophecy of Christ, and erring because they know not the Scriptures,[64] he should have given heed to the very words of the context: "They that are accounted worthy to attain to that world, and the resurrection from the dead, neither marry, nor are given in marriage." Not all in the Millennium will have come there by way of resurrection (for instance, the godly Jews and Gentiles saved out of the Great Tribulation); only the resurrected ones will not marry. Failure to realize more than one group of saints in the period (a result of amillennial oversimplification) accounts for the dilemma, not of the premillennial position, but of the amillennial.

And it is not that Hamilton does not recognize that "of course, there are many passages in prophecy that were meant to be taken literally,"[65] for he lays down the principles that the literal interpretation is to be followed unless there is figurative language (and to that premillennialists agree), or the New Testament indicates a nonliteral sense, or the literal interpretation contradicts truths and statements of the New Testament. In spite of those declared principles of interpretation, he starts with the symbolical interpretation first, and comes to the literal only when he thinks he has to.[66] Such compulsion comes upon him when discussing judgment for Israel. He states:

> But what shall we say about the prophecies concerning the unbelieving Jews? Are they, too, symbolical, or are we to expect a literal fulfillment? Well, in the first place there is no evidence that there is any racial prosperity or national restoration promised to the Jews as a people, apart from their acceptance of Christ as Saviour. . . . It is salvation, not national restoration, that is the great hope of the Jew, and after he is saved, he is on exactly the same basis as the Christian Gentile, as we have shown above. However, for the unbelieving Jew, there are prophecies which we have every reason to expect will be literally fulfilled. Those promises are of wrath and judgment, of being scattered among the nations of the world, and of persecution and tribulation. [What of Romans 11:25-27 alone?] There is no hint or indication anywhere in the New Testament that such prophecies are to be interpreted in any other way than literally. In fact the persistence of the Jewish race in the world and the constant persecution to which they have been subjected, is one of the wonders of prophecy fulfilled before our eyes. Nothing but wrath and destruction awaits the

race unless they turn to Christ and accept him as their Saviour and Messiah.[67]

So Hamilton does believe in literal fulfillments for Israel, but only in the matter of wrath. What shall we do then with a passage like Isaiah 49:14-23?

Murray declares: "If evangelicals complain that liberals rob the Word of God of the meaning which God has meant it to convey, it may well be feared that literalists are guilty of adding to it what God has not put into it; and, while claiming to be fundamentalists and evangelicals, they may be equally blameworthy in the sight of God."[68] Unfortunately, he does not realize that, whereas there are liberals in the amillennial camp (such as Case, to say nothing of Romanists who also have no room for an earthly Millennium), there are no liberals in the premillennial camp; nor does he recognize how one may add to the Word of God by confining it within the limits of some church creed or formula. Furthermore, it can be shown that he misunderstands the principle of literal interpretation; for like other amillennialists, he does not distinguish between literal interpretation and spiritualization, because he thinks literal interpretation can allow for no use of figures.[69]

In another charge Murray indicates that the literalist "is following the Jewish method of interpretation which led its exponents to expect a literal fulfillment of every prophecy and which led them to reject and crucify their Messiah."[70] We should like to ask whether the prophecies of the first coming of Christ were literally fulfilled? They assuredly were, as Matthew testifies again and again. Moreover, Murray manifests he does not understand why Israel rejected their Messiah. Christ Himself gives us the answer in Luke 24:25, where He charges them with not believing all that the prophets had written, namely, prediction of the suffering of the Messiah as well as His reign; and in John 5:40, where He points out that their hardened hearts would not permit them to come unto Him for life.

Berkhof believes that the New Testament rules out literal interpretation. He maintains:

> It is remarkable that the New Testament, which is the fulfillment of the Old, contains no indication whatsoever of the reestablishment of the Old Testament theocracy by Jesus, nor a single undisputed positive prediction of its restoration, while it does contain abundant indications of the spiritual fulfillment of the promises given to Israel. . . . The New Testament certainly does not favor the literalism of the Premillenarians.[71]

Berkhof is surely asking for a great deal in any realm of biblical interpretation when he asks for that which is "undisputed." Are his positions undisputed by the premillennialists?

What does Berkhof make of the positive predictions in Romans 11:25-27 and Revelation 11 concerning Israel? They cannot be made to refer to the church. To claim that the descriptions of the prophets defy literal interpretation, as Berkhof does,[72] is a matter of opinion; it is also noteworthy that he avoids giving his own interpretation of the passages he cites. The interpretation of the literal view is already known. Even he seems to allow for some literal interpretation, for he writes:

> But we are told that all the prophecies fulfilled in the past, received a literal fulfillment; and that, therefore, the presumption is that all prophecies will be so fulfilled. However, though it was but natural that prophecies referring to the near future should be fulfilled in the exact form in which they were uttered, this is not to be expected *a priori*, nor is it likely in the case of prophecies pertaining to the distant future, to a new dispensation with greatly altered conditions.[73]

Several remarks are in order here. First, Isaiah certainly indicated that, because prophecy was fulfilled in a certain manner in the past, one is to look for the same type of fulfillment in the future. Else, how can anyone understand Isaiah 42:9? Second, why make an exception for prophecies relating to the near future? Finally, how were those to whom the prophecies were ultimately transmitted to know when the prophecies were fulfilled? Is that applicable to the mode of death by crucifixion, mentioned in Psalm 22, though that form of death was not known in the history of Israel until centuries later? Under his principle, what happens to prophecy altogether as to value, except for those who can view it after fulfillment?

Allis thinks that the literal interpretation of Scripture exalts the Old Testament above the New.[74] On the contrary, the natural interpretation gives each portion of the Word of God its rightful due; it does not wipe out the testimony of the Old Testament because of a certain view of the New, nor does it destroy the essence of the witness of the New Testament by removing its basis and foundation in the Old. To give specific instances, when he speaks of the Babylon of the book of Revelation, he states: "If Israel must be Israel and Canaan always Canaan, should not Babylon always mean Babylon and Euphrates always mean Euphrates?"[75] And they do, but he has failed to notice that the Revelation speaks of "Mystery Babylon," which is not identical with, but distinct from, literal Babylon. The added word is the clue to another than literal Babylon. Jerusalem is Jerusalem unless one finds a qualifying word or words, as in the phrase "New Jerusalem."

Allis expresses surprise that Darby, "an ardent literalist," should be able to interpret figures when he finds them, and this attitude is taken throughout his work.[76] One who interprets Scripture literally has a right to believe that "the trees shall clap their hands" does not mean that trees have literal hands. As has been noted before, the literal interpretation allows for the natural interpretation of figures as figures according to the accepted canons of rhetoric. Would not Allis's opponents in the liberal camp, who know him to be a defender of the literal interpretations in the matter of the Mosaic authorship of the Pentateuch, the Isaianic authorship of all of Isaiah, the Danielic authorship of the book of Daniel, and other vital matters of Old Testament interpretation, be more than surprised to find him such an ardent opponent of the literal interpretation when it comes to the interpretation of prophecy? Would they not be fairly amazed to find him treating Luke 1:31-33 as definitely literal up to and including the words "Most High," and then by a *volte face* interpreting the rest of the passage as spiritual?

But it is Allis who accuses premillennialists, especially dispensationalists, of strange inconsistency. He declares, "While Dispensationalists are extreme literalists, they are very inconsistent ones. They are literalists in interpreting prophecy. But in the interpreting of history, they carry the principle of typical interpretation to an extreme which has rarely been exceeded even by the most ardent of allegorizers."[77] W. M. Smith feels that charge keenly, for he states:

> For myself, I think we need to give *very* careful attention to the issue Dr. Allis raises, namely, if we agree we find the church in the book of Ruth, typologically, why not in Ezekiel; if the church is prefigured in the marriage of Isaac, why may we not find it prophesied in Isaiah? All these things are important, and we are not dogmatic as to their final interpretation.[78]

But "typology is not spiritualization."[79]

Second, Scripture itself uses historical events of the Old Testament for types. Compare Galatians 4 with its use of Genesis 21; that does not invalidate the historical character of the Genesis narrative. First Corinthians 10 reveals that the events of the Old Testament are to be taken typically. The New Testament refers to Old Testament events, persons, and institutions as types of New Testament truths.

Third, when types are drawn from historical narrative, it is clear what the underlying historical truth is. But when prophecies are allegorized (or made into allegorizations), who can inform the reader then what the underlying truth was meant to be?

Finally, no informed dispensationalist and premillenarian would deny that some overdraw types. Every school of thought suffers from some extremists.

P. E. Hughes, who has recently written on the interpretation of prophecy, believes that the problems of interpretation "are intensified by the consideration that biblical prophecy not infrequently has two stages of fulfillment, a proximate or preparatory stage and an ultimate or consummating stage." That is precisely what the reader is alerted to through the two advents of Christ, through the explanation of the Lord of Isaiah 61:1 and following in the Nazareth synagogue (Luke 4:16-21), and the preparatory fulfillment of Joel 2:28-32 in Acts 2:1-21. Nor is it necessary to underscore the truth of 2 Corinthians 1:19-20 as a guiding principle overriding all others. It is somewhat like the carrying of coals to Newcastle to be told:

The covenant that God made with Abraham was a milestone of the most fundamental importance in the history of prophecy [see chap. 7 for the treatment there]. A right understanding of the significance of the Abrahamic covenant and its implications is conducive to a right understanding not only of the entire prophetic perspective of Holy Sctipture but also of the heart of the Christian Gospel itself in which this covenant comes to full fruition.[80]

That does allow latitude for him to quote Joshua 21:43-45 as the fulfillment of all God's promises to Abraham.

When Hughes comes to the gospels, he maintains, "By the kingdom of *heaven* is meant a kingdom that is not this-worldly and that is eternal because it is the kingdom *of God* (Jn. 3:3, 5)" (italics his).[81] That does not mean the kingdom cannot be on earth, as he denies on the basis of John 18:36. Christ said, "Not of this world," but He did not say, "Not in this world." That shopworn argument against premillennialism could be removed for good, if only the rest of the verse (John 18:36) were considered, for it interprets the first clause of the verse.

But the amillenarian position must be upheld, so Hughes argues further: "The accomplishment of redemption is followed by the enthronement of the Redeemer. This is the setting up of his kingdom . . . [after quoting Heb. 1:3] that is to say, he took his place *on his* throne [italics his], the seat of his sovereign authority."[82] He equates Christ's throne with Revelation 3:21 in spite of Psalm 110:1; Hebrews 1:3; 8:1; 10:12-13; 12:1-2; and definitively Matthew 25:31.

But surely, it may be contended, there is a consummating phase of Christ's kingdom as indicated in 1 Corinthians 15:24-28. When literal interpretation is abandoned, the result is: "His kingdom is not future, but present, extending from his ascension to his return, when he will hand it over to God the Father as universal righteousness is established under the sovereign sway of the trinitarian Godhead."[83] When words are not taken in their natural sense, unless figurative language is clearly indicated, every man's imagination is the final seat of authority. If that method were practiced on the doctrines of redemption, it would make a shambles of the Christian faith.

Because "the kingdom of heaven is at hand" is not found in Acts and the epistles, Hughes holds: "The reason for this, as we have shown above, is that, as the apostles consistently taught, the ascension of Jesus denotes also his enthronement and the inauguration of his kingdom."[84] Not once does he mention Matthew 13 and its application to the question of the kingdom of Christ. Where is the fulfillment of Old Testament prophecies concerning Israel as a nation entering into Messiah's kingdom (Isa. 60—66; Rom. 11:25-27)?

When Hughes confuses the doctrine of resurrection by terminology pertinent to two different transactions, he places the second resurrection at "the moment of Christ's return at the end of this age"[85] (for the believer). And that position is taken in spite of the clear, unmistakable use of ordinal numerals in Revelation 20:5, 6, 14.

Many amillennialists focus their strongest barrages against millennialism at Revelation 20, for that is the Waterloo, the coup de grace, of the antichiliasts. Hughes contends:

> Those who insist on a literalistic principle of interpretation—though it is a principle to which even they find it impossible to adhere with consistency—object that "one thousand years" means what it says. If this is correct, then our understanding of Revelation 20 is clearly invalidated, because now nearly two millennia have passed by since Christ's ascension. . . . To interpret literalistically what is intended symbolically cannot fail to do violence to the sacred text.[86]

The last statement seems as patent an example of begging the question as possible.

After citing a number of similes in Revelation, Hughes concludes: "There is no possibility that the key of literalism will open the secrets of such symbolism; and, in practice even if not in theory, this fact is universally recognized by exponents of this book."[87] First of all, it is clear he does not understand what literal interpretation involves (see McClain's note above). Second, he surely is not concluding by logical induction of facts when he speaks of "universally recognized" by interpreters of the Revelation. Because the number *seven* is used symbolically in Revelation (also 666), he believes the 144,000 of chapters 7 and 14, the 7,000 of 11:13, or the 12,000 stadia of the New Jerusalem of 21:16, and the 1,000 of chapter 20 should be also. Is that true of the two witnesses (chap. 11), the two beasts (chap. 13), and the two resurrections (chap. 20)? Symbolical use of the number *seven*, for instance, does not allow the interpreter to think of ten actual churches in proconsular Asia, or a dozen seals, trumpets, or bowls. Again, beware of that which is too simplistic.

Recently, there appeared a work representing a symposium of four theologians who discussed four views on the meaning of the Millennium.[88] Ladd presents the position of so-called "historic premillennialism." He spends much time opposing the hermeneutic of literal interpretation in dispensationalism. He claims that to insist on a literal hermeneutic and expect others to do so also "amounts to the claim that only dispensationalism, with its literal hermeneutic of the Old Testament, can provide a truly evangelical theology. In my view this simply is not true."[89] "A truly evangelical theology" does not lie in the area just indicated, as literal interpreters of dispensational persuasion know full well. Orthodox men hold varying views on the matter at issue; the crux of the whole discussion is: Which approach best harmonizes the data of Scripture?

] 59 [

Ladd himself admits his ambivalence in interpretation; he claims he is "a nondispensationalist because I do not keep Israel and the church distinct throughout God's program."[90] It is in point to ask, Why not? After declaring that one of the main reasons for literally interpreting Old Testament prophecies regarding the end is because those concerning the first coming of Christ were fulfilled literally, he cautions, "This, however, is an argument which must be closely examined. The fact is that the New Testament frequently interprets Old Testament prophecies in a way *not suggested by the Old Testament context.*"[91]

Two observations are in order. First, Ladd's stricture must be used with caution, because it is an argument which amillennialists use and carry to allegorizing extents, as seen above in the work of Wyngaarden. Second, as a Greek scholar he knows full well that Old Testament passages are employed in the New Testament in a number of ways. They can be discerned as statements of exact fulfillment (Matt. 1:22,23), as illustrative (1 Cor. 9:7-10), as contrasts (cf. Rom. 10:5-10 with Deut. 30:11-14), and as a consensus of testimony (Matt. 2:23), among others, but not for purposes of allegorization or for emptying a prophecy of its valid prediction. Instead of developing a system for his so-called "historic premillennialism," he labors to refute dispensationalism and its literal interpretive principle.

The reader is told, "The Old Testament is reinterpreted in light of the Christ event."[92] How that works out is seen in such a statement as: "Isaiah 53 is not a prophecy of the Messiah. *Messiah* [italics his] means 'anointed' and designates the victorious, anointed king."[93] First, Ladd has no valid basis for using "Messiah" in one of its three meanings and to disallow the other two. Second, by this reasoning Israel may be completely exonerated for not accepting Jesus of Nazareth as Messiah in His first advent. Finally, the prolonged discussion seems unaware that the Old Testament prophecies revealed a twofold ministry of Messiah in two appearings: to redeem and then to reign.

Once the nonliteral approach is started, it leads directly to a hermeneutical cul-de-sac. Ladd continues: "I do not see how it is possible to avoid the conclusion that the New Testament applies [notice the word] Old Testament prophecies to the New Testament church and in so doing identifies the church as spiritual Israel."[94] Not a verse of Scripture is given in proof, because there is none.

In a manner of recapitulation Ladd holds: "Here is the basic watershed between a dispensational and a nondispensational theology. Dispensationalism forms its eschatology by a literal interpretation of the Old Testament and then fits the New Testament into it. A nondispensational eschatology forms its theology from the explicit teaching of the New Testament."[95] That type of interpretation leads him to assert, "There are unavoidable indications that the Old Testament promises to Israel are fulfilled in the Christian church. The alert reader will say, 'This sounds like amillennialism.' And so it does. I suspect that the amillennial writer will heartily agree with all that has been said thus far."[96]

Several objections are in order here. First, if fault is found with a literal interpretation, which, it is said, fits the New Testament into it, how is a biblical induction to be achieved? Is it to be feared that the Old Testament and the New Testament will be found in conflict with each other? Second, to assert that nondispensational eschatology is built on the "explicit" teaching of the New Testament is without proof, is an oversimplification, and should seriously indicate the employment of a dual hermeneutic. Third, there is not a scintilla of evidence that the promises of Israel in the Old Testament are fulfilled in the Christian church. The position has been repeated many times, but where is the foundation in fact? Finally, it is strange that a declared premillennialist should be complacent that his position sounds like that of the opposing camp. There must be a fuzziness or blurring of distinctives to achieve such an impression.

In countering the position of Herman Hoyt, the amillennialist Anthony Hoekema discerns the essential difference: "My disagreement concerns primarily [note this] his method of interpreting Scripture."[97] But it is interesting and strange to hear Hoekema affirm: "It is a gross oversimplification to suggest that the main issue between dispensationalists and nondispensationalists is that of a literal versus a nonliteral interpretation of Scripture. Dispensationalists sometimes interpret nonliterally, and nondispensationalists sometimes interpret literally."[98]

To dispel the confusion, a few points need to be made. First of all, Hoekema is surely out of step with his colleagues in the amillennial camp when he gives so little weight to the difference in interpretation between the two eschatological positions. Second, when he charges that dispensationalists "sometimes" interpret nonliterally, he needs to define his terms more clearly to substantiate his claim. Finally, in all fairness he should indicate that many nondispensationalists interpret literally as a last resort.

How did the amillennialists come to accept a nonliteral interpretation of the Bible? Actually, John Calvin and the Reformers were declared literalists, but they forsook the literal interpretation in eschatology to preserve the position of Roman Catholic eschatology in which they saw no harm.[99] G. H. Hospers gives an example from Romans 9 to 11, which is Calvinistic in character but will not allow of spiritualization at the end any more than at the beginning, where the doctrine of election is discussed. He states, "A careful examination of Hodge's excellent commentary on Romans will show, in these passages, how near he is compelled, on his own principles, to approach the Chiliastic position, and the step by which he avoids landing in their camp is so transparently evasive as to strike one dumb with amazement."[100]

Why is spiritualization so dangerous?

[It] is attributing another and a special sense to the original terms. It partakes of the Swedenborgian principle of hermeneutics which holds to four senses of every Scripture. It is a great pity that so acute a mind as Calvin, after having given such clear and strong testimony in favor of a single fundamental interpretation of Scripture, should after all have fallen into so much spiritualization that even Kuyper took exception to it. He warned against "soul-killing spiritualizing."[101]

Amillennialists need to be reminded, moreover, that "there is nothing low or unworthy about any part of God's material creation as such."[102] The literal, material, earthly is not to be avoided per se, for avoidance savors of the Gnostic abhorrence of the material. It can be shown that, if the spiritualizing principle be admitted into all realms of Christian doctrine, every orthodox doctrine would be eliminated.[103]

In conclusion, we must agree with the words of Homer Payne:

It is not only true that there is an affinity between premillennialism and fundamentalism, but it does not seem too much to say that the great strength of modern liberalism had its spring and finds its support in post- and amillennial circles. This is due in large measure to the fact that the literal interpretation of the Scripture has been set aside and thus the door has been thrown open to all other error.[104]

NOTES

[1]B. Ramm (*Protestant Biblical Interpretation* [1974 reprint], p. 113) assigns the statement to an "old adage."

[2]J. H. Todd, *Principles of Interpretation,* p. 20.

[3]E. M. Milligan, *Is the Kingdom at Hand?* p. 24.

[4]R. B. Girdlestone, *The Grammar of Prophecy,* p. 48; M. S. Terry, *Biblical Hermeneutics,* p. 405. Cf. also B. Ramm, *Protestant Biblical Interpretation* (1970 ed.), pp. 241-75.

[5]Bibliographic details unavailable at this writing.

[6]S. H. Kellogg, *Are Premillennialists Right?* pp. 82-83. Cf. also S. Leathes, *Old Testament Prophecy,* pp. 275-91; see also pp. 292-305.

[7]N. West, *The Thousand Years in Both Testaments,* pp. 91-95.

[8]G. Vos, "Eschatology of the New Testament," ISBE, 2:979.

[9]Ibid., p. 980.

[10]W. Masselink, *Why Thousand Years?* p. 168.

[11]G. H. Schodde, "Interpretation," ISBE, 3:1490.

[12]The expression "potentiation of ecumenicity," evidently referring to universality raised to the highest power, was employed by R. Kliefoth in his *Revelation of John* (German), 2:153, cited by Nathaniel West, *The Thousand Years in Both Testaments,* p. 332.

[13]M. J. Wyngaarden, *The Future of the Kingdom in Prophecy and Fulfillment*, p. 85.

[14]Ibid., pp. 88-134.

[15]G. P. Mains, *Premillennialism: Non-scriptural, Non-historic, Non-scientific, Non-philosophical*, pp. 56-57.

[16]C. Hodge, *Systematic Theology*, 3:866.

[17]Masselink, p. 34.

[18]Terry, pp. 173-74, 203-10.

[19]Cf. I. Walton, *The Works of Richard Hooker*, 3 vols.

[20]Quoted in West, *The Thousand Years*, p. 462.

[21]Ibid.

[22]Joseph Milner, *The History of the Church of Christ*, 1:221. Cf. also *Works of Martin Luther*, 2:190, 276; also 6:367, 453. Muhlenberg Press, Philadelphia, 1943. See J. A. Neander, *General History of the Christian Religion and Church*, pp. 388, 552-57, 711-22.

[23]Mains, p. 58.

[24]C. K. Lehman, *The Fulfillment of Prophecy*, p. 27. The ramifications of the interpretive principle are, indeed, far-reaching as Walvoord has maintained: "The controversy between pretribulationists and posttribulationists is, in miniature, a replica of the larger controversy of premillennialism and amillennialism as far as principles of interpretation are concerned" (J. F. Walvoord, *The Rapture Question*, p. 60).

[25]H. L. Payne, *Amillennial Theology as a System*, p. 33.

[26]G. E. Ladd, *Crucial Questions About the Kingdom of God*, p. 138.

[27]Lehman, p. 8.

[28]L. Berkhof, *The Kingdom of God*, p. 22.

[29]Ibid., p. 23.

[30]W. H. Rutgers, *Premillennialism in America*, p. 64.

[31]Ibid., p. 71.

[32]O. T. Allis, *Prophecy and the Church*, p. 124.

[33]Ibid., p. 125.

[34]Ibid.

[35]C. H. Toy, *Quotations in the New Testament*, p. xxx.

[36]Ibid., p. xxxi.

[37]Rutgers, p. 138.

[38]Lehman, p. 6.

[39]Ibid., p. 17.

[40]G. L. Murray, *Millennial Studies: A Search for Truth*, pp. 44, 46.

[41]Allis, p. 135.

[42]Ibid., p. 136.

[43]Ibid., pp. 136-37.

[44]Ibid., p. 158.

[45]Ibid.

[46]Ladd, *Crucial Questions,* p. 137. In another work Ladd stated: "The author takes it as a basic hermeneutical principle that in disputed questions of interpretation, the simpler view is to be preferred; *the burden of proof rests upon the more elaborate explanation* [italics his]" (Ladd, *The Blessed Hope,* p. 165). The issue is not so simple. Is it true in textual criticism that the simpler is the more correct? In interpretation, was the simplistic view of Job's sufferings the true one?

[47]Ladd, *Crucial Questions,* p. 138.

[48]Ibid., p. 139.

[49]Ibid., p. 141.

[50]S. H. Wilkinson, *The Israel Promises and Their Fulfillment,* p. 128.

[51]S. J. Case, *The Millennial Hope,* p. 178.

[52]Ibid., p. 215.

[53]Ibid., p. 216.

[54]Rutgers, p. 137.

[55]Ibid., p. 138.

[56]Ibid., p. 263.

[57]Ibid., p. 150.

[58]Ibid., p. 138.

[59]Ibid., p. 139.

[60]F. E. Hamilton, *The Basis of Millennial Faith,* p. 38. Bass must concede: "One great impetus to its [dispensational premillennialism] growth has been an invariable insistence that the Bible must be taken literally as the Word of God, and its meaning must not be 'spiritualized' " (C. B. Bass, *Backgrounds to Dispensationalism—Its Historical Genesis and Ecclesiastical Implications,* p. 21). He laments the fact that "literal interpretation became synonymous with valid interpretation. Naturally this affected his [J. N. Darby's] general eschatological outlook, since symbolism is an inherent part [sic] of prophecy" (ibid., p. 130).

[61]Hamilton, p. 40.

[62]Ibid. Ryrie cogently answers Hamilton's charge: "It must suffice to show that only dispensationalism consistently [note this] employs the principles of literal interpretation" (C. C. Ryrie, "The Necessity of Dispensationalism," in J. F. Walvoord, ed, *Truth for Today,* p. 45). Furthermore, even "premillennialists who are not dispensationalists also have to depart from literal interpretation at certain points in their eschatology" (p.46).

[63]Ibid., p. 46.

[64]Ibid., p. 47.

[65]Ibid., p. 53.

[66]Ibid., p. 59.

[67]Ibid., p. 58.

[68]Murray, p. 24.

[69]Ibid., pp. 36-38. In speaking of the literal method of interpretation, McClain has rightly stated: "This method, as its adherents have explained times without number, leaves room for all the devices and nuances of language, including the use of figure, metaphor, simile, symbol, and even allegory" (A. J. McClain, *The Greatness of the Kingdom,* p. 139).

[70]Ibid., p. 40.

[71]L. Berkhof, *Systematic Theology,* p. 713.

[72]Berkhof, *The Kingdom of God,* p. 163.

[73]Ibid., p. 165.

[74]Allis, p. 48.

[75]Ibid., p. 31.

[76]Ibid., p. 179.

[77]Ibid., p. 21.

[78]W. M. Smith, "Israel and the Church in Prophecy," in *Sunday School Times,* p. 958.

[79]G. H. Hospers, *The Principle of Spiritualization in Hermeneutics,* p. 18.

[80]P. E. Hughes, *Interpreting Prophecy,* pp. 9-10, 15.

[81]Ibid., p. 24.

[82]Ibid., p. 25 f.

[83]Ibid., p. 27.

[84]Ibid., p. 28.

[85]Ibid., p. 122.

[86]Ibid., p. 123.

[87]Ibid., pp. 125, 125-26.

[88]R. G. Clouse, ed., *The Meaning of the Millennium,* 1977.

[89]Ibid., pp. 19-20.

[90]Ibid., p. 20.

[91]Ibid.

[92]Ibid., p. 21.

[93]Ibid., pp. 21, 22. That this position is not a *lapsus calami* or *lapsus memoriae* can be seen from his further statement: "Isaiah 53 is not, in its own historical setting, a prophecy of Messiah. It becomes such only when it is interpreted in light of the Christ event. This clearly establishes the principle that the 'literal hermeneutic' does not work" (ibid., pp. 22-23). Incredible reasoning.

[94]Ibid., p. 23.

[95]Ibid., p. 27.

[96]Ibid.

[97]Ibid., p. 104. Even the postmillennialist Loraine Boettner has to admit: "It is generally agreed that if the prophecies are taken literally, they do foretell a restoration of the nation of Israel in the land of Palestine with the Jews

having a prominent place in that kingdom and ruling over the other nations" (ibid., p. 95).

[98]Ibid., p. 107.

[99]H. L. Payne, pp. 87-88.

[100]G. H. Hospers, *The Calvinistic Character of Premillennialism*, p. 8.

[101]Hospers, *Spiritualization in Hermeneutics*, p. 12. See A. Kuyper, *Chiliasm or the Doctrine of Premillennialism*.

[102]Ibid., p. 14.

[103]Ibid., pp. 39-40.

[104]H. L. Payne, p. 366.

3

Dispensationalism

Closely, if not inseparably, related to the vital theme of biblical interpretation, which has been treated in detail, is that of dispensationalism. Dispensationalism as a method of Scripture interpretation, though employed for centuries as will be shown later, has come in for vehement attack in the last thirty or more years. The present tactics of some amillennialists are designed to divide premillennialists on the issue of dispensationalism.[1] Actually, the confirmed amillennialist finds chiliasm as unpalatable without dispensationalism as with it.

The common charge against dispensationalism is its alleged newness or recent character. J. E. Bear begins his treatment of dispensationalism with the statement: " 'Dispensationalism' as we know it today is of comparatively recent origin, having had its beginnings in England in the last century among the Plymouth Brethren."[2] Would that in itself disqualify the view? As far as Bible truth is concerned, the Plymouth Brethren can lay as large a claim to it as any group. But Bear's aim is to show that premillennialists today who are dispensationalists also, do not hold the same premillennial scheme that was prevalent in the early church. He must admit, however, "Of course, doctrines may be new and yet not untrue."[3] As a matter of fact, the new doctrine could be a further development of a previously held truth. Even if it contradicted previous views, it could still be true if in accord with the Scriptures on the subject.

Ladd tells us, "A little over seventy-five years ago, there arose a type of premillennialism which has exercised great influence both in England and America."[4] He makes that type so distinct that he gives it a separate category, dividing conservative interpretations of the kingdom of God into postmillennial, premillennial, dispensational, and amillennial. To do so is both arbitrary and unwarranted, as is evident from his later statement:

> It is not important for the present purpose to determine whether the views of Darby and Kelly were original with them or were taken over from their antecedents and made popular by them. Sources to solve this historical problem are not available to the present writer. For all practical purposes, we may consider that this movement—for dispensationalism

has had such wide influence that it must be called a movement—had its source with Darby and Kelly.[5]

Allis is not so gracious in his appraisal when he contends: "Dispensationalists have accepted the prophetic teachings of the Brethren but until recently have shown themselves decidedly unwilling to disclose the source from which they derived them."[6] It is too bad he did not indicate the reason for their recent change, if one has taken place.

Is dispensationalism new, as its opponents claim? The reader will be interested to know that even some amillennialists do not believe it is of recent origin. Rutgers writes:

> One of the more objectionable and novel features in the development of modern Pre [sic] in America is the doctrine known as *dispensationalism*. It at once exhibits Judaism, and that in its last stage of Rabbinism, and biblicism. It is novel and modern in the sense that its widespread acceptance among Christians in America dates from the last decade of the nineteenth century. . . . Dispensationalism as such, however, is not an invention of these few decades.[7]

A. Reese, whose aim is avowedly to expose the alleged errors of the dispensational system, speaks of those views thus: "It matters not that they are new and novel, and have never been heard of in the whole history of the Christian Church since the Apostolic Age. What men call heresy sometimes proves to be the truth of God."[8]

D. H. Kromminga, who probably more than any other in recent years has carried on extensive research into the historical features of premillennialism, assures us: "Subdivision of the dispensations had already been made by Tertullian and Joachim, and multiplication of dispensations had likewise appeared in Origen."[9] He honestly states that fact, though he himself takes the anomalous position of seeking to wed premillennialism to the Reformed doctrine of the covenant of grace. The truth of the matter is that dispensations were recognized in the early centuries of the church, but they have received a more detailed and thoroughgoing treatment in more recent years. Too, "It is not much over a century since the last of the crust of misinformation succeeding the advent and official recognition of the spiritualizing theory, was broken through."[10]

Lewis Sperry Chafer was probably the great teacher of dispensational truth in his generation. Fortunately, he has left us his mature conclusions, not only in his monumental theology, but also in his study entitled *Dispensationalism*. Here he points out one of the reasons dispensationalism appears new to many. He rightly maintains, "In the recovery of vital truth in the Reformation dispensational distinctions, like various other doctrines, were not emphasized."[11] This explains why those who are wedded to Reformation creeds and formulas, but not always willing to concede the Reformation principle of the right of the

individual to interpret the Bible for himself under the leading of the Holy Spirit, find dispensationalism such a novelty. Chafer points out: "To a considerable degree, all Christians are dispensationalists," because
(1) Any person is a dispensationalist who trusts the blood of Christ rather than bringing an animal sacrifice. (2) Any person is a dispensationalist who disclaims any right or title to the land which God covenanted to Israel for an everlasting inheritance. And (3) any person is a dispensationalist who observes the first day of the week rather than the seventh.[12]
The validity of that position is amply attested when the antidispensationalist Hamilton sets forth three dispensations in his scheme: (1) pre-Mosaic; (2) Mosaic; and (3) New Testament.[13]

Kromminga is very emphatic that premillennialism need not be dispensational, when he holds:

> Premillennialism need not be dispensationalistic, as its history shows. And when men *insist* on a conflict between the Reformed Covenant-doctrine and the premillenarian *dispensationalism* . . . then, though they are right, it is time to remind them of that history and to ask whether they are not really proceeding from the Anabaptist conception of the Church also. As yet, the assumption of an inherent conflict between the millennium and the covenant is unproven.[14]

His position is untenable as will be seen later; it is an attempt to harmonize irreconcilables. Reformed covenant doctrine cannot be harmonized with premillenarianism.

Ladd, though defending premillennialism, says, "Masselink made the mistake, so often made by amillenarians, of identifying premillennialism as such with its dispensational form."[15] Whether Masselink was wrong will soon be seen. It will not do to lament the exclusive identification of premillennialism in America with dispensationalism,[16] for until recently, when new-premillennialism made its appearance—a form of premillennialism that seeks to make itself more acceptable to amillennialism—the normative premillennial view has been the dispensational.

To all attempts to inject a wedge between premillennialism and dispensationalism, Chafer has the sufficient answer. He contends,

> Another claim has been made in recent discussions: "I am a premillennialist, but not a dispensationalist." This statement evidently supposes that premillennialism is a belief in an event which is isolated from all that precedes and all that follows it. The term *premillennial* conveys the thought that Christ comes before the millennium. In reality premillennialism becomes a dominating feature of interpretation since it bears on the whole divine program from its beginning to its end. As well might it be argued that though the sun rises in the morning it will neither be preceded by darkness nor accompanied by light as to contend that Christ

will come to the earth again, as the Scriptures relate that coming to all that precedes it and all that follows, without causing the most stupendous dispensational changes.[17]

Allis has taken much pain to level extended and serious charges against dispensationalists. He claims: "Dispensationalism has become increasingly in recent years a seriously divisive factor in evangelical circles."[18] The cliché is in point here that all others are divisive when they differ with us. A more serious accusation is that modernism (higher criticism) and dispensationalism share a common error.[19] Allis knows full well that the amillennial camp includes, along with orthodox men, avowed liberals like Case and the general run of modernists, as well as Romanists. No amillennialist can show such variegated complexion in dispensational premillennialism. Dispensationalists hold to all the cardinal doctrines of the faith. "It is the dispensationalists who are promoting Bible study movements over the whole land and they are the major factor in all evangelistic and missionary activity today. Dispensationalism has always been disastrous to theological dicta that cannot stand the acid test of biblical proof."[20] And again,

> There is a reason why churches are filled, souls are saved, and the interest in missionary work thrives, where the whole Bible with its vital distinctions is faithfully preached. Agreement cannot be accorded to recent writers who accuse the faithful Bible expositors and evangelists of this and past generations of being modernists, and only because they stand for that form of doctrine and recognize those distinctions which are invariably discovered when the whole Bible is considered and believed and when it is given its plain and reasonable interpretation.[21]

Furthermore, instead of hopelessly dividing the Word of God, dispensationalism, by its proper and warranted divisions, manifests the inner and basic unity and continuity of the Bible. It reveals clearly that man, no matter under which regime or test he is placed, is hopelessly inadequate to become righteous in the sight of God and must always ultimately come to God for the bestowal of His righteousness.[22] Ladd is assuredly right when he credits dispensationalism with "the support of some of the most godly ministers and Bible teachers America has ever known," and affirms, "It is doubtful if there has been any other circle of men who have done more by their influence in preaching, teaching and writing to promote a love for Bible study, a hunger for the deeper Christian life, a passion for evangelism and zeal for missions in the history of American Christianity."[23]

Allis charges all dispensationalists with antipathy to creeds. That argument can be a two-edged sword, for the Roman Church has her creeds too. Are we prepared to incorporate all of them into systems? Standing in the tradition of the Reformation, it is vital to be sympathetic toward the teaching of Scripture, rather than to be prejudicially bound by creeds of men at the outset. Rutgers exhibits a misunderstanding of some of the basic tenets of dispensational premillennialism in speaking of the dispensations: "Applied, this means that in the law age there was no grace, and *vice versa,* in the grace or present period there is no law."[24] He would probably be highly offended if charged with misunderstanding the dispensational position, but let the reader judge on reading: "We are plainly taught that the law is a necessary part of [God's redemptive plan], a savor of life unto life [to those who obey it]."[25] Could anything be more erroneous, unscriptural, or misleading than this last statement when considered in the light of 2 Corinthians 3? Who do you think are the legalizers and Judaizers?

Berkhof has this to say:

> This dispensational principle of interpretation has a deplorable effect on the understanding of the truth revealed in the Bible. It tends to obscure and even to undermine the unity of the revelation of redemption, as it appears especially in the doctrine of the covenant of grace, and insofar also the unity of the Bible. Its application engenders a piecemeal or fragmentary study of the Bible as a whole. It encourages a search for historical rather than for absolute truth, and thereby limits and endangers the normative character of the Bible as a whole.[26]

As already seen above, the dispensational method of Bible study reveals the unified and ultimate purpose of God in spite of failure by man in every age. The true effect of dispensationalism is the direct opposite of that which Berkhof claims. Bible study flourishes in premillennial, dispensational churches.

There will be numerous issues upon which antidispensational amillennialism and dispensational premillennialism will be in conflict, as will be seen in later discussion, but for the moment two illustrations can be given from Allis's work where the dispensational system is supposed to be in error.

In treating Psalm 51 Allis states, "The fact that the most spiritual of Christians have been able to make this entire psalm their own is a proof that this verse [he is referring to verse 11] does not have the meaning Dispensationalists give to it."[27] Without a scintilla of Scripture proof, Allis believes he has proved his case as far as verse 11. That will not suffice to demolish the dispensational argument that verse 11 is not applicable to the believer today. Proof is available from John 14:16-17. Furthermore, if spiritual Christians make the entire psalm their own, do they include verses 18 and 19 also? or must they be spiritualized to mean something else? How much better to recognize the primary application of such passages, then to glean abundant spiritual truth wherever the principles of grace for this age are not compromised. Admittedly, the Psalm 51 passage is important, but only incidental to the main argument.

However, Allis comes to what he believes is the basic idea in discussing Acts 3:24:

What does Peter mean by "these days"? The whole question at issue between the Dispensationalists and their opponents is brought to a focus in these words. By "these days" does Peter mean days that are now present, a period that has already begun, or does he refer to a future time? . . . the fact that he immediately appeals to his hearers as "the sons of the prophets, and of the covenant," and cites that part of the Abrahamic covenant which predicts the universal scope of the gospel, makes the inference a natural, if not a necessary one, that by "these days" Peter means the gospel age of the Great Commission. The words, "unto you first," indicate that Peter, as later Paul, recognized that, until they finally rejected it, the Jews, as individuals, not nationally, were entitled to be the first to hear the gospel message.[28]

Acts 3:24 is indeed a pivotal passage, and will not at all bear the interpretation or "the inference a natural, if not a necessary one" that he places upon it. The portion is found in the discourse of Peter after the healing of the lame beggar. Peter offered his hearers, upon repentance and faith, the fulfillment of the things spoken by the prophets (Acts 3:19-21), including Samuel and his successors who "told of these days." Allis understands "these days" to refer to the present age, when in fact they refer to the days of the "times of restoration of all things" plainly spoken of in the passage. Peter is speaking of the days of Messiah's appearance to Israel; the two advents are telescoped as in Isaiah 61:1-2. Certain expressions used by Allis in his argument are puzzling. What is meant by "until they finally rejected it?" Why must it be "as individuals and not nationally?" Why, in view of their rejection of their Messiah are they "entitled to be the first to hear?" Besides, had that generation not heard already? Instead of adhering to the obvious meaning of the passage, he has created a number of problems of his own choosing.

Any discussion of dispensationalism would not be complete if it did not take cognizance of the dispensationalism of the Scofield Reference Bible. Few, if any, writers on dispensationalism fail to mention that work. Often writers expose themselves in characterizing Scofield's splendid reference work. A notable example is A. Pieters in his lecture entitled *A Candid Examination of the Scofield Bible* before a ministerial association of the Christian Reformed Church on June 1, 1938.

Pieters is chosen here because of the extreme character of his remarks, although others approximate him when discussing dispensationalism and the Scofield Bible. First, Pieters admits Scofield's great piety and earnest devotion to the gospel.[29] He is prepared to class the Scofield Reference Bible as perhaps the most influential single work in the religious life of America in this century.[30] He characterizes the users of the work as "among the best Christians in our churches, those with the deepest faith in the Holy Scriptures and with the most sincere devotion to the Lord."[31] Before long, however, he accuses Scofield of assuming "superiority over his brethren,"[32] and then passes on to abusive language unbecoming a scholar. He claims, "It seems like a harsh judgment, but in the interest of truth it must be uttered: Dr. Scofield in this was acting the part of an intellectual charlatan, a fraud who pretends to knowledge which he does not possess; like a quack doctor, who is ready with a confident diagnosis in many cases where a competent physician is unable to decide."[33] Even though Pieters has to admit that Scofield consulted eminent teachers on the great doctrines of the faith, he still holds that Scofield speaks only for himself. It would do all critics of the Scofield Bible good to consult the list of consulting editors of that reference work, then proceed to investigate the amount of time, research, and travel spent in America and Europe on that gigantic project. When Pieters comes to discuss the dispensational scheme, he thinks that such an extensive system should have ample scriptural authority, but claims to find none. He goes on to a discussion of the different dispensations, closes with that of promise, and concludes that the scheme "breaks down completely."[34] In spite of the alleged complete breakdown, it is surprising to find him admitting five of Scofield's eight covenants.[35] For him the final authority is "general Christian exposition down the centuries" and "the Reformed doctrine."[36] That sounds strangely unlike the principle of the Reformation movement.

In recent years some have loosely used the word *ultradispensationalism* for others when they wanted to admit some dispensations in the Bible themselves. Some scholars today class those as ultraconservative who believe in the Mosaic authorship of the Pentateuch, because they wish to be classed as conservative while denying such authorship. It is the same practice at work. Kromminga, for instance, classes Scofield as an ultradispensationalist.[37] J. B. Graber has adequately shown the difference between normative or conservative dispensationalism and the abuse of it in ultradispensationalism. He defines ultradispensationalism,[38] outlines its origin,[39] and sketches clearly its distinctive beliefs and differences from normative dispensationalism.[40] Allis may believe that dispensationalists cannot refute Ethelbert Bullinger without harming their own cause,[41] but abuse of a doctrine has never been sufficient moral ground to abandon a doctrine. There is abuse of the doctrines of the moral responsibility of man and the sovereignty of God. Would he be willing to relinquish them because of extremists? There are abuses in practices as well as doctrines. Who will be willing to forego the practice of the Lord's Supper and baptism just because certain abuses have arisen in those ordinances, and that even in apostolic times (witness the condition of the Corinthian church)?

Though the implications of dispensationalism have been repeatedly explained, Barton Payne reveals misunderstanding of the issues in his opposition. He claims: "Indeed, the unity of the whole course of redemptive history was involved, for, if pressed to its logical end, dispensationalism must limit the cross to the parenthetical dispensation of the church, a divine afterthought to the 'kingdom gospel' of prior revelation."[42]

In reply, it must first be emphatically affirmed that, when the dispensational method of interpretation is understood, it will be seen to accord the greatest unity to the whole course of redemptive history, which must issue in the greatest glory to God. Second, in discussions of Scripture truth necessity is laid upon all to carry data, not to a "logical end," but only to that point which biblical data will allow. Else, what would eventuate if Calvinism or Arminianism were carried to their "logical ends?" Third, if dispensationalism were comprehended, the charge could never be leveled that dispensationalism has to limit the cross to the parenthetical dispensation of the church. No dispensationalist worthy of the name has ever held such a view. Fourth, how much reverence is exhibited when God can be accused of an "afterthought?"

Barton Payne, lending his voice to the charge of recency for dispensationalism, writes: "Not that major doctrines may not take long in their development, but dispensationalism involves the interpretation of the whole Bible. Could a matter so important have been missed so long? Scripture alone has the authority to decide the issues that church history raises."[43] It must be pointed out that so vital a doctrine as justification by faith, which moves majestically from Genesis to the Revelation, was submerged and encrusted with human error even from apostolic times until the Protestant Reformation. No man can lay down rules for the development of either ideas or events in the course of human history. The final issue is, "What saith the Scripture?"

In discussing the works of dispensationalists, among whom the present writer is included, Barton Payne says: "These very titles indicate dispensationalism's characteristically eschatological emphasis, though many would question their identification of premillennialism with what is peculiarly Darbyite interpretation."[44] A few comments are in order. First, it is not a characteristic emphasis of dispensationalism to focus on the realm of eschatology. Dispensationalism is as distinctive in the theological disciplines of bibliology, anthropology, soteriology, and ecclesiology, as it is in the area of eschatology. Second, it is only in comparatively recent years that some have tried to divorce premillennialism from dispensationalism. It is an interesting commentary to learn that many of those brethren came originally to premillennialism through the gateway of dispensationalism. Finally, Barton Payne has a tendency to use "Darbyite" in a manner implying "guilt by association." In the discussion below it will be seen conclusively that dispensationalism antedates Darby by centuries, not just years.

Ladd, commenting on the book of Revelation, defines thus:

> A variant form of premillennialism is Dispensationalism, which sees the millennial kingdom primarily in terms of God's theocratic promises to Israel. The entire book of Revelation is interpreted in terms of these

dispensational presuppositions and is concerned with the fate of restored Israel in the last days and not with the church. In many circles the only form of premillennialism known is Dispensationalism. The form of pre-millennialism which sees the Revelation as a prophecy of the destiny of the church is not widely held today.[45]

Those acquainted with the features of dispensationalism will immediately recognize that Ladd has severely oversimplified that method of biblical interpretation. Two questions keep thrusting themselves to the fore: Why is it that the best known form of premillennialism is the dispensational one? Why is his position held by so few?

Clarence Bass has written at length on the background and origins of dispensationalism. Many of his statements are refuted, not only by adherents of dispensationalism, but by nondispensationalists as well. He defines his aim in writing: "The purpose of this book is to explain the historical setting out of which dispensationalism has grown, and to analyze its implications."[46] He claims dispensationalism came from the nineteenth century and was unknown before that in the history of Christian thinking. It arose in an atmosphere of theological controversy.

In further defining the purpose of his book, Bass states: "The purpose is not to construct a case against dispensationalism."[47] It is difficult to find a work less objective on the subject than his, especially because he claims to have gone to the original sources in study abroad and thinks his volume is "the most unbiased and accurate account yet written."[48] When he declares: "No dispensational writer has ever been able to offer . . . a single point of continuity between what is today known as dispensationalism and the historic premillennial view,"[49] he may be excused for not being acquainted with the work of Charles C. Ryrie, which will be treated below, since it appeared some five years after his. Even then, Bass has never retracted any position erroneously taken in his original work. But how does it happen that he indicates no knowledge of the work of Arnold Ehlert written long before his book?[50]

From page 48 through page 98 Bass labors to join dispensationalism almost entirely with the Plymouth Brethren, all the while underscoring the internal divisions that marked the movement. All that is clearly intended to demonstrate that dispensationalism is divisive to the core and to be shunned as a plague.

One need not scrutinize contemporary evangelical church life too closely to see this principle at work today. Nor does it take more than a casual survey of the history of theology since Darby's day to trace the continuity of his view of separation in our day. There exists a direct line from Darby through a number of channels—prophetic conferences, fundamentalistic movements, individual prophetic teachers, the Scofield Reference Bible, eschatological charts—all characterized by and contributing to a spirit of separation and exclusion. The devastating effects of this spirit upon the total body of Christ cannot be underestimated.[51] What oversimplification to accuse dispensationalism with the spirit of separation in the church! The devastation supposedly wrought is overdrawn and overdramatized.[52]

Let us turn to specifics: Can anyone compute how many men and women have been challenged in prophetic conferences to trust Christ for salvation, to make their Bible study more meaningful, to answer the call of God to the mission fields of the world, to live lives honoring to the Lord? Let Bass or any other nondispensationalist name one study Bible with as much blessing spread to the people of God as the Scofield Reference Bible. As for divisions in the Christian church, have the divisions in the Presbyterian, Baptist, Methodist, Episcopal, and independent denominations been caused by adherence to dispensational theology? The controversies have been over personalities, polities, practices, liberalism versus orthodoxy, rather than over dispensationalism. In the heat of controversy let no one overstep the bounds of truth. *Magna est veritas et praevalabit!* (Great is truth and will prevail!)

The worst statement in Bass's work, as this writer evaluates it, is this: "Has not dispensationalism contributed largely to this default of the church's mission [of taking the gospel to the world], and made of it a detached, withdrawn, inclusively introverted group, waiting to be raptured away from this evil world?"[53] This writer has for almost half a century read missionary literature from around the world on a daily basis, and he can assert without equivocation that dispensationalists are in the forefront of evangelical missions everywhere. Man for man they far outnumber nondispensationalists. Did it ever occur to minimizers of Scofield and his theology to ascertain that he was the founder of the Philadelphia School of the Bible (now the Philadelphia College of Bible, a school with an illustrious past, an enviable present, and a bright future), as well as the Central American Mission?

Antidispensational strictures have not found dispensational exponents without adequate refutations. Hoyt discerningly states: "I find it hard to understand why one system is labeled dispensational and others escape that description. For the facts are these: Not one view of the millennium . . . is without some arrangement of dispensations; and most certainly the very mention of an eschatological millennium imposes another dispensation."[54] McClain speaks knowledgeably to those who would denigrate dispensationalism because of the use of charts by some. He maintains, "The different ages of God's dealings with men are not always sharply divided with no transitional stage."[55] Such elements can be elucidated with or without the use of visual aids.

In the judgment of this writer no recent author on the subject of dispensationalism equals the insights and lucidity of Ryrie. His contribution is mainly found in a chapter in a symposium and then in an entire volume on the dispensational system.[56] At the outset there needs to be a clearing of the atmosphere, so he states, "Though the statement is bold, it may be stated without fear of controversy that there is no interpreter of the Bible who does not recognize the need for certain basic distinctions in the Scriptures."[57] Even covenant theologians hold to different divisions or stages in the unfolding of the "covenant of grace." When the dispensationalist uses the term "dispensation," he realizes that theologically the emphasis is not on the notion of time, but a clear and distinctive administration of God in His progressive dealings with man.[58]

As has been stated above, the great divide between pre- and amillennialism is attributable to the different interpretive principles employed by the respective adherents. But there is a sense in which that is a result of an overarching initial presupposition; that is, the philosophy or goal of history inherent in each view. Ryrie explains:

> Concerning the goal of history, dispensationalists find it in the establishment of the millennial kingdom on earth while the covenant theologian regards it as the eternal state. This is not to say that dispensationalists minimize the glory of the eternal state, but it is to insist that the display of the glory of the God who is sovereign in human history must be seen in the present heavens and earth as well as in the new heavens and earth. This view of the realization of the goal of history within time is both optimistic and in accord with the requirements of the definition. The covenant view, which sees the course of history continuing the present struggle between good and evil until terminated by the beginning of eternity, obviously does not have any goal within temporal history and is therefore pessimistic.[59]

Along with a proper goal of history a valid philosophy of human history must manifest an adequate unifying principle.

> In covenant theology the principle is the covenant of grace ... the unifying principle of covenant theology is soteriological. In dispensationalism the principle is the theological or perhaps better eschatological, for the differing dispensations reveal the glory of God as He shows off His character in the differing stewardships culminating in history with the millennial glory. If the goal of history is the earthly millennium, and if the glory of God will be manifested then in the personal presence of Christ in a way hitherto unknown, then the unifying principle of dispensationalism may be said to be eschatological (if viewed from the goal toward which we are moving) or theological (if viewed from the self-revelation of God in every dispensation).[60]

Just as in nature, so in the realm of Scripture revelation, there is a principle of progress in revelation. For the first realm see Mark 4:28; for the second see Isaiah 45:15 with John 1:18 and 14:8-9. In that area of truth only the dispensational approach fulfills the requirements. True, covenantism allows for different phases of administration of the program of God, but it must be noticed carefully that all transpires within the limited and restricted sphere of the covenant of grace. Such a condition imposes certain strange and strained interpretations of large portions of the Scripture.

Dispensationalism, on the other hand, can and does give proper place to the idea of development. Under the various administrations of God different revelation was given to man, and that revelation was increasingly progressive in the scope of its content. Though similarities are present in various dispensations, they are part of a true development and not a result of employing the unifying principle of the covenant of grace. The particular manifestations of the will of God in each dispensation are given their full yet distinctive place in the progress of the revelation of God throughout the ages. Only dispensationalism can cause historical events and successions to be seen in their own light and not to be reflected in the artificial light of an overall covenant.[61]

Pursuant to the discussion of progress in doctrine in the Bible is the answer to the nondispensationalist charge that dispensationalism is novel in the arena of interpretation. It is forgotten that, "Like all doctrines, dispensational teaching has undergone systematization and development."[62] A living organism must ever grow and develop. Misunderstandings and misrepresentations of dispensationalism, even though unintentional, account for much of the criticism of the system.[63] It is to be expected that opposition will issue from certain quarters: (1) theological liberals, who do not agree with literal interpretation or fundamental doctrines of the Bible; (2) amillennialists, because dispensationalists are consistently premillennial; (3) those who believe dispensationalists have not gone to the logical conclusions in their teachings; and (4) those who want to be premillennial but not dispensational, because dispensational premillennialism is not "classical or historic" premillennialism. Dispensationalism has been attacked as a heresy or cult; guilt-by-association has been practiced with reference to it; it is accused of being divisive. There have been the "intellectual" attack, because it is supposed to be unscholarly; the historical attack (recent, so not true); ridicule-of-doctrine attack (two ways of salvation supposedly taught by it); and others.

The values of dispensationalism, as set forth by Ryrie, are: (1) it answers the need of biblical distinctives. All must admit differences between the Old and New Testaments; even covenantists find different periods of God's administration, as shown above. (2) Dispensationalism answers the need of a philosophy of history. There is a vindication of God's purposes in time, whereas covenant theology/amillennialism postpones it to the eternal state.[64] In any philosophy of history there must be a unifying or cohesive principle (see Albright's "organismic" view of history).[65] In covenantism the rigid rule of the covenant of grace (soteriological) is employed, whereas in dispensationalism the binding element is theological (cf. Rom. 11:36).[66] God's revelation moves progressively to its goal; in dispensationalism only can historical events be seen in their contribution to the intended consummation. (3) Dispensationalism furnishes a consistent hermeneutics, instead of the dual hermeneutics of covenant theology, which allows so much latitude for subjectivity. Whereas dispensationalism maintains a consistent literal interpretation, as seen in detail in a previous chapter of this volume, amillennialism depends heavily on allegorical interpretation, especially in the sensitive area of prophecy. When you find a premillennialist who claims to be nondispensational, you may be sure that somewhere in his presentation he abandons literal interpretation for nonliteral.[67]

A failing of nondispensational covenant-theology amillennialists is their practice of reading back the New Testament into the Old, sometimes called "Christianizing" the Old Testament. That is contrary to the valid laws of a proper logical induction, resulting in a mixture of factors that are meant to be separate. Post-Calvary and post-Pentecost conditions cannot be read back into the Old Testament without definite harm to the beautiful fabric of self-consistent Bible doctrine.[68] Covenant theologians constantly cry that the dispensationalist is destroying the inner unity of the Bible. Those dear brethren are unaware that their fears are actually for the imposed unity of their covenant of grace, which appears to be in mortal danger when divisions are made in God's administrations with man. Ryrie rightly points out: *"Variety can be an essential part of unity"* (italics his).[69] Concern has often been voiced that dispensationalism fragmentizes the Scriptures. That charge can arise only when many continuing and durative principles throughout the ages are lost sight of.[70] To sum up, the three basics of dispensationalism are: (1) differentiation between Israel and the church; (2) the normal, literal hermeneutical principle; and (3) the underlying purpose of God in history as His glory, not primarily the salvation of man (Rom. 11:36).

It is usual to find in the works of antidispensationalists the charges that dispensationalism arose in the nineteenth century among the Plymouth Brethren (because recent, therefore nonbiblical), and they were (and are) a separatist movement (hence to be avoided by those seeking unity among believers).[71] First, knowledgeable dispensationalists do not assert that their whole system has been taught from postapostolic days. To Darby must go the credit for formulating the system. Is that sufficient to make it contraband, any more than the fact that covenant theology was organized by Cocceius of the seventeenth century? It cannot be denied that elements of the dispensational scheme are discernible in the early church, as will be presently demonstrated.[72] Let it be remembered that not all that came from the early church was in accord with the Scriptures, for example, Gnosticism, Ebionitism,

Galatianism, and others. The final court of authority is the Bible and that alone.

Recognizing the work of Ehlert in the bibliography of dispensationalism, Ryrie traces the line of indisputable evidence that dispensational truths "were held early and throughout the history of the church."[73] Such concepts are found in Justin Martyr (110-165), Irenaeus (130-200), Clement of Alexandria (150-220), Samuel Hanson Coxe (1793-1880), who followed Clement's views, Augustine (in his *To Marcellinus,* CXXXVIII, 5, 7), Pierre Poiret, French philosopher (1646-1719), John Edwards (1639-1716), Isaac Watts (1674-1748), and John Nelson Darby (1800-1882), the systematizer of dispensationalism in modern times. It is interesting to find that Scofield followed the dispensational scheme of Isaac Watts, the great hymn writer, rather than that of Darby. Why, then, the new awareness of dispensational matters? "Undoubtedly the recency of systematic eschatology partly accounts for the relative recency of systematic dispensationalism."[74]

The accusation against the divisiveness of dispensationalism has been sufficiently spoken to above. But there is yet another feature of the system that angers nondispensationalists, and that is the doctrine of the apostate church. Often the credentials for orthodoxy are sadly lacking among those so sensitive to that concept. It should be pointed out that emphasis on the apostasy of the church came to the fore at the rise of the prophetic conferences as an antidote to the false optimism of postmillennialism.[75] Clarification is needful at this point: dispensationalism *does not teach* that the entire church in any century is apostate. It does teach that the last days of the church age will witness a great apostasy from the ranks of the church, and that is abundantly attested by Scripture (see 2 Cor. 11:14-15; 2 Thess. 2:1-12; 1 Tim. 4:1-3; 2 Tim. 3:1-9, 13; 4:3-4; James 5:1-5; 2 Pet. 2:1-3; 1 John 2:18-29; 4:1-6; Jude 3-4; Rev. 2-3).

When the dispensational scheme is studied carefully and without prejudgment, it will be found to embody the key principle to the interpretation of the entire Bible. It will be found to be a method gleaned from the Bible, and not a system foisted upon it.

NOTES

[1]See D. B. MacCorkle, *A Study of Amillennial Eschatology,* p. 117.
[2]J. E. Beer, "Dispensationalism and The Covenant of Grace," in *The Union Seminary Review,* July 1938, p. 2.
[3]Ibid., pp. 3-4.
[4]G. E. Ladd, *Crucial Questions About the Kingdom of God,* p. 48.
[5]Ibid., p. 49, fn. 15.
[6]O. T. Allis, *Prophecy and the Church,* p. 13.
[7]W. H. Rutgers, *Premillennialism in America,* p. 172.

[8]A. Reese, *The Approaching Advent of Christ*, pp. xi, 29.
[9]D. H. Kromminga, *The Millennium in the Church*, p. 289.
[10]R. J. Reid, *Amillennialism*, p. 59.
[11]L. S. Chafer, *Dispensationalism*, p. 10.
[12]Ibid., p. 9.
[13]F. E. Hamilton, *The Basis of Millennial Faith*, pp. 26-27.
[14]D. H. Kromminga, *The Millennium*, pp. 57-58.
[15]Ladd, *Crucial Questions*, p. 53.
[16]Ibid., p. 49.
[17]Chafer, *Dispensationalism*, pp. 12-13.
[18]Allis, p. vi.
[19]Ibid.
[20]Chafer, *Dispensationalism*, p. 12.
[21]Ibid., p. 106.
[22]Ibid., p. 105.
[23]Ladd, *Crucial Questions*, p. 49.
[24]Rutgers, p. 176.
[25]Ibid., pp. 180-81.
[26]L. Berkhof, *The Kingdom of God*, p. 138.
[27]Allis, p. 45.
[28]Ibid., p. 139.
[29]A. Pieters, *A Candid Examination of the Scofield Bible*, p. 4.
[30]Ibid.
[31]Ibid., p. 5.
[32]Ibid., p. 9.
[33]Ibid.
[34]Ibid., pp. 15-16.
[35]Ibid., pp. 16-17.
[36]Ibid., pp. 26-27.
[37]Kromminga, *The Millennium in the Church*, p. 248.
[38]J. B. Graber, *Ultra-Dispensationalism*, pp. 1, 6.
[39]Ibid., p. 22.
[40]Ibid., pp. 25, 29, 34 ff., 52.
[41]Allis, pp. 159-64.
[42]J. B. Payne, *The Imminent Appearing of Christ*, pp. 31-32.
[43]Ibid., p. 42.
[44]J. B. Payne, *The Theology of the Older Testament*, p. 40.
[45]G. E. Ladd, *A Commentary on the Revelation of John*, p. 261.
[46]C. B. Bass, *Backgrounds to Dispensationalism—Its Historical Genesis and Ecclesiastical Implications*, p. 7.
[47]Ibid., pp. 7-8.
[48]Ibid., p. 10.

[49]Ibid., p. 14.

[50]C. C. Ryrie's work is *Dispensationalism Today* (Moody Press, 1965). Arnold Ehlert's study of the history of dispensationalism appeared as "A Bibliography of Dispensationalism," in *Bibliotheca Sacra,* 1944-1946, more than a dozen years before Bass's work.

[51]Bass, p. 99.

[52]Ibid., p. 144.

[53]Ibid., p. 149.

[54]Clouse, *The Meaning of the Millennium,* p. 42.

[55]A. J. McClain, *The Greatness of the Kingdom,* p. 372.

[56]C. C. Ryrie, "The Necessity of Dispensationalism," pp. 39-50, also C. C. Ryrie, *Dispensationalism Today* (1965).

[57]Ryrie, "Necessity of Dispensationalism," pp. 40-41.

[58]Ibid., p. 41.

[59]Ibid., p. 43.

[60]Ibid., p. 44.

[61]Ibid., pp. 44-45. It is not denied that certain elements of particular dispensations overlap. A balanced dispensationalism differs from ultradispensationalism, because the latter unfortunately does "fail to recognize the difference between the progress of doctrine as it was during the time of revelation and the representation of it in the writings of the Scripture" (ibid., pp. 49-50).

[62]Ryrie, *Dispensationalism Today,* p. 9. Cf. 1 Cor. 13:12.

[63]Ibid.

[64]Ibid., pp. 15-18. Cf. also A. J. McClain, "A Premillennial Philosophy of History," *Bibliotheca Sacra,* Apr. 1956, pp. 113-14. See also his *Greatness of the Kingdom,* pp. 528-31.

[65]W. F. Albright, *From the Stone Age to Christianity,* pp. 82-126.

[66]See the criticism of covenant theology on that score by the nondispensationalist James Orr in his *The Progress of Dogma,* p. 303.

[67]Ryrie, *Dispensationalism Today,* p. 20.

[68]Ibid., pp. 34-35.

[69]Ibid., pp. 35-36. Witness that in the material creation and the Bible.

[70]Ibid., p. 40.

[71]C. Bass rings the changes on those two concepts again and again. See discussion above.

[72]Ryrie, *Dispensationalism Today,* pp. 65-66. Calvin had to answer a charge of newness against the teachings of the Reformers; cf. *The Institutes,* Vol. I, "Prefatory Address—" p. 3, cited by Ryrie, p. 67.

[73]Ibid., pp. 67-68. Contra especially Bass and Ladd.

[74]Ibid., pp. 69-77, esp. p. 77.

[75]Ibid., p. 82.

4
Covenantism

Just as premillennialism is linked to dispensationalism, so amillennialism is joined to covenantism or covenant theology. Many amillennialists do not attempt to prove the validity of the covenant system; they assume it proved at the outset. J. E. Bear claims:

The Bible is the final authority. However, in the brief space at my command I am going to limit our discussion to the teaching of Dispensationalism and one of the great doctrines of the Church which is commonly spoken of as the Covenant of Grace. . . . In discussing Dispensationalism and the Covenant of Grace, it will *not* be our purpose, then, to *prove* the Covenant of Grace from Scripture. Such evidence is set forth in the standard works of theology produced by the great Reformed Theologians. . . . It will be our purpose, rather, to examine this doctrine and see if the Dispensational teaching is in accord with it or not.[1]

Thus at the very outset he makes a doctrine never mentioned in the Bible normative in the discussion, and that immediately after he has stated that the Bible is the final authority. He himself must concede that "the term Covenant of Grace is not found in the Bible, but our Church has always believed that it stood for a doctrine which is clearly taught in the Bible."[2]

The main burden of Bear's argument, and indeed his surprise, is that dispensationalists, not holding to one covenant throughout the Scriptures, nevertheless, do not teach two ways of salvation.[3] To him that is "a radical inconsistency." Dispensational premillennialists maintain that the one great objective of God is to save men by faith alone through the Savior's work, through placing them in different ages under different tests to show them their helplessness and need of His saving grace. Covenantal amillennialists have never explained how one can believe that without calling God's plan the "covenant of grace" (terminology not found in the Bible) and at the same time doing away with such vital distinctions as those between law and grace, the church and Israel, or the kingdom and the church. Bear believes, furthermore, that "the Dispensationalists have no monopoly on the word 'dispensation.' It has been used for generations in the Church to indicate that God dealt with men in somewhat different ways in different periods. *But the Church was not teaching 'Dispensationalism.'* "[4] If he will consider carefully the dispensational position, he will find that dispensationalists claim that "God dealt with men in somewhat different ways in different periods," but they do not proceed to obliterate distinctions clearly set forth in the Word.

Bear's reasoning is that the church has always maintained that God had one plan of salvation for all sinful men, and that must be embodied and circumscribed by the covenant system. Therefore, when dispensationalists do not hold to covenantism, he concludes: "We are led to the conclusion, then, that the Dispensational teaching about 'dispensations' gives *two methods* of salvation, works and grace."[5] In order for him to be logical and consistent in his own contention, he ought to charge the dispensationalist with seven ways of salvation, if each dispensation means a new way of salvation. Those were rather ways of condemnation and not means of salvation. The case is that of Romans 2. Does he find more than one way of salvation in Romans 2? The apostle Paul is pointing out only the basis for condemnation. It does not help the covenantist's argument to be speaking again and again of "the covenants" and at the same time stress *the covenant* of grace.

The blame, according to Bear, is to be laid to the distinction dispensationalists make between law and grace. He states, "Moreover, it seems to be this distinction which they make between grace and law which makes them reject the Covenant of Grace."[6] How can such diametrically opposite principles be incorporated into one covenant and then that covenant be called the covenant of grace? Do dispensationalists make a greater line of cleavage between law and grace than Paul does in Romans 11:6? How do covenantists explain such a passage? If grace was not manifested in a new way through the death of Christ, what is the meaning of John 1:17 after all? or 2 Corinthians 3:7? Chafer was surely right in contending, "The theologian who draws his proof as much from the standards of his church as from the Bible is slipping from the true Protestant position."[7]

Apparently, the chief concern of the covenantists is that in the dispensational system there seems to be no unifying principle in Scripture, therefore they propose to embody such a principle in the covenant of grace interpretation. But that can be shown to be wholly unnecessary. There is no need to superimpose upon the testimony of Scripture a principle that, though it seems to unify the Scriptures, does so only at the expense of the obliteration of some of the most clearly defined distinctions in the Word of God. The remedy is worse than the supposed disease. There is a unifying principle, and it lies not in the direction of covenantism. A. G. Hebert has surely discerned it when he maintains, "The Messianic Hope is the central theme of the Bible. It is that which gives to the two Testaments their unity."[8]

True, it is the person and work of the Lord Jesus Christ that give the Old and

New Testaments their inner and indestructible unity. But let it not be supposed that there is consistency on the matter of the one covenant even among amillennialists. Hamilton contends, "There have been several covenants, but no change in the way of salvation."[9] Why, then, is it not permitted to dispensationalists to hold that there have been several dispensations, but no change in the way of salvation? Yet the amillennialists will not allow this.

Berkhof has, perhaps, given us as detailed and clear a picture of covenantism as any. As to the origin of the covenant system, he finds that "the covenant relationship between God and man existed from the very beginning."[10] That is supposed to be taught in passages like Ephesians 1:4 and following, and 3:11, together with Romans 5:12-21 and 1 Corinthians 15:22.[11]

But we must distinguish between a possible covenant in the Godhead, based on those passages, and the assumption of a covenant relationship between God and man in Eden from the very beginning. Payne has rightly pointed out,

the very terminology used in relation to covenant making in the Old Testament would seem to indicate that there was no covenant in Eden before the fall . . . [Note Genesis 15:9-17 and Jeremiah 34:18]. There is no record of any such sacrificial procedure in connection with Adam's establishment in the garden. Not only so, it is contrary to the entire situation, as death was foreign to the earthly scene prior to the entrance of sin.[12]

It will be remembered that covenantists maintain that the dispensational system is too involved and departmentalized, but note Berkhof's discussion of the relation of the counsel of redemption to the covenant of grace:

1. The counsel of redemption is the eternal prototype of the historical covenant of grace. . . . The former is a compact between the Father and the Son as the Surety and Head of the elect, while the latter is a compact between the triune God and the elect sinner in the Surety. 2. The counsel of redemption is the firm and eternal foundation of the covenant of grace. . . . The counsel of redemption makes the covenant of grace possible. 3. The counsel of redemption consequently also gives efficacy to the covenant of grace, for in it the means are provided for the establishment and execution of the latter.[13]

As important as the covenant of grace is to the covenantist, he must admit, "It is not easy to determine precisely who the second party is. In general it may be said that God naturally established the covenant of grace with fallen man."[14] It is the considered opinion of the dispensationalist that the difficulty in determining the identity of the second party arises from the fact that the covenant has no basis nor proof in Scripture. Berkhof makes clear concerning the covenant of grace that "it is essentially the same in all dispensations, though its form of administration changes."[15]

Those changes of administration sound very much like dispensational changes held by the dispensationalists. Proof for one covenant is supposed to be demonstrated in that "the Bible teaches that there is but a single gospel by which men can be saved. And because the gospel is nothing but the revelation of the covenant of grace [this remains to be proved], it follows that there is also but one covenant."[16] That is a stringing together of non sequiturs involving the very heart of the problem. He denies that man is continually on probation as the dispensationalists affirm. His contention is that man was on probation in Eden and has been in a state of ruin ever since.[17] Surely there is nothing irreconcilable about man's being on probation even while he is in a fallen state. God wants man to see the experimental outworking of his own depravity, a fact known always to God (see Romans 3:19).

In the course of his discussion Berkhof reveals he misunderstands some of the basic elements of the dispensational scheme. For example, he writes:

> Those parts of Scripture that belong to any one of the dispensations are addressed to, and have normative significance for, the people of that dispensation, and for no one else. . . . Since the dispensations do not intermingle, it follows that in the dispensation of the law there is no revelation of the grace of God, and in the dispensation of grace there is no revelation of the law as binding on the New Testament people of God.[18]

But he allows himself some distinctions that surely border on the dispensational divisions when he notes, "On the basis of all that has been said it is preferable to follow the traditional lines by distinguishing just two dispensations or administrations, namely, that of the Old, and that of the New Testament; and to subdivide the former into several periods or stages in the revelation of the covenant of grace."[19]

Moreover, there must be a recognition of some change with the law of Moses. Can that still be the covenant of grace in all its primary and original force? Berkhof replies, "The Sinaitic covenant is an interlude, covering a period in which the real character of the covenant of grace, that is, its free and gracious character, is somewhat eclipsed by all kinds of external ceremonies and forms which, in connection with the theocratic life of Israel, placed the demands of the law prominently in the foreground, cf. Gal. 3."[20] Note carefully how that conforms to Romans 11:6; the apostle makes grace and works antithetical, not a "somewhat eclipsed" arrangement. It would be well to mark that the law itself placed to the fore external ceremonies and forms, and not the people of Israel themselves, as some amillennialists have stated.

But confusion reigns when he comes to discuss the Galatians 3 passage, for it gives the coup de grace to any view that maintains the present validity of the law of Moses for the believer. He holds, "But it should be noted that the apostle does not contrast with the covenant of Abraham the Sinaitic covenant as a whole, but only the law as it functioned in this covenant, and this function only as it was misunderstood by the Jews."[21] There is not a scintilla of evidence for these unfounded distinctions. The claim is that all Paul was denouncing was Israel's misconception of the law, and that to Gentile believers in Galatia, you note, and not the law itself as inapplicable to the life of the believer today in this age of grace. For Berkhof, the Sinaitic covenant was a blessing of God bestowed on Israel,[22] but that is impossible in the light of Deuteronomy 27:26 and Galatians 3:13, as well as Romans 5:20, where man is seen to be a dismal failure under that test. At length Berkhof attempts to show that law and grace are essentially the same, but different.[23] The argument is far from convincing, because it flies in the face of too many pronouncements of the New Testament that reveal those principles to be mutually exclusive.

A tertium quid has been proposed by Kromminga. With his background in Reformed covenant theology and yet his discernment that the Bible clearly teaches a millennial reign of Christ on earth, he seeks to reconcile covenantism with premillennialism. He is surprised that such a harmonization has not been set forth before this.[24] He feels encouraged in his attempt by the fact that Irenaeus was a premillennialist and laid the foundations for "the Reformed doctrine of the Covenants."[25] His views have had little acceptance, and for the good reason that he has tried to pair two irreconcilables. Nor will the proposal be more appealing even if the Millennium is not considered a full dispensation on a par with "the Old Dispensation of Promise and the New Dispensation of Fulfillment, which are bound together by the one Christ, common to them both."[26]

There is a failure here, and that is even more common with amillennialists than with Kromminga, to realize that premillennialism does not hinge upon a simple and single device—one passage of Scripture or the inclusion or exclusion of one dispensation—but upon an entire view of the Scriptures. Actually, before the discussion is concluded Kromminga calls for a "subdivision" of the New Dispensation, just as the Old Dispensation is divided by him into pre-Mosaic, pre-Abrahamic, pre-Babylonian, and antediluvian.[27] In another place it is reduced to the Old Dispensation with the Patriarchal and Israelitish periods, and the New Dispensation with the church and the kingdom of Christ.[28] Try as they may, even those who oppose divisions of the Scriptures ultimately make them themselves.

On the subject of the covenants Allis begins his treatment with the Abrahamic covenant. He objects, first of all, to the premillennial claim that that covenant was unconditional. He declares, "Those who insist that the Abrahamic covenant was wholly unconditional, do not really so regard it is shown also by the great importance which Dispensationalists attach to Israel's being 'in the land' as the pre-condition of blessing under this covenant."[29] There is a failure here to recognize that ownership of the land depended upon the Abrahamic covenant, and that in perpetuity; whereas occupation of the land depended and still depends on the Palestinian covenant of Deuteronomy 28 to

30, which demands obedience as the prerequisite. Allis questions why, if the Abrahamic covenant is supposed to be unconditional, Esau is excluded from the terms of the covenant. After all, he was a son of Isaac, as well as Jacob.[30] The sufficient answer to that is found in Romans 9, and should not be difficult of comprehension to a Calvinist. Blessing was in the line of promise alone but according to the choice of God. "So then it is not of him that willeth, nor of him that runneth, but of God that sheweth mercy" (Rom. 9:16).

When Allis comes to treat Exodus 19:5 and the word "covenant" there, he claims: "It is to be noted that in the Old Testament this word is always in the singular, never plural. The natural explanation is that all of God's covenants with His people (cf. *e.g.*, Deut. xxix.1 f.) are in reality one and the same covenant, whether made with Abraham, with Moses, or with David. The form and details may vary: the covenant is essentially the same."[31] That is the normative position of the covenantist, but it is susceptible of a twofold refutation. In the first place, in each instance where the word "covenant" is used in the Old Testament, the context makes clear what covenant is referred to. If the reference to "my covenant" in Exodus 19:5 is considered, it will be readily seen that it cannot be confused with the Abrahamic covenant or the Davidic covenant or the Palestinian covenant; it is clearly a reference to the Mosaic covenant then in forming. Second, the Old Testament may use the singular "covenant," but what does Allis do with Romans 9:1-5 where we read of "covenants"? We do not form a hermeneutic on the Old Testament or the New Testament alone, but upon both.

His discussion of the new covenant on the basis of Hebrews 8:8-12 fares no better. He says, "It would be hard to find a clearer reference to the gospel age in the Old Testament than in these verses in Jeremiah; and the writer of Hebrews obviously appeals to it as such."[32] He has overlooked three facts. First, those who are primarily addressed in the epistle to the *Hebrews* are not noticed. Second, he has not mentioned that the covenant is expressly said to be made with the house of Israel and the house of Judah. Is that to be taken as another name for the church? Third, he fails to note with what the covenant has been contrasted—the one at Sinai, which was surely made with Israel alone, not with the Gentiles nor with the church. Last, he does not accept the harmonization of the Old Testament passage with the Hebrews passage in this manner: the covenant was made with Israel originally by the Lord Jesus Christ. When they rejected it, it flowed out in blessing with all salvation's benefits to believing Jews as individuals and believing Gentiles as individuals. The ratification of that covenant in the life of Israel as a nation will take place in the millennial kingdom (which Allis rejects, so he must place all of the covenant's force in the present age of the church), as is attested by Romans 11:25-27.

As an end to all controversy Allis quotes the Westminster Confession of Faith to show that the Protestant position is that which takes one covenant throughout the Bible. Actually the Bible itself, then, should never have spoken of an old covenant and a new covenant (which it does so clearly) "but one and the same under various dispensations."[33] Let the reader note too that the Confession mentions "various dispensations."

If the position of the covenantist appears confusing and contradictory, it is because of his reasoning in a circle. With real insight Payne has summarized the situation for us:

> They begin by arbitrarily establishing the grounds for proving the existence of a covenant; from this they proceed to set up a covenant nowhere mentioned as such in the Scripture yet of greater significance and outreach than all those which are specifically mentioned; then to complete the circle of fallacy they arbitrarily declare, again without Scriptural support, that the covenant thus introduced includes all those which are plainly set forth in the Word and so claim the passages related to the bona fide covenants as argument for their own invention.[34]

Is the matter we have been treating in this chapter of such vital importance? Indeed, it is. According to Chafer,

> The advocates of this interpretation [covenant of grace] oppose every earthly feature of the divine program. They disregard or ignore the earthly covenants and promises; they spiritualize or vaporize the vast body of Scripture bearing on the Davidic throne and kingdom; they present no specific reason why Christ was born as the Son of David; and they recognize no earthly glory or purpose in His second advent.[35]

That is too expensive an interpretation for one who wants every portion of the Word of God to have its full weight and significance.[36]

It has been a constant charge by covenantists against dispensationalism that, not only is it unnecessarily complex and overly fragmentizing of Scripture, but it is suspect because of its recent origin. Ryrie has presented the sufficient refutation here:

> Systematized covenant theology is recent [so Cornelius Van Til, a covenant theologian, in his entry "Covenant Theology," *Twentieth Century Encyclopedia* (Baker, 1955, 1:306)]. It was not the expressed doctrine of the early church. It was never taught by church leaders in the Middle Ages . . . not even mentioned by the primary leaders of the Reformation. Indeed, covenant theology as a system is not any older than dispensationalism is. This does not mean it is not biblical, but it does dispel the notion that covenant theology has been throughout all church history the ancient guardian of the truth which is only recently being sniped at by dispensationalism."[37]

The covenant view arose "sporadically" late in the sixteenth century. Thus, if lack of age and absence of developed expression of position are fatal to the validity of dispensationalism, it is equally so for covenantism.[38]

Furthermore, looking at all Scripture through the spectacles of the covenant of grace, its advocates have been compelled to interpret the Old Testament by the New. All agree that the New Testament is the guide and light to a comprehension of the Old Testament, but that is no excuse for the practice of "Christianizing the Old Testament," which results in forced exegesis with which even nondispensationalists find fault.[39]

In summary, then, it is affirmed that covenant theology is recent, is not specifically revealed in Scripture, places biblical data in a hermeneutical straitjacket, and "occasionally speaks about salvation by the Mosaic law."[40]

NOTES

[1]J. E. Bear, "Dispensationalism and the Covenant of Grace," pp. 4-5.

[2]Ibid., p. 5. Ryrie has clearly shown that even formal definitions of covenant theology are difficult to discover even in the works of covenant theologians, although all realize that as a system of theology it rests on the two covenants of works and grace as the determinative guides for the interpretation of the Scriptures. It should be stated that the concepts in a covenant of works and a covenant of grace are not unbiblical; however, nowhere can one find them systematized into covenants in Scripture. Even the nomenclature of the covenants never occurs in the Bible (Ryrie, *Dispensationalism Today*, pp. 177, 183-84). It needs no argument to prove that dispensations are found in the Bible (cf. Eph. 1:10; 3:9). It is passing strange that Scripture nowhere mentions either a covenant of works or a covenant of grace as it does a covenant with Abraham, the covenant with Moses at Sinai, or the new covenant (ibid., p. 186).

[3]Ibid., p. 8.

[4]Ibid., pp. 10-11.

[5]Ibid., pp. 10-11, 14. No dispensationalist will allow covenant theologians to misunderstand the dispensational position on one method of salvation. Ryrie's refutation is unanswerable: "Indeed, the law was a declaration of the will of God for man's salvation, and if sins could be forgiven via the ritual law [so J. Barton Payne, *Theology of the Older Testament*, p. 414], then covenant theology must be teaching two ways of salvation—one by law and one by grace! Covenant theology seems to teach the very 'heresy' it accuses dispensationalism of teaching!" (ibid., p. 190).

[6]Ibid., p. 17.

[7]L. S. Chafer, *Dispensationalism*, p. 16.

[8]A. G. Hebert, *The Throne of David*, p. 39.

[9]F. E. Hamilton, *The Basis of the Millennial Faith*, p. 27.

[10]L. Berkhof, *Systematic Theology*, pp. 263, 264.

[11]Ibid., p. 266.

[12]Homer L. Payne, *Amillennial Theology as a System*, p. 142.
[13]Berkhof, *Systematic Theology*, p. 270. P. E. Hughes, a more recent writer on covenantism, expresses dissatisfaction with "the convoluted eschatology of those who belong to the 'dispensationalist' school. Many of these seem to regard the premillennial creed as an authenticating mark of those who are acceptable as fully orthodox" *(Interpreting Prophecy,* p. 102). He allots less than three pages in his work to a discussion of dispensationalism. He is guilty, as are most covenant theologians, of oversimplification, which results in an unfounded homogeneity that refuses to recognize explicit scriptural distinctions. Note how he speaks of the dispensational treatment of the period of the church: "a period which, as we have indicated, is *outside the scope of biblical prophecy* and to which Christ's kingdom teaching has *no application . . ."* (ibid., pp. 102-103, italics added).
[14]Ibid., p. 273.
[15]Ibid., p. 279.
[16]Ibid.
[17]Ibid., p. 291.
[18]Ibid., pp. 291-92.
[19]Ibid., p. 293.
[20]Ibid., pp. 296-97.
[21]Ibid., p. 297.
[22]Ibid., pp. 297-98.
[23]Ibid., pp. 299-300.
[24]D. H. Kromminga, *The Millennium*, pp. 5, 61.
[25]Ibid., pp. 61-62.
[26]Ibid., pp. 62-63.
[27]Ibid., p. 63.
[28]Ibid., p. 64.
[29]O. T. Allis, *Prophecy and the Church*, p. 34.
[30]Ibid., pp. 35-36.
[31]Ibid., p. 59.
[32]Ibid., p. 154.
[33]Ibid., pp. 165-66.
[34]H. L. Payne, p. 145.
[35]Chafer, *Dispensationalism*, pp. 107-8.
[36]Even the oft-repeated accusation of covenantists against dispensationalism cannot compensate for the loss in vital biblical distinctions. Hughes writes: "But we fear that the dispensationalist method of interpretation does violence to the unity of Scripture [by this he evidently refers to the alleged "covenant of grace" from Genesis to Revelation] and to the sovereign continuity of God's purposes, and cavalierly leaves out of account a major portion of the apostolic teaching—that, chiefly, of the Acts

and the Epistles—as unrelated to the perspective of the Old Testament authors" (Hughes, p. 104).

[37]C. C. Ryrie, *Dispensationalism Today*, p. 179.
[38]Ibid., p. 183.
[39]Ibid., pp. 187-88.
[40]Ibid., p. 190.

5
The Historical Argument
for Premillennialism

Until comparatively recent times the consensus of opinion of those writing on the millennial question was that the early church was premillennial with but few exceptions. Authorities like Adolf Harnack, Philip Schaff, and a number of others could be cited to prove the early appearance of premillennialism in the history of the church. Today amillennialists take strong exception to that affirmation. Let us review the situation from a number of writers in order that our position taken in the early part of this work may be seen to be amply substantiated.

H. C. Thiessen holds that "the Early Church was premillennial," and points to Fisher as authority for the wide diffusion of the chiliastic belief as found in Justin, Irenaeus, and Tertullian.[1] Reid quotes early authorities in the church to show the apostolic character and origin of premillennialism.[2] He notes, "Amillennialism was the *Modernism* of the fourth century, superseding 'the old Millenarianism' that had strengthened the hearts of the Lord's own prior to their nestling in the lap of political favor."[3] Although the premillennial position "appears to have been the reigning sentiment of the orthodox believers," a change came with Augustine.[4]

D. Bosworth gives the testimony of Papias, Justin Martyr, Irenaeus, Tertullian, and Lactantius among others to evidence the early origin of chiliasm.[5] Hospers, basing his conclusions on the authority of historians, states: "The Premillennial idea, crude and underdeveloped as might naturally be expected, was prevalent in pious circles, and dates from the days of the Apostles," and does not hesitate to pronounce that *"Premillennialism is really the Reformed doctrine in Eschatology."*[6] He also attributes the change in eschatological viewpoint to the influence of Augustine. S. J. Case, who is not a premillennialist, plainly declares, "Within Christianity belief in the temporary character of the present age clearly assumed a form known as the millennial hope." And again, "Christian hopes for the next two generations revolve about this primitive notion of the heavenly Christ soon to return to inaugurate a new regime upon a miraculously renovated earth."[7] He rightly traces the early opposition to chiliasm to the Gnostics with their doctrine of the inherent evil of matter, and the later opposition to the popularity of Christianity when Constantine espoused it as the religion of the state. Nothing was left to be hoped for; the golden age had arrived.[8] The same position is taken by H. L. Payne,[9] Chafer,[10] and Ladd.[11]

The amillennialist Berkhof is not willing to concede all that. He maintains, "During the early Christian centuries the prevailing, though not officially recognized view of the Kingdom of God, was eschatological, and in some cases Chiliastic."[12] His reasons are far from satisfactory. Later he refers to the work of Kromminga and comes to the conclusion that "while a few of the early Church Fathers were clearly chiliastic in their teachings, they formed exceptions rather than the rule."[13] Pieters contents himself with the assertion that the usual premillennial contention cannot be substantiated from the evidence at hand.[14]. Rutgers concedes that historians like Neander, Mede, Schaff, and Harnack claim the first three centuries of the Christian era were premillennial, then adds: "The prevalence therefore of chiliasm in the early centuries of the Christian era is admitted, but it must be asserted, however presumptuous it may seem, with greatest respect and esteem for the learning and scholarship of the church historians cited, that this prevalence has been unduly exaggerated and must be cut down appreciably."[15] Before he concludes he tries to show that the views of the historians are in error. He also denies the conclusions that premillennialists draw from the historical argument.[16] This argument is eagerly seized upon in favor of a doctrine held by the opposition. When he comes to pronounce on the chiliasm of the early American settlers,[17] his remarks are so unfounded and wide of the mark, that Smith gives him the coup de grace on the whole historical argument.[18]

A discussion of the historical argument for premillennialism would not be complete without a survey of the material set forth by Kromminga in his studies in the history of chiliasm. He is most irenical in his approach, and often concedes positions unnecessarily, but comes to the conclusion in the early part of his work that we have "the notable phenomenon, that the chiliasm of the ancient period was primarily premillenarian and the chiliasm of the medieval period was primarily postmillenarian, while in the modern period both the premillenarian and the postmillenarian streams of chiliasm have continued to flow side by side from the Reformation down till the present."[19] He agrees with other historians that a change came with Augustine.[20] In spite of previous statements, however, he seeks to be acceptable to both viewpoints, when he declares: "But, whether we like it or not, the facts look very much indeed as if Amillennialism made its appearance in early extra-canonical Christian literature fully as early as did any chiliasm."[21] He does not substantiate his position adequately, and there will be few, if any, historians who will go along with him here.

In one place he agrees with Pieters in his conclusions in his articles in *The Calvin Forum* (1938),[22] then states to the contrary that "the paucity of chiliastic material in the Apostolic Fathers does not mean, that chiliasm was not rather extensively present in the ancient Church at the very early period when these men wrote."[23] That shifting back and forth of position tends to render the force of his work rather ineffective. Kromminga believes that the most that can be said for the situation is this:

> The evidence is uniformly to the effect, that throughout the years from the beginning of the second century till the beginning of the fifth chiliasm, particularly of the premillenarian type, was extensively found within the Christian Church, but that it never was dominant, far less universal; that it was not without opponents, and that its representatives were conscious of being able to speak only for a party in the Church.[24]

Kromminga sheds some light on the question as to whether present premillennialism is wholly divorced from early premillennialism, and presents great variety today whereas ancient chiliasm was uniform. In speaking of Lactantius (A.D. 260-330), he states: "It is quite plain, that Lactantius represents the traditional and current type of Premillennialism. His views are so much like modern premillenarian views, that it must be acknowledged, that these were in all their essentials current in the ancient Church."[25] In the matter of uniformity we learn: "It has already become apparent that in ancient chiliasm there was proportionately about as much variation of detail[26] as there is among the various premillenarian schemes of the present time."[27]

Kromminga points out in detail how the change from the early position took place. It transpired in the fourth century, and the responsible persons were Origen, Constantine, and Augustine. Origen, alienated from chiliasm because of the grossly materialistic character of the view of his day, resorted to the method of allegorization of Scripture, thus cutting the Gordian knot. That was a drastic means, and the church naturally suffered from it. It had definite kinship with the Gnostic abhorrence of the material as inherently and innately evil.[28] When Constantine made Christianity the favored religion of the Roman Empire, such a change was bound to have its effect upon Christian outlook and hope. Why look forward to a future kingdom? Were they not realizing that blessing then and there?[29] Augustine, who declared he would not believe the gospel unless the authority of the church were behind it, revolted at what he termed excessive carnal expectations. That led him to treat the passage in Revelation 20 in a twofold way: the first resurrection is spiritual regeneration and takes place by means of baptism; the second is physical resurrection by means of the final judgment. "The rule with Christ Augustine understands in a threefold way: it comprises at the same time the conquest of lusts by the believer, the government of the Church by its office-bearers, and the blessed state of the departed saints, especially of the martyrs."[30] Though that was surely a latitude of opinion on one passage, the influence of Augustine predominated in his day, and indeed throughout the Middle Ages. Premillennialism was lacking in the church of the Middle Ages.[31]

When we come to modern times,

the fact is well known, that modernism or neo-protestantism has adopted the Christian concept of the kingdom as the symbol for its own cultural hopes and has thereby temporarily given great encouragement and deceitful friendship to the Postmillenarians. When neo-protestantism at the beginning of the present century began its triumphant march through America, the association of liberalism with Postmillennialism [and he could have added, with amillennialism also] and, by way of reaction, of fundamentalism with Premillennialism became practically unavoidable.[32]

Kromminga goes on to point out how American evangelism after 1843 has never lost the premillennial emphasis, for the noted evangelists have been uniformly premillennial. It is most interesting that Kromminga has not explained why fundamentalism should be linked with premillennialism. The reason was certainly more than "by way of reaction." Why did not fundamentalism "by way of reaction" turn to amillennialism? It is clear that he is dealing with effects and not causes. The sober fact is that, although the historical argument cannot be made to stand alone, it reveals that fundamentalism has every right and warrant to be linked with premillennialism, for the very good reason that the latter is in line with apostolic teaching.

NOTES

[1]H. C. Thiessen, *Introductory Lectures in Systematic Theology*, p. 470.
[2]R. J. Reid, *Amillennialism*, pp. 64-66.
[3]Ibid., pp. 66-67.
[4]Ibid., pp. 68-69.
[5]D. Bosworth, *The Millennium and Related Events*, pp. 19-21, 23-24, 34.
[6]G. H. Hospers, *The Calvinistic Character of Pre-millennialism*, pp. 1-2, 5.
[7]S. J. Case, *The Millennial Hope*, pp. 2, 117.
[8]Ibid., pp. 155, 172, 179.
[9]H. L. Payne, unpublished dissertation, pp. 13-14.
[10]L. S. Chafer, *Dispensationalism*, pp. 11-12.
[11]R. G. Clouse, *The Meaning of the Millennium*, pp. 23, 25, although his tone is not so certain on pp. 155-56. In more recent writings he has coined his own phrases such as "historic premillennialism" and "classic premillennialism," which have not gone unchallenged. Hoyt replies to Ladd: "Re-

ference to 'historic' premillennialism suggests something that I do not believe is true. . . . Any fundamental validity that is truly historic is to be found in the New Testament—something that was espoused by the early church and persisted for several hundred years" (R. Clouse, p. 41). In another context Walvoord has well stated the case: "One of the most eloquent testimonies to premillennial truth is found in the absolute silence of the New Testament, and for that matter the early centuries of the church, on any controversy over premillennial teaching" (J. F. Walvoord, *The Millennial Kingdom,* p. 118.)

[12]L. Berkhof, *The Kingdom of God,* pp. 21-22.

[13]Ibid., pp. 132-33.

[14]A. Pieters, *A Candid Examination of the Scofield Bible,* pp. 17-18.

[15]W. H. Rutgers, *Premillennialism in America,* p. 52.

[16]Ibid., p. 132.

[17]Ibid., p. 81.

[18]W. M. Smith, "The Prophetic Literature of Colonial America," *Bibliotheca Sacra,* 100: (Jan.-Mar., 1943), 72-74.

[19]D. H. Kromminga, *The Millennium in the Church,* pp. 27-28.

[20]Ibid., p. 29.

[21]Ibid., p. 33.

[22]Ibid., p. 41.

[23]Ibid., p. 42.

[24]Ibid., p. 51.

[25]Ibid., p. 76.

[26]Contra G. L. Murray, *Millennial Studies; A Search for Truth,* p. 12.

[27]Ibid., p. 77.

[28]Ibid., pp. 102, 104.

[29]Ibid., pp. 107, 286.

[30]Ibid., pp. 109-11.

[31]Ibid., pp. 114, 164.

[32]Ibid., p. 239.

6

Pre- and Amillennialism as Systems

Before turning to specific contrasts between premillennialism and amillennialism, it may be well to consider some general features of those systems in a summary manner. Though differing radically with the premillennial viewpoint, based on the literal interpretation of the prophets and the dispensational approach to the Scriptures,[1] Berkhof fairly judges that "it renders valuable service by emphasizing anew the supernatural and catastrophic elements in the establishment of the Kingdom. The doctrine, so favored in many circles today, that the Kingdom of God must be set up by man, and will by a natural process of evolution grow into perfection, is decidedly unscriptural, and the sooner this is admitted, the better it will be."[2]

Murray must acknowledge that "in no school of Christian thought can one find less liberalism than among the premillennialists."[3] In that same vein Rutgers concedes, "It is perhaps no exaggeration to assert that American Christianity is Premillenarian; the Fundamentalists have included it in their creed."[4] There is also a recognition on his part that more than one passage in the book of Revelation is involved in the premillennial position; it touches the whole scope of theological truth.[5]

But he characterizes premillennialism in strong language when he states: "Chiliasm is an underground stream, alternately rising to the surface and then again disappearing, with each overflow depositing sediment which breeds poisonous malaria."[6] If this were true, it would speak ill for American Christianity of the fundamentalist stamp. But, of course, no proof is given, for none is forthcoming. Rutgers goes on to accuse premillennialism of a reactionary attitude that is wholly negative, because it is permeated with pessimism.[7] In whatever respects premillennialism may be termed pessimistic, the pessimism is surely born of the statements of Scripture concerning the last days of this age. Remember also that it places before the believer the true optimism of the imminent coming of the Lord Jesus Christ. As a friend so aptly used to say, "There is no use trying to be optimistic with a misty optic." We can face the issues straightforwardly, because we have the God-given remedy.

Another charge made frequently against chiliasm is that it is Judaistic in origin and tendency[8]—that it has transplanted to Christianity the carnal mis-understanding of the glorious prophecies of the Messianic Kingdom;[9] and that it is nothing more than the distorted view of the scribes and Pharisees, which departs from the Word of God.[10] Those charges ask for reply. If chiliasm is accused of Judaistic origin and tendency, where will that charge end? It is such in the same sense that the Bible is. Was it not our omniscient Lord who uttered the words of John 4:22? If there was a transplanting of a carnal misunderstanding of the words of the prophets concerning the kingdom, is that to be laid at the door of the apostles? Were they wholly without the understanding vouch-safed to expositors today? As for the Pharisees, the distinction should ever be made that the denunciations of our Lord against them were leveled more at their formalistic and hypocritical worship than at their mistaken doctrinal views. But before the end of the discussion in his work, Rutgers accuses premillennialists of "Israelolatrie."[11]

All who have read premillennial literature to any extent are aware of the abundant use of Scripture to be found there. That also is a basis of criticism with Rutgers, who calls it "Biblicism."[12]

For amillennialists there exists no need for a Millennium, because they claim a fulfillment of the Davidic Covenant in New Testament times. Murray is frank to confess, "We have never been able to see the purpose of such a reign, nor can we understand how the Lord's physical presence, visible to a compara-tively small number of His people, could mean more than His spiritual pres-ence experienced by them all, unless we choose to dispense with faith and walk by sight."[13] We may be allowed a few observations on that statement. First of all, God has purposed to vindicate His Son and set Him on David's throne. There will be the fulfillment of Psalm 2:6; Luke 24:26 as well as 1:32-33; and 1 Peter 1:11. The sufferings were literal; the glories will be also. Second, we are nowhere informed that Christ's presence will be visible to a comparatively small number of His people. Third, where is the Scripture that compares that physical presence to the present spiritual presence as to degree of significance? Finally, we thank God for the hope that faith some day will be swallowed up by sight (Rom. 8:23-25 and 1 John 3:20. And that sight is nowhere indicated in Scripture as a lower level of spiritual experience and enjoyment.

When Murray informs us that amillennialism is the only view taught or implied in the great creeds of the church,[14] we are constrained to reply that, first of all, the creeds of the church are valuable, but they are not all-determining. No creed or number of them gives us all the doctrines of the faith. Has there ever been a general council of the church that has pronounced on the number of books in the inspired canon? He does not mention the creed or creeds that do teach or imply amillennialism. In common with others Mur-ray never erects a system of his own.

When Payne comes to discuss amillennial theology as a system, he purposes to examine the systematic character of amillennialism, believing that no such examination has yet appeared.[15] It will be readily seen that the subtitle to our original work was a comparison of the two systems. But after further study and research in amillennial literature since the writing of our first edition, we are more and more convinced that the word *system* when used in connection with amillennialism is only an accommodation and concession. Amillennialism is no system. The main works on that viewpoint treat only phases of the subject by attacking certain positions of the premillennialist. We are inclined rather to agree with D. B. MacCorkle that "amillennialism is a reactionary movement [even in the fourth century] without biblical system."[16]

Payne correctly enumerates features of the amillennial view of the kingdom, as "1. The kingdom is heavenly rather than earthly. 2. It is spiritual rather than political. 3. It is present rather than future. 4. Its point of inauguration is the first rather than the second advent. 5. Its king is in heaven rather than in Jerusalem. 6. Its subjects are found in the church of God rather than the nation Israel."[17]

Even such a summarization can suffice to show that amillennialism does not compare with premillennialism as a system that utilizes all the biblical data. Premillennialism is often accused by amillennialism as being too detailed and too full of program. A broad, general plan full of oversimplifications as the amillennial viewpoint is with its covenant of grace, may be appealing at first glance, but what becomes of the Scripture that is left untreated? Recall that Hamilton stresses in his work the supposed discrepancy between the premillennial interpretation of Isaiah 65:20 and the words of our Lord in Luke 20:35, and then never gives us his own exegesis of the very passage in Isaiah upon which he hinges his argument! No, we are compelled to agree with MacCorkle: *"Amillennialism cannot present a scientific system . . . At this hour no monumental work exists which sets forth a system known as amillennialism."*[18]

If that be considered too summary a fashion in which to deal with the question, note the considered comments of Smith in reviewing Allis's work: "On the one hand, he is himself unable to present a constructive arrangement of the great prophecies of the Bible concerning the future. His book is a criticism of the premillennial view, that the Church and Israel are distinct, but it does not offer a constructive interpretation of the prophecies which he refuses to accept as supporting the dispensational view."[19] Not only so, but Allis ignores the present apostasy.[20] It is definitely not safe to allow any church creed, however good, to shape our thinking on the whole range of Bible truth.[21]

Kromminga, though a premillennialist, cannot be accused with his covenant of grace position, of an animus toward amillennialism; therefore, his general characterization of amillennialism is worthy of consideration. It is well known how often premillennialists are confronted with the variations of views in their school of thought. The impression is that amillennialism is as uniform as could be desired. He contends,

> Hamilton does not recognize variations in Amillennialism. It is a recommendation for the view, if it is really well unified and uniformly held. But fact is, that there is need of recognizing variations in Amillennialism. It is far from being a perfectly unified system or scheme of eschatology. It is quite clear that Hamilton limits the thousand years of reign with Christ to the disembodied spirits in heaven; but it is equally certain, that this is not what Augustine, the father of the amillennial view, did. He embraced in that reign also the believers who do battle here on earth with lusts, and the elders who rule in and over the churches. In a sense, the elimination of these two modes of ruling with Christ may be hailed as a simplification and improvement upon the Augustinian Amillennialism; but it should at any rate be recognized, that it is not the only type of Amillennialism and that it is not fully Augustinian.[22]

That contention is true and leads us to ask why amillennialists will accuse premillennialists of departing from historic premillennialism, when they themselves have left Augustinian amillennialism. And how does the case stand with premillennialists on the matter of uniformity of opinion? It must be conceded that "with all this variation within its ranks Premillennialism has about as much of a chance to present to the outsiders a united front and to avoid the danger of falling into internal strife as has Protestantism or Christianity as a whole."[23] Moreover, premillennialism has the advantage of a full-fledged biblical system, which treats seriously all the data, as over against amillennialism, which is a negation without an orderly theological system.[24]

NOTES

[1] L. Berkhof, *The Kingdom of God*, p. 160.
[2] Ibid., p. 159.
[3] G. L. Murray, *Millennial Studies: A Search for Truth*, p. 14.
[4] W. H. Rutgers, *Premillennialism in America*, p. 10. Ladd, speaking of the 1920 Fundamentalist Convention in Buffalo, recalls that Curtis Laws wrote: "Premillennialists were much in evidence because premillennialists are always sound on the fundamentals . . ." (Ladd, *The Blessed Hope*, p. 60).
[5] Ibid., p. 12. The breadth of the subject has well been stated thus: "The second coming of Christ is thus both the Blessed Hope of the Church and the hope of human history. His coming will mean both salvation and judgment . . . it may be designated by the term *premillennialism*" (Ladd, *The Blessed Hope*, p. 7).
[6] Ibid., pp. 90-91.
[7] Ibid., pp. 132-33.

[8]Ibid.

[9]Ibid., p. 133.

[10]Ibid., p. 136.

[11]Ibid., p. 192.

[12]Ibid., pp. 150-51. Walvoord notes: "Amillennialism has not arisen historically from a study of prophetic Scripture, but rather through its neglect. . . . It becomes apparent early . . . that amillennialists have no guiding principle in spiritualization and that they come to widely different conclusions" (J. F. Walvoord, *The Millennial Kingdom,* p. 67). Furthermore, he declares: "Amillennialism, being a negative affirmation, does not have the power to create a complete system" (ibid., p. 70).

[13]Murray, pp. 19-20.

[14]Ibid., p. 87.

[15]H. L. Payne, *Amillennial Theology as a System,* p. 7.

[16]D. B. MacCorkle, *A Study of Amillennial Eschatology,* p. 87.

[17]H. L. Payne, pp. 21-22. The amillennialist Hoekema summarizes five major teachings of dispensational premillennialism, which he rejects as not in harmony with Scripture: "1. *The Old Testament predicts Christ's millennial reign*[italics his, here *et passim*]" For him the Old Testament says nothing of a millennial reign, because passages which do depict the millennial reign are by allegorization made to describe the new earth or the final state. "2. *There is a sharp separation between Israel and the church in God's redemptive program, so that Israel is said to have a future quite distinct from the future of the church.*" The only refutation he offers is Ephesians 2:14, 16, 19, a passage that sets forth conditions only in the church, not those between a literal Israel and the Body of Christ. On the basis of Romans 11 he equates the New Testament church with spiritual Israel, an identification nowhere stated or implied in Scripture. "3. *Old Testament prophecies about Israel are always interpreted literally.*" According to Hoekema the New Testament itself rejects that hermeneutical principle. If so, what of "seed" in Galatians 3; "new" in Hebrews 8; "I am" in John 8? He makes a shambles of Acts 15 in its use of Amos 9:11. That is poor exegesis. "4. *There is a future centrality for Israel as a nation.*" He even denies that Romans 11:26 teaches a future conversion of Israel. "5. *The mediatorial kingdom of God is only future.*" There is a misunderstanding here of the premillennial position, which holds that only the consummating phase of the mediatorial kingdom of God is future. Ladd's criticism of the postmillennial view is equally true of Hoekema's amillennial stance: "There is so little appeal to Scripture that I have little to criticize." Cf. Robert G. Clouse, ed., *The Meaning of the Millennium,* pp. 108-12, 144.

[18]MacCorkle, *Amillennial Eschatology,* p. 126.

] 103 [

[19]W. M. Smith, "Israel and the Church in Prophecy," *Sunday School Times,* December 1, 1945, p. 957.

[20]Ibid.

[21]Ibid., p. 958.

[22]D. H. Kromminga, *The Millennium in the Church,* p. 259.

[23]Ibid., p. 265.

[24]A common error among amillennialists is their taking the position that millennial issues reside exclusively, or almost so, in the realm of eschatology. Walvoord has the sufficient reply to that fallacy: "It is not too much to say that ecclesiology may be characterized as being either amillennial or premillennial. . . . Many of the important aspects of premillennialism are determined in ecclesiology rather than in eschatology" (Walvoord, *The Millennial Kingdom,* p. 221). See below the discussion in Part Four, chapter 15.

Part Two

Analysis of the Premillennial System

7
The Kingdom in the Old Testament

It is the claim of all informed premillennialists that if we do not and cannot find the kingdom or Millennium in the Old Testament, then we have no basis upon which to expect that it will be found in the New Testament.[1] The unwavering contention is that it is to be clearly seen in both Old and New. We have not found any premillennial discussion that begins with Genesis 3:15, but we believe that it is from that point that we must set out. The privilege of beginning here may be denied us by some, because there is no clear mention of the kingdom here, but we must not expect to find all the elements of the kingdom in one verse. One link in any chain never constitutes the whole chain.

The protevangelium of Genesis 3:15 is interesting from a number of angles After God had viewed His finished and perfect creation with manifest satisfaction, and after man had been placed in the central and commanding position in His finished work, man in his innocent state was put to the sole test of unfeigned and wholehearted obedience to his Creator, who rightly expected his allegiance. After man fell there was but one gleam of hope vouchsafed by God, and that was in the announcement of Genesis 3:15. God assumes the role of prophet and, knowing the end from the beginning, predicts that there will be enmity between the serpent and the woman and between its seed and her seed. The serpent's seed will bruise the heel of the woman's seed, and the latter will bruise the former's head. The word translated "bruise" is really "to lie in wait for" (*shuph*), suggesting the idea of prolonged conflict with the element of expectancy. Here then are set up two contending forces, headed by Satan on the one hand and Christ on the other, which are to flow on throughout the entire Word until the serpent's seed is finally and eternally consigned to the lake of fire. The triumph of the seed of the woman through His great redemption is the marvelous story of the Word of God, and here in Genesis 3:15 we have the seed plot that is to unfold through a revelation to be given "by divers portions and in divers manners" (Heb. 1:1). When Genesis 4:1 records that upon the birth of Cain, Eve said: "I have gotten a man, the LORD" (NASB marg.), it is possible that she was looking to the fulfillment of the word given to her by God.[2] But God's thoughts are not our thoughts, and Eve was soon to realize how ill-timed was her expectation.

It was not long before the deadly nature of the virus of the first man became manifest. The first transgressor of the law of God gave birth to the first murderer, who in turn went out from the presence of God to institute a citied civilization apart from God. Time alone was needed to reveal that man's wickedness was such that God could see every imagination of the thoughts of his heart as only evil continually (Gen. 6:5). But even the flood did not change the nature of man, for in the descendants of Noah we find a Nimrod (from *maradh,* "to rebel") who began a kingdom in the land of Shinar, or Babylon. That is the first mention of any kingdom in the Bible, and it is the kingdom of idolatrous Babylon, the seat and source of all idolatry (Zech. 5:5-11; Rev. 17:3-6; 18:24). From that place of iniquity God called Abram to go to the land of Canaan (Gen. 12:1).

When God laid His hand upon Abram in Ur of the Chaldees, He made an unconditional promise to him of the greatest and weightiest import.[3] The promise concerning the seed of the woman was narrowed down to the family and descendants of Abram. The covenant of God guaranteed to Abram that he would be the father of a great nation; that the blessing of the Lord would be his; that his name would be made great; that he would be a blessing; that the curse of God would rest upon those who cursed him, and the blessing of the Lord would be the portion of those who blessed him; and that in him all the families of the earth would be blessed. The phrase "in thee" is later explained in Galatians 3:16 as referring to Christ, who is to be the source of blessing for both Jew and Gentile. That covenant has never been abrogated by God and can be shown, if it were the present purpose to do so, to be the seed of all the later covenants of the Word. It was not set aside by the law from God's side, as Paul conclusively proves in the third chapter of Galatians, and it can never be nullified by man, because it is not conditioned upon any faithfulness or obedience of man. It is unconditional in every sense of the word.

That the covenant with Abraham involved three of the essential elements—a land, a nation, and a seed—of the kingdom was made clear from the later confirmations of it; first to Abraham, afterward to Isaac, and then to Jacob (Gen. 12:1-3, 7; 13:14-18; 15:18-21; 26:1-5; 28:13-15). Each time of course, it was God who ratified the covenant. In Genesis 13:14-18 Abraham was told to view the land northward, southward, eastward, and westward, for to him and to his seed it was given in perpetuity. God further revealed to him that his seed was to be as numberless as the dust of the earth. Once more God confirmed the covenant to Abraham, whom He delighted to call His friend, when he had obeyed the Lord even to the point of offering up his son. That offering the Lord refrained from accepting, for He had already—from before the foundation of the world—provided Himself with the Lamb who takes away the sin of the world (Gen. 22:15-18).

There in the land of Moriah Abraham was reassured that his seed would be as the stars of heaven and as the sand of the seashore and that in his seed all the families of the earth would be blessed. Because Isaac was the promised seed through whom in a future day in the person of the Redeemer the covenant blessings would be actualized and realized, we should expect God to put him in remembrance of the covenant. So we find God speaking to Isaac in Gerar, not only warning him not to go down into Egypt, but declaring that He would bless him and multiply his seed as the stars of heaven according to the oath made to Abraham (Gen. 26:1-5). The promise was once more endorsed to Isaac upon his return from Gerar to Beersheba with the usual mention of "thy seed" (Gen. 26:24). Nor was Jacob left without a word concerning the covenanted blessings. The oath was confirmed to him in Bethel and later upon his coming out of Padanaram, each time with the repetition of the key words "thy seed" (Gen. 28:13-15; 35:11-12).

The aged Jacob, upon his deathbed, foretold the fortunes of his sons (Gen. 49:3-27). The blessing upon Judah and the prophecy concerning him are of special interest for our study (vv. 8-12). It narrowed down the promised seed to the tribe of Judah and added another and most important element of the kingdom, the King. The twelve sons of the patriarch were told that the sceptre, the emblem of regal authority, would not depart from Judah nor one who issues decrees, until Shiloh came, to whom the gathering of the people would be. Many believe Shiloh is the One to whom reference is made in Ezekiel 21:27, where the prophet exclaims: "I will overturn, overturn, overturn, it: and it shall be no more, until he come whose right it is; and I will give it him." That would make the word *Shiloh* equivalent to *shelo*. Others believe that Shiloh refers to the man of peace and rest, deriving in this case Shiloh from *shalah*. In either case many students of the Word are of the opinion that direct mention is here made of the Messiah who was to come of the line of Judah. The extent of His authority is revealed: "Unto him shall the gathering of the people [the nations] be" (Gen. 49:10). The peaceful character of His kingdom and the plenty that will be present in it are all alluded to in the binding of a foal to the vine and the colt of an ass to the choice vine, and in the washing of His garments in wine and in the blood of grapes.

Finally, the surpassing beauty of the King is also mentioned in highly figurative language. Besides Genesis 49:10-12 there is one more reference to the King in the Pentateuch, in Numbers 24:17-19. The prophecy came from the lips of Balaam the son of Beor, a Mesopotamian from Pethor, who had been hired by Balak, king of Moab, to curse the children of Israel, who were journeying from Egypt to the promised land. After Balaam had blessed Israel three times, he said to the infuriated Balak: "Come therefore, and I will advertise thee what this people shall do to thy people in the latter days" (Num. 24:14). In his next vision Balaam saw a star coming out of Jacob, alluding to the heavenly dignity of the one to come, and a sceptre rising out of Israel. This view of the coming King is not occupied with peaceful representations, but rather with the conquering might of the King in battle as He smites the corners of Moab, both Edom and Seir are vanquished, and Israel is elevated triumphantly to a place of preeminence. Then He who comes from Jacob will have dominion.

The thread of the story is once more taken up when God condescended in His grace to make an unconditional covenant with David of the tribe of Judah (2 Sam. 7:10-16). That time the promised seed was narrowed down to the house and dynasty of David. The basis of the covenant, to be sure, was in the fathomless grace of God. Although David was a man after God's own heart, he was not free from sin, for we note that not long after God's covenant with him he fell into the darkest of transgressions. His heart, like that of all men everywhere and at all times, was deceitful above all things and desperately wicked, so that he himself did not know it. There was absolutely nothing in him, therefore, that would obligate God to enter with him into covenant relations of such vast and far-reaching implications and provisions. The Davidic covenant rests upon exactly the same basis as the Abrahamic, the ineffable grace of God. Those covenants have never, and can never, be broken because they do not depend in the slightest particular upon any act or performance of man, but are rooted and grounded in the immutable promise and oath of God. The provisions of the covenant are, furthermore, unmistakably clear.

First of all, David, whose desire had been that the Lord might have a fitting place in which to dwell in the midst of Israel, was told that the Lord would appoint a place for His people Israel where they would be established and where they would be at peace from all their enemies who had afflicted them.[4] Their settlement in the promised land was to be permanent.

The second provision of the covenant was a Davidic house or dynasty. David's seed would be set up after his death, and the Lord would establish his kingdom. The primary application, of course, was to Solomon who would be used to set up that house, the throne of which God would establish forever. The second provision included the throne and the kingdom that are necessarily linked with the dynasty.

Another feature of the promise was chastisement upon the Davidic house for disobedience. Although a paternal relationship was to exist between the seed of David and God, they would receive chastening from the rod of men and from the stripes of the children of men. That that cannot possibly refer to the Lord Jesus is evident from the clause "if he commit iniquity." The chastisement was carried out in the division of the Solomonic kingdom and the Assyrian and Babylonian captivities.

Still another point of interest in the promise was the assurance that sin in the Davidic line would not abrogate or disannul the covenant (2 Sam. 7:13-16, esp.). The final provision of the oath, and indeed it runs throughout the passage, was that all its features, except the chastisement, were to be eternal (cf. Psalm 89). Amillennialists—to digress here for a moment—accuse the premillennialists of taking prophecy in its literal sense and yet shortening the eternal kingdom of Christ to a mere thousand years. We shall deal with that question more fully later, but here let it suffice to say that we hold Christ's kingdom to be eternal even as it is here declared by God. We can well imagine, to resume the discussion where we left it, the impression made upon David by that revelation.

It warms the heart to read the words of David as he went in and sat before the Lord in grateful adoration. He recognized that it was not the manner of man, but that God was doing all for His Word's sake and according to His own heart. Here, then, are all the elements necessary for the kingdom—the land, the nation, the dynasty, the throne, the kingdom, and the King. In light of that, those who oppose the doctrine of the Millennium are mistaken to claim that the doctrine is first gleaned, and that not legitimately from the laws of exegesis, from a single passage in the Revelation and then read back into the rest of the Bible.

Just as the Abrahamic covenant had its confirmations in the lives of Abraham, Isaac, and Jacob, so the Davidic covenant has its endorsements in the Word. Apart from the prophetic books we find it confirmed in 1 and 2 Chronicles and the Psalms. The covenant as recorded in 1 Chronicles 17:9-15 is practically word for word what we have in 2 Samuel 7, with this interesting difference: In the passage in 1 Chronicles, God seems to link Himself with the kingdom more closely, if possible, when He says: "I will settle him in mine house and in my kingdom for ever" (v. 14). The house and kingdom are not merely David's, but God's also. When Solomon the king was dedicating the Temple he had built to God, he began by blessing the Lord God of Israel who had with His hand fulfilled that which He spoke with His mouth to David. He went on to narrate how God chose Jerusalem where His name might dwell and David to be over His people, showing how God has performed His Word in raising up a seed to David to sit on his throne in conformity with His promise that David should not lack a man to sit upon his throne (1 Kings 8:12 ff.).

When one turns to the Psalms, he finds confirmations of the covenant on every hand. In the second psalm the scene is set in the far future, in a day when the nations are raging and are in great tumult with their hearts intent upon throwing off the rule of God and His Christ. Then we are permitted to view God's attitude toward an uprising and ungodly confederacy. The Lord who sits in heaven—He need not even arise to destroy them—shall laugh and have them in derision. Then He shall make known to the nations the fierceness of

His anger and the terror of His displeasure. For despite the opposition of Satan-motivated men and nations, God has set His King upon His holy hill of Zion. That is the pronouncement of God, who calls those things that are not as though they were, because He knows full well the immutability and stedfastness of those things that He has willed. In the verses following, the Son speaks, announcing the decree and the law of God that promise to give to His wellbeloved Son the nations as His inheritance and the uttermost parts of the earth as a possession. Those that will not obey willingly will be broken with a rod of iron and dashed in pieces like a potter's vessel. The warning of the Spirit to the kings is, therefore, that in view of the futility of attempting to thwart the covenanted purposes of God in His King, they do well to serve the Lord with fear and rejoice with trembling.

Of the many other wonderful psalms that speak of the King Messiah we choose only three. Those will suffice to show how the book of Psalms confirms the covenant of God with David. At the thought of the good word he is to speak, the heart of the psalmist (Psalm 45) bubbles over with joy (*rahash,* mildly translated "inditing"). Then follows a description of the beauty of the King that beggars the Hebrew tongue, so that the Holy Spirit coins a new and intensive word for beauty (*yaphyaphitha*), doubling the ordinary word to better convey the thought of the King's surpassing beauty. His grace, might, glory, majesty, warfare, and victory for the sake of truth, the eternal character of His throne, the righteousness of the rule of His kingdom, and His anointing of God with the oil of gladness, are all fittingly brought forth to portray the King in His glory.

The time seems to be the marriage feast of the King when His garments, in Oriental fashion, smell of the myrrh, aloes, and cassia that have been sent to Him from the palaces of kings and whereby He has been made glad. The obedience of those kings to the King is hereby implied. Then attention is drawn to the bride of the King who forsakes her own people and father's house, so that she may be wholly given over to the King. The retinue and clothing of the queen are described as well as the joy and gladness that attend her entrance into the King's palace. The psalm closes with the mention of the everlasting name and eternal praise of the King. Little wonder it is that the psalmist tells us his heart "bubbled and boiled over" with his good matter concerning the King.

If Psalm 45 depicts the marriage of the King, Psalm 72 speaks of the character of the reign of the King. The title, rather than pointing to Solomon as the one addressed, may be better understood as assigning to him the writing of the psalm. By no stretch of the imagination can the statements recorded be applied to Solomon. They are as high above him as the heaven is above the earth. The reference is undoubtedly to the King Messiah. The writer, first of all, requests that the judgment and righteousness of God will be given the King. That the prayer is answered is evident from what follows. The King will righteously and judiciously vindicate the cause of all that are afflicted, oppressed, and needy. The result will be that all men will reverence the King whose very presence will be refreshing. In the days of His reign the righteous will flourish, so that violence, wickedness, and oppression will be supplanted by abundance of peace. His dominion shall stretch from sea to sea and from the river unto the ends of the earth. Animal creation is yet to yield Him obedience. All kings shall worship and all nations shall serve Him. So righteous will be His reign that prayer will continually be made to God for the perpetuation of His rule. Great prosperity and abundance will attend His glorious government, and all nations shall call Him blessed when the whole earth is filled with His glory.

Before passing from the Psalms it is vital to consider Psalm 89. Ethan the Ezrahite takes occasion to praise God for His mercies and faithfulness, which are best exemplified in the covenant made with David, His servant, that his seed should be established forever and his throne to all generations. After extolling God for the beauty and wonder of His Person, the psalmist returns again to the theme of the sure mercies of God to David, representing God as saying: "My mercy will I keep for him for evermore, and my covenant shall stand fast with him" (v. 28). Mention is made once more of chastisement in the Davidic line for sin, and again it is noted that God will nevertheless neither take His lovingkindness from His chosen servant, nor allow His faithfulness to fail. For the covenant-keeping God declares: "My covenant will I not break, nor alter the thing that is gone out of my lips" (v. 34). Man may be faithless and is, but God cannot lie; He has sworn by His holiness. Surely, no one could obtain more certain corroboration and confirmation in any matter than did David in the unconditional and gracious covenant God made with him concerning a future King and His kingdom.

But the truth of a Messianic kingdom is not solely dependent upon the links that have been forged in the progress of this study. The prophets of God in Israel also wove that theme into the fabric of their incomparable prophecies. Now it is time to see what Isaiah has to say concerning a future visible, earthly, and glorious kingdom. Isaiah was a prophet to the Southern Kingdom of Judah and was a contemporary of the prophet Micah. The prophecy of Isaiah is the fullest of all the prophecies, covering a time period from his own day to the creation of the new heavens and new earth, the present age excepted. He is one of only three writers in the Word (the others are Peter and John) who mention the new heavens and new earth.

The first part of the message of Isaiah is taken up in the main with the subject of judgment and the future captivity in Babylon; the latter part, with the glorious future for Israel and the Gentiles through the suffering and glorified Servant of Jehovah. The vision of the prophet opens with a rebuke of the disobedience and stubbornness of Israel in departing from the way of the

Lord. Their sacrifices and offerings and appointed feasts are no longer sources of delight to God, for the hearts of the people are not right with God, and violence and oppression fill the city. Along with the warning of punishments, the prophet adds that God will restore Judah's judges as at the first and her counselors as at the beginning, so that the city will be called "The city of righteousness, the faithful city" (1:26). From the contemplation of the present state of Judah and Jerusalem, the eyes of the prophet are raised to see the vision of the latter days when the mountain of the Lord, symbolic in prophetic Scriptures of a kingdom, shall be established above all kingdoms and all nations shall be drawn as in a river *(wenaharu)* to it. It will be known to all that out of Zion comes forth the law and the word of the Lord from Jerusalem. Then will there be righteous judgment among the nations of the earth, and peace will so prevail that swords and spears, implements of warfare, will be converted into implements of productive industry. War will be outlawed and learned no more.

There follow prophecies dealing with punishment for existing sin in Israel, which reveal the low and degraded spiritual condition of the nation. Between messages dealing with the campaign of Rezin the king of Syria and Pekah the son of Remaliah against Jerusalem and the threatening invasion of Judah by the Assyrian forces, Isaiah gave Ahaz a sign, although he disdained to ask one of the Lord (7:10-16). It was the sign of the virgin birth of the King, as Matthew confirms in the first chapter of his gospel (1:22-23). In Isaiah 9 there is a continuation of the subject of desolation awaiting Judah in the Assyrian invasion, but in the midst of it the prophet portrays a scene of victory that will come to Israel because a child is born (speaking of the virgin birth) to the nation and a son is given (referring to the gift of God's eternal Son). He will sustain the government by His own power, for He is the Wonderful Counselor, the mighty God, the Father of eternity—perhaps alluding to the fact that His kingdom will go into the ages of the ages—and the Prince of peace. His government shall increase without end, and peace shall universally prevail as He rules upon the throne of David and upon his kingdom to order and uphold it with judgment and justice forever. And none of that is dependent upon the will or designs of man, for the zeal of the Lord of hosts will bring it all to pass.

In chapter 11 Isaiah prophesies again of the kingdom of the King Messiah. The first verse of the chapter must be coupled with the last verse of the preceding chapter to bring out the striking contrast. When the Lord is casting down the strong and haughty enemies of Israel and the thickets of the forest are being cut down with iron, there shall come forth a twig out of the stump of Jesse and a shoot out of its roots shall be fruitful. That is a picture of the forsaken and degraded position of the Davidic dynasty at the time the King comes to His kingdom. He is to be equipped with the sevenfold plentitude of the Holy Spirit; the Spirit of the Lord, the spirit of wisdom and understanding, the spirit of counsel and might, the spirit of knowledge and of the fear of the Lord. With such equipment He will be able to refrain from judging merely from outward appearances and from reproving from hearsay and rumor. His kingdom will be one in which the poor are judged with righteousness, a blessing rarely granted them, and the meek and humble of the earth will have their causes adjudicated with uprightness.

That will necessitate punishment and even death, which will be speedily meted out to the wicked. The peace and tranquillity of His kingdom will even reach to and pervade the animal kingdom, so that the wolf and the lamb, the leopard and the kid, the calf and the young lion, the cow and the bear, the predator and the prey, will be able to dwell in safety and peace together. None shall desire to hurt or destroy, for the earth will be as full of the knowledge of the Lord as the waters cover the sea. When that root of Jesse is raised up, not only will Israel come from Assyria, from Egypt, from Pathros, from Cush, from Elam, from Shinar, from Hamath, from the islands of the sea, and from the four corners of the earth, but the Gentiles also will seek after Him whose rest is glorious. The order in His kingdom is: blessing upon Israel and through them blessing to all the nations. What a remarkably detailed picture Isaiah has given here of the King and His kingdom on the earth!

But the prophet has not yet said his last word on the subject. In chapter 14 Isaiah predicts the restoration of Israel from all the lands of their captivity; their settlement in their own land; and the peace that will be manifest throughout the nation and the whole earth. "Yea, the fir trees rejoice at thee, and the cedars of Lebanon, saying, Since thou art laid down, no feller is come up against us" (v. 8). Surely no one could say that state of affairs exists in Israel today, a nation still scattered, peeled, and oppressed on every side. Going on through the book of Isaiah, in the midst of the burden or vision concerning Moab, these words are found, which can apply only to the covenanted kingdom: "And in mercy shall the throne be established: and he shall sit upon it in truth in the tabernacle of David, judging, and seeking judgment, and hasting righteousness" (16:5). One might expect the prophet to complete his messages of doom and destruction, and then turn his undivided attention to a portrayal of kingdom conditions, but the mind of the Holy Spirit finds it wise and proper to insert those rays of hope all along the way.

So the word is recorded in 24:23: "Then the moon shall be confounded, and the sun ashamed, when the LORD of Hosts shall reign in mount Zion, and in Jerusalem, and before his ancients gloriously." What could the prophet say of a kingdom age that would be more explicit than that which he has already declared? But the end is not yet. The theme in chapter 25 is a day when death is swallowed up in victory, God has wiped away all tears from all faces, and Israel is glad and rejoicing in the long-awaited salvation of the Lord. The minor note becomes prominent again as the prophet pronounces trial and woe upon

Jerusalem and Ephraim (chaps. 28-31), only to brighten as he speaks of a King reigning in righteousness and princes ruling in judgment (32:1), when the wilderness and the solitary place shall be glad for Israel, delivered from her surrounding enemies, and the desert shall rejoice and blossom as a rose (35:1).

The glory of Lebanon and the excellency of Carmel and Sharon will be given to the desert, and at that time the eyes of the blind will be opened, the ears of the deaf will be unstopped, the lame man will leap as an hart, and the tongue of the dumb shall sing (Isa. 35:2, 5, 6). "And the ransomed of the LORD shall return, and come to Zion with songs and everlasting joy upon their heads: they shall obtain joy and gladness, and sorrow and sighing shall flee away" (v. 10). Before Isaiah presents that unsurpassed portrait of the suffering Servant of the Lord, he addresses a most comforting and consoling message to the captive daughter of Zion of the time when messengers shall publish salvation and say to Zion, "Thy God reigneth!" (52:7). That will be a day of comfort and redemption for the people of the Lord in Jerusalem. The testimony of the prophet Isaiah to the reality of a covenanted kingdom need not be prolonged. Chapters 54, 60, 61, and 66 could be added, but what has already been advanced from the writings of the prophet must surely suffice for the mind of the serious student of the Scriptures.

But if one believes Isaiah is alone in this witness, he is sadly mistaken. His messages are more full and extensive on the kingdom than those of the other prophets, but they are by no means the sole testimony to the glorious, earthly reign of the King. Jeremiah has his word to say on the subject. That prophet, ministering also to the Southern Kingdom, prophesied much later than Isaiah. He began in the days of Josiah the son of Amon and continued through the reign of Jehoiakim the son of Josiah until the Babylonian captivity at the end of the eleventh year of Zedekiah the son of Josiah. He ministered for a little while during the captivity until his death. His messages, largely denunciatory, were not well received, and he himself met with opposition and persecution. At one time he decided to refrain from telling forth the message of the Lord, but the word of God was in his heart as a burning fire, and he could not forbear any longer. From the beginning of his prophecy through chapter 22 there is one continuous and unbroken message of judgment, of infidelity to God, and of warning concerning the Babylonian captivity. But in chapter 23 the prophet, after denouncing the destroying, faithless pastors of the sheep of the Lord, makes known that God Himself will in a coming day regather the scattered sheep and not only set over them shepherds who will have their welfare at heart, but will also raise up to David a righteous Branch (Jer. 23:1-8).

A King will then reign and be successful in executing judgment and justice, not in heaven, but in the earth. "In his days Judah shall be saved, and Israel shall dwell safely: and this is his name whereby he shall be called, THE LORD OUR RIGHTEOUSNESS" (v. 6). The same theme is returned to in chapters

30 and 31 after sundry messages and signs on coming judgment and chastisement. After an unprecedented time of sorrow and tribulation, Israel shall come back to serve the Lord her God and David her king who will be raised up over her (30:7-9). Her captivity will be brought to an end by the gracious interposition of God who will restore her to her health and heal her of her wounds (30:12-17). The virgin of Israel, a most loving appellation, will again be built and adorned. Joy and singing will take the place of sorrow and weeping. Redeemed Zion is to sing and rejoice as only the redeemed know how. The land will no longer be abandoned and desolate but will bring forth plenteously (31:4-14).

The final message of Jeremiah on the subject of the kingdom is to be found in chapter 33. While he was shut up in prison, the Lord revealed to him that, although Judah was in captivity and the covenanted promises seemed abrogated, God nevertheless intended to cause the captivity of Judah and the captivity of Israel to return. He would cleanse them of their iniquities and pollutions, that the blessing and joy of God might be theirs in abundance. The reason God is to do that in behalf of Israel is because of His purpose to perform that good thing He promised to the house of Israel and the house of Judah (v. 14). It is made clear that the "good thing" is the Branch of righteousness that will be raised up to David, and He will execute judgment and righteousness in the land. Jerusalem in her safety will then be called by the name of her King, The Lord Our Righteousness (vv. 15-16). All that is in conformity with and in fulfillment of the word of the Lord to David that he should never want a man to sit upon the throne of the house of Israel. So firm and established is that fact in the eternal plan of God that it can no more be set aside or invalidated than God's covenant of the day and His covenant of the night can be broken, so that there should be neither day nor night in their season (vv. 17, 20 ff.). What surer confirmation could Israel have had than that which God gave by the mouth of the prophet Jeremiah when he foretold of the coming kingdom?

The next to take the witness stand to testify concerning the earthly kingdom is the prophet Ezekiel. Does he confirm in his prophecy the fact of a promised earthly kingdom to be governed by a King of the seed of David? Ezekiel was one of the exilic prophets; at the very outset of the prophecy he is among the captives by the river Chebar in Babylon. He appears to minister to the whole nation, for he is sent to the house of Israel and is designated by God as a watchman of the house of Israel. The prophecy is couched in highly symbolic language, which is difficult of exact exposition. From the general symbolism of prophecy we gather that his early chapters are occupied with messages of the visitation of Israel by God with judgment for their multitudinous sins and departures from the true worship of the living God. Judgment is pronounced as well against the Ammonites, against Moab, Edom, Philistia, Tyre, Sidon, and Egypt.

After his disclosure of the unfaithfulness and avarice of the shepherds of Israel, whose chief concern is for their own sustenance and comfort, the prophet, in words similar to those of Jeremiah, predicts that the Lord will gather and deliver His sheep from all the places where they have been scattered in order to settle them in peace in their own land where He Himself can feed them of His bounty (34:1-10). Then He will set up a shepherd who will care for the sheep, His servant David. Showers of blessing will make the land productive where the people of Israel will no longer be a prey he nations about them (vv. 23-26). The blessings of God that will attend the visible kingdom of the King of the lineage and house of David are further set forth in the lengthy and detailed account in chapter 36.

In Ezekiel 37, the prophet records the vision of the valley of dry bones and its explanation, then interprets the sign of the two sticks upon which he has been commanded to write. The gathering of those two sticks into one is said to represent (note how Scripture is explicit in the explanation of its symbols) the regathering of the children of Israel from among the nations to be one nation in their own country, and "one king shall be king to them all" (v. 22). But it is not left to us to surmise who that king may be, for we are unequivocally told that the Greater David will be king over them and will shepherd them in the statutes and judgments of God. The earthly David will be their prince forever. Following the prophecy against Gog, Ezekiel gives us a most elaborate and minute picture of the Temple of the Davidic kingdom. Through nine chapters (40-48) the prophet describes not only the Temple building itself, but also the place of the throne, the altar, the appointed offerings, the priests, the worship of the people of the kingdom, and the prince who will rule over them all.

Daniel, too, has his distinctive message relative to the kingdom. He is an exilic prophet, having been taken captive to Babylon by Nebuchadnezzar in the time of Jehoiakim. His prophecy is remarkable among other things for the light it throws upon the times of the Gentiles and Gentile domination. It was in the second year of his reign that Nebuchadnezzar dreamed a dream and, unlike Pharaoh of old, forgot its content. When the magicians, astrologers, and sorcerers of Babylon showed their inability to meet the request of the king to recount the forgotten dream and give its interpretation, Daniel came forward, relying upon the help of his God, and promised to comply with the king's demands (2:24-45). After prayer he was given the vision and interpretation from God. The image that Nebuchadnezzar had seen had a head of fine gold, breast and arms of silver, belly and thighs of brass, legs of iron, feet part of iron and part of clay. A stone cut out without hands smote the image upon its feet and broke them to pieces. The iron, clay, brass, silver, and gold were all broken at the same time, and the wind carried them away, while the stone that struck the image became a great mountain that filled the whole earth.

The king was told that he was the head of gold to whom was given dominion over men, beasts of the field, and fowls of the heaven. That is confirmed by the prophecy of Jeremiah in 27:4-8. The Babylonian kingdom under Nebuchadnezzar was the first world empire. It was to be followed by a kingdom inferior to it, represented by the silver. The trend of the metals to the baser reveals the degradation in the procession of those empires upon the scene of history. The second empire, as corroborated by secular history, was the Medo-Persian, and the third was the Greco-Macedonian. The fourth empire was represented by the basest metal, but the one greatest of all in strength. Notwithstanding its strength, the kingdom was to be, and in point of fulfillment was, divided into the Eastern and Western Roman empires. Those two in turn are divided into ten kingdoms. The iron is mixed with clay, a combination of strength and weakness. Some believe reference is here made to a coexistence of both monarchical and democratic forms of government in the Roman Empire. In the days of those last ten kings and their kingdoms, the God of heaven will set up a kingdom that shall never be destroyed, symbolized by the stone that became a great mountain.

The stone represents the coming King who is not made by human agency, but comes from the glory of the Father. It is swift in its movement, and the destruction that it accomplishes is sudden. God's kingdom is to be set up by no progressive and gradual process or development; it is unexpected and instantaneous. The stone smites the feet but brings about the collapse of the whole world rule and system. It does not build upon the wreckage thus effected, which is completely done away with, but is the source of a new kingdom that fills—note—the whole earth (2:35). To Daniel, then, it is granted to reveal the relationship between the kingdom of the King and the governments of this world under Gentile domination and ascendancy.

In Daniel 7 the same subject is treated from a different angle. This time it is the prophet himself who has the dream, and the vision is under the figure of four beasts, denoting God's appraisal of the moral character of the kingdoms of the world. The Babylonian Empire is represented by the lion, who is chief among the animals, even as that first kingdom was among its successors. The second beast like a bear speaks of the cruelty of the Medo-Persian Empire. The swiftness of the leopard characterizes the world-empire of Greco-Macedonia. The fourth beast, which is the most important of all for it is farther along in the prophetic time scheme of the ages, is so terrible and dreadful that there is no beast to describe it. It displays tremendous strength in its rapaciousness. The beast, unlike the others in that particular, also has ten horns which are revealed as ten kings, answering to the ten toes of the image. From among these ten horns there comes up a little horn that plucks up three of the other horns and has eyes like a man and a mouth that speaks great things.

While the prophet beheld, thrones were set and the Ancient of Days sat in judgment with the result that the beast was slain and destroyed, and dominion was taken from the rest of the beasts. Then one like the Son of man, a name connecting Him with the seed of the woman of Genesis 3:15, came with clouds of heaven to the Ancient of Days, who gave Him dominion, glory, and a kingdom that all nations should serve Him, which dominion and kingdom are everlasting and indestructible. In the interpretation Daniel is told that the saints of the Most High (some translate *'elyonin,* "most high places," which is possible from the text) shall take the kingdom and possess it forever and ever. The prophet is also made to understand that the great things of the little horn are blasphemies against the Most High, and that the time of his power, delegated to him, will be until a time and times and the dividing of time, which is found to be three and a half years by comparison with other prophetic Scriptures (Dan. 12:7; Rev. 11:2; 12:6, 14; 13:5). But his dominion shall be speedily taken from him, and the kingdom and dominion, on earth to be sure just as was that of the little horn, will be given to the saints of the Most High, whose kingdom is an everlasting kingdom. With such evidence there need be no hesitation to assert that Daniel too bears undiminished, forceful testimony to an earthly kingdom.

Among the twelve so-called minor prophets abundant and clear predictions of the kingdom of the Davidic King exist, which entitle them to be considered as legitimate links in the long chain of Old Testament teaching concerning a glorious earthly reign in Jerusalem over the regathered people of Israel. Of those twelve prophets there was but one, Malachi, who did not directly or by type speak of the kingdom age, although he dealt with the Day of the Lord and the fact of the visible coming of the Sun of righteousness with healing in His wings.

Hosea heads the list of the minor prophets in the English canon. His ministry was cast with the Northern Kingdom of Israel. His message was particularly taken up with the thought of the unfaithfulness of the children of Israel to their God. The relationship set up between them and the Lord is analogous to that between a man and his wife. Israel because of her infidelity is compared to an adulterous wife, a woman of many loves. Because of constant and persistent going astray, Israel has rightly been given the name *Lo-ammi,* not my people (1:8-9). But the day will yet come when Israel will be as the sand of the sea which can neither be numbered nor measured; then they will be called the sons of the living God (1:10). That those words cannot be legitimately applied to the return from the Babylonian captivity is seen from the content of the next verse. Here it is said that the children of Israel and the children of Judah will be gathered together and have one head over them (1:11). The comment of the Holy Spirit in Romans 9 is to the same effect (vv. 25-26).

In Hosea 3, the prophet was commanded of God to buy a woman beloved of her friend, yet an adulteress; that the prophet did, saying unto her that she should abide for him many days without playing the harlot. The reference of that symbolical transaction is, of course, to Israel and her relation to the Lord. For in a similar manner the children of Israel were to be, and have been, many days without a king or a prince, any governmental authority, and without a sacrifice and without an image, any true worship or idolatrous worship, and without an ephod and teraphim, any means of priestly ministration. After that long period the children of Israel will return and seek the Lord their God and David their king. In the chapters following, the prophet poured out his divinely-given indictment against the sin and degradation of the nation. Then he turned at the close of his prophecy to the consoling promise of God with reference to the day when He will be their King after He has healed their backsliding. In language most beautiful Hosea pictured the fruitfulness of Israel in the kingdom. He will grow as the lily; his branches shall spread; his beauty will be as the olive tree; and his smell shall be as Lebanon (14:4-7).

Joel, a prophet to the Northern Kingdom also, dealt in his short prophecy with the insect plague at that time and the desolation and havoc it created throughout the land. From a contemplation of the destructive agencies then at work, the prophet gazed into the future and revealed in telling terms the dreadfulness of the Day of the Lord. The great and terrible conflict of that day was described, and then the deliverance was referred to. The Lord Himself, the hope and strength of the children of Israel, will roar out of Zion, and the voice of the God of Israel shall speak forth from Jerusalem (3:16). At that time Israel will be holy, and such will be the plenty of the land that the mountains will drop down new wine, and the hills will flow with milk. All the rivers of Judah shall flow with waters, and a fountain will come forth of the house of the Lord. Judah, cleansed and purified, shall dwell forever, and Jerusalem from generation to generation (3:18-20).

Amos, a prophet to the Northern Kingdom before the exile, was occupied with the pronouncement of God's coming judgment upon Damascus, Gaza, Tyre, Edom, Ammon, Moab, Judah, and Israel. After a detailed accusation of the heartless worship in Israel the prophecy foretells of the sifting of the house of Israel among the nations (9:9). Afterward the promise of the Lord is: "In that day will I raise up the tabernacle of David that is fallen, and close up the breaches thereof; and I will raise up his ruins, and I will build it as in the days of old" (9:11). That the reference is unmistakably to the kingdom is made clear by the final words of the prophecy. The land will be so fruitful and productive that the plowman will overtake the reaper, and he who treads the grapes will overtake him that sows the seed. Israel's captivity will be ended; the desolations of the land will be rebuilt; the forsaken cities will be inhabited; Israel will be planted in their land; and they will no more be pulled up or dispossessed of their land (9:13-15).

In the short prophecy of Obadiah, Edom was called to account by God. After the sin of Edom had been laid bare, the prophet predicted that upon Mount Zion will be both deliverance and holiness; then the house of Jacob shall fully enter into their possessions. Israel shall inhabit and possess the land, "And saviors shall come up on mount Zion to judge the mount of Esau; and the kingdom shall be the LORD'S" (v. 21).

When we turn to the prophet Jonah we find no definite and explicit prophecy of the covenanted kingdom of David. But there is much in the book by way of type. Many agree that the sole purpose of the message is not to show the bigotry of the prophet, or even how God accepts true repentance. As for the latter, we learn from Nahum that destruction was eventually meted out to Nineveh, who returned to her sinful ways. Nor is the only purpose of the book to reveal that God is the God of all nations. If Jonah had never been written, that would have been known from other parts of the Word of God. What more, then, is included in the prophecy? The message of Jonah typifies in a remarkable manner the life history of the nation of Israel. Israel, like the prophet, was chosen of God for a mission and entrusted with a message for the whole world. The nation was disobedient to her high and noble calling and was consequently cast out of her land into the midst of the nations. She will yet be gathered out of her captivity into her own land, where, having learned the price of disobeying the command of God, she will preach God's message to the nations in the kingdom, as confirmed by Isaiah and others. Jonah, then, is a typical book demonstrating Israel as fulfilling her God-given and long-rejected mission in the age of the kingdom.

Micah was another prophet to the Southern Kingdom of Judah. The woes and judgments that Micah pronounced upon Israel are as penetrating and piercing as any in the prophetic Scriptures, but he did not confine his message to those. In the fourth chapter of his prophecy he centered his attention fully upon the kingdom. He predicted that in the last days the mountain of the house of the Lord will be established above all the mountains; many nations shall come to the mountain of the Lord to be taught of His ways in order to walk in His paths, for out of Zion will go forth the law and the word of the Lord will be proclaimed from Jerusalem; the King will judge all the nations with equity so that the learning of war will be done away with; and the peace of the kingdom with its well-founded security will allow every man to sit under his vine and under his fig tree, none making them afraid (4:1-4). At that time and in those days God will regather Israel that has been driven out and afflicted, "and the LORD shall reign over them in mount Zion from henceforth even for ever" (4:7, 8).

The prophet went on in the same vein when he prophesied in the next chapter the birth of the King in Bethlehem Ephratah in Judah, for out of her was to come forth He that was to be ruler in Israel, even He whose goings forth have been from everlasting. That shepherd will stand and feed Israel in the strength of the Lord, in the majesty of the name of the Lord His God. They shall abide, for He will be great unto the ends not of heaven but, on the contrary, of the earth (5:1-4).[5] The prophecy of Micah closes with the word of assurance that God will perform the truth, even the oft-repeated and oft-confirmed promise, to Jacob, and the mercy to Abraham, which God endorsed with an oath involving His transparent and unapproachable holiness (7:20).

Nahum prophesied of the coming destruction of Nineveh as God's visitation of her for her sins. In the midst of his message, however, he interjected a word concerning the kingdom, calling the attention to the messengers who bring good tidings and publish peace (1:15). That that was a reference to the kingdom is corroborated by the fact that in practically the same words Isaiah predicted the message to be given out in the kingdom, the context making it unquestionably certain that the kingdom is in view throughout (Isa. 52:7).

Habakkuk, who is probably best remembered for his indelible words "the just shall live by his faith" (2:4), of which so much is made in the New Testament revelation, began with a great problem confronting him. He could not see how God, who is of purer eyes than to behold evil and cannot look on iniquity, permitted evil to go on without judgment being meted out. But he ended his message with a song of praise in which he said: "God came from Teman, and the Holy One from mount Paran. Selah. His glory covered the heavens, and the earth was full of his praise" (3:3). Those and similar words assure us that the kingdom is in the mind of the prophet. No wonder then that he could say referring to present conditions, that even if the fig tree would not blossom, nor the vines give their fruit, nor the olive trees give their increase, nor the fields yield their food, nor the flock be in the fold, nor the herd in the stalls, yet would he rejoice in the Lord, even the God of his salvation (3:17-18).

Zephaniah was a prophet of Judah called upon to bear witness to Israel of the coming captivity, not omitting at the same time to remind the surrounding nations of the judgment of God in store for them. Before he closed his message and laid down his pen, he poured out words of infinite comfort and solace. He called upon the daughter of Zion and Jerusalem to sing and be glad and rejoice, for "the king of Israel, even the LORD, is in the midst of thee: thou shalt not see evil any more" (3:14-15). The Lord Himself will save Israel, rejoice over her, and cause her to get fame in every place where she has been put to shame (3:17, 19). God promised her this blessing: "I will make you a name and a praise among all people of the earth, when I turn back your captivity before your eyes" (3:20).

The prophecies of Haggai and Zechariah, postexilic prophets, are yet to be considered before the prophetic testimony and witness to the kingdom are completed. The burden of Haggai's message was the need to finish the work already begun, and later interrupted, on the restoration of the Temple. At the end of his prophecy he mentioned the overthrow of the throne of kingdoms and the destruction of the strength of the kingdoms of the nations, which time is known from the prophecy of Daniel to coincide with the establishment of the kingdom of the rightful King of the earth.

Five of the fourteen chapters of Zechariah speak of the kingdom. In the third chapter, the prophet is speaking of the peace and security of the kingdom, when every man will have his own vine and fig tree (3:10); in the eighth chapter, reference is made to God's dwelling in the midst of Jerusalem, the city of truth, which shall be thickly populated and become the source of spiritual power and witness throughout the entire earth (8:3, 20-23); in the ninth chapter not only is the presentation of the King set before us, but with reference to His kingdom it is also said: "His dominion shall be from sea even to sea, and from the river even to the ends of the earth" (9:9-10); in the twelfth chapter the establishment of the Davidic kingdom after the great war of the nations is brought before us (12:7-10); and in the last chapter the prophet concludes with the record, among other definite details, that "the LORD shall be king over all the earth: in that day shall there be one LORD, and his name one" (14:9).

It has been the purpose of this chapter to show by a consistent and connected study of the Old Testament Scriptures that the kingdom finds, not accidentally or incidentally, but purposely and intentionally, a place in God's revelation preparatory to the New Testament age. Writer after writer and prophet after prophet added a line here and a line there to complete the Old Testament picture of a kingdom under the King of the Davidic line. With such a prophetic testimony to guide them and shape their thinking, what kind of kingdom were the Jews of those days and those who study the Word in this day, to expect? Were the Jews at fault in expecting God to fulfill His oft-reiterated word and guarantee that on the throne of David in Jerusalem, over regathered and cleansed Israel, there would one day reign in unexcelled glory and righteousness a King of the house of David? No one can reasonably explain away all the various and painstakingly minute prophetic utterances that have been perused.[6]

NOTES

[1]McClain has discerningly pointed out: "The field of Old Testament is not only the largest but also in certain respects the most important area in the entire investigation of the future Mediatorial Kingdom of God" (A. J. McClain, *The Greatness of the Kingdom*, p. 135). That accounts for the detail employed in this chapter. On the other hand, in spite of the voluminous and precise character of the predictions of the Old Testament,

the amillennialist, realizing he cannot deny such testimony and maintain his genuine regard for the infallibility and inerrancy of Scripture, pleads for the introduction at this point of a new hermeneutical principle, specifically, the allegorizing one. No wonder that the results are "often arbitrary, mystical, and far-fetched" (ibid., pp. 259-60).

[2]There are some who argue that *'eth* (usually the mark of a definite direct object) has rather the prepositional force of "from" or "by." That position seems lacking in proof, and a stronger alternative is the prepositional force of "with."

[3]The issue has not been overstated by Walvoord: "In the controversy between premillenarians and amillenarians, the interpretation of this covenant more or less settles the entire argument" (J. F. Walvoord, *The Millennial Kingdom*, p. 139). The pivotal significance of that covenant has not been lost on the amillennialists. The three essential elements are a land, a nation, and a seed, and Hughes treats them in order. First, he asks what Abraham himself expected in the light of the promises. By allegorization he decides that Abraham did not look forward to any territorial possession, but, because of the future fiery judgment on all the earth, he was expecting an everlasting possession of a nonearthly character (P. E. Hughes, *Interpreting Prophecy*, pp. 38-39). The same argument can be leveled against the promises concerning heaven. He equates the New Jerusalem with the new heaven (Heb. 11:13-16; 12:22 f.). They are clearly distinct (Rev. 21:1-2). In order to preserve some logic to the language of promise, Hughes assures us that the everlasting possession had for Abraham "a *sacramental* significance" (ibid., p. 41). What does that mean? Simply that the land was "a pointer to that transcendental reality of joy and peace for which every human heart has a longing" (ibid., p. 42). Now what becomes of the promise of a nation? His reply is: "To spurn the covenant is to forfeit its blessings and to cut oneself off from the line of promise" (ibid., p. 50). Thus in one fell swoop the natural seed is dispossessed to make room for a new people of God. How sad not to recognize that, although unbelief can never expect blessing from God, the Lord would sovereignly find those believing hearts in Israel to whom He could and would fulfill all the promises. And what of the promise of the seed? It is admitted by all that, although Isaac was that seed in the immediate future (Gen. 21:12, last clause), the ultimate reference is to Christ (Gal. 3:16). That is no ground to claim: "Christ, and Christ alone, is the true 'remnant.' He alone is born of God. The theological implications of this truth are of the utmost importance. . . . Jesus Christ . . . is the sole faithful 'remnant' " (ibid., pp. 59-60). We are unable to find even one scripture verse upon which to hang that exegetical oddity.

[4]The reader should notice especially that twice (2 Sam. 7:10) at the outset of

the covenant God emphasizes "a place." That is in direct opposition to recent claims that the concept of the kingdom is mainly, if not exclusively, an abstract one. McClain believes that such efforts need not claim too much attention. Says he, "The great ideas of the Bible are concrete rather than abstract; and such terms as the *Kingdom of God* are intended to convey meanings which are pertinent to actual situations in the world of reality with which common men are somewhat familiar" (McClain, p. 17). Not only is the promise couched in terrestrial terms, but its realization will be also. "It is here that the great purpose of . . . the *Mediatorial* Kingdom appears: On the basis of mediatorial redemption it must 'come' to put down at last all rebellion . . . finally bringing the Kingdom and will of God *on* earth as it is in heaven. When this purpose has been fully accomplished, the mediatorial phase of the Kingdom will disappear as a separate entity, being merged with the Universal Kingdom of God" (ibid., p. 35).

[5]Again and again, writers who discount a literal kingdom on earth do so on the ground that it would be unspiritual. This writer has never been able to conceive of any earthly kingdom over which the Lord Jesus Christ rules in righteousness and equity as lacking spirituality. McClain agrees: "Wherever and whenever we find God establishing a direct and personal relationship between Himself and other personalities, whether as individuals or as a group, regardless of place or conditions, such a relationship must be regarded as basically *spiritual* in nature" (McClain, p. 66). The contrary position reveals the influence of Platonic philosophy on many theologians who see the material as always "non-spiritual" or unspiritual.

[6]From a study of the kingdom in the Old Testament and the additional revelation in the New Testament, some have erroneously concluded through their allegorizing that the mediatorial kingdom is not terrestrial, but celestial. A few have even taken the position that Christ offered only a celestial kingdom, but that the Old Testament prophecies will be fulfilled in the future in a terrestrial kingdom. In both cases faulty hermeneutics has led well-meaning men astray. The Bible knows of only one mediatorial kingdom.

McClain puts it forthrightly: "Certainly, the future kingdom is to be a genuine revival and continuation of the 'throne of David.' In a very real sense there is but one Mediatorial Kingdom of God" (McClain, p. 42). No knowledgeable premillenarian doubts that there are phases (a mystery form and a consummating form at least) of the one kingdom. Again, McClain guides aright: "But it is highly relevant here to observe that perhaps the most important guiding principle suggested by an examination of the Old Testament material is that the Mediatorial Kingdom of the prophets is *one* [italics his] Kingdom, not two kingdoms. This one Kingdom has various aspects . . . but these aspects must not be pluralized into different kingdoms, the one *spiritual* and the other *earthly*" [italics his]. (McClain, p. 146.) In discussing Amos 9:11 (to this writer the passage is one of the most crucial on the coming kingdom), McClain states that the coming kingdom "will maintain an unbroken historic connection [see Acts 1:6 and the force of the Greek verb in the question] with a kingdom which once existed 'in the days of old.' This is a biblical fact beyond dispute which must be taken into account as a guiding principle in all attempts to understand the Kingdom set forth in Old Testament prophecy" (ibid., p. 148). We could not be in heartier agreement.

8

The Kingdom Offered, Rejected, and Postponed

From the standpoint of a study of the kingdom there is probably no book in the entire revelation of God that is of more importance or more decisive than the gospel of Matthew. Its exact interpretation is a matter of more than ordinary moment for the present study and discussion. It is by no mere chance that it is found at the head of the New Testament revelation. The Holy Spirit saw to it that this book, without which the message of the New Testament would be incomplete and disorganized, was placed where it is now in our canon. Much is being made of its position, because it is pivotal.

An honest and conscientious reader of the Old Testament among Israel must have felt, after the close of the Old Testament canon, which took place before any of the New Testament was written, that God had given a revelation that bore every mark of incompleteness as far as the facts of a future king and kingdom were involved. There was a promise that David would have a man to sit on his throne, but the King had not yet appeared. According to the delineations in the prophets there were certain revealing characteristics to be seen in the Messiah King that could not be attributed to anyone who had already come upon the horizon of Jewish life. There was a guarantee of a Davidic throne in Jerusalem, but Israel was still groaning and laboring under the distasteful Roman yoke. Promises there were by the scores of the future blessedness of the land, but no man believed himself in the day when every man would sit under his vine and fig tree and fear for nothing (Mic. 4:4). Was there a need for more promises? Decidedly no! All that was to be reasonably expected was a fulfillment of those things that were spoken by the mouth of the prophets.

So upon turning to the gospel according to Matthew we find it preeminently a book of fulfillment. The first verse not only furnishes the keynote of the book, but outlines Matthew's treatment of the person and work of the King. It reads: "The book of the generation of Jesus Christ, the son of David, the son of Abraham." One would expect the writer to have placed the sonship of Abraham before that of David. But there is reason for the present order.

Matthew purposes, first of all, to relate the Christ to the Davidic Covenant and then to the Abrahamic Covenant. First, He comes to offer Himself as the covenanted King, then upon His rejection He becomes the source and fount of worldwide blessing to all nations. To one who has had the Old Testament promises burned deeply into his heart and mind, those words come with forceful impact and joyous realization. However, to claim that one is the King Messiah and to prove that claim are too widely different propositions. Many may be classified under the first heading, but just one under the second.

So Matthew proceeds to prove by an incontestable genealogical table that Jesus the Christ is both the son of David and the son of Abraham, but primarily the former. Nor is that an unnecessary and superfluous task: the King must be of the house and lineage of David in order to fulfill to the very letter all the Old Testament predictions of the coming King who is to set up the kingdom. But to satisfy minds that the Christ is a lineal descendant of David is not all that is required, for there were many kings born in the line of David who were not the covenanted King. The King must be born in a specific way and in a designated place. Matthew relates that Christ was born of a virgin to fulfill the prophecy of Isaiah (Matt. 1:22-23); Luke adds the annunciation by the angel Gabriel to the Virgin Mary wherein he foretells that Jesus would be great and should be called the Son of the Highest (Luke 1:31-33). The Lord God will give to Him, continues the word of the messenger, the throne of His father David, so that He will reign over the house of Jacob forever. Of His kingdom there will be no end. That descendant of the house and dynasty of David, then, is connected by the Word at the very outset with all the prophecies relating to the future Messianic kingdom. That He was born in Bethlehem of Judah, as prophesied by Micah, is confirmed by both Matthew and Luke (Matt. 2:6; Luke 2:4-11, 15, 16). Our minds can rest assured, therefore, as to His person.

After all the blessing that was promised to Israel through her King, one might expect that the nation would rise up as one and receive Him with open arms. But the record reads otherwise. Israel, far from being ready to welcome Him, was first informed of the birth of the King through wise men from the east. For shame, to be caught napping in such a vital matter! But surely there followed a time of great exultation and praise to God that He had kept His word and brought to fulfillment the sure mercies of David. On the contrary, when Herod, the king, heard the inquiry of the wise men, he was greatly troubled and all Jerusalem with him. Still later when the king saw that his nefarious designs had miscarried, he sought to make certain the death of the King by a slaughter of all children in Bethlehem from two years old and under. The safety of the child King was effected through a revelation from God. Such was the preliminary reception, or better, rejection, of the King.

But despite the oppositions of man, the Word of God must have its fulfillment, so the forerunner of the King came upon the scene next, fulfilling the closing prophecies of Malachi (3:1). More interesting than the person of the forerunner, was the message he bore to the nation. When John the Baptist came preaching in the wilderness of Judea, he said: "Repent ye: for the kingdom of heaven is at hand" (Matt. 3:1-2). No explanation is offered as to the meaning of the "kingdom" in his message, for the people knew what was implied by his words.[1] After a study of the Old Testament prophetic Scriptures, what else could one expect him to say? There was no need to describe the conditions and characteristics of the kingdom, for that had been done so repeatedly and minutely. Nor was it necessary to inform them that the kingdom could not and would not be established without the rightful King. John's words implied that the very kingdom that had been promised to Israel was now at hand in the person of the King whose forerunner and herald he was.

National repentance was the condition for the setting up of the kingdom, but that did not necessarily call for generations of time in which it was to be accomplished.[2] The kingdom—note that it was not merely a kingdom, for the definite article is qualifying and defining—was at hand (lit., had come near). Furthermore, it was the kingdom of the heavens, calling attention to its source and heavenly origin.[3] It was the rule of the heavens on earth, administered by one chosen from heaven and at the same time of the seed of David. But repentance was far from the minds of those religious leaders who had entrenched themselves in the highest ecclesiastical offices and believed that the kingdom was due them because they were of the seed of Abraham. They were warned that coming judgment and the poured-out wrath of God were to be their portion.

Then the King came upon the horizon! Surely pomp and splendor were in His train and thousands of thousands waited upon Him and His pleasure. Not so, for the King came in the form of a servant and seeks to be baptized of John (Matt. 3:13-15). Many and differing explanations have been given for that action of the King. Some hold that Christ submitted Himself to baptism in order to fulfill the prophecy of Daniel that the Messiah would fulfill all righteousness. Others contend that His induction into the priestly office is signified, thus connecting the Matthew passage with Psalm 110. Still others maintain that it was the act of identifying Himself with the sinful human race. To the last view we are inclined. It is, of course, possible that all those conceptions are included; surely none is of necessity excluded.

In Matthew, the King, who is to dwell in the midst of Israel and who, it was predicted, is to be their Redeemer, meets His people in the place of their need. As they come to the baptism confessing their need, He meets them there to redeem them from that lost condition and estate in which they admit they now find themselves. His baptism composes His formal induction into office, at which time God Himself sets His seal upon the King, for God the Father declares Him to be His beloved Son, and God the Spirit comes in visible form like a dove to rest upon Him for every good word and work (Matt. 3:16-17).[4]

God has made His pronouncement concerning the King; Satan contests it. The moral right of the King to rule is tested. He is tempted in every point as was the first Adam and, unlike him, He is found wanting in none (Heb. 4:15). The lust of the flesh, the lust of the eyes, and the pride of life are appealed to and evoke no response from Him. As Isaiah had foretold, the Spirit rests upon Him and the fear of the Lord is His portion (Isa. 11:2). There need be no fear as to the moral fitness of that King to rule in righteousness and judgment. What will be His first word to His people? We need not read far to find it, for—despite the fact that the King's forerunner has been cast into prison, a most unseemly treatment for the herald of the King—Jesus departs into Galilee in fulfillment of the prophetic word and begins to preach: "Repent: for the kingdom of heaven is at hand" (Matt. 4:17). That is exactly the same message as that of John.

Have we any right to assume that Christ meant something altogether different in the employment of those words than did John? Nor did Christ explain what was meant by those words; His hearers knew full well their import. How unwarranted is the assertion, then, of those who find that Christ's ideas and conceptions of the kingdom involved something far removed from the thought of His hearers. Yet they declare that Christ never held to the essentially earthly or material character of the kingdom.[5]

Mains in his discussion of the question concedes that there is possibly an indication in the early ministry of the King that the thought of a temporal and earthly kingdom, "as a temptation," made its appeal to Him. But the actual and full meaning of the kingdom for Christ was simply the rule of God in the hearts of men everywhere.[6] Thus by a process of hermeneutical alchemy the numerous prophecies of a literal, earthly kingdom are transmuted into mere poetry and Oriental symbolic drapery.

Every king must have laws for the regulation of conduct in his kingdom. Is the kingdom of the son of David to be otherwise? For answer one need only study the Sermon on the Mount, so well known and so little understood. That portion of the gospel of Matthew has probably been misapplied as much as any other part of the Word. It is a result of a failure to consider the context, immediate and broad, of the passage. The King is still offering the covenanted kingdom to those to whom it was promised. Now He promulgates laws for the carrying on of that kingdom. There is no message of salvation in that sermon. It tells us not how to be acceptable to God, but it does reveal those who will be pleasing to God in the kingdom. All the laws found in the passage are not steps whereby man finds favor with God; they are rather an enumeration of the points in which man in his natural state falls short of the requirements and demands of a holy and righteous God. The Sermon on the Mount is legal in its character; it is the law of Moses raised to its highest power. These all are righteous laws, for they are given by the righteous King in seeking to establish His righteous reign over Israel.[7]

In chapters 8 and 9 the King is seen performing mighty works in attestation of the fact that He is that one spoken of by the prophets. Christ heals the leper, the servant of the centurion who is palsied, Peter's wife's mother who is sick of a fever; He casts out demons from the two men of Gadara and restores sight to the blind. The King shows His power to destroy the havoc and ruin wrought by sin in the human race (cf. 1 John 3:8). His power over nature is demonstrated in His stilling of the waves of the sea. These were just representative cases, for He went about all the cities and villages teaching in the synagogues of the Jews, preaching the gospel of the kingdom, and healing all manner of sickness (Matt. 9:35).

But it was not the intention of the King to confine the preaching of the gospel of the kingdom to His own ministry. So it is recorded that He appointed His twelve disciples to the same task. His words to them were most instructive and illuminating. They were told not to go into the way of the Gentiles, nor into any city of the Samaritans, but rather to the lost sheep of the house of Israel (Matt. 10:5-6). That was surely because all the promises concerning the King and kingdom were given to Israel and applied directly to them in the first instance. They were not left to prepare their own message, for He instructed them to preach as they went: "The kingdom of heaven is at hand" (v. 7). The messages of the forerunner of the King, of the King Himself, and of the twelve disciples were absolutely identical.

What were the disciples to understand by those instructions? Did they need to be enlightened as to the actual import and content of the subject of their preaching? They evidently understood full well what was involved, for they asked no questions. If they had wrong ideas of the kingdom, that would have been a most opportune moment to dispel them from their minds. Did Christ disillusion them as to their mistaken and earthly conceptions of the kingdom?[8] He did not, for their understanding of the nature of the kingdom was the proper, legitimate, and reasonable one. Yet Masselink feels called upon to say of them that even they, who presumably should have known better, were not entirely free from the mistaken earthly conception of His kingdom.[9] Those who reject the earthly kingdom of the Messiah make much of the contentions among the disciples for supremacy in the supposed future earthly kingdom. What gross and insupportable views they and all the Jews had of the kingdom, it is claimed. But it appears never to have occurred to those who find fault with the disciples in their view of the kingdom, that Christ never once corrected the Jews for their belief in an earthly kingdom. He did reprove them for not believing all the prophets had foretold of Him, that is, that He should first suffer and then enter into His glory. Ottman has put the case well when he states:

> The Messiah's sorrows, which had so perplexed the prophets, did not enter into the popular conception of the Messianic mission, but the failure to discern this necessity of suffering does not prove that the national hope was in other respects without justification, and false. The apostles went forth to the Jewish people with a message of definite meaning, and this message was accredited by signs and wonders done by them. They did not understand the manner in which the kingdom was to be introduced: for this involved what they were yet in ignorance of—the suffering, death, resurrection, and second advent of the King: but none the less true was their message, and it was designed to evoke the hostility of the nation, and thereby accomplish the determinate counsels of God.[10]

The disciples were not sent out upon their mission, however, before it had been made clear to them that theirs was not an easy task and that the price of discipleship was nothing less than utter self-effacement in the service of the King (Matt. 10:16-23).

From that point Matthew begins to draw attention to the dark clouds appearing on the horizon. The forerunner of the King was cast into prison, and while there, himself questioned the genuineness of the claims of the King. The King most graciously sent a message of assurance and confirmation, then turned to pour out His word of wrath and impending doom upon those cities that had not received His message and in which most of His mighty works had been performed (11:1-6, 20-24).

Then He injected a new element into His message: He appealed to all those who were weary and heavy-laden to come to Him for rest (11:25-30). He was certainly not preaching the gospel of the kingdom (cf. 3:2; 4:17; and 10:7), for the message was a personal invitation to fill individual need. The King was evidently turning from the purpose first outlined in His coming; undoubtedly, God was revealing the introduction of a new element in the mission of the King, that had not been inculcated into the Old Testament prophecies. In chapter 12, the opposition to the King and His message went on apace. Finally, He severed every earthly tie, announcing that whoever did the will of His Father in heaven was His brother, sister, and mother (12:46-50). The King had been rejected. Impossible as it may seem, it was sadly true.

What was to become of the kingdom that the Old Testament men of God so faithfully, painstakingly, and vividly described? Was it to be forgotten or replaced by something altogether different? It must first be stated that the rejection of the King by Israel could not possibly abrogate the unconditional covenant made with David. God had covenanted that David should never lack a man to sit on his throne, regardless of Israel's acceptance or rejection of Him.

Let there be no misunderstanding on that point. There is no intention to imply that God was going to thrust the King upon Israel contrary to their willing acceptance of Him. If that had been God's purpose, it could have been accomplished at the first coming of the King regardless of Israel's attitude. But what did the rejection of the King entail? In failing to receive the King, that particular generation of Israelites lost the kingdom He was about to establish. What happens to the kingdom will be seen later in the discussion.

In chapter 13 of his record, Matthew set forth what are so well known as the mystery parables. C. I. Scofield has said: "At no other point has the false system of interpretation forced upon those who start from the presupposition that the church and the kingdom are one, so fatally perverted our Lord's words as in the interpretation of the parables of the kingdom."[11] What was the occasion for them? Because Israel was intent on His rejection, lightly esteeming His person and refusing to receive His testimony and work, the Lord began an altogether different phase of His work, in which He was designated as the "son of Abraham" as well as the "son of David." The rejection of the King by the nation after so many signs and verifications of His claims was not evidence that the testimony of the King was lacking in some vital particular, but it revealed the hardness of heart that had gripped the nation as a whole.

What was the purpose of the parables? There is difference of opinion among interpreters upon this score, but it appears that the point is made clear in the passage. When the disciples asked the Lord why He spoke in parables, He answered: "Because it is given unto you to know the mysteries of the kingdom of heaven, but to them it is not given" (Matt. 13:11). The nation had refused the clear and simple testimony that had been given, but the disciples had accepted it. To those who had, more was to be given. As for the others, who would have none of Him or His message, Isaiah had prophesied that their hearts would be hardened by their lack of obedience, that their eyes would be closed, and that their ears would be dull of hearing (Isa. 6:9). It was a deplorable spiritual condition into which they had allowed themselves to fall. But the disciples must not be refused the further light, so the message of the King as to the immediate future of the kingdom was couched in mysteries of the kingdom of heaven.

The essence of a mystery is not something hidden and secret, which only a few know. The Scriptures use the word in a technical sense to denote some truth that has been hidden previously, but now is brought to light (cf. Rom. 16:25-26; Eph. 3:4, 5). Christ was revealing, then, in the mystery parables certain facts concerning the kingdom that had always been in the mind and plan of God. That does not mean that the features of the kingdom predicted in the Old Testament are done away with or abolished, as has been shown throughout. The kingdom now takes a form in which its administration is in the hands of men while the King is rejected and absent from the kingdom, a period not described in the Old Testament.

If the occasion and purpose of the parables have been matters of controversy among interpreters of the sacred Word, then how much more the interpretation of the parables themselves? The first is the parable of the sower who sowed seed, some of which fell by the wayside, and the fowls came and consumed them. Some fell on stony places where there was no depth of earth, and soon they were withered by the scorching sun. Others fell among thorns and the thorns choked them. Still others fell into good ground and brought forth fruit in various proportions. That parable and the one following it are not left for the reader to interpret for himself. The Lord, the covenanted King, explained them, and any interpretation of the rest of the parables that does not tally with those that the King gave the first two, stands condemned. For in all those parables the Messiah King was evidently speaking of the same period of time and the same sphere of profession, namely, professing Christendom, which is not the kingdom as we know it in the Old Testament, although it has points of similarity with it.

The first parable emphasizes the method of ministry in the mystery kingdom and the results that flow from it. It should be noticed that the seed is the same whether it fell by the wayside, on stony places, among thorns, or into good ground. The seed is the Word of the kingdom. There are four classes of people to whom it comes. The first class receives it, does not understand it, and permits the wicked one, Satan, to catch it away. There is no fruit or profit received from the Word, because the heart is not responsive. The seed falling on stony places represents the man who hears the Word and receives it with joy, but his reception is a superficial one, for when adversities and trials come because of the Word, he forsakes his stand. He is willing to accept the Word if the reception of it does not cost him any personal inconvenience or pains. The seed falling among thorns and being choked speaks of the man who receives the Word, but he is so taken up with the things of this world and its cares, that the Word has no place in his life. There is no room or time for it at all. He is preoccupied with other affairs. The seed that falls into good ground and brings forth much fruit is the man who hears the Word, understands it, and brings forth fruit in his life and service. It is to be understood, then, from that parable that during the time the kingdom is not established on earth as prophesied, there will be only a partial success for the Word that is preached. In the parable of the sower and the one following, the emphasis of truth seems to be placed upon the beginning of the kingdom in mystery form.

In the second parable the King likened the kingdom of heaven to a man who sowed good seed in his field, but while men slept his enemy came and sowed tares among the wheat. When the field brought forth its fruit, the tares were found among it. When the servants of the householder questioned what should be done with the darnel, he commanded them to allow the wheat and the darnel to grow together until the harvest, at which time the tares would be gathered together and burned. In the interpretation of that parable to the disciples, the King explained that the sower is the Son of Man and the place of His sowing is the world. The good seed represents the children of the light, and the tares refer to the children of the wicked one. The enemy that sowed the tares is Satan. The harvest is the full end of the age, and the reapers are the angels, whom the Son of Man will send forth at the consummation of the age to gather out of His kindgom all things that offend and those that do iniquity. Those will be cast into a furnace of fire, while the righteous, who are the wheat and the children of the kingdom, will shine forth as the sun in the kingdom of their Father. The parable reveals that professing Christendom will be the sphere of activity, not only for the Son of Man and His servants, but also for the devil and his emissaries. Good and bad will be found in the kingdom in its mystery form from the beginning to the end. Only the harvest in a coming day will reveal who are the good and who are the bad.

There are other distinctive features of the kingdom of heaven during the absence of the King that He made known to them by the following parables. The kingdom of heaven was next compared to a grain of mustard seed, which a man took and sowed in his field. That particular seed is very small in size, but when it is grown it is the greatest among the herbs, becoming a tree where the birds of the air come to lodge. That mystery reveals the great external growth of the kingdom. It has a small beginning but grows outwardly so rapidly that it includes within its compass the bad as well as the good. The kingdom in mystery comprises the church invisible, but it also has many who, like the birds of the air who seek lodging in the mustard tree, are mere professors and not really children of the kingdom.

In the fourth parable He said: "The kingdom of heaven is like unto leaven, which a woman took, and hid in three measures of meal, till the whole was leavened" (Matt. 13:33). Of all the parables that is probably the one about which there has been most contention or difference of opinion among students of the Word. The principle set down at the beginning of the discussion on the parables still applies: Any interpretation of the seven parables that does not agree and conform to that which the King gave in regard to the first two, cannot be accepted as the correct explanation. There are those who make leaven in that parable the gospel, which will through generations and ages of preaching finally permeate the world, resulting in the conversion of the whole world.[12] There are serious and weighty objections to be lodged against that interpretation, which cause us to believe it untenable.

First of all, nowhere in Scripture can leaven be shown to mean anything other than evil. Why should the instance in Matthew 13:33 be an exception? Does the context warrant it? We think not, and that leads to a second objection. If the parable teaches the final triumph of the good over evil, it contradicts outright the teaching of the other parables, which show the presence to the end of both good and evil. Third, such an interpretation contradicts large portions of the Word of God that speak of the end of this age as well as the end of the Jewish age.[13] It is, therefore, an inadmissible interpretation. The parable speaks of the condition of the teaching within the church during the mystery age. The woman represents either woman out of her place in the church in teaching doctrine or represents the church as a whole. The meaning intended to be conveyed, then, is that during the history of the church on earth there will be the introduction of false doctrine, symbolized by the leaven as in the reference to the leaven of the Pharisees and the Sadducees, which will in time permeate the whole church. That does not necessarily imply that every individual in the invisible church will be astray in his doctrinal conceptions, but the church in its entire scope will feel the presence of false teaching in its midst. How true that is today no one needs to be informed.

The next three parables are not spoken to the whole multitude, but to the disciples only (Matt. 13:36-52). The fifth parable likens the kingdom of heaven to a treasure hid in a field. When the treasure was found, the man finding it hid it and sold all that he had to buy the field. It is the worst exegesis possible to make that represent the sinner buying salvation, and reveals a lamentable ignorance of the essence of the gospel, which is founded in the grace of God. The King was here speaking of the nation Israel, the peculiar treasure of the Lord, hidden as it now is throughout the world, but yet to be brought forth for blessing attendant upon the establishment of the kingdom in the earth. The following parable of the pearl of great price has reference to the church, for which the King gave himself.

The last parable deals with the end of the age. The gospel of the kingdom is seen under the figure of a net, which when cast into the sea gathers up in its meshes both good fish and bad fish. A separation takes place when the net is dragged ashore; so will there be a separation of the good and the bad at the end of the age. Those who were mere professors in the kingdom in its mystery form will be cast into the furnace of fire. In Matthew 13 the King not only reveals—and it had never been revealed before by any of the Old Testament prophets—that there will be a period during which the kingdom will be postponed, but He outlines clearly the course of affairs on earth during that particular period.[14]

The rejection of the King continued, and He foretold, after the great confession of Peter, that upon His deity He would build His church and the gates of hades would not prevail against it (16:18). There are several points of interest here. That is the first mention of the word "church" in the Scriptures.

Many argue, however, and the amillennialists are among them, that the church must have been in existence before that time or the disciples would have asked concerning its nature. That they did not is proof positive that they already knew of the existence of the church. That that was not the case is manifest from the question of the disciples in the first chapter of the book of Acts, as well as from the tense of the verb "build," which is in the future. He did not say that He had been building it, but that He was yet to do so.

Another point of interest is that the King Himself was to undertake the building of the church, and that body was to be His in a peculiar sense—"my church." The basis of that church is in His deity, and the security of it is expressed by the fact that the gates of hades will not close upon one of its number. At that time the Lord gave Peter "the keys of the kingdom of heaven," about which more later. Immediately followed the prediction of the sufferings, death, and resurrection of the King. That was totally out of the range of the outlook of the disciples, but it was not without the scope of the eternal purpose of God, which He had determined in that King, whom He would yet place upon His holy hill of Zion (Psalm 2:6).

Yet Israel was not to be left without a further opportunity to accept Him as their King, and that publicly. So the King presented Himself to the nation, fulfilling the words of the prophet Zechariah (9:9-10). But there was a notable omission (Matt. 21:4-5). The words "having salvation" are absent from the record in Matthew, for in the first coming of the King that portion of the prophecy was not fulfilled to Israel. In a few days the nation had not only finally rejected Him, but also had brought about through the medium of the Roman government the crucifixion of their King; yet not until He had left a word as to the future fulfillment of the covenanted promises involved in the setting up of an earthly, glorious kingdom (chaps. 24-25).[15] Their sole accusation against Him was that He was the King of the Jews. So He had been declared by the angel Gabriel before birth; so He claimed for Himself throughout His ministry; and upon that ground was found the desired pretext for ridding themselves of the One who claimed to be their King.

But God's plans are not so lightly disposed of. Shall all the multiplied promises of God of the Old Testament, which involve His faithfulness and everlasting divine holiness—for because He could not swear by a greater He swore by His own holiness—with relation to the covenanted and prophesied kingdom of the son of David be forever unrealized? Strange as it may seem, the King was dead. The nation had wrought its own undoing, for He, upon whom all their hopes depended, was gone. But that also was in the determinate counsels and foreknowledge of God, for in that manner salvation was to be accomplished for all the world. And, furthermore, the resurrection of the King had been predicted as well as His death. In the resurrected King, then, all the covenanted promises would have to be fulfilled.

With the death of the King the hopes of the disciples were dashed to the ground. In despair, they did not know which way to turn. Truly, the shepherd had been smitten and the sheep were scattered (Zech. 13:7). When Christ joined Himself to the disciples going to Emmaus, with sorrow and anguish of heart they expressed themselves: "But we trusted that it had been he which should have redeemed Israel" (Luke 24:21). But great was their joy when their risen Lord appeared to them from time to time.

The book of Acts indicates that the resurrected Christ taught His disciples forty days concerning the kingdom of God (1:3). Evidently, He had not told them the time of the future kingdom, for they asked Him one day: "Lord, wilt thou at this time restore the kingdom to Israel?" (1:6). It is true that the disciples, so enamored of the many Old Testament prophecies of the glory of the coming King, had failed to understand adequately and allow for the references to His vicarious death in the Old Testament revelation. But now that those things were fulfilled, what could possibly hinder the speedy establishment of the kingdom by the King at that time? So there was ample ground for the question of the disciples. Note that they referred to a specific kingdom, "the kingdom." The verb "restore again" is also full of significance. They did not ask about a kingdom that had never had a beginning, but there was to be a restoration of something that had already existed. In what sense that is meant will presently be seen. The verb *(apokathistaneis)* literally means "to restore to its former state."[16]

The kingdom that was to be instituted was recognized as having a beginning in the kingdom of David, of whose seed Jesus Christ was made according to the flesh. In a real sense the kingdom yet future will be the Davidic kingdom, ruled over by the son of David. Furthermore, the disciples realized that the kingdom, if it were to be set up at all, would not be the product of their strivings and labors, but must be set up by the King Himself. Therefore, they inquired: "Wilt thou?" The chief point in questioning was to ascertain not the fact or the reality of the future kingdom, but the exact time of its erection and establishment. Finally, they showed that they knew the kingdom was to be restored to Israel to whom it was promised. Far from being an inappropriate and foolish question, as some have laboriously sought to prove, the problem occupying the minds of the disciples was legitimate and important.

If their question is interesting, the answer is all the more so. Consider it negatively first. Let it be noted that Christ did not answer that the kingdom had been entirely given up and was being displayed in the formation of the church. The Lord did not rebuke them for asking foolish and impertinent questions. He did not inform them that there was to be no future kingdom at all for Israel.

Finally, He did not even mention anything that would cause us to believe that their ideas relative to the kingdom were erroneous and false. If the disciples were in serious error on that vital point, of all times that was the time when Christ might be expected to correct them. He was soon to leave them and be veiled from their physical sight. But what did He say? He merely answered that the times and seasons were not for them to know, because the Father had reserved them in His own power and desired them to be secret. Then He turned their minds to the present duty immediately before them, that of witnessing to His death and resurrection to the ends of the earth. The query of the disciples, then, coming as it did after the death, resurrection, and forty day postresurrection ministry of the Lord, is of importance for our study.

When the appointed time had come on the day of Pentecost, the Lord graciously poured out His blessed Spirit on the disciples as they tarried in Jerusalem, according to the express command of the risen and ascended Lord. The joy and enthusiasm of the Spirit-filled disciples attracted the attention of those multitudes of Jews who had come up to Jerusalem, according to the injunction in the law, to celebrate the feast of Pentecost (cf. Deut. 16:16).

Their comment on the phenomenon before them led to the sermon of Peter. That his address was a masterful one is the unanimous opinion of all who have studied it. The aim of the apostle was to bring his hearers to the point where they realized that God had made that same Jesus whom they crucified, both Lord and Christ. The Holy Spirit spoke through him to the accomplishment of that end. First, the apostle showed the folly of the accusation of the crowd as to the cause of the phenomenon before them. Then he pointed to the partial fulfillment—for he did not use the regular clause "that it might be fulfilled," which is generally found in New Testament fulfillments of Old Testament prophecies—of the prophecy of Joel concerning the gift of the Holy Spirit. There followed a logical recital, beginning with reference to the miracles and signs and wonders wrought by Jesus of Nazareth, of the death, resurrection, and ascension of the Messiah, all of which were in the determinate counsel and foreknowledge of God and prophesied of in their own Scriptures.

Peter emphasized the resurrection to show that God had in mind a resurrected Christ to sit on the throne of David, when He promised with an oath that David should have a King to sit upon his throne. That Christ was truly resurrected was further proved by the fact that He had shed forth that which He promised He would. Peter followed that with a reference to Psalm 110.

What followed the message is of particular significance. It had so pricked the hearts of the apostle's hearers that they asked what they were to do. He did not tell them: "Repent ye: for the kingdom of heaven is at hand." He did speak, however, of repentance and baptism in the name of Jesus Christ for the remission of sins and the reception of the gift of the Holy Spirit (Acts 3:18-21). Peter here used one of the keys of the kingdom of heaven in its mystery form, which were delivered to him by the Lord when He first spoke of building His church. The other key would be used to open the door to the Gentiles in the house of Cornelius, the centurion of the Italian band (Acts 10:34-48).

Is it to be concluded then from Peter's message that the kingdom, since it had been so often and so persistently rejected by Israel, was no longer to be offered to them? The answer is found farther along, beginning in Acts 3 when Peter and John went up to the Temple at the prayer hour. The healing of the lame man at the gate called Beautiful was the occasion for Peter's second sermon. After summarily accusing his hearers of killing the Prince of life, he concluded that the things that the prophets had prophesied concerning the sufferings of Christ had been completely fulfilled. There remained now for them but to repent, so that their sins would be blotted out. The rendering in the Authorized Version of the remainder of verse 19 is poor and is not true to the construction. According to J. H. Thayer the words *hopos an* never mean "when," as they are here translated.[17] The proper translation would be "in order that," with the idea of purpose. The aorist verb points to a definite time in the future for the accomplishment of that which follows in the verse.

What the "times of refreshing" are that come from the presence of the Lord, has been the subject for various opinions. Henry Alford, who shows genuine insight into the passage, believes that the definite arrival refers to the spiritual blessing that will attend the conversion of Israel, which will in turn be the motivating cause for the sending by God of the same Christ who was preached to Israel.[18] That Christ the heavens must receive until the times of the restitution of all things. The word for "restitution" occurs only here in the New Testament, although the verb is found, among other places, in Acts 1:6.[19] That connects what is said here with the question of the disciples as to time. The restoration referred to is that of the kingdom to Israel as well as the blessing to be showered upon creation. The "all things" are limited by the clause "which God hath spoken by the mouth of all his holy prophets since the world began."[20]

With the preceding chapter of this study in mind, there is no need to ask what those things can be. In spite of those facts, Kuyper, in commenting upon the so-called external and carnal expectations of the disciples, laments the fact that even as late as the day of the ascension, when surely they should have known better, according to his way of thinking, the disciples still showed the same interest in a kingdom for Israel. He consoles himself, however, with the false assurance that after Pentecost it "is never mentioned among the Apostles any more."[21] That statement is contrary to the teaching of Scripture, as is manifest from the passage in Acts 3 that has just been under consideration. Apart from that passage, the apostles did mention the kingdom after Pentecost, and several examples can be referred to in passing. Paul mentioned the kingdom of Christ the King in 1 Corinthians 15 and in 2 Timothy 4, among other instances; James spoke of the kingdom in writing to the twelve tribes scattered abroad; Peter referred to the everlasting kingdom of our Lord and Savior Jesus Christ; John pointed out a time when "the kingdoms of this world are become the kingdoms of our Lord, and of his Christ; and he shall reign for ever and ever" (Rev. 11:15). Pentecost evidently does not mark the last mention of the kingdom on the part of the apostles. If Kuyper's contention were true, we would be hard put to it, as he is, to explain why all the explicit Old Testament prophecies have vanished into thin air.

NOTES

[1]That the position stated is not the writer's personal unwarranted inference is confirmed by McClain: "The absence of any formal definition of the Kingdom in its initial announcement indicates that the Jewish hearers were expected to know exactly what Kingdom was meant" (A. J. McClain, *The Greatness of the Kingdom*, p. 276). And the implications of that fact are vastly more far-reaching than appears at first, for "since there is no record of any formal definition in these initial announcements of the Kingdom, it is highly improbable that any was given. Obviously, such a definition would have been absolutely necessary if Christ had entertained a radically novel conception of the Kingdom of God" (ibid.).

[2]All the gospels indicate that the establishment of the mediatorial or Messianic kingdom on earth is ethically conditioned, that is, on man's acceptance of it by faith (cf. McClain, p. 304).

[3]In rabbinic literature also "the kingdom of heaven" *(malkhuth shamayim)* denotes the rule of the heavens (i.e., God) on earth (cf. Dan. 4:32). McClain has summarized the concept well: "Thus, read in the light of its evident Old Testament context, the phrase 'kingdom of heaven' does not refer to a kingdom *located* [italics his] in heaven as opposed to the earth, but rather to the coming to earth of a kingdom which is heavenly as to its origin and character" (McClain, p. 280).

[4]If ever confirmation were needed that the King was baptized for a reason other than that which was true for His countrymen (Matt. 3:6), it is amply supplied by the unequivocal attestation of the Father and the Spirit to His undisputed sinlessness.

[5]Ladd, rejecting Hoyt's position that Christ's concept of the kingdom was no different from that of Old Testament prophecy, declares: "This in my view misses the central message of the Gospels." Then in attempted refutation of Hoyt's view he quotes Matthew 12:28, concluding, "Here is something utterly different from the prevailing Old Testament hope" (R. G. Clouse, *The Meaning of the Millennium,* pp. 85, 94). Decidedly to the

contrary, Christ's word is absolutely consonant with the Old Testament expectation that Messiah would perform miracles at His appearing to Israel.

Hoyt's position is impregnable: "At no point does Christ ever intimate that his conception of the kingdom is any different from that in Old Testament prophecy" (ibid., p. 85). It will take more than an ipse dixit to refute this claim. Scripture must be forthcoming to demolish the argument, but where is it presented by the opposing camp?

Note how literally the Old Testament predictions were honored and fulfilled in the events of our Lord's earthly life. There was a literal virgin birth; it was in literal Bethlehem that He was born; He was literally betrayed by a friend and sold for thirty pieces of silver; He literally rode into Jerusalem on a donkey; He was literally crucified and that between transgressors; He was literally raised from the dead; He literally performed miracles before His death and after His resurrection (ibid.). Observe how Old Testament prophetic features received their full and proper realization in Christ's ministry: (1) the priority of the spiritual (John 3:3-5); (2) highest ethical standards (Matt. 5:19-21, 27); (3) proper social conditions (Matt. 13:41-43; Luke 6:20-21); (4) religious purity (Mark 11:15-17); (5) political restructuring (Matt. 19:28; 25:31); (6) changes in the physical realm (Matt. 9:35; 10:5-8). Cf. Hoyt.

McClain, the mentor, colleague, and predecessor of Hoyt, is as clear in those sensitive and determining areas as anyone this writer has studied. First, he shows our Lord never hinted that His view of the kingdom varied in any way from that of the Old Testament prophets (McClain, p. 277). Second, His rejection by Israel did not change His attitude one whit. His people refused Him, not because His perspectives on the kingdom differed from the prophets, but because of their "tunnel vision" in not seeing the entire organismic delineation foretold by the prophets (cf. ibid., p. 278; Luke 24:44). Third, phrases like "kingdom of heaven" and "Son of man" employed in announcing the kingdom, could have no meaning outside the context of Old Testament prophetic testimony (ibid., p. 279). Fourth, Christ's royal claims are interwoven with Old Testament prophetic confirmations (ibid., p. 280; cf. Luke 4:18-21; 7:24-27; 20:41-44; 24:44). Finally, the several announced elements of the King and His kingdom bear a singularly and consistently literal identity between the kingdom preaching of the gospels and that of the Old Testament prophets' predictions.

To particularize, these factors are distinctly present: (1) the spiritual element, repentance (Matt. 3:2; John 3:3); (2) the moral element (Matt. 5:21-44); (3) the social element (Matt. 5:21-28; Mark 10:13-16; Luke 14:13); (4) the ecclesiastical element, i.e., the externals of religion (Matt.

5:17-19; Luke 2:21-24, 41-42); (5) the political element (Luke 1:31-33; 19:11-19; 20:13-18). Matthew 21:23 does not mean that the kingdom was taken from Israel, for believers in Israel cannot be excluded from Col. 1:13; but from its then present rulers—see Matt. 21:45); and (6) the physical element (Matt. 9:35; John 20:30-31; 21:25). Cf. ibid., p. 286.

[6]His statements are: "There would seem possibly some indication that in the initial days of his mission the thought of a temporal kingdom may, as a temptation, have thrust itself upon him. . . . It would be nearly a perfect definition of Christ's thought of the kingdom if we were to say that it meant to him simply God's reign in the human heart" (G. P. Mains, *Premillennialism*, pp. 114-15).

[7]It is wrong to hold that the Sermon on the Mount has no relevance or profit for the believer today. Interpretation is one; application is manifold. It is difficult to see how Psalm 23 (given under the law era) can have meaning for saints now, and not Matthew 5-7. Has none of the Old Testament value for a Christian today? To ask the question is to answer it.

[8]There is no validity in Ladd's contention, who in commenting on the Acts 2:34-35 quotation of Psalm 110:1 states: "Peter, under inspiration, has transferred the throne of David from Jerusalem—Zion (Psalm 110:2)—to heaven. In his session, Jesus has been made Lord. He has also begun his reign as the Messianic, Davidic King. He has entered upon his reign as Lord and Christ" (Clouse, p. 31). That is not "historic" premillennialism, but undiminished and recognizable amillennialism. Nor is there proof that "*Christ* [italics his] means 'anointed one' and refers to His role as the anointed Davidic King" (ibid). That is a far too restricted use of that crucial term in the light of the threefold office clearly presented in Isaiah 50:4-5 (Prophet) and Psalm 110:2, 4 with Zechariah 6:12-13 (Priest and King).

[9]W. Masselink, *Why Thousand Years?* p. 25. But see Luke 24:25-27.

[10]F. C. Ottman, *Imperialism and Christ*, p. 122.

[11]Complete bibliographical data not available at this writing.

[12]A basic pillar in the postmillennial structure of interpretation.

[13]Among others are 1 Tim. 4:1-3; 2 Tim. 3:1-17 (esp. v. 13); 4:3-4; 2 Pet. 2:1-3; 3:3-4; 1 John 2:18-24; 4:1-3; and Jude 3-16, 18-19.

[14]The concept of a postponed kingdom appears to exasperate amillennarians and nondispensationalists alike. Let it be understood that as far as God is concerned, who knows the end from the beginning, nothing is postponed. But Scripture views events from the divine perspective as well as the human standpoint. Notice that even with the central doctrine of justification: the divine approach (Paul in Romans) and the human (James in his epistle). Hughes, however, asks: "Would that kingdom have been set up on earth there and then if their response had been positive? Was God's

position one of doubt and uncertainty, so that he had to wait and see what the answer of the Jews would be? And when it turned out to be a negative answer was he forced to resort to an emergency measure until such time as he could put his original plan into effect? We may assume that it is not the intention of dispensationalists to diminish the competence and sovereignty of Almighty God and the immutability of his purposes; but their explanation of the sequence of events can hardly fail to arouse questions such as these" (P. E. Hughes, *Interpreting Prophecy*, pp. 104-5).

When Hughes does marshal "proof" that the apostles did not see the era of the church as a parenthesis, he cites Joel 2:28-32 and Psalms 16 and 110. Notice that not one of those passages speaks even remotely of the church age. He concludes, nonetheless, "Neither here nor elsewhere is there any mention of a postponement of the kingdom or a change of plan on God's part" (ibid., pp. 105-6). We should like to ask Hughes, a confirmed Calvinist, a few questions. When God had His Lamb slain from eternity (cf. Matt. 25:34; 1 Pet. 1:19-21; and probably Rev. 13:8), why did He place Adam and Eve under a test of obedience in the Garden of Eden? Because He knew beforehand the certainty of their failure, was His test any the less bona fide? When God promised Israel deliverance from Egyptian bondage and entrance into their promised land, was He or was He not aware of their coming rebellion at Kadesh-barnea, which postponed the actual entry of Israel until the older generation had died? What is to be done with the interpretation of the postponement parables (Luke 19:11-27—"went to a distant [far] country"; Matt. 25:19—"after a long time")? What was the purpose or meaning of the mystery parables of Matthew 13? What of the cases where the gospel invitation was rejected as definitely as the offered kingdom? In view of Matthew 23:39 was not something postponed? (Cf. Matt. 21:33-46; 22:1-14.) God makes no mistakes, knows all things potential or actual, and surely is not in need of our feeble, unnecessary theodicies.

McClain answers the critics of the postponement view because of their disregard of the different aspects of the mediatorial kingdom. He holds: "(1) During the present Church age, from Pentecost to the second coming of Christ, the Mediatorial Kingdom must be said to be in *abeyance,* in the sense of its actual establishment on earth. (2) In another sense, however, it might be said that the Mediatorial Kingdom does have a present *de jure* existence, even prior to its establishment. This is true, first, in the sense that God is today saving and preparing in the *ekklesia* the members of the royal family who are destined to rule with Christ in the future established Kingdom; and, second, in the sense that, as those born into the royal family, we enter *judicially* into the Kingdom before its establishment, a divine action so remarkable that Paul speaks of it as a translation (Col. 1:13)" (McClain, pp. 439-40).

It is true that the church in this age is enjoying many of the *spiritual* blessings that the Old Testament connects with the future Messianic kingdom, such as pardon for sin (Isa. 55:4-7), justification by faith and imputed righteousness (Jer. 23:6), regeneration (Ezek. 36:24-28), and the coming of the Holy Spirit on men (Joel 2:27-28). Some of those blessings were possible to believers in the time of Abel (Heb. 11:4) and Abraham (Rom. 4:3), long before Moses and David.

[15]That there is yet a final, consummating phase of the kingdom in the future, McClain cogently sets forth: "But if that Kingdom was established at the first coming of our Lord, as some affirm, it becomes impossible to explain why following His rejection by Israel all New Testament Scripture agrees in setting the goal, not in the present world order, but in the future at His second coming" (McClain, p. 335). The point at issue is further underscored thus: "The essential point, which cannot be reasonably disputed is this: the Mediatorial Kingdom of Old Testament prophecy, which was announced in our Lord's early ministry as 'at hand,' was not established because of Jewish unbelief, and its arrival is now set definitely at the second advent of the King" (ibid., p. 355).

In addition, if the kingdom Christ offered at His first advent is now realized, as amillennialists hold, then there are several irreconcilable problems that face serious students of the Scriptures. How are the tribulations and trials of this life (Rom. 8:18) to be reconciled with the position that Christ is presently reigning with His saints "in a Messianic Kingdom allegedly established on earth at His first advent" (ibid., p. 377)? It is, indeed, "one of the mysteries of theological opinion" (ibid.). Furthermore, God's throne in heaven and David's throne on earth are never employed in Scripture as synonymous or identical (Rev. 3:21; cf. also Acts 2:30, 34). Indisputably, the phrase "kingdom of God" in Acts (Orr claims it is almost always found in an eschatological context) is never mentioned by the apostles as already established (ibid., p. 425. See Acts 1:6-11; 3:19-21; 15:13-16). Such realization awaits the return of the King from heaven. Moreover, is it not strange that no New Testament letter is addressed to the saints in "the kingdom of heaven?" Finally and conclusively, "The theory that Christ and the saints are now reigning in a present kingdom of God on earth, is specifically refuted by the Apostle Paul" (McClain, p. 433). Cf. 1 Cor. 4:8; 2 Tim. 2:12. In Rom. 15:12 Paul is not claiming the fulfillment of that prophecy now.

[16]J. H. Thayer, *A Greek-English Lexicon of the New Testament,* renders *apokathistèmi,* as in Greek writings, "to restore to its former state," used

"of the restoration of dominion, Acts i.6 (1 Macc. xv.3)," p. 62, *sub voce.* H. G. Liddell and R. Scott, *A Greek-English Lexicon,* define it as "reestablish, restore, reinstate," in 1:200, *s.v.* J. A. Alexander, *Commentary on the Prophecies of Isaiah,* 1:205, comments correctly on Isa. 9:6 (Heb.): "The two reigns are identified, not merely on account of an external resemblance or a typical relation, but because the one was really a restoration or continuation of the other."

[17]Thayer, p. 450, col. 2.

[18]H. Alford, *The Greek Testament,* 2:37f.

[19]Thayer, pp. 62-63; W. F. Arndt and F. W. Gingrich, *A Greek-English Lexicon of the New Testament,* pp. 91-92; Liddell-Scott, 1:200-201.

[20]C. I. Scofield, *The Scofield Reference Bible* (1917), p. 1153, fn. 2; *The New Scofield Reference Bible* (1967), p. 1166, fn. 2.

[21]A. Kuyper, *Chiliasm or the Doctrine of Premillennialism,* p. 6.

9
The Church Age and the Church

A dispensational study of the Scriptures reveals that the age following the ministry of the King, that age in which we now live, is different from any other age preceding or succeeding it. It is called the church age because of the presence in it of a body of people, the church, that has not been seen on earth in any previous dispensation. First Peter 1 states that what puzzled the Old Testament prophets was not the fact of the sufferings of the Messiah and the glory that should follow, but the time and way in which they would be accomplished. Upon the horizon of their outlook there loomed large the two advents of the King; the one for the purpose of suffering for the sin of the world, and the other for the purpose of reigning as the Son of David upon His throne. Any intervening period was foreign to them, because it had not been revealed by God.

In Matthew 13 the King is seen disclosing things that had been kept secret from the foundation of the world (vv. 34-35). Christ is the first in Scripture to make known that there is a church age to follow His earthly life and ministry. When the prophets and the Jews of ancient times read and studied the words found in Isaiah 61:1-2, they did not understand, and one could not expect them to have understood, that there was to be a great interval between "the acceptable year of the Lord" and the "day of vengeance of our God." It was only when the King had come and made it known in the synagogue at Nazareth, that the Scripture was ever rightly understood, and then, we may suppose, only by a limited few (Luke 4:16-21). The prophecy in Daniel 9:24-27 also allows for that intervening period, disclosing too the consummation of the Jewish age.

When that crucial prophecy is studied, it is seen that, after the prophet had studied the prophecy of Jeremiah relative to the end of the desolations of Jerusalem, and after he had earnestly poured out his heart before God in true confession of his sins and those of his people, God sent Gabriel to give him understanding in his perplexity. The angel revealed to him that seventy weeks were determined upon his people and the holy city for a sixfold purpose; namely, to finish the transgression, to make an end of sins, to make reconciliation for iniquity, to bring in the righteousness of the ages, to seal up the vision and prophecy, and to anoint the most Holy. From the going forth of the commandment to restore and build Jerusalem unto Messiah the Prince, there were to be seven weeks, and sixty-two weeks. And after sixty-two weeks the Messiah was to be cut off, but not for Himself. That would be followed by the destruction of the city and the sanctuary by the people of the prince that should come. The end of that destruction would be war, the desolation that had been determined. Verse 27 speaks of the confirmation of a covenant made by one with many for one week, which agreement is broken by the covenantor in the middle of the week.

The interpretation of all the details of that wonderful prophecy is without the range of the present purpose. Attention must be directed to certain particulars. It is evident that the prophecy concerns the nation Israel, for Gabriel speaks of "thy people," Daniel's people. Furthermore, the weeks spoken of (*shabhu'im*) are not meant to be seven-day weeks. They are rather heptads of years, or 490 years. (That is substantiated by Daniel 10:2, where "three full weeks" is a translation of *sheloshah shabhu 'im yamim* or "three weeks of days." In that case the weeks are seven-day weeks.) The division of those weeks is as follows: (1) seven weeks, or 49 years, (2) sixty-two weeks, or 434 years, (3) one week, or 7 years. The beginning of the reckoning is the time of the decree to restore and build Jerusalem, which was in the twentieth year of Artaxerxes, or 445 B.C. (Neh. 2). From that time till Messiah the Prince there were to be sixty-nine weeks, or 483 years, and it is only another proof of the infallibility of the Word of our God that the Lord Jesus Christ entered Jerusalem (according to the calculations of Sir Robert Anderson), at the consummation of the sixty-ninth week.[1] Then appears the prophecy of the death of the Messiah and the destruction of Jerusalem. There remains now but one week of the prophecy, and from the nature of its prediction it is readily seen that it has not been fulfilled. The clock of God stopped at the end of the sixty-ninth week and the Jewish age has been interrupted. That interval is the church age, not foreseen in the Old Testament.[2] It is that interval that solves the problem that troubled the prophets when they searched for the specific time of the sufferings of Christ and of the glory that should follow. The church age began, then, when Daniel's sixty-nine weeks were finished and will come to an end before the beginning of the seventieth week.[3]

It is not to be inferred, however, that this age receives its nature or characteristic features from the church present in it. For the nature of this age is said to be evil. In writing to the Galatian believers, Paul saluted them with grace and peace from God the Father and from the Lord Jesus Christ, "Who gave himself for our sins, that he might deliver us from this present evil world [lit. age], according to the will of God and our Father" (Gal. 1:4). The church age, like other ages before it, is evil because it is under the domination of the god of this age, Satan. The world system in this age, directed by Satan, seeks to detract from the glory of God. The underlying principles upon which it is built are apart from God. This age is also characterized as to its nature as evil, because the mystery of iniquity is working its steady course through it (2 Thess. 2:7). That process will culminate in that day when a man claims to be God and seeks divine honors and worship from all; it is the consummation of evil in the man of sin, the son of perdition.

God has a purpose, moreover, in this age as He has had in former ages and will have in the future ages. The exact nature of that purpose is best ascertained by its setting relative to the ages before it and those subsequent to it. That is best accomplished by a resumé of the dispensational scheme.

H. C. Thiessen in his careful research on the dispensations points out clearly that in each of the seven dispensations in time God is working out His purpose to reveal experimentally and practically that man can never become right before God in his own strength or through his own deeds. Each age reveals God's plan worked out in four particulars: first, a special test; second, a grievous failure; third, a righteous judgment; and fourth, a gracious intervention.[4]

In the age of innocence, man was tested as to whether he would obey the voice of God under the most favorable of circumstances. He failed by heeding instead the voice of Satan. The judgment executed upon man was expulsion from the garden with his wife; sorrow in the life of the woman and subjection to her husband; burdensome labor for the man in making a livelihood; and enmity between the seed of the serpent and the seed of the woman. Grace was manifested in that God did not wipe out the human race, but even furnished a covering for the man and his wife, typifying the robe of salvation through sacrifice and shedding of blood. He also granted them the hope of a coming redeemer (Gen. 3:15).

In the age of conscience, man was tried as to whether he would by the aid of conscience choose to do that which is pleasing to God. Failure under that system is seen in the killing of Abel by his brother Cain and the gradual degeneration in the human race until God saw that every imagination of the thoughts of man's heart was only evil continually (Gen. 6:5). God's righteous judgment was poured out upon the race by the sending of a flood in the time of Noah. His grace, however, was manifest here also, for Noah and his house were preserved from the deluge.

The third dispensation was that of human rule. The test in that age was whether man by legislation and law enforcement could become righteous before God. The result is seen in the Tower of Babel and the confounding of human languages together with the widespread dispersion of man. God graciously intervened yet again and chose Abraham for His purposes (Gen. 11:27-32).

In the following age of promise, God was testing man to reveal whether by promises of every nature, he would seek to be pleasing in the sight of God. That man failed even under those favorable circumstances is evident from the departures from the land of promise on the part of the three patriarchs, as well as the lapses of faith in the lives of each of those men and their posterity. The crowning failure was the descent into Egypt, which carried with it the judgment, the enslavement of the nation of Israel to the Egyptians. Again God graciously intervened and raised up a deliverer in His chosen servant, Moses.

The fifth age revealed in the Scriptures is that known as the law, in which the test was whether man, after he had been the recipient of grace (Ex. 19:4) and had willingly accepted the law, could make himself acceptable to God by means of works of merit that he could perform. The failure under that system is most evident from the disobedience to the commands of God in the wilderness until the culmination in the crucifixion of the promised King. Judgments attended the failures of Israel throughout their way until, consequent to the rejection of the King, they were scattered throughout the world. When the law age is resumed—the Jewish age has been cut short as noted in Daniel's prophecy—judgment will follow upon Israel in that time known as the "time of Jacob's trouble" (Jer. 30:7). The gracious intervention of God is seen in every instance of disobedience and unbelief, but nowhere so markedly as in the death of the King, which God has made a source of blessing to all. The wrath of man will praise God, and the remainder He will restrain (Psalm 76:10). In the end of that dispensation of law there will be tokens of grace also in the ministry of the tribulation remnant and God's care for them (Rev. 7:1-8), as well as the multitude saved out of the nations upon the earth.

The present age is the age, or dispensation, of the church. The test in this age is whether man will accept by simple faith the gift of God, salvation in Christ Jesus. There is failure in this period also, as all know so well. The righteous judgment of God will be manifest in the Tribulation period toward all of professing Christendom, the nations, and Israel (Rev. 6-19). The last dispensation will be dealt with later. The aim here has been to show what the purpose of the church age is.

There remains now to consider the course and end of this present age. It has been touched upon from various angles in the study already, but only in a cursory way. From Matthew 13 it was learned that the kingdom in mystery form, which includes the invisible church, has throughout its course the presence in it of good and evil. Those go on side by side until they are separated at the end. The end of the mystery parables does not coincide, however, with the end of the church age, because the tares and bad fish are disposed of after the end of the church age. The tares of the mystery kingdom, a part of professing Christendom, continue on and are absorbed in mystery Babylon, which is destroyed during the Tribulation period. But for the most part the course of the mystery parables tallies with that of the church age.

In Revelation 2 and 3 there is given to us a marvelously accurate outline of the spiritual course of the church age, so much so that some church historians have taken it for the outline of their works.[5] The letter to the church at Ephesus shows the condition of the church at the end of the apostolic age; she had lost her first love and was growing colder in her orthodoxy. The Smyrna church represents the time of the Roman persecutions in the church. The letter to Pergamum reveals the condition in the church when it unites with the state. Some believe that condition goes on to the end, as in the Church of England and the state church of Scandinavia. Thyatira is a church illustrative of the corruption and degeneration that came into the church when Rome held unrivaled sway during the Middle Ages. The letter to Sardis discloses the course of the church during the Reformation period, which was lacking in emphasis on the Holy Spirit and the subjective side of salvation. Philadelphia represents the presence in the professing Church of the true church. Laodicea speaks to us of the low spiritual state of the church in the last days of the present age. This is supported by the prophecies in 2 Thessalonians, 2 Timothy, and 2 Peter. The church age is not one in which the good finally triumphs over the evil and all along the way things get better and better in the world. Exactly the opposite is true of the course of the church age.

Thus far in this chapter the church age has been treated; it is now time to consider the church herself. To speak of the church age is not synonymous with referring to the church, the Body of Christ. First, notice her origin. Those who seek to find the church in the Old Testament are hopelessly at sea. There is no mention or prophecy of the church in the Old Testament Scriptures. There are figures and types of the church, but no direct reference to the church. How does one substantiate such a claim?

First of all, Christ spoke in Matthew 16:18 of building the church in the future tense. It is incomprehensible that He should do so if the church had its origin in the Old Testament. Second, the disciples displayed no knowledge of the truth of the church's existence, and they were acquainted with their Scriptures. Third, that truth is definitely declared to be a mystery (Rom. 16:25-26; Eph. 3:1-12). Paul explains that "a mystery" is that which was kept secret since the world began, but is now made manifest and known by the Scriptures of the prophets. In speaking particularly of the church, the apostle mentions again that the mystery is that which in other ages was not made known but is now revealed to His holy apostles and prophets by the Spirit. Fourth, the church as a body is impossible without the death of Christ through whom she is reconciled to God; without the resurrection of Christ by which she partakes of His resurrection life; without the ascension of Christ by which she is assured of a Head;[6] and without the descent of the Holy Spirit by which she is formed into an organism through the baptism of the Holy Spirit. The church has her origin, then, with the descent of the Holy Spirit of God on the day of Pentecost.

The Scriptures reveal in 1 Corinthians 10:32 that there are three groups of people in the world: Jews, Gentiles, and the church of God. It is not an ethnic division, nor a geographical one, but a religious one. The Jews are those who trace their ancestry to Abraham; the Gentiles are all other nations apart from the Jews; the church is made up of both believing Jews and Gentiles.

Paul disclosed in Ephesians 3 that the mystery of the church is that the Gentiles should be fellow heirs and of the same body, and partakers of the promise in Christ by the gospel. How is that brought about? Recall the words of the apostle who told of the privileges of Israel to whom pertain the adoption, the glory, the covenants, the giving of the law, the service of God, the promises, the fathers, and the honor of being the channel for the birth of the Christ (Rom. 9:1-5). On the other hand, the same apostle depicted the miserable plight of the Gentiles who were without Christ, aliens from the commonwealth of Israel, strangers from the covenants of promise, without hope, and without God in the world (Eph. 2:11-12).

How, then, do those vastly differing groups combine to constitute one body? First, God refuses to recognize any merit or privilege in any individual or group of individuals, but places all under sin. Second, He is rich in grace unto all that call upon Him, for whoever calls upon the name of the Lord is saved. Third, the same Spirit of God baptizes both Jew and Gentile alike into the Body of Christ (1 Cor. 12:13).

A vitally important Scripture in that connection is Acts 15:13-18. That it is often misunderstood goes without saying. The circumstances that called forth the Jerusalem Council are well known. Contention had arisen between Barnabas and Paul on the one side and certain of the sect of the Pharisees on the other, the former denying and the latter affirming that it was necessary for the Gentiles who were being brought into the faith to be circumcised and to keep the law of Moses. Peter told of his experience in preaching among the Gentiles and suggested that no yoke be placed upon the new converts that neither they, the Jews, nor their fathers could bear. Paul and Barnabas recited what the Lord had done through them in behalf of the Gentiles.

It was left to James to make the concluding remarks. He pointed to the testimony of Peter, which showed conclusively that God was visiting the Gentiles "to take out of them a people for his name." Then followed his statement as to the harmonization of that with the return of the Lord and the setting up of the Davidic kingdom with the conversion of those in Israel and the Gentiles also.

Scofield has said, "Dispensationally, this [Acts 15:13-18] is the most important passage in the N. T."[7] It is essential to ask the place of Israel in this age, and why Israel is not mentioned here. Is it because Israel had been completely rejected, and the church was constituted from among the Gentiles?[8] Israel is not mentioned because there was no question as to the position of Israel in the church; it was Israelites who were deciding as to the status of the Gentiles. So we conclude from those passages considered that the church is made up of Jews and Gentiles who have placed their faith in a crucified and risen Savior and Lord.

What is the purpose of the church? Some have believed that the specific purpose and aim of the church are to make the world a better place in which to live. Others have decided that the goal of the church's activities should be the ushering in of the kingdom. Neither of those constitutes a biblical representation of the purpose or work of the members of the Body of Christ. The chief end of the life of each individual in the church, for the command is personal to every redeemed heart, should be to make Christ known. The last command of Christ to preach the gospel to all creatures is still in force and has never been abrogated or altered. Besides making Christ known to all who do not know Him by saving faith, the believer is to "live soberly, righteously, and godly, in this present world; looking for that blessed hope, and the glorious appearing of the great God and our Saviour Jesus Christ" (Tit. 2:11-14). Christ died to purify to Himself a peculiar people, which God had foreordained to be zealous and walk in good works. God not only purposes in the church to have a channel whereby Christ may be made known and a people that will glorify Him by their good works, but also intends to show in the ages to come the exceeding riches of His grace in His kindness to the church through Christ Jesus (Eph. 2:7). Only eternity will reveal how good and merciful God can be to hell-deserving sinners. God has a present and an eternal purpose in His called-out people.

Not only are the origin, constituency, and purpose of the church declared in the Scriptures, but her destiny also. The combined testimony of the Word is that the church is a heavenly group. Her Head, the Lord Jesus Christ, is in heaven seated at the right hand of the Majesty in the heavens where He ever lives to intercede and advocate for His Bride. She has been raised up to sit together with Christ in the heavenlies. Her life is hidden with Christ in God, and as a result she is exhorted to set her affections on things above. All her spiritual blessings are in heavenly places in Christ Jesus, and her warfare is not against flesh and blood, human agencies, but against spiritual wickedness in heavenly places. Every phase of her life, therefore, is connected with heaven, and her destiny is no exception. It is a heavenly destination to which the church is traveling. Our citizenship, the apostle Paul informs us, is in heaven from whence we look for the Savior, the Lord Jesus Christ, who will change the body of our humiliation and will fashion it, by His boundless power, to be like the body of His glory. Christ promised His disciples before He left them that He would come again and receive them unto Himself, that where He is there they might also be. In His prayer to the Father in John 17 He asked: "Father, I will that they also, whom thou hast given me, be with me where I am" (v. 24). That prayer is to be answered finally when all the redeemed of this age are in the presence of their Lord. The destiny of the church, then, is heaven in the enjoyment of the immediate and ever-blessed presence of Christ and the Father.

Contrary to the belief of many, the Word teaches that the church is not to remain on earth indefinitely. The termination of the church's sojourn on earth has been clearly set forth in the Scriptures. Paul revealed that the rapture will end the earthly pilgrimage of the church. After the apostle's ministry in Thessalonica, his converts there were troubled about the fact that some of their saved loved ones had died. They appear to have been under the impression that they would all be alive at the coming of the Lord. Paul wrote to reassure them that they need not sorrow as others that have no hope. For at the coming of the Lord, living believers will not precede those who have fallen asleep in Jesus. He Himself will descend from heaven with a shout, with the voice of the archangel, and with the trump of God. The dead in Christ will rise first, then living saints will be caught up together with them in the clouds to meet the Lord in the air. Both parties will ever be with the Lord (1 Thess. 4:13-18).

In writing to Corinthian believers on the matter of the resurrection, the same apostle laid emphasis more particularly that time on the condition of living saints. He revealed a mystery that not all believers will pass through the experience of death, but there will some day be one generation of saints that will be changed in the twinkling of an eye, in a moment, at the last trump. At the sound of the trumpet the dead will be raised to incorruption and those alive will be changed (1 Cor. 15:50-58). Nowhere in Scripture is the time of that event made known. It is imminent at all times, certain at one time hidden in the counsels of God. The church had her beginning on earth when the Third Person of the Trinity descended to undertake her formation; she will have her termination on earth when the Second Person of the Trinity comes to take her to Himself.

The presence of the redeemed of this age in heaven will be followed by the adjudication of rewards for faithful service. The Scriptures are one in declaring over and over again that believers will not come into condemnation or judgment (Rom. 8:1). All the condemnation or judgment that all our sins deserved was poured out without reserve upon the head of the matchless, undefiled Son of God, the Lamb of God who came to take away the sin of the world. As a result, those who accept the finished work of Christ for their sins are said to have passed into life and are not coming into judgment. There is no judgment now or in eternity for those who are in Christ Jesus. It would thwart the very purposes of God's eternal plan to judge Christ for our sins and then charge us with them in a coming day of judgment.

To what purpose, then, is there a judgment for believers? The judgment is solely for rewards for work done, not before salvation, but after the individual has been saved. Paul wrote to the Corinthian believers that it should not be a matter of concern to them whether they were present in the body or absent from it. Present in the body meant absent from the Lord; absent from the body was to be present with the Lord. The matter of importance is that in their labor they may be accepted of Him. The reference is to the judgment seat of Christ before which all believers will be manifested to receive the things done in the body, whether good or bad (lit., useless or profitless) (2 Cor. 5:6-10).

The apostle explained the question of the Christian's judgment more fully in 1 Corinthians 3. After he had called attention to the carnality present among them because of their contentious parties, Paul showed that it is God who is the determining factor in all Christian service. The work of the believer is merely to cooperate with God, building upon the foundation that has already been laid, Jesus Christ Himself. But there are various ways of building upon the one foundation. The service of some will be such that it can be compared to gold; that of others silver, precious stones, wood, hay, or stubble. Each and every work will be tried in the Day of Christ as to what sort it is. If it is of the nature of gold, silver, and precious stones, it will be able to stand the probatory test of the fires of judgment, and the believer will receive reward. If not, the believer loses his reward. It is not a matter here of losing his salvation for that is steadfast and secure, depending upon the work and merit of Christ and not the works of any believer.

There is an encouraging word added in the next chapter, which shows that at the time of judgment "then shall every man have praise of God" (1 Cor. 4:5). The nature of those rewards is also revealed in the Scriptures, but the present study limits its discussion to the fact of the rewards of the individual members of the church in a future day, the Day of Christ when He comes to gather His own to Himself.

In order to complete that consideration of the church, there is need but to mention here the marriage of the church. Throughout the New Testament the church is viewed as the future Bride of Christ. Paul was jealous over the believers in Corinth with a godly jealousy, for he had espoused them to one husband, that he might present them as a chaste virgin to Christ (2 Cor. 11:2). The Bride of Christ, which is His Body, has not been completed yet through these many centuries; when she is complete and gathered to her Lord and Head, and when her works have been judged for rewards, then will follow, as John reveals in the book of Revelation, the marriage of the Lamb (Rev. 19:7-9). The union, consummated thus, will go on in ever-growing blessedness throughout the endless ages of eternity.

NOTES

[1]Sir R. Anderson, *The Coming Prince,* pp. 122-28.

[2]Ladd has stated it plainly: "It should not trouble us that the New Testament for the most part does not foresee the millennial kingdom any more than the fact that the Old Testament does not clearly predict the Church Age" (R. G. Clouse, *The Meaning of the Millennium,* p. 39). Even those who may not concur fully with the first portion of the comparison, may acquiesce with the latter part. Again, he emphasizes the last clause: "The Old Testament does not foresee or precisely predict the Church Age" (ibid., p. 190).

[3]It is, then, eminently correct for Hoyt to say, "The present age is to be regarded as a period of transition for the mediatorial kingdom" (Clouse, p. 88).

[4]H. C. Thiessen, Lecture Notes on the Dispensations.

[5]The term "church" in the book of Revelation, it is vital to remember, is *never* used of believers in heaven, only of local churches on earth (A. J. McClain, *The Greatness of the Kingdom,* pp. 446-47).

[6]It is impossible biblically and logically to have a body without a head, and Christ did not become the Head until in resurrection glory (Eph. 1:20-23). Even in the material creation God did not make Adam or Eve a body without a head (Gen. 2:7, 21-23).

[7]C. I. Scofield, *The Scofield Reference Bible* (1917), p. 1169, fn. 1; see also *The New Scofield Reference Bible* (1967), p. 1185, fn. 1.

[8]Recent attempts by some hardy souls to revive the long moribund postmillennial view scarcely know what to do with that question. One late endeavor claims: "The fact is that when Christ came and was rejected, he deposed the leaders of apostate Judaism, the Pharisees and elders, and appointed a new set of officials, the apostles, through whom he established his church." Then quoting Matt. 21:43 and 1 Thess. 2:16 without benefit of exegesis, he concludes: "That leaves no space for a future nationalistic conversion" (Boettner in Clouse, p. 101). Sad it is that he has completely overlooked or ignored the great statement of Paul in Romans 11:25-27.

10
The Tribulation Period

The word "tribulation" is derived from the Latin *tribulum,* which means a threshing-sledge. The term is used in the Scriptures in a general and specific sense. When David had spared the life of Saul for the second time, he expressed the wish that, as he had spared the life of his enemy God would deliver him out of all tribulation, referring to any kind of adversity (1 Sam. 26:24). In the epistle to the Romans, chapter 5, Paul noted that one of the benefits of justification is that the believer can glory in tribulation, for he knows that it is conducive to patience (v. 3). Here the reference is to any trial or affliction. But the Scriptures evidently use the term in a specific and well-defined sense also. At the end of his prophecy Daniel spoke of a time of trouble, unprecedented in the entire history of his people (Dan. 12:1). Matthew, Mark, and Luke in their respective records of the eschatological discourse of the Lord Jesus revealed a time of tribulation at a definite point in the history of the world and in that of Israel in particular (Matt. 24-25; Mark 13; Luke 21). It is to that particular period that our attention is directed now.

In the earlier study of Daniel's seventy weeks the attempt was made to show that the Jewish, or law, age was brought to a sudden close at the end of the sixty-ninth week with the cutting off of Messiah the Prince. When the church age is brought to a close by the completion of the Body of Christ from Jews and Gentiles, the blindness will be taken away from Israel (Rom. 11:25), and the Jewish clock will again begin to tick. That period is known as the Great Tribulation, which, it is said, is to intervene between the coming of the Lord Jesus for His saints and His coming with His saints. It is the seventieth week of Daniel's prophecy and is referred to in Daniel 9:27.

The first fact of importance in a consideration of the Tribulation period is that the church will not be in that period. Several factors support that position. First, all believers have the promise of God through John that they will be kept from the hour of the trial (the definite article is in the original), pointing to a definite and specific time of trial that will come upon the world to try those that dwell (lit., are fully settled down, as the church is not because of its pilgrim nature) upon the earth (Rev. 3:10).

Second, the nature of the seventieth week of Daniel (9:24-27) would cause one to believe that the church will not be found in it. The Body of Christ was not found in the sixty-nine weeks, and it is highly improbable on that account that she will be found in the seventieth week. God does not have two mutually exclusive governing principles as law and grace operative in one period.

Third—and here the arguments given by Thiessen are in order—the nature and purpose of the Tribulation militate against the church's being found in it.[1] That period is a time of judgment and chastisement for the ungodly world. God never punishes His own children with the world. The Tribulation period is expressly spoken of as the "time of Jacob's trouble" and the "time of the heathen (lit., Gentiles)," but it is never spoken of as the "time of the church" (Jer. 30:7; Ezek. 30:3). Why have the two other divisions of the human race been designated in that connection and not the church, if there is not meant to be left the impression that the church is to be delivered from the time of trial?

Fourth, the position and constituency of the twenty-four elders favor our position. Many commentators hold that those elders represent the whole body of the redeemed in heaven, the church of Christ. There is proof for that view. (1) The white raiment is the righteousness of the saints only (Rev. 19:7-8). (2) Crowns are nowhere promised in Scripture as rewards for any but those who are in the church (1 Cor. 9:25; Phil. 4:1; 1 Thess. 2:19; 2 Tim. 4:8; Jas. 1:12; 1 Pet. 5:4; Rev. 2:10). (3) Their song is one of redemption, for they have been redeemed by the blood of the Lamb from every kindred, tongue, people, and nation. (4) When the multitude that has been saved out of the Tribulation gives thanks to God, the elders and the angels are seen about the throne and give separate thanks and praise. (5) When the 144,000 stand on Mount Zion (Rev. 14:1-5), they are apart from the elders and sing their song before the four living ones and the elders. (6) When the elders give thanks in chapter 11 at the sounding of the seventh trumpet, they do not mention their personal participation in the future rewards of those saints and prophets, probably because they have already received theirs. (7) The word "church" does not occur after the third chapter, and the Bride of Christ is not seen on earth until the reign in chapter 20, when she coreigns with her Lord. Throughout the time of earth's judgments the group representing the church is seen in heaven as spectators, who are consciously worshiping their Creator and Redeemer.

There is a fifth reason we believe the church will not go through the Tribulation period: the relation of the Holy Spirit to the mystery of lawlessness. In 2 Thessalonians 2, it is stated that one of the ministries of the Spirit of God is to restrain evil. He will do so until He leaves the earth in the Body of Christ. The man of sin, who is a most important factor in the Tribulation period, is not revealed until the Holy Spirit is "taken out of the way" in the church (2 Thess. 2:1-12). Therefore, it follows that the Tribulation begins after the rapture of the church.

Sixth, if the church is not taken up into heaven before the Tribulation, there is no time before the visible coming of the Lord in glory for inserting the rewarding of the faithful service of the saints and the marriage supper of the Lamb. Surely those events require just such an interval as the period between the rapture and the revelation, and they take place in heaven.

Finally, the many exhortations to constant expectation of the Lord's coming are inexplicable if a period of trial is next on God's program for the church. How can the church be looking for the blessed hope when she is looking for the Tribulation period? The conclusion is, therefore, that the church will not be found on earth during the Great Tribulation.

Norman B. Harrison notes a threefold cause of the Great Tribulation.[2] The failure of Israel to accept her Messiah and the complete moral failure on the part of the Gentiles and professing Christendom will bring about that period (Jer. 30:3; Ezek. 30:3; Rev. 17:5, 14-18). Also, it will be occasioned by an increase in the power and influence of Satan in preparation for the time when he shall reveal his man of sin as the god of the age (2 Thess. 2:7-8) in the middle of the period. Third, it will be occasioned by the plan of God to set His King on His holy hill of Zion (Psalm 2:6).

There will be certain distinct groups in the time of the Great Tribulation. That Israel is particularly in view can be seen from Jeremiah 30:4-7, where the prophet foretold a day when there will be heard a voice of trembling, of fear, and not of peace, when every man will have his hands on his loins as a woman in travail, with his face turned to paleness, because "it is even the time of Jacob's trouble." All the nations that do not profess to be subject to God nor render any allegiance to Him will form a second company, for Jeremiah testified in 25:31 that God has a "controversy with the nations," and Ezekiel spoke (30:3) of "the time of the heathen" (lit., nations). Apostate Christendom (the bad fish and the tares of Matthew 13) will be included in mystery Babylon, which appears to consist of all the false religious systems of all ages.

Finally, there will be the Tribulation remnant of Israel. To ascertain the constituency and purpose of that remnant, Revelation 7 must be considered. A reading of the chapter shows two groups are discernible: the 144,000 and the great multitude from all nations, kindreds, peoples, and tongues. Milligan is of the opinion that the 144,000 sealed ones refer primarily to Jewish Christians but have a wider application as well in the church universal. He dispenses with the difficulty of the Jewish names by claiming that it is customary for John to "heighten and spiritualize all Jewish names."[3] His final conclusion upon the chapter is that the two companies are identical, in the one case being sealed as God's own, and in the second instance having entered into the peace and joy of their Lord. Alford sees in the 144,000 all the elect of God who will be living on earth at the coming of the Lord, "symbolical of the first-fruits of the church." He contends that the groups in chapter 7 are not identical, but that the first is included in the second. He explains further that "out of great tribulation" means "the whole sum of the trials of the saints of God."[4]

Neither of those statements is adequate to explain all the facts presented in the chapter. In the first place, the church is not in view in the Revelation (except as seated in heaven viewing the events upon the earth, as has been shown above) from chapter 4 through 19. In the second place, it is difficult to accept any interpretation that spiritualizes the names of the Jewish tribes into the Israel of God or the church universal. That principle of interpretation is valid that states: "When the plain sense makes good sense, seek no other sense." Concerning the 144,000 sealed ones, one concludes that when the church is caught up to be with the Lord, God will call a remnant of His people—He has ever had a true witness to Himself and His goodness among His people Israel even in the darkest hours of their apostasy and declension—to proclaim the gospel of the kingdom, for "this gospel of the kingdom shall be preached in all the world for a witness unto all nations; and then shall the end come" (Matt. 24:14). The presence of that remnant is brought out in many Old Testament passages and explains the existence and purpose of the imprecatory psalms. The result of their testimony is seen in the great multitude of Gentiles saved (Rev. 7:9-17).

What is the character of the Great Tribulation? From Isaiah 24-28 and from Revelation 8-19, an adequate idea of the characteristics of the period may be gained. But there is much more additional material revealed in the messages of the minor prophets. Isaiah spoke of the period as one in which the earth will be utterly broken down, clean dissolved, and moved exceedingly. It will reel to and fro like a drunkard; it shall fall and not rise again. Then will the indignation of the Lord be upon all nations and upon their armies unto their destruction. The "mountains shall be melted with their blood" (Isa. 34:3). The garments of the Lord will be red like those of one that treads in the winefat; His fury will be poured out without measure (Isa. 63:1-6). Daniel mentioned a time of trouble such as never was since there was a nation, even to that same time (Dan. 12:1). Joel had much to say of the Day of the Lord, of which the Tribulation period is a part along with the millennial reign itself—both are viewed under that caption in Scripture. He described it as a day of darkness and of gloominess, a day of clouds and of thick darkness, a day in which all faces shall gather blackness, a day in which not only the earth will quake but the heavens also will tremble, a day in which the sun and moon will be dark, and a day in which the stars will refuse to give their light (Joel 2:1-6, 30-31).

Amos spoke of the Day of the Lord as darkness and not light. He best depicted the straitness of the times by likening them to a man who fled from a lion and was met by a bear, or went into his house only to be bitten by a serpent upon the wall (Amos 5:18-19). Zephaniah in dealing with the same theme said the day shall be one of wrath, a day of trouble and distress, a day of wasteness and desolation, a day of darkness and gloominess, a day of clouds and thick darkness, a day of war and sieges (Zeph. 1:14-17). Men will walk like blind men, and their blood will be poured out like dust.

The book of Revelation presents from chapter 4 to 19 (or more specifically from chapters 6 to 19) the most detailed account of the ravages to be wrought by that time of unexampled and unprecedented judgment of God upon the ungodly world. Heaven, earth, the seas, and men dwelling upon earth will all be touched and sensibly affected by those events. There will be worldwide woe, universal distress, and unheard-of anguish. Fear and terror will reign supreme. God will by grievous judgments melt the nations, Israel, and all apostate religious systems in a fiery furnace. It will no doubt be a period of trial, sorrow, calamity, spiritual darkness, wickedness, and catastrophe such as the world has never seen nor imagined. The plagues of Egypt will be insignificant in comparison with it, and the Reign of Terror in France during the French Revolution or the unspeakable atrocities of the Spanish Inquisition will not even remotely approximate it. Even the diabolical Nazi holocaust will not equal it.

That the Tribulation period follows a definite course in its development is discernible from the Scriptures. In that connection the eschatological discourses of the Lord in Matthew 24, Mark 13, and Luke 21 are of interest and importance. Girdlestone rightly notes that "the framework of the prophecy appears to be Israelite."[5] After the Lord had pronounced His woes upon the Pharisees and the scribes and left the Temple as desolate, His disciples came to show Him the Temple buildings. To them the Temple was not desolate, with all its fine buildings and masonry, and they wished to call the attention of the Lord to that. But He foretold that it would be completely destroyed. The destruction was actually accomplished in A.D. 70 under the leadership of Titus.

The disciples were not fully satisfied with their understanding of those things, so they asked the Lord as He sat on the Mount of Olives a threefold question, or three questions that were certainly closely related. They asked for the time of the destruction of the Temple and the city of Jerusalem, for the sign of His visible, or second, coming, and for the time of the end of the age. The last question does not deal with the end of the world (as the Authorized Version has it translated), but rather with the end of the age. Of which age were the disciples asking? They were asking of the age in which they were then living, to be sure, and that was the age of the law, or the Jewish age.

Notice carefully the answer to their threefold question. The first part is answered in full in Luke 21 where the siege and destruction of Jerusalem are predicted as being brought about by the encompassing armies of Rome under Titus. The inhabitants would be carried away captive into all the nations, and Jerusalem would be trodden down by the Gentiles until the times of the Gentiles would be brought to a close (vv. 20-24). Next outlined is the course of events that will be signs of the visible coming of the Lord. Matthew's record (24:4-14) seems to point to a preliminary period that, some have believed, refers to the end of the church age. That seems untenable because the Lord was not answering a question concerning that age at all. The primary reference seems to be, if the context is considered, to the end of the Jewish age. There is in the present age, however, a foreshadowing of the things spoken in those verses.

Furthermore, the signs of Christ's visible coming are not discernible in the church age as they will be in the period following this present age of grace. The Lord points out that there will be many who will claim to be Christ; wars and rumors of wars will increase; nation will rise up against nation, and kingdom against kingdom; famines, earthquakes, and pestilences will abound in diverse places. Those signs will be followed by extensive persecutions of the Jews and universal hatred. The gospel of the kingdom will be preached at that time for a witness to all nations, and then shall the end come. Verse fifteen of Matthew 24 begins with the sign of the abomination of desolation spoken of by Daniel the prophet. When compared with other passages of Scripture, particularly those found in the Revelation, the time appears to be the last half of Daniel's seventieth week, known more specifically as the Great Tribulation. That time of three and one-half years is designated as time, times, and the dividing of times; forty-two months; or twelve hundred sixty days (Dan. 7:25; 12:7; Rev. 11:2, 3; 12:6). It will be the period of the most intense judgments and the greatest activity of the beast, the false prophet, or the Antichrist, and Satan himself. So horrendous will be those days that unless they were shortened, no one would be saved. For Israel's sake they are shortened. Immediately after the tribulation of those days the Son of Man will appear, coming in clouds of heaven with power and great glory.

Thus far the outline has been given in general for the course of the Tribulation according to the synoptic gospels. It is necessary now to fill in that scheme with the details gleaned from other portions of the Word. It is revealed that the Jews before the end of the Jewish age will return to Palestine and rebuild the Temple, the Tribulation Temple in which the man of sin will sit boasting of divine prerogatives and demanding divine worship (Dan. 9:27; 2 Thess. 2:3-4; Rev. 11:1-2). The beast will make a covenant with the people of Israel, presumably one for their security and protection. He will break that covenant in the midst of the seven-year period and will be revealed in all his satanic perversity and wickedness. The trumpet judgments (Rev. 8:1—11:19) will be poured out upon the earth, upon the sea, upon the rivers and fountains of waters, upon the solar and lunar systems, and in various ways upon men on earth. The two witnesses of God will be killed and raised (Rev. 11:7-11). An earthquake, disastrous to both men and the city of Jerusalem, will follow.

Thunderings, an earthquake, and lightnings will complete the judgments of the seventh trumpet.

The beast from the sea will be revealed in all his blasphemous pretensions with his coadjutor, or false prophet, who will cause the earth and its dwellers to worship the first beast (Rev. 13:1, 11). The judgments of the seven bowls of wrath will follow in rapid succession (Rev. 16). Babylon, religious and commercial, will be destroyed and the great war in the Valley of Megiddo will be entered upon. The marriage of the Lamb will have previously taken place in heaven (Rev. 19:7-10), and Christ will come in glory to destroy the beast, the false prophet, and their armies (19:17-21). Christ will be followed by His glorified saints, who will be spectators of the immediate victory of their Lord. The beast and false prophet will then be consigned to the lake of fire (19:20). That, by way of rapid survey, is the course of the important period known as the Tribulation.

We turn now to consider the immediate consequences of the period. (1) Israel will be regathered from the ends of the earth whither they have been scattered (Matt. 24:31). They will be judged by the Lord in the wilderness according to the prophecy of Ezekiel (20:33-42) and restored in blessing to their own land, there to be a blessing to all the nations of the earth (Ezek. 37:21-28). (2) Many Gentiles will be saved out of the Great Tribulation as a result of the preaching of the gospel of the kingdom as a witness to all nations (Matt. 24:14; Rev. 7:9-17). (3) The beast and the false prophet will be cast into the lake of fire (Rev. 19:20). (4) Satan will be conquered and bound and consigned to the bottomless pit (Rev. 20:1-3). (5) The war of Armageddon will mark the end of all war on the earth—the attempt at the end of the Millennium on the part of Gog and Magog to compass the beloved city will not really be a battle (Joel 3:1-2, 9-16; Rev. 16:13-16; 19:17-21). (6) Christ Jesus, the one once despised and rejected of men, will come in visible glory with His angels, according to the testimony of many passages of Scripture that need not be alluded to here, as KING OF KINGS AND LORD OF LORDS (Rev. 19:11-16).

Finally, when He sits on the throne of His glory, the nations will be brought before Him to be judged as to the treatment of His brethren, the remnant of Israel, during the Great Tribulation (Matt. 25:31-46). Their attitude toward Israel will evidently be a factor that reveals their heart attitude toward God and His purposes in Christ, for those who are of the "goat" nations will go away into everlasting punishment. Those who are of the "sheep" nations will enter into the kingdom prepared for them from the foundation of the world; they are later said to go into eternal life, which shows a relationship between the King's millennial reign and the eternal reign of the Father (cf. 1 Cor. 15:24-28).

To recapitulate, the church's position in the Tribulation, the causes, the companies, the character, the course, and the consequences of the Great Tribulation have been treated.

While the judgments are taking place (Rev. 4-19), and no mention is made of the church on earth, there are three references to a group of saved in heaven: chapters 4-5, 13, and 19. Compare 2 Cor. 11:2 and Eph. 5:25-27 with Rev. 19:1-9, especially v. 7. Compare Rev. 13:16 with 13:6 and Heb. 9:11. See ASV on 13:16, no *kai* in final clause. Compare Heb. 8:2, 5; 9:3 and 2 Pet. 1:13-14. As to the judgments themselves in Rev. 6-19, McClain has rightly stated: "Regardless of the chronological arrangements which may be made of these judgments, whether some recapitulation or overlapping scheme be adopted, the opening action of chapters 4 and 5 simply cannot be pushed into the picture which follows in 6 to 19."[6] There is an unalterable sequence of events.

Barton Payne, a declared premillennialist, credits dispensationalism with recapturing the truth, held by the early church and the Reformers, of the imminence of the Lord's return. However, his commendation is strongly muted by his belief that the restoration was at the expense of the unity of redemption history and valid exegetical distinctions.[7] In fairness, he has admitted that reacting posttribulationalism, apart from some gains he believes they have made, has lost ground also. He believes: "But its efforts have been predominantly negative and its retention of certain interpretive novelties has resulted in a denial of the imminent return of Christ altogether."[8] Resting heavily on the historical argument, he stresses that the early church expected the Lord's appearing at any hour (2 Tim. 4:8); on the other hand, the Ante-Nicene Fathers held to a posttribulational hope.[9]

After an evaluation of the influence of Augustine on eschatology and the Brethren movement's view of the local church, Barton Payne concedes: "The majority of American premillennialists are still pre-tribulationist in their interpretation."[10] But he follows with a logical non-sequitur to which no dispensationalist can subscribe: "Dispensational pre-tribulationism is committed to a thoroughgoing futurism in its exegesis of biblical prophecy. It is therefore forced to deny the imminence of the appearing of Christ, which cannot be impending until the close of the future tribulation . . . it presents the innovation of a rapture for the church that is kept distinct from the remainder of the eschatological complex, and which is thus made capable of occurrence at any moment."[11] It is evident that his difficulty stems from his inability to distinguish between Christ's coming for His saints and then His coming with them.[12] Between those important events must occur the tribulation period, just as in premillennialism between the first and second resurrection there must intervene the kingly reign of Christ on David's throne.[13]

Since Barton Payne has placed so much stress on the historical argument, it is surprising to hear him declare: "Prior to the rise of Irving and Darby a century and one-quarter ago, all premillennialists were post-tribulational, that is, they located the rapture of the church at the same time as the appearing of Christ, after the tribulation."[14] On the basis of "higher scholarship" he divides Darby from premillennialists. Then he makes an amazing admission: "The one subject about which reacting post-tribulationists show the most disagreement is that of the tribulation. A few identify it with the whole of church history; others do the same, but with a terminal portion of unprecedented extent in the times of the final Antichrist while the large majority restrict *the* [italics his] tribulation to a period of several years that are yet future."[15] His evaluation of modern posttribulationism in its literature is that it is "predominantly negative," and its writers have been "extravagant in their debate."[16]

Barton Payne states that the majority of dispensational pretribulationists are guilty of "uncritical acceptance" of their view, and that their leaders "feel they are now fighting for its very existence."[17] Scholars have enough of a task in serious discussion of Scripture without indulging themselves in wishful thinking. Payne himself tries to see the Tribulation as already past. He coins the expression "classical interpretation" for his view.[18] Thus he preserves the imminence of Christ's appearing, but on what basis? He judges from the perspective of Christians suffering in different areas of the world. That argument has been and is used often, but it rests on a faulty perspective. Who is to judge that the sufferings of believers today, real and incredible as they are in so many parts of the world, equal the horrendous events of the Tribulation period? Those living during World War I thought they were experiencing the Tribulation, then those in World War II, then those in the Indo-China conflicts, then those in the atrocities recently perpetrated in Africa, to say nothing of the agonies of the Middle East wars, but who can legitimately equate them with Daniel 12:1 and Matthew 24:21? Who can presume to know how grievous is suffering "such as was not since the beginning of the world to this time . . . nor ever shall be"? Only Deity can speak here with finality on such a span of history. Let all men refrain from interpreting Scripture in the light of current events, rather than events in the light of Scripture. The latter course is the only trustworthy one.

When Ladd comes to his discussion of the blessed hope, he spends considerable time on a refutation of a pretribulation rapture, using extensively the historical argument. He argues that the program of pretribulationists "included important elements which are not found in the early church. Among these were the teachings of the Rapture of the Church at the beginning of the Tribulation and the expectation of an any-moment secret coming of Christ for the purpose of rapturing the Church."[19] He concedes that the question of the rapture of the church, as all biblical issues, must rest on the clear teaching of the Word, yet he emphasizes at length the views of interpreters of early

Christian times. Scarcely a posttribulation writer varies from that method, yet in their conclusions they effectively cancel out each other's positions.[20]

Before any exegesis is attempted or a logical induction drawn from Scripture data, Ladd clearly posits his objective: "The central thesis of this book is that the *Blessed Hope is the second coming of Jesus Christ and not a pretribulation rapture* [italics his]. The Blessed Hope is not synonymous with pre-tribulationism."[21] Having stated that objective, he strangely declares: "For the most part, the Word of God is not explicit about the order of events. Matthew 24 says nothing about the resurrection; the book of Revelation says nothing about the Rapture of the Church; Paul's epistles say nothing about the resur-rection of the unrighteous. Our problems arise when we begin to ask questions which were not in the minds of the authors."[22]

It is axiomatic that no important doctrine of Scripture can be gleaned from one passage alone. There is a need for a collation of evidence. As a New Testament scholar, Ladd is fully aware that no gospel gives a full chronology of the life of our Lord; a harmony of the gospels is absolutely necessary. It is fallacious to maintain: "We hold that pretribulationism is an inference and not the explicit teaching of the Word of God. Therefore, it is not to be identified with the Blessed Hope."[23] In all fairness, is posttribulationism more than an inference? Is it as well substantiated from the full-prophetic testimony as is pretribulationism?

Ladd states: "The hope of the Church throughout the early centuries was the second coming of Christ, not a pretribulation rapture. If the Blessed Hope is in fact a pretribulation rapture, then the Church has never known that hope through most of its history, for the idea of a pretribulation rapture did not appear in prophetic interpretation until the nineteenth century."[24] Could that argument not be leveled against the specifics in the premillennial position to which he does subscribe? What orthodox scholar today, thoroughly committed to the doctrine of justification by faith, would be willing or content to allow even Luther's treatment of the doctrine to be determinative or definitive for him? What about the doctrines of pneumatology and eschatology that have come down to this generation? It must ever be recognized that in doctrine there must be progression, on the basis of clearer understanding of Scripture, whereby truth is honed, polished, and clarified.

Ladd admits that the early Fathers did believe in the imminence of Christ's return. He strongly declares: "Let it be at once emphasized that we are not turning to the church fathers to find authority for either pre- or post-tribulationism. . . . While tradition does not provide authority, it would nevertheless be difficult to suppose that God had left His people in ignorance of an essential truth for nineteen centuries."[25] Has not truth been lost and recovered? In the time of the Judges? In the wilderness journeys before that? Was not the book of the Law, no one knows how long, lost—in the Temple, mind you—and then recovered in Josiah's day to be interpreted by Huldah the prophetess? Coming to modern times, did the Reformers recover truth long lost in monasteries and churches? Ladd's treatment of the historical data leaves much to be desired.[26] He is willing to hold to a posttribulation premillennialism at the price of a dual hermeneutic, that is, equating Israel with the church.[27]

Some writers introduce into their discussion of doctrine the practice of counting noses. Ladd cites those who were premillennial, but not pretribulational. It is interesting to notice that of the dozen some names mentioned, only two or three are still living.[28] The use of terms like "uncritically" and "a sound premillennialism" is also not likely to advance the cause of truth regarding the pretribulation rapture.[29] What is of inestimable value, however, for the attainment of correct doctrine would be to realize and act upon the truth that words (i.e., *parousia* [coming], *apokalupsis* [revelation], and *epiphaneia* [manifestation], vital terms of eschatological discussion) may have more than one meaning, depending on usage and context.[30]

At the outset of his discussion of the rapture and the Tribulation, Walvoord correctly evaluates the question: "The rapture question, while neglected by modern liberals, is one of the main areas in dispute in conservative eschatology."[31] He discerningly realizes the matter has important doctrinal and practical ramifications, impinging upon bibliology (hermeneutical principles), ecclesiology, and eschatology.[32] Once an interpreter keeps clear the distinctive terminology in the Scripture for Israel and the church, he is well on the way to a valid solution of the problems connected with the Tribulation period.

It is essential to realize that "never are tribulation saints referred to as a church, or as the body of Christ, or as indwelt by Christ, or as subject to translation, or as the bride."[33] Biblical phraseology here is explicit and exact, so that those living on earth in the Tribulation are designated as Israelites, Gentiles, and saints without any reference to the redeemed of the church age. Those who demand specifics of pretribulationism from the fathers are lacking in historical perspective. Where can one find developed premillennialism in the early centuries, even so-called classical premillennialism? Centuries are required for such developments and refinements of doctrines. As examples, the basic doctrine of the Trinity was not formulated until the Council of Nicaea (A.D. 325), the doctrine of total depravity in the fifth century, and the doctrines of justification by faith and of the priesthood of believers in the sixteenth century (the Protestant Reformation).[34] However, it cannot be validly denied that the keystone of pretribulationism—the doctrine of imminence—is unmistakably present in the literature of the early church, even if precise terms are lacking.[35]

In posttribulationist writings there is a serious defect in not realizing that between Christ's coming for His saints and then with them, there is needed an indispensable interval for (1) the judgment seat of Christ (2 Cor. 5:10; cf. also 1 Cor. 3:14-15; 1 Pet. 5:4; Rev. 4:4; 22:12), (2) the marriage of the Lamb to His Bride (Rev. 19:6-8), (3) the judgment of Israel (Ezek. 20:34-38), and (4) the judgment of the nations (Matt. 25:31-46).[36] Moreover, to join the two phases of Christ's return results in inescapable embarrassment to posttribulationists. Walvoord has pointed out:

> If the translation takes place *after* [italics his] the tribulation, the question facing the posttribulationists is a very obvious one: Who is going to populate the earth during the millennium? The Scriptures are specific that, during the millennium, saints will build houses and bear children and have normal, mortal lives on earth. If all believers are translated and all unbelievers are put to death at the beginning of the millennium, there will be no one left [in unresurrected bodies] to populate the earth and fulfill these Scriptures (cf. Isa. 65:20-25).[37]

Although it is undeniable that most of the church holds to posttribulationism, and has for some time, it is also demonstrably true that the position is that of almost all postmillenarians and amillenarians. It is inevitable that in time posttribulationists land in the cul-de-sac of nonmillenarianism, a truth visible today on the theological scene both in Canada and the United States. There is an inescapable logic affinity between a literal hermeneutic, premillennialism, and pretribulationism, as there is between a dual hermeneutic, posttribulationism, and nonchiliastic positions.[38] When posttribulationists, for instance, blur the solid distinctions between Israel and the church, they are ready to embrace one people of God in both Testaments, then one covenant throughout Scripture, and ultimately nonmillenarianism.[39]

The omission from the discussion of the partial rapture and midtribulation views has been purposeful, because the proponents of those positions are decidedly in the minority today.

Among the most recent advocates of posttribulationism is Robert H. Gundry, whose extended treatment calls for a lengthy rebuttal in view of the genuine pains to explicate the position and the absence, in true scholarly fashion, of vituperation and denigration of opposing views.[40] Early in his discussion Gundry states clearly the issue he confronts in his work and declares himself a premillennialist.[41] He has felt the need for his written contribution because Ladd's work on the blessed hope is not sufficient by reason of its general historical approach, and Alexander Reese's volume is not only outdated but employs an "embarrassingly bombastic style."[42]

Concisely, his goal is stated:

> The present thesis is threefold: (1) direct, unquestioned statements of Scripture that Jesus Christ will return after the tribulation and that the first resurrection will occur after the tribulation, coupled with the absence of statements placing similar events before the tribulation, make it a

natural to place the rapture of the church after the tribulation; (2) the theological and exegetical grounds for pretribulationism rest on insufficient evidence, *non sequitur* reasoning, and faulty exegesis; (3) positive indications of a posttribulational rapture arise out of a proper exegesis of relevant Scripture passages and derive support from the history of the doctrine.[43]

In view of such statements it is strange to find early in the treatment a hermeneutical tempering of vital distinctions and definitions. "Israel" is referred to not only as the physical descendants of Abraham through Isaac and Jacob, but also by extension as those "either nationally considered or ideally considered as a spiritual body of redeemed people."[44]

That is undeniably the introduction of a vital element of covenant theology and amillennialism. It is unacceptable for one seeking to maintain the norms of dispensationalism with its single hermeneutic. Moreover, in any attempt to substantiate a certain theological position from Scripture evidence it is harmful to the presentation to beg the question at any point in the argument. Yet Gundry writes: "The terms 'second coming' 'return,' 'advent,' and 'Parousia' all refer to the posttribulational return of Christ with attendant events unless qualified otherwise by the immediate context. The alleged pretribulational advent, resurrection, translation, and rapture of the Church are always so qualified by modifiers or by context."[45] And more:

> In the chronological question concerning the rapture, the dispensational issue centers in the field of ecclesiology. An absolute silence in the OT about the present age, a total disconnection of the Church from the divine program for Israel, and a clean break between dispensations would favor pretribulationism: the Church would not likely be related to the seventieth week of Daniel, or tribulation, a period of time clearly having to do with Israel. But a partial revelation of the present age in the OT, a connection (not necessarily identification) between Israel and the Church, and a dispensational change involving a transitional period open the door to the presence of the Church during the tribulation.[46]

Those lengthy quotations are necessary because throughout his volume Gundry elaborates and defends those basic guidelines. A number of observations are in order. (1) He has introduced into the discussion, not lost on a student of logic, a number of adjectives—"alleged," "absolute," "total," "clean," "not likely," "partial," (and an adverb) "not necessarily"—all of which are tendentious. (2) Have other posttribulational writers laid down such a group of options before? Why does he depart from their approach? (3) His terms need clarification. (4) He is laboring to extricate himself from a theological straitjacket of his own making: he desires to remain a dispensationalist and yet accepts covenant theology postulates. (5) Where in the treatment of the subject is there a recognition of the vital relevance of Ephesians 3:1-7? (6) It is easy to claim that in the pretribulational system "the dealings of God with the Church are severed from His dealings with Israel."[47] But the statement is neither exact nor accurate.

Gundry adduces another argument against pretribulationism: "Both parties [pre- and posttribulationists] agree that a large number of Gentile saints (whether or not they will belong to the Church) will live on earth during the Tribulation (so, clearly, Rev. 7:9-17). But do any tribulational passages in the OT mention those Gentile saints? No such passages are adduced."[48] Carrying the argument further, it is maintained: "If none exist, pretribulationists should hardly argue from a mysterious silence in the OT concerning the Church, because the OT remains silent also concerning the Gentile saints whom we know to be on earth during the tribulation."[49] No one denies that those of Rev. 7:9-17 are Gentile saints from the clear statements of the passages, but it cannot be denied that they entered the Tribulation as unsaved Gentiles; otherwise, they would have been included among the saints of 1 Thess. 4:13-18. That unsaved Jews and Gentiles will be in that period is clearly stated in Jeremiah 30:3 and Ezekiel 30:3. How can one overlook so patent a proof in order to build an argument from silence, which is always precarious because of its two-edged force? It is well to remember it is not our prerogative to dictate the revelation of Scripture, but to expound it.

Moreover, it is not enough to state they are Gentile saints, leaving it to be inferred that they are saints of the church. Where does Revelation 7 or any other passage designate them as members of the church, the Body and Bride of Christ? Where is it indicated that they have been baptized into the Body of Christ (1 Cor. 12:13), the unmistakable and indispensable characteristic of believers of the church age? Furthermore, the "mysterious silence in the OT concerning the Church" is explicable on the evidence of Matthew 13:17; 16:18 ("will build"); Ephesians 1:22-23; and 3:9 ("hid in God"). In almost fifty years of research this writer has never seen an explanation from a scholar who believes that the church is in the Old Testament, implicitly or explicitly, as to how there could be a Body of Christ on earth before the Head became such in resurrection glory, lucidly stated in Ephesians 1:22-23. In the physical realm God did not create Adam a body without a head, nor in the spiritual realm would He create the Body (the church) without the resurrected, glorified Head.

In his attempt to blur dispensational distinctions, although few dispensationalists deny there is a bridging or phasing from one age to the next (see Acts 2, then 3:1), Gundry tries to find "mysteries" distinctive of the church in other ages, such as the mystery of lawlessness (2 Thess. 2:7), the mystery of God (Rev. 10:7), and the mystery of Babylon (Rev. 17:5-7), along with others. From that he concludes that the "mystery of the church" was also present in the Old Testament. As a New Testament scholar he knows well that that extrapolation cannot stand. By definition "a mystery" is something revealed, an additional disclosure to what may have been revealed in the Old Testament. However, the New Testament mystery of the church is not a parallel case; in those areas mentioned old truth was built upon, but with regard to the church it is explicitly stated that it was "hidden in God" (Eph. 3:9). The other mysteries could be hidden in the Old Testament to be further amplified and searched out; but truth "hidden in God" is entirely new in the sense of requiring a revelation from God in order to be known at all. After all that discussion, for Gundry to declare "that the Church *as such* [italics his] is never designated a mystery" is surely not apropos in the light of Ephesians 3:3-5 where the word occurs not once, but twice.[50]

In order to make a place for the church in the Tribulation period, which is a part of Israel's age, Gundry attempts to mingle those companies in the past as he claims they will be in the future. He states: "The subsequence of the revelation that Gentile converts should compose one body with the Jews (Eph. 3:3, 6) does not alter the fact that OT prophets predicted the salvation of Gentiles during the Church age."[51] The blending of things that differ reveals an amazing blind spot in his thinking. Old Testament prophets, of course, predicted the salvation of Gentiles. See, for example, Isaiah 65:1 and numerous other references. Even more, long before the galaxy of Old Testament prophets appeared, the salvation of Gentiles was undeniably foretold in Genesis 12:3. But where is there a statement or even a hint that those Gentile believers would be united inextricably with Jewish believers in an eternal Body of Christ as stated plainly in Ephesians 3:1-6? Neither in the Old Testament period nor in the Millennium are those saved groups baptized into one spiritual entity. Otherwise, what are the meaning and purpose of the "mystery" of the church? Christ's coming and finished work made more of a difference than Gundry or amillennialists like Allis (see above) are prepared to admit. And why in Luke 4:20-21 did Christ interrupt the reading of Isaiah 61:1-2 where He did, if He did not intend to illustrate dramatically a distinct change in economies in human history?

Yet the contention moves relentlessly on to say, "There are clear indications that the change from Israel to the Church took place over a prolonged period of transition dating from early in Jesus' ministry to a time posterior to Pentecost."[52] It is apropos at this point to ask why there was a need at all for Pentecost. The "entrance of grace" in John 1:17 cannot be made equivalent, as Gundry hopes, to the presence of the church on earth. There is no proof that the apostles constituted the "Church in embryo" until the Day of Pentecost, as he thinks. No wonder he adds to confusion in maintaining that, although "many features about the Church and this age are unique . . . the Scriptures also teach the essential unity of all saints."[53] It must be declared that he cannot have it both ways. Either he has a single hermeneutic, a distinction between

Israel and the church, and a consistent dispensationalism/premillennialism, or he must opt for a dual hermeneutic, a blurring of the differences between Israel and the church (see below Part Four, chap. 15), a covenant theology, and an ultimate capitulation to amillennialism. He himself realizes the affinities in his assertion: "The distinctiveness of the Church tends toward pre-tribulationism. The oneness of the Church with saints of other dispensations tends toward posttribulationism."[54] He could have added also that the latter position ("oneness" needs explication here) leads in time to covenantism and even amillennialism.

Gundry sees no incongruity with God's working simultaneously with two covenant peoples, Israel and the church, in the Tribulation, because millennialists of all kinds, including pretribulationists, recognize that the church will rule on earth in the Millennium (1 Cor. 6:2; Rev. 5:10) as well as Old Testament saints (Rev. 20:4, 6). It has escaped him that the millennial conditions do not mean tribulation for either group as is true in the time of God's wrath in the Tribulation period. Determined to blend Israel and the church in different stewardships of God's program, he cites the fact of Israel's return to the land, though in unbelief, at a time when God is still dealing with the church, as a necessary preliminary step to the predicted Tribulation.[55] But this age is not the Tribulation period by any definition of terms. Besides, God is not dealing today with Israel as a nation, but as individuals (cf. Rom. 9-11). The inescapable fact remains that the church is never spoken of as a participant in the Tribulation. Exegetical pandemonium can only result when one holds that "the tribulation knows only one group of redeemed people, the Church. The regenerate Jewish remnant will belong to the Church then as now (Rom. 11:5) and will be raptured at the posttribulational advent of Christ."[56]

Notice, first, the departure from a literal hermeneutic to a covenant position of one redeemed people for all ages. That is a logical necessity for post-tribulationism and its postulates. Second, the Jewish remnant of the church age is correctly an integral part of the Body of Christ as in Romans 11:5 and Galatians 3:28, but where is a corresponding Scripture that places the Jewish remnant of the Tribulation period in the church? Third, it is poor argumentation constantly to be begging the question. Why is it so hard to fathom that God does not have two governing principles and companies center stage, as it were, at the same time (cf. Rom. 11:6 with John 1:17)? It is no wonder that interpretive problems surface when there is gratuitous injection of a company where they are not placed by Scripture. Posttribulationism can only introduce disharmony into Scripture when it seems at the same time to accord with dispensationalism, because dispensational distinctives are entirely incompatible with dual hermeneutics and a covenantal framework.[57]

Because he knows that posttribulationism jeopardizes the biblical doctrine of imminence, he enters arguments on suddenness and unexpectedness that he believes bring the pretribulational argument to "an obvious and critical limitation."[58] That is not logical reasoning but wishful thinking on his part and another example of setting up a straw man. Next, he treats what he calls "the strongest and most extensive warnings to watch in the entire NT in the Olivet Discourse" where, he claims, Christ gave no hint of a pretribulational rapture, whereas "a very full description of the posttribulational Parousia forms the climax."[59] Here his exegesis is most reprehensible, for as an exegete he has violated the basic law of context.

First, he disregarded the point of the disciples' question: "the end of the age." The significant word "end" occurs in verses 3, 6, 13, and 14. They were not speaking of the end of the church age, in which they were not living, but the end of the then-present Jewish age. Second, Christ was not foretelling events related to the church by His use of "the holy place" (v. 15), "in Judea" (v. 16), and "on a Sabbath" (v. 20). Third, by transferring all the specifics to the church he is satisfied to come up with the climax of a "posttribulational Parousia." That is not exegesis but eisegesis. The admonitions of the Olivet Discourse cannot defensibly be identified with those of the epistles; the former refer to Israel, whereas the latter relate to the church. It is here at Matthew 24-25, by his own choosing, that his entire eschatological program receives its coup de grace. That is not putting the case too strongly, for he commits the same exegetical error in designating "the major portion of Revelation" with its Tribulation events as "signs for the Church."[60] He pursues an ignis fatuus by seeking to divorce expectancy from imminence. His posttribulational arguments and nuances are so novel, that he disagrees with Barton Payne and Ladd of his own posttribulational camp. When he argues, "If a delay in the Parousia of at least several years was compatible with expectancy in apostolic times, a delay for the several years of the tribulation is compatible with expectancy in current times. Jesus clearly indicated to the early disciples that His coming would be delayed for some time."[61] He extrapolates incorrectly.

One of the serious errors Gundry makes, as does Ladd, is in his definition of the wrath of Satan versus the wrath of God in the events of the Tribulation period. He writes, "Not until the final crisis of Armageddon . . . will God pour out His wrath upon the unregenerate. . . . The tribulation of the seventieth week has to do, then, not with God's wrath against the sinners, but with the wrath of Satan, the Antichrist, and the wicked against the saints."[62] First, how has it escaped his attention that Revelation 6:15-17 speaks of "the wrath of the Lamb," which can never be made to mean "the wrath of Satan"? Also, the wrath of God is surely indicated before Armageddon in descriptions of peace taken from the earth (6:4), death's power over the earth (6:8), convulsions in the heavenly bodies (6:12-14, esp. v. 14), and the consumption of the third of the earth, a third of the trees, and all green grass by fire (8:7). It is indicated in the turning of a third of the sea into blood (8:8), the death of a third of marine life and the destruction of a third of the ships (8:9), the embitterment of a third of the rivers and springs of waters (8:10-11), the smiting of a third of the sun, moon, and stars with consequent partial darkness both day and night (8:12), and the horrendous locust plague (9:3-11). The slaughter of a third of mankind (9:15-19) and the fall of a tenth of the city of Jerusalem (11:13), as well as the hellish authority of the beast over all earth dwellers (13:7), the slaying of those who refuse to worship the beast's image (13:15), the economic boycott of all men without the beast's name or number of his name (13:16-17), and the blood bath of the land of promise for a distance of 200 miles (14:17-20), will occur, and all before Armageddon is introduced either proleptically (16:13-16) or actually (19:17-18). Do those events picture the wrath of Satan or the wrath of God? If the former, as Gundry explicitly holds, then how in reason can these be explained: "the wrath of the Lamb" (6:16); "the great day of his wrath" (6:17); "Thy wrath came" (11:18); "the wine of the wrath of God" (14:10); "winepress of the wrath of God" (14:19)? Concerning the bowl judgments it is explicitly stated that "in them the wrath of God is finished" (15:1), not begun. It has been the experience of this writer that posttribulationists to a man fail to indicate why the church must endure the Tribulation. What is the purpose of it all? Does it perform the function of a purgatory for that one of all Christian generations? It will not satisfy the requirements of the case to attempt to mitigate the severity of the afflictions, as has been clearly demonstrated.

When Gundry attempts exegesis of passages like Luke 21:36; 1 Thessalonians 1:10; and Revelation 3:10 (especially the last reference) one recognizes a faulty exegesis. The length of the treatment of the last citation shows the stringency under which he labors.[63] The interpretation of Revelation 4:1 and the twenty-four elders constitutes a curious refuge to escape the position that they represent the church; he denies the elders are human, because for him they are "a celestial order of beings." He has departed here from an axiom of Revelation interpretation, that is, that figures and symbols in the book may be understood from their usage elsewhere in the Old and New Testaments. Where in all Scripture do elders represent nonhuman creatures?[64] He realizes how damaging to his whole argument would be the position he opposes. He would be checkmated on the spot. Once he has eliminated the church from Revelation 4:1, he finds a curious dilemma: no mention of the church in earth, in heaven, or in the air. As a scholar he should admit the precarious nature of the argument from silence, but he pursues it to the hilt, again and again.

Question after question fairly occurs to the reader. Two examples follow: "In posttribulationism, the redeemed multitude who come out of the great tribulation constitute the last generation of the Church (7:9-17)."[65] It is apropos to ask, Why was it, then, that John did not recognize them as such and had to ask their identity? Further, "To press woodenly the marital relationship of both Israel and the Church to the Lord would be to say that God is a bigamist."[66] Scripture is careful to indicate that Israel is the wife of the Lord in the Old Testament (Isa. 62:5), and the church is the Bride of Christ (never Israel, cf. Eph. 5:25-27, 32). Furthermore, he should credit students of Scripture with the knowledge that the relationships are symbolic. Dealing in oversimplifications, he sees no distinction between "Day of Christ" and "Day of the Lord." Why not include "Day of God" (2 Pet. 3)? It also is in a clearly eschatological context.[67]

After treating the three synoptic accounts of the Olivet discourse; 2 Thessalonians 1:7-10; and Revelation 19:11-16, he affirms: "These passages and 1 Thessalonians 4:16, 17 share the implication that He will come all the way down. Thus, the saints will meet Christ in the air to join in His continued descent."[68] One of the most mystifying elements in the posttribulation system, to which all its adherents adhere, is that of the continued descent of Christ and His church after the meeting in the air. What was the purpose of the catching away in the first place? What is to be accomplished by the descent either by Christ or the church? To those relevant, insistent questions the posttribulationists give no answer, but they continue the position in order to blend rapture and visible appearing (Revelation) in one to have the church continue on earth through the Tribulation.[69]

Gundry wonders why the rapture can be mentioned in John 14:1-3 and not in the Olivet discourse in view of the fact that both are in the gospels. That is, indeed, a strange dilemma for a New Testament scholar. Again, there is failure to see that John 14-17 is on church (postresurrection, 17:4) ground, whereas Matthew 24-25, as has been shown above and innumerable times by pretribulationists, are answering questions on the end of the Jewish, not church, age (Matt. 24:1-3).[70] Yet he insists there is only one place in the New Testament where the eschatological significance of "end" can be ascertained exactly, and he finds it in the Olivet discourse, a passage that has no reference to the church age, because Christ was answering questions of an altogether different nature.

In the opinion of this writer the worst exegetical oddity in the book is his treatment of John 14:1-3. Almost fifty years of close study and research in eschatology have not witnessed such an interpretation. Notice with extreme care: "He is going to prepare for them *spiritual abodes within His own person* [italics his]."[71] Imagine such a conclusion when the passage keeps stressing (see also last verses of chapter 13) "place," "places," and "Father's house"! That is the method some use to rid themselves of the reality of heaven itself. Being of undoubted orthodox persuasion, he must rid himself of such connotations. First, he declares: "Jesus could hardly have made it clearer that the abode of a disciple in the Father's house will not be a mansion in the sky, but a spiritual position in Christ."[72] He hastens to retrieve himself by this defense: "We are not to deny a literal heaven, of course." Wisdom would have indicated a far better use of words based on more solid exegesis of the context.[73]

In the discussion of the doctrine of judgment the reader is bound to be surprised that a premillennialist could maintain: "The understanding of one general judgment at the end of the millennium does not merit the designation 'amillennial,' for the early champions of premillennialism in modern times held to this view."[74] First, if the position of one general judgment does not merit the designation "amillennial," what does it merit? His saying so does not make it so. Second, has the amillennial literature been carefully studied? Third, if the champions of premillennialism were early, how could they be in modern times? Fourth, strangely, the statement concerning the alleged champions appears without the needed documentation. Fifth, has it not been firmly stated above that posttribulationism has an affinity toward amillennialism plus a dual hermeneutic plus covenantism?

In reading polemical works it is always wise to search diligently until the catalyst or actuating cause for the writing is discovered. In this case it surfaces in these words: "This is mentioned only lest too much stock be placed in the present popularity of pretribulationism within a large segment of American evangelicalism."[75]

NOTES

[1]H. C. Thiessen, "Notes On the Dispensational Approach to the Bible."
[2]N. B. Harrison, *His Sure Return*, pp. 32-42.
[3]E. M. Milligan, *Is the Kingdom Age at Hand?* pp. 194, 197, 262.
[4]H. Alford, *The Greek Testament*, 4:624, col. 1.
[5]R. B. Girdlestone, *The Grammar of Prophecy*, p. 138.
[6]A. J. McClain, *The Greatness of the Kingdom*, pp. 465-66, 472.
[7]J. B. Payne, *The Imminent Appearing of Christ*, p. 7.
[8]Ibid.
[9]Ibid., p. 14.
[10]Ibid., p. 35.
[11]Ibid., p. 36.
[12]For a detailed discussion see Part Four, chap. 17.
[13]See the elaborate treatment in Part Four, chap. 18.
[14]Payne, *Imminent Appearing of Christ*, p. 36.
[15]Ibid., pp. 37-38.
[16]Ibid., p. 38. Among the writers he cites Alexander Reese and George Ladd.
[17]Ibid., p. 39.
[18]Ibid., p. 41.
[19]G. E. Ladd, *The Blessed Hope*, p. 8.

[20]Compare the approaches and conclusions of Barton Payne and Ladd, both posttribulationists. As for the historical argument, it may well be asked whether those scholars hold to the teaching of baptismal regeneration, which was so rife in the early church. See ibid., pp. 10-11.

[21]Ibid., p. 11.

[22]Ibid., p. 13.

[23]Ibid.

[24]Ibid., p. 19.

[25]Ibid., pp. 19-20.

[26]Ibid., pp. 20-31. He confuses tribulation(s) with the Great Tribulation, a grave error that confuses the whole issue of the rapture (esp. p. 21). His evaluation, that if the church is prepared with faith fixed in God, it need not dread the Tribulation, reveals a lack of comprehension of the actual gravity of the Tribulation period (p. 24).

[27]Ibid., p. 31.

[28]Ibid., p. 45 ff.

[29]Ibid., p. 51.

[30]Ibid., pp. 62-63.

[31]J. F. Walvoord, *The Rapture Question*, p. 8. In 1945 the present writer was discussing theological areas with Dr. Lewis Sperry Chafer, founder and first president of Dallas Theological Seminary. Dr. Chafer calmly said, "The center of conflict in theology between orthodox men in the foreseeable future will be the relation of the Rapture to the Tribulation period." At the time the writer thought Dr. Chafer was overreacting to certain publications at the time, so the subject was not pursued. But the more than a quarter of a century since then has proved that he spoke with his usual insight and foresight.

[32]Ibid., p. 10.

[33]Ibid., pp. 39, 43. Furthermore, where are they said to be baptized of the Holy Spirit? Cf. 1 Cor. 12:13.

[34]Ibid., p. 52.

[35]Ibid., pp. 53-54.

[36]Ibid., p. 89.

[37]Ibid., p. 93.

[38]Ibid., pp. 95, 127.

[39]Ibid., pp. 143-45. It must be stressed that "the precise teaching of the translation of the Church is never found in passages dealing with the return of Christ to establish His kingdom on earth" (ibid., pp. 169-70, 199).

[40]R. H. Gundry, *The Church and the Tribulation.*

[41]Ibid., pp. 9-10.

[42]Ibid.

43Ibid., p. 10.

44Ibid.

45Ibid., pp. 10-11.

46Ibid., p. 12.

47Ibid.

48Ibid., pp. 12-13, 13.

49Ibid., p. 14. The passages he cites do not deal with the church.

50Ibid., p. 16.

51Ibid., p. 19.

52Ibid., pp. 19, 21.

53Ibid., pp. 21-22.

54Ibid., p. 23.

55Ibid., p. 24, also p. 26. His questions concerning the witnesses of the gospel of the kingdom from among Israel are clearly answered in Rev. 6:9-11, as well as in Matt. 24:14, where the issue is the end of Israel's age. Cf. p. 27.

56Ibid., p. 28.

57Ibid., pp. 29-33.

58Ibid., pp. 33-34.

59Ibid., pp. 36-37.

60Ibid., p. 37.

61Ibid., pp. 45-49.

62Yet that is precisely the argument in ibid., pp. 49, 51. He must admit, too, as we have claimed above: "Some have turned from pre- to post-tribulationism and finally to amillennialism" [as in Canada, England, and the USA], ibid., p. 52.

63Ibid., pp. 53 ff. Rev. 3:10 alone is discussed from pp. 54-61.

64Ibid., p. 70.

65Ibid., p. 78.

66Ibid., pp. 80, 85.

67Ibid., p. 97.

68Ibid., p. 104.

69See the fuller discussion below in Part Four, chapter 17. In that area Gundry follows Reese's argument, ibid.

70Ibid., pp. 134-35.

71Ibid., p. 154.

72Ibid., p. 155.

73Ibid.

74 b ., pp. 163-64.

75Ibid., p. 185.

11

The Millennium

All premillennialists consistently hold that the coming of Christ in glory will usher in the long-awaited and covenanted kingdom of the son of David. They find the closing and final links of the chain of their evidence in the book of Revelation. Let us turn now to a consideration of the book. As might be expected, the amillennialists and premillennialists differ widely upon the interpretation of Revelation. Perhaps that is the point of greatest difference between the two views of biblical interpretation. Milton S. Terry claims that no other portion of the Word of God has been more controverted and variously interpreted than the book of Revelation.[1]

There are certain preliminary considerations in the treatment of the book that ought to be touched upon here. First, the book is not apocryphal (lit., hidden), but it is a revelation, a disclosure. Many amillennialists seek to evade the force of much of the teaching found in the book by referring to the "obscure" nature of the book. If the book is meant to reveal and disclose, how can it be said to be obscure? God is not hiding the person of Christ in the book, but He is, on the contrary, unveiling Him in all His beauty and glory. Second, the place of the book in the canon is of great importance. It presupposes all that goes before it. For a proper and adequate interpretation of the Apocalypse, the entire Word must be studied. It is the culmination and capstone of the whole revelation of God. Third, the message is "signified," which means it is conveyed by means of signs. Fourth, it is expressly spoken of as a prophecy.[2] Finally, the idea of completion runs throughout the book, being brought out by the repeated use of the number seven, the number of dispensational fullness.

There are at least four general hermeneutical approaches to the book of Revelation. The first view is known as the *historical.* It holds that the message gives the entire history of the church and pictures the antagonism of the forces of evil in the world against the church. The *preterist* approach interprets the greater part of the prophecies as having been fulfilled in the struggles of the past, particularly in the conflict of the church with the Roman Empire. Those who explain the Revelation *ideally,* or *spiritually,* see in the book nothing more nor less than the final triumph of truth over error. The *futurist view,* to which this writer adheres with the great majority of premillennialists, maintains that all is future and prophetic from chapter four to the end. It is evident that not all of those views can be defended with equal satisfaction to the one who is persuaded of the literal interpretation of Scripture.

A fourfold purpose is discernible for the writing of the book. (1) It was meant to encourage believers in times of the great Roman persecutions by showing them the final victory of Christ. (2) It aims to confirm all of the Old Testament prophecies and to add to them in regard to the future. (3) It purposes to present an unveiling of the Lord Jesus Christ. It is remarkable how that purpose of the book is lost sight of. In the many controversies and debates over the details of the book, the person of Christ, whom the book is intended primarily to unveil and reveal, is relegated to an insignificant place, if He is not neglected altogether. (4) The book aims to show how Christ enters upon His terrestrial purchased possession and comes into the actual investiture with His rightful kingdom. Such a book, then, will bear close and diligent scrutiny.

The imagery of the book of Revelation is a phase of the interpretation of the book that is vital, because it is made the basis, not only for various and conflicting opinions, but it is used as an excuse to rid some of the admission of the existence of the doctrine of the Millennium in the Apocalypse. Caldwell sees in the book, for the most part, a series of repetitions descriptive of the period between the first and second advents of the Lord.[3] Kuyper admits first that he believes in the authenticity of the book, but he finds it impossible to harmonize a literal interpretation of the book and its figures with the plain teachings of Christ.[4] He notes that it was for that very reason—that is, the attempt was made in the early church to harmonize a literal interpretation of the book with the rest of the New Testament teaching—that the Revelation had such a late admission into the canon. Mains feels that John cannot possibly be made to speak of things relative to the twentieth century, because the book is full of hyperbole of the first Oriental order.[5] The purpose for which that style was used was to give the message impulse and drive into the hearts of those who read the book. In that and similar fashion is the imagery of the book employed to allow for all kinds of interpretations of the contents of the message. Perhaps as unfounded a view as any is that of Warfield, who when writing on the Millennium and the Revelation, says: "The ascertainment of the meaning of the Apocalypse is a task, that is to say, not directly of verbal criticism but of sympathetic imagination: the teaching of the book lies not immediately in its words, but in the wide vistas its visions open to the fancy."[6]

Imagine interpreting the Word of God by "sympathetic imagination!" That certainly is taking unwarranted advantage of the imagery of the book. It is preferable to hold with Girdlestone[7] and Ironside[8] that there is no figure or symbol in the book but what is explained, alluded to, or found in germ somewhere else in the Scriptures. As for the numbers found in the book, they are to be treated as all numbers are in the figurative and symbolic passages of the Bible; that is to say, they are to be given their literal value, and then the figure or symbol is to be drawn from that. There are literally seven stars, seven lampstands, seven epistles, seven churches, seven spirits, seven seals, seven trumpets, seven bowls, and seven plagues. Any symbolism that may be gleaned from those cannot change the seven to ten or five or any other number. The reason numbers symbolize anything in the Apocalypse is because of their literal character. Let that suffice for the presence of imagery in the book.

For many interpreters, the book of Revelation has no order whatsoever, but that is a strange anomaly, for the book has a well-defined order. It is, in the view of many, one of the most orderly books in the Bible, Delitzsch in speaking of the Apocalypse said that it represented the Old Testament eschatology placed in its "future temporal succession and order."[9] From that angle the book becomes the key to prophetic study. In seeking to find the plan of the book, one is met at the very outset with the needed outline. In the nineteenth verse of the first chapter the apostle is told to write the things he has seen, the things that are, and the things that will be hereafter. That forms the threefold scheme of the book, and it is in that order that the revelation of the future things proceeds.[10]

The things John had "seen" were the glorified and resurrected Lord Jesus, the seven stars, and the seven lampstands. The "things which are" included the seven messages to the churches in Ephesus, Smyrna, Pergamum, Thyatira, Sardis, Philadelphia, and Laodicea. Those seven churches of proconsular Asia bear their message for the whole church age, as has been noted before. There are several divisions under the "things which shall be hereafter." First, the rapture of the church takes place. Then follows the seventieth week of Daniel or the Tribulation period from chapter four to nineteen. There are parenthetical visions, to be sure, as in chapters 7 and 14, but they can be discerned from the subject matter and the context in which they are found. They in no way hinder the orderly progress of the revelation. The twentieth chapter speaks of the Millennium, and the last two chapters deal with eternity to come. Could anyone expect the last book of the Bible to be more orderly? The book of Revelation rounds out the Word of God in a perfect way.

Since the twentieth chapter deals with the kingdom, or the Millennium, it must be researched carefully.[11] Before doing so, however, one should consider the proleptic view of the kingdom given in the eleventh chapter. The earlier part of the chapter speaks of the ministry and fortunes of the two witnesses, after which the second woe is announced. Then follows the seventh trumpet sound when great voices in heaven are heard saying: "The kingdoms [better, "kingdom"] of this world [lit., world-system] are become the kingdoms [better, "is become the kingdom"] of our Lord, and of his Christ; and he shall reign for ever and ever" (v. 15). The twentieth chapter reads:

> And I saw an angel come down from heaven, having the key of the bottomless pit and a great chain in his hand. And he laid hold on the dragon, that old serpent, which is the Devil, and Satan, and bound him a thousand years, and cast him into the bottomless pit, and shut him up, and set a seal upon him, that he should deceive the nations no more, till the thousand years should be fulfilled: and after that he must be loosed a little season. And I saw thrones, and they sat upon them, and judgment was given unto them: and I saw the souls of them that were beheaded for the witness of Jesus, and for the word of God, and which had not worshipped the beast, neither his image, neither had received his mark upon their foreheads, or in their hands; and they lived and reigned with Christ a thousand years. But the rest of the dead lived not again until the thousand years were finished. This is the first resurrection. Blessed and holy is he that hath part in the first resurrection: On such the second death hath no power, but they shall be priests of God and of Christ, and shall reign with him a thousand years (vv. 1-6).

All the Old Testament prophecies that spoke of a kingdom were at one in declaring that it would not be brought about except by the visible presence of the King. In chapter 19 of the Revelation Christ is seen returning to earth in glory as King of Kings and Lord of Lords. What does there remain to be fulfilled yet before the kingdom is ushered in? Nothing whatever. So we find accordingly that after the binding of Satan, the saints reign with the King for a thousand years. The first resurrection is complete before the thousand years begin. All Old Testament saints are raised some time after the Tribulation, probably immediately after, according to Daniel 12:2, which follows the prophet's word on the time of trouble (12:1). All New Testament saints that fell asleep in Jesus were raised at the rapture when the living saints were changed and caught up. There remains now only the question of the resurrection of the saints martyred during the Tribulation period. It is found in the twentieth chapter now before us. The reason the other groups are not mentioned as raised here is that their resurrection has been spoken of elsewhere and has already been accomplished. For a prophecy to be certain of fulfillment it is necessary that God mention it once. That makes it as steadfast as if it were recorded many times.

In the first seven verses of the chapter the phrase "thousand years" is referred to six times. From those references the word "millennium" is derived. But millennium and kingdom indicate exactly the same ideas. What is the addition of Revelation 20 to the doctrine of the Millennium, above what has been studied concerning the kingdom in the Old Testament? Or is one constrained to believe that here is the first and only mention of a millennial reign of Christ? With the Old Testament study of the kingdom fully in mind, the answer with unreserved confidence is that Revelation 20 is neither the first nor sole mention of the reign of Christ.

But the passage does add something: the time period of the kingdom reign. All other prophecies of the kingdom mentioned it and described it with great detail, but never once spoke of the length of time that it would cover. That fact is revealed in this passage. Instead of giving the whole doctrine of the Millennium, then, the text adds only the last element of the time. The termini of the age are brought before us in the passage. They are the premillennial coming of Christ, the premillennial resurrection of martyred saints and of Old Testament saints, the premillennial judgment of Israel, and the premillennial binding of Satan. They also include the postmillennial resurrection of the wicked, the postmillennial loosing of Satan and his final doom, and the postmillennial judgment of all the wicked dead. Between those termini, well-defined and clear, is the thousand-year reign of the King with His Bride and His subjects.

When the Old Testament prophecies were surveyed to find in them confirmation of the Davidic covenant, again and again the characteristics of the millennial age were touched upon. But the treatment was far from systematized in a definite order, because every prophet interspersed—as is the case with all doctrines of the Bible—here and there throughout his message different characteristics of the kingdom. We shall now gather them up to receive the full force of their combined and harmonious testimony. In this discussion Nathaniel West will be followed, though not exclusively.[12]

Satan, the great deceiver and adversary, will be cast into the bottomless pit for the entire period of the kingdom. In that age God will be testing man to see if, even with Satan out of the way to tempt and harass him no longer, he will be acceptable before God. The uprising at the end of the age will reveal the failure of man again. With Satan consigned to the pit, the nations everywhere will be out of the power of Satan. There will be no more rival kingdoms or a succession of kingdoms. The stone that becomes the mountain will break all others to pieces (Dan. 2:44-45). Christ's reign will be undisputed and unhindered from opposition from any other government or reign on earth. There will be no cause for a divided allegiance to God's King, the Man of His choice.

The false religious cults and systems that are springing up now everywhere on such a colossal scale will be done away with, and the knowledge of God will cover the earth as the waters cover the seas (Isa. 11:9). No man will need to instruct his fellow man in the things of God, for they will all know Him from the least to the greatest (Jer. 31:31-34). Israel will be restored to Jehovah, purged from her sin (Ezek. 36:24-27). The days of her wandering will have come to a close. The prophecy of Daniel 9 will be operative in the life history of Israel: transgression finished, sins ended, iniquity atoned for, and everlasting righteousness and holiness effected. War will exist no more; all nations will be at peace under the rule and righteous reign of the Prince of Peace (Isa. 2:2-4; Zech. 9:9-10). There cannot and will not be peace until He comes to govern in peace. Vain are the peace plans of men without the presence of the King to rule in peace.

Nature will be rejuvenated, and harmony will once more reign (Isa. 35:1; Rom. 8:19-22). The curse will be removed from the ground, and the desert and wilderness will be abundantly fruitful and productive (Zech. 14:11). Animal creation also will experience a change in which animals of rapacious appetites will become meek and tame. The age of man will be lengthened, for a man of one hundred years will be esteemed but a child (Isa. 65:20).[13] No longer will there be a division in the midst of Israel, but Israel and Judah will be united and will dwell together in their own land of blessing (Ezek. 37:15-22).

The coming of the King to the Mount of Olives will bring about physical changes in the land that will alter its contour (Zech. 14:9-10). The city of Jerusalem will be built again, adorned, and be fruitful as never before (Zech. 1:16-17; 2:4-5).[14] The nations in the kingdom will recognize the favored condition of Israel when God wipes away forever their reproach and uses them in the conversion of the Gentiles (Zech. 8:20-23). The land will be redistributed among the twelve tribes, and the Temple will be rebuilt with the sacrifices, as memorials, reinstituted (Ezek. 40-48).[15] Yearly the nations will go up to Jerusalem to worship the Lord in the Feast of Tabernacles (Zech. 14:16-19). The Bride of Christ will reign with Him, and Israel will also rule over the nations under the direct command of the King. All nations will dwell in obedience and submission to the righteous King. Surely that partial picture—for it is only that—of the millennial age and its characteristic features should suffice to show that not only is that age not in progress now on the earth, but it has never been. It is definitely and conclusively a future age.

Before this chapter on the Millennium is concluded, a glance at the purpose of the age and the events following it will be helpful. The aim of God in the millennial age will be to test man with a last test to see if he will serve and obey Him. He has been tested in innocency, under conscience, under human government, under promise, under law; he is being tested now under distinctive grace. Then he will be tested in an age of righteousness. The test will show whether man under the most favorable of circumstances—with Satan bound and rendered harmless, with a renovated earth, with a harmony present throughout nature, and with the righteous King ruling and governing in righteousness, judgment, and justice—can be found to be well-pleasing in the sight of God. Man will fail, for he will still have the sin nature present with him. Another purpose of the age will be to fulfill God's oath and promise to David. God declared time and time again that He would not lie to David. The millennial reign will prove that He did not lie to him. A third purpose, perhaps included in the one just mentioned, will be to fulfill all the numberless prophecies of the Old Testament to Israel for her blessing. If the kingdom age is never to be realized, what do we make of the immutability of the counsels of His will? If the kingdom age is being realized now, how is the Bible to be understood in any of its statements of fact? If God promises Israel a literal kingdom and then gives the world a spiritualized kingdom in this present age, what becomes of the promises of God? We prefer to rest the case here with the concluding word that the Millennium is followed by the uprising of Satan and his hosts, the judgment of the wicked, and the new heavens and the new earth. The premillennial view of interpretation consistently adds link upon link to a long chain of evidence, reaching directly from Genesis to Revelation. It proves that the Word of God teaches a literal, actual, and world-wide Millennium, or kingdom age, under the personal reign of the King, the matchless and peerless son of David.

Notes

[1]M. S. Terry, *Biblical Hermeneutics,* p. 466.
[2]After Augustine's time and throughout the Middle Ages, the Revelation was interpreted on so-called spiritual lines. His amillennial view was that the thousand years started with the earthly ministry of Christ and would continue to the end of the church age. That became the "predominant interpretation" (G. E. Ladd, *The Blessed Hope,* p. 31). But with the beginning of the nineteenth century there came a movement that returned to the original position of the church, that is, the futurist view of the Revelation. That strong reaction affirmed the importance of the second coming of Christ with emphasis on the place of His earthly kingdom after His return (ibid., p. 35). Before long many periodicals and books appeared that treated the exposition of prophecy and the "heralding [of] the imminent return of Christ" (ibid.).
[3]L. S. Chafer, *Must We Dismiss The Millennium?* p. 5.
[4]A. Kuyper, *Chiliasm or the Doctrine of Premillennialism,* pp. 11, 12.
[5]G. P. Mains, *Premillennialism,* pp. 24, 39.
[6]B. B. Warfield, "The Millennium and the Revelation," p. 646, in *Biblical Doctrines* (N.Y. 1929), pp. 643-64. That chapter is a reprint of an article in *The Princeton Theological Review* 2 (1904): 599-617. Strange language this is for one who believed so strongly in the infallibility and inerrancy of the inscripturated Word.
[7]R. G. Girdlestone, *The Grammar of Prophecy,* pp. 48-53.
[8]H. A. Ironside, *Lectures on the Book of Revelation,* pp. 13-14.
[9]Fuller bibliographic data not available.
[10]Hughes's view is totally insupportable, when he finds fault with another age

beyond the present age in a millennial era, because the New Testament speaks of believers now upon whom "the ends of the world are come" (1 Cor. 10:11). To oppose the Millennium "as the climactic age of human history" on such flimsy basis reveals poor exegesis indeed of Paul's statement (P. E. Hughes, *Interpreting Prophecy,* pp. 126-28). The Millennium is decidedly the culminating of all human history, because in it is found the vindication of (1) God's covenant to David (2 Sam. 7:10-17), (2) His promise to saints of this age (2 Tim. 2:11-13), (3) His declaration of the utter subjugation of all sin and sinners (1 Cor. 15:24-28), (4) His promise of the renovation of the earth (Isa. 35:1-10), (5) His prediction of the liberation of all animal creation (Isa. 11:6-9; Rom. 8:19-22), (6) His promise of sovereignty to His people Israel (Deut. 26:19; 28:1, 13; Isa. 60:5, 10, 12, 14, 16; Dan. 7:22, 27) in their regenerate condition (Ezek. 36:23-29; 37:26-28; Rom. 11:25-27) on their own land (Isa. 49:11-20; Jer. 23:7, 8; Ezek. 37:25; Amos 9:14-15), (7) His declared commitment to the exaltation of Christ (Luke 24:25-26; 1 Cor. 15:24-28; Phil. 2:5-11; Rev. 19:11-16).

[11]McClain has correctly observed: "There have been minor differences among premillennial interpreters with reference to some details of Revelation 20, but these are as nothing when compared to the confusion which reigns among postmillennial and amillennial writers who attempt to expound the chapter" (A. J. McClain, *The Greatness of the Kingdom,* p. 476). He has further pointed out the overall salient features of the pivotal chapter: "The unique contributions of Revelation 20 are at least two: first, a *chronology* of the coming Kingdom; and, second, a concise *outline* [italics his] of constitutive events in their proper order, so clear that there should be no cause for misunderstanding" (ibid., pp. 476-77).

[12]N. West, *The Thousand Years in Both Testaments,* pp. 286-94.

[13]According to the prophetic Scriptures, even sickness will not be known any longer (Isa. 33:24). Hoekema finds fault with premillennialists and with the New Scofield Reference Bible in particular, because they interpret Isa. 65:17-25, so that verse 17 refers to the new heavens and new earth, whereas verses 18-25 describe millennial conditions. For him such exegesis is capricious or arbitrary, to say the least (Clouse, *The Meaning of the Millennium,* pp. 174-76). But note that verse 17 specifically mentions "I create new heavens and a new earth." However, verses 18-25 indicate terrestrial, this-worldly elements—Jerusalem, infants, old men, a hundred years, death, houses, vineyards with their fruit, the days of a tree, the wolf, the lamb, the lion, the bullock, the dust as the serpent's food, and God's holy mountain, indeed, all features of this mundane world. McClain, furthermore, answers Hoekema's argument long before the latter wrote it: "It is apparent . . . that Isaiah saw *together* [italics his] on the

screen of prophecy both the Millennial Kingdom and the Eternal Kingdom; but he expands in detail the former because it is the 'nearest-coming'
event and leaves the latter for fuller description in a later New Testament
revelation" (McClain, p. 138). Allegorization in the interpretation of
Scripture is never called for.

Ladd objects to the "Jewishness of the millennial kingdom." He claims, "This
is made impossible by Hebrews 8:13" (Clouse, p. 94). Two observations
may be made here: (1) A careful exegesis of Hebrews 8:13 will show a
contrast is being made between the age of law and the age of the church,
not between the church age and the kingdom age; (2) it is interesting to
recall that in Ladd's earlier work on crucial matters of the kingdom, he did
yeomanly service in support of the "Jewishness of the millennial kingdom."

Hughes summarily dismisses the Temple of Ezekiel 40-48 thus: "The fact,
however, that throughout the book of Ezekiel there is so much detailed
and graphic imagery makes it intrinsically unlikely that the prophet's vision
of the temple is meant to be interpreted in a literal manner" (Hughes, p.
129). It is noteworthy that not once does he give his own interpretation of
those nine chapters, an important division of that great prophetic book
(cf. this author's, *The Prophecy of Ezekiel*). He only expresses opposition to
"a reversion to Judaism" (who advocates this?), and disallows a com-
memorative offering of sacrifices because of "the sacrament of holy communion." Although the church has commemorated the death, resurrection, and coming again of Christ in the Lord's Supper, Israel evidently is
allowed no memorial of any kind. Hughes says further, "But people do
not commemorate one who is present with them. . . . This being so, it
does not make sense to talk of commemoration" (Hughes, p. 130). A few
observations are in order. First, if we want to be strictly accurate, we need
to recall that Christ instituted the Lord's Supper in the very presence of
the disciples. Could He not have easily instructed them in that commemoration without actually performing it? Second, is not Christ in us and
with us when we gather to celebrate the blessed Lord's Supper? Third, it is
never ours to dictate what should be revealed, but to interpret and expound the content of the revelation. What is Hughes' interpretation of
Ezekiel 40-48? For him the vision of the Temple corresponds to the new
heaven and new earth in Revelation. He maintains that on the basis of the
chronological [?] sequence of Ezekiel 38, 39, and 40-48. In Revelation 20
the Gog and Magog episode (equated with those of Ezek. 38-39 in spite of
clear geographical delineations in Ezekiel) is followed by the new heaven
and new earth, so q.e.d. To justify his handling of the passage, he affirms,
"Premillennialists, however, disregard the significance of this sequence in
Ezekiel's prophecy" (Hughes, p. 132). One wonders about the depth of

research that could come to such an unfounded statement.

The chronological sequence in Ezekiel, according to premillenarians, is this: after denunciations against Israel for their sins and predictions of judgment, chapters 36 and 37 (which Hughes does not touch) detailedly present the regathering, reunion of Judah and Israel, and the regeneration of the nation with blessing flowing out to the nations of the world; chapters 38 and 39 predict the invasion of resettled Israel from the north (not all parts of the world) with its neighboring allies and the subsequent thoroughgoing judgment on the godless invaders; chapters 40-48 in perfect sequence set forth in detail the distribution of the land among the tribes and the carefully ordered worship in the land of Israel during the Millennium.

Hughes and fellow amillenarians fail to see that the Temple of Ezekiel is on earth and not commensurate with the eternal new heavens and new earth (ibid, p. 132). In fairness it must be stated that some premillenarians deny sacrifices in the Millennium (Clouse, p. 26). How consistent to view Old Testament sacrifices as promissory notes (Rom. 3:25) of the coming all-sufficient redemption, and millennial sacrifices as receipts. Amillennialists reveal a remarkable parallel to the disciples in Christ's day: the latter wanted to overleap an age (Acts 1:6), and the former today overleap the consummating millennial age by passing from the kingdom of grace to the kingdom of glory, omitting the kingdom of righteousness in the glorious reign of Christ on His rightful earthly throne (Matt. 25:31).

Part Three
Analysis of the Amillennial System

12
The Covenant of Grace

The literature on the subject of the amillennial approach to the Scriptures, compared with the numerous works on the premillennial position, is rather scanty. Some have thought that, since there is a comparative lack of literature on the amillennial interpretation of the Bible, the view itself is a very recent one. The view is not recent, although it has come into greater prominence in recent years. That can be explained from the fact that the two views that held the center of conflict for many, many years, were the premillennial and postmillennial. In point of time, the amillennial view was in existence before Daniel Whitby ever presented his "new hypothesis."[1] In fact, B. B. Warfield is quoted as having once said that the amillennial view "has the best right to be called the historic Protestant view." Some of its advocates, if not all, find seeds for such a view in the teachings of Augustine in the fourth century of the history of the church.

In our own day many of the postmillennialists have gone to the amillennialist camp, even though they are designated in some quarters by their former name. Of the three main works on the amillennial view—there are, to be sure, some articles and shorter discussions—the fullest discussion of the subject is to be found in the work of Masselink entitled *Why Thousand Years?* The other two works on the subject are *The Future of the Kingdom* by Wyngaarden to whom we have already referred, and *The Pauline Eschatology* by Vos. The latter was the teacher of both Masselink and Wyngaarden. The reason we mention that fact is that in general the view held by Vos, considered by all as the outstanding amillennial authority of the day, is that held by his pupils. They show in their works traces of their teacher's opinions and positions.

In our discussion, in order to give a fair and impartial presentation of the amillennial approach, we follow the work of Masselink. It is held by amillennialists themselves to be an able exposition of their side of the question. The works of Vos and Wyngaarden also deal with circumscribed phases of the subject and not the whole field. In the one case Pauline eschatology is the theme of discussion; in the other, the general method of spiritualizing interpretation with regard to the elements of the kingdom. Surely we shall not have a partial presentation of the opposing view, if the exponents of it themselves are allowed to speak for themselves in their own way.

Masselink's treatment of the subject starts out with an appreciation of the premillennial position as a happy contrast and antidote for modernism, as a warning against the present tendency in the church to an unscriptural optimism in spite of the evident apostasy, as a proper reemphasis of the truth of the second coming of Christ, as a protest against the lack of spirituality in many churches, and as a stimulus to the eschatological research of the Scriptures. So much may be true of the premillennial view, but it is deficient, he claims, in its whole scheme of Scripture interpretation. We are inclined to ask how the premillennial view could do all he says it does, and then be so sadly lacking in the vital matter of biblical interpretation as a whole, but we turn to a setting forth of his position.

After he points out the main feature of the millennial doctrine and its history through the ages of the church, he takes time to deal with the supposed error of explaining the Scriptures in a literal manner. He assails the dispensationalism of the Scofield Bible as contradicting and denying the organic development of the revelation of God, as well as the unity of the entire Word. With considerable pains he sets forth the progressive character of the organic revelation of God. Just as there is gradual growth from the blade to the ear then to the full grain in the ear, so with the seed thoughts in the Bible. That is illustrated by the first prophecy of redemption to be found in Genesis 3:15. To that germinal thought were added later in due order and in differing form all the Old Testament Messianic prophecies from Genesis 49:10 on through the book of the prophets. Each step along the way presupposes that which has gone before and then adds something more.

The organic and progressive revelation of God consists in a unified plan of salvation through covenant relationship. The salvation of Scripture is dependent everywhere and at all times upon the covenant of grace. God never deals with man under any circumstances except by means of a covenant agreement. Adam was first dealt with in the Garden of Eden under the terms of the covenant of works. When that was broken and abrogated, God made another covenant, the covenant of grace, with the last representative of the race, the last Adam. That covenant is said to be made in the blood of Christ, hence we find the expression "the blood of the everlasting covenant." It is only by entrance into the covenant of grace that there is any hope for men throughout the history of mankind. It is the only basis upon which God will condescend at any time to deal with men and have communion and fellowship with them. The many times the word "covenant" is to be found in the New Testament is proof that it is of primary significance. The entire religion of the Bible is a covenant religion, and all God's dealings on earth with man are upon the principles to be found in the covenant.

It has been noted that the covenant of works was made with Adam before his fall. When he by disobedience fell, God could no longer deal with him on the basis of that covenant. He had forfeited any benefit that the covenant could afford him or his posterity, since he represented the whole race of mankind. What was to be done now? God must have another covenant in order to be able to deal with man at all. The covenant of works was then displaced and superseded by the covenant of grace. In its more circumscribed sense the agreement was made between God the Father and Christ as the head of the church, which is His Body. In its broadest sense the contract was made between the three Persons of the Godhead and believers and their seed. Under the first sense, then, we find such analogies in Scripture as "the vine and the branches" and the "head and the body." In the second sense, God's relationship with Israel is always viewed as a covenant relationship. When the New Testament identifies the Christian church with the true Israel of Old Testament times, all believers are then recognized as children of Abraham, with whom first the covenant of grace was formally established. What happened to the covenant of grace from the time of Adam to the time of Abraham if it was only formally established with the latter? And their children as well?

But the covenant of grace itself is in turn based upon what is called the council of peace or the covenant of redemption. That covenant was made within the Godhead between God the Father, God the Son, and God the Holy Spirit. It is not mentioned frequently in Scripture, but traces of it are seen throughout the revelation of God. At that time Christ agreed to effect the work of redemption, and for it God the Father promised Him the Messianic glory as an everlasting reward. That is, then, the foundation for the covenant of grace. The Last Adam agreed to die for the sin of the world, and in actually doing so ratified the covenant agreement made with the Father before the world began. Both the Father and the Son are now bound by the covenant. The only part of it that remained to be accomplished in time was completed when Christ cried: "It is finished." Now it stands steadfast and firm forever. That is the basis for the covenant of grace. A surer foundation it could not have.

The first actual revelation of the covenant of grace is to be found in Genesis 3:15. In that instance God placed Himself on the side of His fallen creature and assured him of victory over the devil and his powers. The verse predicts an endless hatred between the church and the world, which God Himself placed there. It is also to be noted from the text that Satan, by attempting to undo the Son of Man, works out his own destruction; for in seeking to bruise the heel of the woman's seed, he has his own head crushed. In that promise the defeat of the powers of darkness is guaranteed, a partial fulfillment of which took place at the cross of Calvary, and the complete fulfillment of which will be effected at the return of the Lord Jesus to put down the last enemy.

] 195 [

We are next told that the covenant of grace appears in the time of Noah. After God had brought a flood upon the earth because of the insufferable wickedness and corruption of the heart of man, He promised never to destroy the world again with a flood. As long as the earth remains, the Word of God assures us, there will be seed-time, harvest, cold, heat, summer, winter, day, and night. That agreement is called the covenant of nature, but it is really closely related to the covenant of grace, because God made it for the sake of His church. When the church of God is complete, the covenant of nature will be consummated and the world will come to its end as Peter tells us in his second epistle. The covenant of nature is, therefore, one of the auxiliaries of the covenant of grace and one of the media for its realization.

In the time of the patriarch Abraham the covenant of grace comes again into the greatest prominence. It is formally established with Abraham, and he is given the covenant sign, which is circumcision. The covenant is instituted between Abraham and his seed as an everlasting covenant. Peter is said to refer to that when he spoke of the promise to Israel and their children and all that were afar off. For the assertion that the Abrahamic Covenant was not exclusively national, proof is advanced along several lines. Premillennialists, who are extreme in their position, are supposed to deny the lasting nature of the covenant and make it merely a national covenant with Israel. The first proof adduced that the covenant is not exclusively national is that Israel as a nation was not actually organized until the time of Moses, which is some four hundred years after the establishment of the covenant with Abraham. Second, to say that God had in mind merely a national seed for Abraham is to undervalue the great spiritual blessings included in the covenant.

The words "to be a God unto thee and to thy seed after thee" contain all the future blessings of the covenant of grace. In it are included regeneration, eternal life, forgiveness of sins, and many other unmentioned blessings. Moreover, the sign and seal of the covenant, the rite of circumcision, meant more than an indication of membership in the commonweath of Israel. It set forth cleansing from sin and removal of the uncleanness of the flesh. That that is the spiritual meaning of circumcision is brought out time and time again in the New Testament. In the first instance, circumcision had a spiritual significance and not a national one. Finally, circumcision was a seal to Abraham of the righteousness of faith. It was God's appointed way of manifesting to Abraham that he was a believer and approved of Him. The covenant of grace established with Abraham was exactly the same as revealed to Adam and later spoken of by Peter as including the promise of eternal salvation to the true Israel and their children after them.

But the covenant of grace is not to be thought of as discontinued during the period of Moses. When God revealed Himself as the "I AM THAT I AM," He meant to imply that He was the unchangeable covenant-keeping God. His purpose now was to keep His promise with regard to the land, thus showing the covenant made at Mount Sinai to be "essentially the same" as that first set forth in Eden and continued to Abraham. The Mosaic period may emphasize the Law, but it must be remembered that it is with the most gracious design.

The Law, it is claimed, meant to teach the people of Israel a beneficial rule of life and show them the need of Christ. It is true that that was not realized in the lives of the carnal in Israel, but God is not to blame. He intended to lead them to repentance. In truth, the Law was God's way of manifesting grace to Israel along several lines. It helped them to understand more clearly God's attributes of mercy and justice; it gave them an insight into God's method of atoning for sins; it provided them with a sanctuary, priesthood, altar, and sacrifices; it contained the promise of God to make them a kingdom of priests and a holy nation. In short, it may be considered the supreme manifestation of the grace of God to the people of Israel.

Thus the covenant of grace is carried forward another step in its history. In the final prophecies of the Old Testament there is said to be a threefold development. Covenant theology teaches that the particularism of the Old Testament—that is, the limitation of redemption to the nation Israel—will be replaced by the universalism of the New Testament, when redemption is offered to the whole world with the covenant blessings available for all. Second, more stress is laid upon the faith of the individual than upon that of the nation. Finally, it is unequivocally foretold that the external ceremonial nature of religion will become spiritual and internal.

When we come to the New Testament revelation, we find immediately that the link that connects it inseparably with the Old Testament revelation is the covenant of grace. In the New Testament the covenant of grace reaches its last and final stage of fulfillment. For that reason the New Testament period is far superior to the Old Testament dispensation of the Law, and is spoken of as better. Especially is that brought out in the epistle to the Hebrews.

Several proofs demonstrate the superiority of the New Testament dispensation over the Old. In the first place, the Old Testament contained only the prophecies of the blessings of the New Testament, whereas the latter contains the blessings and privileges themselves. The Old Testament is the shadow; the New is the reality. In the Old Testament economy it was a tabernacle made with hands in which God dwelt; in the New, Deity took on flesh and tabernacled among men.

In the second place, the limitation of God's grace to Israel in the Law dispensation is displaced by the universal offer to all. That feature of the covenant of grace had been foretold to Abraham when he was promised that he would be a father of many nations. The restriction of the blessings of the covenant to Israel was never intended to be permanent, as evidenced in the case of Jonah.

In the third place, the New Testament economy puts the emphasis upon the gracious character of the covenant and connects it with the Abrahamic covenant rather than with the Sinaitic covenant. We are not to understand that the Law is excluded from the New dispensation. When Paul contrasts it with the gospel in the epistle to the Galatians, Masselink contends, he is actually referring to the Law as understood by the Jews of the time, who thought of the covenant at Sinai as a covenant of works.

In the fourth place, the New Testament dispensation provides richer blessings than the Old Testament period. In the former we have the work of redemption an accomplished fact, whereas in the latter it was merely in the stage of anticipation. In the former the Holy Spirit is graciously poured out, whereas in the latter His coming was merely predicted.

In recapitulating, proofs are advanced to show the covenant of grace is identical in all dispensations. (1) The idea of the organic unity of the covenant is expressed throughout the whole Bible. Paul makes clear to the Galatian believers that Gentile Christians belong to the same covenant that was made by God with Abraham, demonstrating the unity, vital and unbroken, between the Old Testament church and the New Testament church. Just that is meant by God's preaching the gospel to Abraham.

(2) The New Testament covenant of grace and the Old Testament covenant are linked together by the song of the virgin Mary in Luke 1. She sang of God's mercy from generation to generation, which He spoke to the fathers, to Abraham and to his seed forever.

(3) The New Testament church and that of the Old Testament are one and the same, because Peter declared, in the book of Acts, that they are the children of the prophets and of the covenant that God made with the fathers, when He promised blessing to all the kindreds of the earth.

(4) All the New Testament blessings are none other than those that are comprehended by God's statement in Genesis 17. Furthermore, the underlying unity of the New Testament church with that of the Old is seen in the word used for "church." It refers to those called out of the world.

That thought was not only implied in Genesis 3:15, but put into practice when Abraham left Ur of the Chaldees, when Israel left Egypt for the land of Canaan, and when Israel was told by God that He meant for them to be a peculiar people to Him out of the nations of the earth. The purpose of their calling was a church purpose; namely, to witness to the truth of God among the nations. An authorized definition of the church must include the people of God under the Mosaic Law. The unity of the Old Testament and New Testament church is seen in Paul's picture of the olive tree in Romans 11. Here is seen the root from which both bodies sprang, that is, the root of Abrahamic blessing. A further proof that the church in both dispensations is the same is seen from Paul's statement in Ephesians 2:14 that the middle wall of partition has been broken down between Jew and Gentile, peace having been made between them.

(5) The sacraments of the old economy are essentially the same as those of the new. Circumcision, symbolizing the cleansing from sin, is preserved in the rite of baptism. The Passover, speaking of atonement for sin through blood and deliverance from bondage, is said to find its counterpart in the ordinance of the Lord's Supper. Moreover, the means of salvation in both dispensations is the gospel of the Lord Jesus Christ. When Paul warned the Galatians against a gospel that was not a gospel, it is claimed that he was referring directly to the Jewish deception that his gospel was different from that in the Old Testament. That there is but one Mediator for the New Testament church and for the Old is to be gleaned from the symbols of the Old as well as from the fulfillment of the New. Furthermore, all the blessings promised to Abraham are seen as realized in the New Testament. The innumerable seed and the blessing of redemption through Christ are main elements of the covenant; they are still in force.

Finally, that the New Testament church rests upon the covenant with Abraham is plain from the whole testimony of Scripture, as well as from the very substance of the gospel. Christ claimed that He came not to destroy, but to fulfill, for the Old Testament spoke of Him.

Such, then, is the importance attached to the covenant of grace and the place assigned to it in the amillennial system of biblical interpretation. We reserve comment upon the subject until later in our discussion.

Notes

[1] D. Whitby in G.N.H. Peters, *The Theocratic Kingdom*, 1:525, 528, 530, 532-34.

13
The Kingdom in the Old and New Testaments

In their discussions of the kingdom amillennialists note at the first the two facts that are presupposed by the premillennialists in regard to the Messianic kingdom. The first is that the kingdom is not now on earth, but is future, beginning with the second advent of Christ. The second is that the kingdom is not spiritual but earthly.[1] From that preliminary word the study goes on to a consideration of the kingdom in the Old Testament. The kingdom of God, they believe, was actually realized in the Garden of Eden. There God ruled and reigned supreme, with all His subjects giving Him the proper obedience that is befitting a King. All the blessings that can flow from the kingdom of God on earth were there. Nevertheless, the highest ideal had not been reached. Eternal life depended upon the perfect obedience of man, and, had that been forthcoming, the everlasting kingdom would have come into existence with all its glory.

When sin entered, it meant nothing more nor less than that man was ridding himself of the sovereign rule of God, his King. That disobedience was the occasion for the setting up in the world of another kingdom, that of Satan himself. Since the fall of man there have been two kingdoms in the world, the kingdom of this world and the kingdom of God, the kingdom of darkness and the kingdom of light. The kingdom of the world is ever seeking to snatch the glory from God. The institution of the kingdom of God is the church of Christ. The aim of the world is to bring God's kingdom into conformity with itself and thus rob God of His rightful glory.

But God did not leave man in his fallen estate without any help. Immediately, God placed Himself under covenant relationship with man and announced redemption through the seed of the woman. That was the first and initial step in the kingdom of God. God's kingdom is coexistent with the covenant of grace; the two are inextricably interwoven. The setting up of the kingdom of God was to be a process, gradual in its unfolding. The Old Testament theocracy was another stage in the progress of the establishment of the kingdom of God on earth.

When Samuel was troubled that Israel should ask for a king as the other nations had, God told him that they had not rejected him, Samuel, but had rejected God that He should not be King over them (1 Sam. 8:1-7). Yet the underlying principle of the theocracy was never absent from the history of Israel, for He still remained their King during the time of Saul, David, and the other kings of Israel. They were actually representing God, so that God's sovereignty continued over Israel as heretofore.

In the Old Testament revelation, however, the kingdom of God never reached its final consummation. The prophets were united in foretelling a future display of His glory. The emphasis in their messages was placed upon the spiritual nature (in contrast to the outward and external nature of it in the Old Testament) of the future kingdom when the law of God is to be written on the hearts of the people.[2]

There is a certain peculiarity in the Old Testament kingdom that must be pointed out. The kingdom of the Messiah as predicted by the prophets is only partially realized in the New Testament dispensation. For that reason the New Testament revelation speaks of the kingdom as that which is present and then again as that which is future. When Christ cast out demons, He told the Pharisees that it was a sign that the kingdom of God had come to them (Matt. 12:28). Yet in speaking of the kingdom in the future aspect, He foretold that many would come from the east and west to sit down with the patriarchs in the kingdom of heaven (Matt. 8:11). In that way Christ spoke of His kingdom as present and then as future.

In the Old Testament those two phases of the kingdom are often seen against one background and must be distinguished. The well known prophecy of Isaiah 61 has both aspects of the kingdom blended together. That part of it was fulfilled with the first appearance of Christ is certain from the words of the Lord in the synagogue at Nazareth (Luke 4:16-21). The remainder of the prophecy awaits fulfillment at the second coming of the Lord. The same is true of the prophecy of Joel, part of which was realized at Pentecost and part of which is yet to be fulfilled in the future Messianic kingdom when changes in the elements will take place (Joel 2:28-32). When the ministry of John the Baptist is studied, the same practice is in evidence. He spoke first of the kingdom of heaven as at hand and then mentioned the laying of the axe to the root of the trees and the casting of the bad tree into the fire, a clear representation of the future judgment at the second appearing of Christ.

If the doctrine of the kingdom of God is of importance in the Old Testament, it is given no less prominent a place in the New Testament. The entire ministry of Christ was bound up with the kingdom. He preached the fulfillment of the time for the kingdom of God, and mention was made in His Sermon on the Mount of those who will inherit the kingdom of heaven. The many kingdom parables reveal the importance attached to the kingdom by our

Lord. The Messianic work of Christ is to establish the kingdom of God which is effected when Christ delivers over the kingdom to the Father that God may be all in all (1 Cor. 15:24-28). The preaching of Christ and that of John the Baptist were intended to acquaint Israel with the fact that the Old Testament Messianic prophecies were about to be fulfilled in the establishment of the mediatorial kingdom of Christ. The so-called carnality of the Jews of the time was the reason for their failure to recognize Him as their promised King. They were too much taken up with their own conception of the national and external glory that was to come to Israel. The emphasis on the kingdom of God revealed that it was not national but rather universal. The nation had really failed to comprehend in a spiritual manner the words of their prophets; their rejection of the King followed as a logical consequence.

The contention of premillennialists that the "kingdom of Christ" is used exclusively to designate the future kingdom and must be differentiated from the "kingdom of God," is said to be wholly without warrant or support in the Scriptures. As a matter of fact, both are identified time and time again. When Christ spoke of the tares, in Matthew 13, He stated that the angels will gather them out of His kingdom, and then the righteous will shine as the sun in the kingdom of their Father. Paul spoke of evil men as having no inheritance in the "kingdom of Christ and God" (Eph. 5:5). The apostle sometimes spoke of the kingdom of God as present and at other times as future. The same is true with regard to Paul's mention of the kingdom of Christ.

In the gospel according to Matthew the kingdom is designated in the main as the kingdom of heaven, whereas the kingdom of God is mentioned but a few times. The explanation of G. Vos is offered.[3] Matthew was writing to the Jews who had a peculiar reverence for the name "God"—note this, in spite of their most evident lack of perception of the true nature of the kingdom—and would easily understand the meaning of "the kingdom of heaven." Mark and Luke, on the other hand, were writing to Gentiles, so they used the phrase "kingdom of God" rather than the other.

The kingdom is characterized as the kingdom of heaven, because it is patterned after heaven and its perfection. Reference is also made in that name to the eternal and lasting value of the dominion. Furthermore, there is involved the thought of the heavenly origin and source of the kingdom; the God of heaven is He who will set it up.

The name "kingdom of God" is employed because it points to the spiritual character of the reign and dominion. The glory of God is its chief and sole object. Christ's work, in which He seeks only to glorify His Father, is completed when God is all in all; His work is complete when God is glorified. That is the purpose of the kingdom of God. Apart from that it has no legitimate reason for existence. The chiliasts, however, in referring to Israel's glory as the main purpose of the kingdom are transferring, without right or warrant, the glory of God to the glory of Israel.[4] It is a serious error, according to the amillennialists, and shows the revival in the minds of the millennialists of the old long-discontinued Jewish hope of the disciples of Christ (Acts 1:6).

The spiritual nature of the kingdom, however, is not only brought out by the use of the names "the kingdom of heaven" and "the kingdom of God," but there are also other considerations that lead to the same conclusion. When Christ told the Pharisees that the kingdom of God was in them, He surely was not intimating that it was to be instituted with power or glory (Luke 17:21).[5] The parables of the kingdom stress that selfsame characteristic of the kingdom; because they were not fully comprehended by the multitude is proof of their spiritual content.

The gospel according to John also makes clear the true nature of the kingdom. The unregenerate and spiritually unenlightened man can neither see nor enter the kingdom of God. Whenever John speaks in his record of eternal life, he is substituting that phrase for the kingdom. They are interchangeable.[6] The greatest blessings in the kingdom are eternal life, communion, and the fellowship of God with man. When Matthew makes entrance into the kingdom of heaven dependent upon conversion, he is also pointing to the spiritual nature of the kingdom (Matt. 18:1-3). Furthermore, the definite word of Christ is that His kingdom is not of this world, by which He means that His kingdom is not earthly but heavenly, not material but spiritual (John 18:36).[7] Since it is not of this world, it is not to be set up by worldly means of propagation and expansion. Paul adds his word of testimony when he says that the kingdom of God is not meat and drink, but righteousness, peace, and joy in the Holy Spirit (Rom. 14:17).

Not only is the nature of the kingdom spiritual, but its blessings are as well. The glory of God is the chief end in the establishment of the kingdom, and that in itself bespeaks blessedness for man. Salvation is the greatest possible blessing that can come to man and undoubtedly is the most honoring to God. God's unrivaled rule in the hearts of men is the normal state of affairs. That is the work accomplished by salvation, part of which is realized in this life. Christian joy is here and now unspeakable and full of glory. Another blessing that comes with salvation is the relation that the believer sustains to God as his Father, called the divine Fatherhood. In God's kingdom He is our Father as well as our King and Sovereign. As a child by natural generation shows the nature of the parent, so does the believer by spiritual generation, or better regeneration, reflect the nature of his Father in heaven. The incalculable blessing of the kingdom is disclosed by the parable of the pearl of great price and the parable of the hidden treasure (Matt. 13:44-46). Those parables seek to convey the idea of inestimable value. The blessings of the kingdom are so worthwhile, because God prepared it for His own before the foundation of the world.

Furthermore, earthly blessings for Israel under an earthly rulership were not in the mind of the Lord Jesus. In all Christ's teachings He displayed no special patriotism for the Jewish nation.[8] When He spoke of His future Messianic kingdom, even then He did not single out Israel for particular blessing, but rather said that the children of the kingdom would be cast out (Matt. 21:43).[9] Far from the kingdom being originally or solely intended for the people of Israel, it was to be taken away from them and given to the Gentiles who will bring forth fruit, appropriate and adequate for the occasion. It therefore is evident that the materialistic, earthly conception of a Jewish empire with Christ as a temporal king finds no basis in the Scriptures and is directly foreign and opposed to all that the Word has to say on the question of the kingdom. The kingdom of God is nothing more nor less than the rightful inheritance of those who are saved by the gospel of God's grace in Christ Jesus, and it is definitely not connected with the restoration of the Jewish national existence and kingdom.

Thus far the attempt has been to show that, contrary to the view of the premillennialists, the kingdom of the Lord is not material, external, or earthly, but is positively and absolutely spiritual in its character. But that is not all. The chiliastic conception of the kingdom that makes it a thing of the future entirely is also erroneous and untenable. As a matter of fact, the kingdom is a present reality and actually in existence. The claim is made that that is the testimony of the Scriptures everywhere. Zechariah had foretold of the coming of the lowly King with salvation, and in Matthew's gospel the multitudes recognized Him in the King that came in the name of the Lord. When Christ began His ministry, we are told that He began to preach the acceptable year of the Lord (Isa. 61:2). That meant the presence of the kingdom. In answering those who accused Him of casting out demons by Beelzebub, the Lord made clear that Satan was not divided against himself, and added that if He was casting out demons by the Spirit of God—the implication being, of course, that He certainly was—then the kingdom of God was upon them (Matt. 12:22-28).

That must also mean that the kingdom was then present and is now in existence as well. But the end of the nonmillennial position is not yet. The Sermon on the Mount, with its final exhortation to seek first the kingdom of God and His righteousness, implies throughout that the kingdom is here. The kingdom must be a reality in order to be sought after. When Christ, furthermore, was on trial before Pilate and asked whether He was a King, He answered unhesitatingly that He was a King (John 18:37). He could not say that if the kingdom were something of the future.

But the words of Peter in the book of Acts clinch the whole matter and prove conclusively that the kingdom is present (Acts 2:29-33). In speaking of the resurrection of Christ, the apostle goes on to reveal the exaltation and session of the Lord Jesus. In that passage the resurrection of the Lord is spoken of in connection with His sitting on the throne, which is assuredly most fatal to the theory of the millennialists that Christ is to sit on the throne of David when He comes again to establish His monarchy in Jerusalem.[10] The amillennialists give that much proof for their contention that the kingdom, covenanted of old to David, is a present reality.

Before passing on to the amillennial conception of the future of the kingdom after the return of Christ, one needs to consider the amillennial view of the course and end of this age, the church age. Amillennialists are careful to make clear that they do not agree with postmillennialists with regard to that matter. Masselink thinks there is nothing more foolish than the postmillennial view of the Scriptures.[11] He claims it is quite senseless to hold that the world is getting better and better until it will reach perfection or a stage approximating it, at which time Christ will return. Suppose all the world were truly converted. That would not do away with the problem of sin. Regenerate people still have enough difficulty with sin in themselves. Sin is not to be dealt with in that manner. It requires the intervention of God to bring about a state of perfection.

The amillennialists do not content themselves with the statement that the kingdom is only or entirely a present reality; they believe there is a future aspect or phase of the kingdom revealed in the New Testament as well as in the Old Testament.[12] That is spoken of as the eschatological side of the kingdom in that it touches upon things future. The future kingdom is to be ushered in when Christ returns in glory. At that time the dead of all ages will be raised together and judged together, there being one resurrection and one general judgment. After those events the kingdom will be ushered in, not on earth, but in heaven. Many will then come from the east and the west (Matt. 8:11); the righteous will shine as the sun in the kingdom of their Father (Matt. 13:43); the meek will in truth inherit the earth (Matt. 5:5); the pure in heart will see God (Matt. 5:8); there will be such a thing as sitting on the right hand of Christ (Matt. 20:23); and the future joy of the disciples is described as eating and drinking with Christ in His kingdom (Matt. 26:29).[13]

At that point several distinctions are pointed out. Christ, as the second Person of the blessed Trinity, is with the Father and the Holy Spirit, King over the whole created universe. It is His natural kingship and is eternal in its extent. There is also, however, a Messianic kingship that rightfully belongs to the Lord Jesus, because He is the Messiah. In the Messianic kingship there is a twofold distinction to be made between the "Kingdom of Power" and the "Kingdom of Grace." The kingdom of power is Christ's Messianic kingdom as related to the whole creation. That was in view when He said: "All power is given unto me in heaven and in earth" (Matt. 28:18). By that kingdom Christ exercises sway over both heaven and earth. The question may be asked: "Does not that power belong to Him by His natural kingship?" There is a distinction, for here it is said that the power is "given," and in the natural kingship it belongs to Him because of His divine nature.

In conjunction with the kingdom of power there is Christ's kingdom of grace wherein Christ exercises His kingly rule over the church. That was referred to when God said in the second psalm: "Yet have I set my king upon my holy hill of Zion" (v. 6). The kingdom of power will some day come to an end when Christ delivers the kingdom to God. His Messianic rule over the whole creation will be returned to the Father and not His rule over the created universe that belongs to His natural kingship.

After the kingdom of power has come to an end, the kingdom of grace will still go on, for it is to be an eternal kingdom. The kingship of Christ over His church, the kingdom of grace, will merge or issue into the kingdom of glory in heaven. We have then the natural kingdom of Christ by virtue of His deity, which is everlasting; the Messianic kingdom is divided into the kingdom of power and the kingdom of grace. The kingdom of power is returned to the Father at the second appearing of Christ, and the kingdom of grace, which is concerned with the church in its present aspect, will go into the future kingdom of glory. With that we close our discussion of the amillennial view as it is outlined and presented by one of that group. Masselink is recognized by others as setting forth the view in its proper light and also acknowledges his direct indebtedness to Vos, the chief authority on this particular position of biblical interpretation. Our comments are reserved for the next section of the study on the comparison of the two views.

Notes

[1]W. Masselink, *Why Thousand Years?* pp. 13-19. Though there are more recent treatments than that work presents, they lack the breadth it affords.

[2]Hoyt has evaluated the position well: "Amillennialists center their attention upon the spiritual elements, bypassing the social and political, and call it the New Testament kingdom" (R. G. Clouse, *The Meaning of the Millennium,* p. 84).

[3]G. Vos, *The Pauline Eschatology,* p. 12.

[4]That is a gross misunderstanding of the premillennial position. Because the Scriptures give prominence in the kingdom to Israel (Isa. 60 in its entirety), is no reason to claim, by extrapolation, that premillenarians transfer the glory of God to Israel.

[5]That type of exegesis lacks a basis both in logic and, more importantly, in Scripture.

[6]It is well to notice how often amillenarians equate one term with another and use them interchangeably. That is forced upon them by their uniformitarian approach and their constant oversimplification of things that differ.

[7]It is more than strange that amillennialists in their exegesis have not seen that Christ clearly explained what He meant by "not of this world." By no stretch of the imagination can it be made to teach that He was declaring that His kingdom would not be *in* this world.

[8]That is impossible of substantiation in the light of Matt. 23:37-39 and Luke 19:41-44. Could such a position explain the reason amillennialists are not noted for their interest in Jewish evangelization?

[9]The exegesis of that important passage has been given earlier.

[10]It is impossible exegetically to equate the throne of David on earth (Acts 2:30-33) with the Father's throne in heaven. Compare Psa. 110:1-2 with Rev. 3:21 and Matt. 25:31.

[11]Masselink, p. 214. His actual words are: "To our mind there is nothing more foolish than what popularly passes as the post-millennium view. . . . Now nothing could be quite so senseless."

[12]Amillennialist Hoekema believes "that the millennium of Revelation 20 is not exclusively future but is now in process of realization" (Clouse, p. 156).

[13]Hoekema attempts to set forth the amillennial system, but it is noticeable how sketchy the treatment is. He explains: "My discussion of the amillennial understanding of the millennium will include the following topics: the interpretation of the book of Revelation, the interpretation of Revelation 20:1-6, a look at two Old Testament passages commonly viewed as predicting an earthly millennial kingdom, a brief sketch of amillennial eschatology, and a summarizing statement of some of the implications of amillennial eschatology" (Clouse, p. 155). First, he finds fault with long-recognized terminology: "The term *amillennialism* is not a happy one" (ibid.). He suggests (after Jay E. Adams) that the term be exchanged for "realized amillennialism." Hoekema next outlines his scheme of explanation: "The system of interpretation of the Book of Revelation which seems most satisfactory to me (though it is not without its difficulties) is that known as *progressive parallelism* [following William Hendriksen] . . . the book of Revelation consists of seven sections which run parallel to each other, each of which depicts the church and the world from the time of Christ's first coming to the time of his second" (Clouse, pp. 156-57). The seven sections are set forth as: (1) chaps. 1-3; (2) chaps. 4-7; (3) chaps. 8-11; (4) chaps. 12-14; (5) chaps. 15-16; (6) chaps. 17-19; (7) chaps. 20-22. His purpose is to show the seven sections as parallel to each other, but "they also reveal a certain amount of eschatological progress. The last section, for example, takes us further into the future than the other sections" (ibid., p. 158). If the Revelation does not speak of future events (cf. Rev. 1:19), why call it a "prophecy" (Rev. 1:3) in the sense of prediction?

Part Four

Comparison of These Systems

14
Law and Grace

The purpose in the preceding parts of this discussion has been to present, after an appropriate introduction to the whole question, the premillennial and amillennial systems of biblical interpretation. The attempt was made to analyze the systems as they are set forth by their respective advocates. The sum of the matter is: the premillennial approach to the Scriptures teaches that after the return of the Lord Jesus Christ in glory to the earth, there will be set up in Jerusalem the throne of David upon which He will reign, with His saints, for a thousand years; the amillennial view holds that there is to be no such period of one thousand years on earth. The two views are diametrically opposed to each other, and there are basic points upon which they differ. Those points of difference are to be dealt with at this time.

Premillennialists and amillennialists disagree in their conceptions of law and grace. Not all premillennialists hold the same position as that to be set forth here, nor do all amillennialists maintain exactly the same position as does Masselink, but the positions to be contrasted are fairly general for both views.[1]

Someone wisely said that the man who knows the relationship between law and grace has the key to true theology. Amillennialist Masselink begins his discussion on the premillenarian confusion of law and grace by criticizing the Scofield Bible for its statement that God offered Israel at Sinai the choice between law and grace, and they hastily and rashly accepted the law, which was a poor selection. He claims the premillennialists contend that the law is utterly abrogated and abolished. Therefore, proof is advanced to show the perpetuation of the law.[2]

First of all, the Ten Commandments are grounded and based upon the moral nature of God and the relationships that exist between men everywhere, he claims. Right is always right, and wrong is always wrong. It was just as contrary to God's will for Adam not to love God, as it is for anyone not to love God. As long as God is the Creator and man is the creature, there is a necessity for the law; as long as human relationships last, the law must be perpetuated.

Second, the law was unchangeable when it was first given. That is evident from the record of the transaction on Mount Sinai. The tables of the law were written on both sides to reveal, we are told, that nothing was either to be added or subtracted therefrom. The finger of God wrote them to show the powerlessness of man to erase anything. They were written on stone to indicate their lasting and permanent obligations.

Third, the repudiation of the Ten Commandments is in direct conflict with the practice of the Christian church. The commandments, so the church has held, are as binding today in their exactions as they have ever been.

Fourth, the Lord Jesus Himself never abolished the law, for He declared that He purposed to fulfill it in His coming, and did not intend to abolish. He explained its inner spiritual content, as in the Sermon on the Mount, which proved that He had no idea of annulling it.[3]

Fifth, Jesus explained the moral law because of the corruptions of His day. Because the Jews had completely lost sight of the purpose of the Sabbath, the Lord revealed to them that the Sabbath was made for man, thus making it legitimate for all men to perform works of piety and love for which the Sabbath was instituted. The Jews thought the commandment forbidding killing meant only murder, but the Lord pointed out that even anger against a brother was a violation of the commandment.

Sixth, to alter the law of God is dangerous work. Who would decide where to begin? For God to alter His law would be tantamount to an admission that it was imperfect in the first place.

Seventh, the Christian needs the law to convict him of sin. Whenever a child of God falls into sin, he needs just such a "stern pedagogue" as the law is to bring him back into fellowship with Christ. Law abrogation implies that the Christian is no longer in conflict with Satan and sin, which is perfectionism. Moreover, the commandment given to love one another, which is called the new commandment, does not mean that the law is abolished. That new commandment merely sets forth the new motive in the keeping of the law. Furthermore, if the believer loves Christ, he will keep his Lord's commandments, for the Word says that is the whole duty of man. Again, in Romans 8 the apostle Paul points out that the law is fulfilled in the believer through the Spirit, because Christ fulfilled it representatively for all believers in His earthly life.

Finally, the new nature implanted in the believer at the time of salvation delights to obey the law of God. The apostle Paul declared that with his mind he himself served the law of God.[4]

Not only has the law been perpetuated, but the Christian, although not under the law for salvation nor because of fear of God nor the curse of the law, must keep the law, says Masselink.[5] There are definite reasons for his assertion.

In the first place, every believer is a subject of the kingdom of God. His law in His kingdom is the commandments, particularly the Ten Commandments.

Every Christian in order to bring glory to God is willing to grant obedience to the law of God. The righteousness of God is made manifest in His law, and the saved man is told to seek first the kingdom of God and His righteousness (Matt. 6:33).

Second, the believer is a child of God and loves to obey, or should, the commandments of his Father. He is God's child; now it behooves him to walk so before the world that others may know for a surety that God is his Father.

Third, the Christian keeps the law to obtain reward. Of course, he is not legal about it as were the Jews, for he recognizes that even the smallest of rewards is a matter of grace. But in his obtaining reward, God is further glorified.

Fourth, the believer is glad to obey the law because of the gratitude in his heart for the redemption that the Lord Jesus Christ wrought out for him on the cross when he was in a deplorable, lost state.

Furthermore, the child of God renders obedience to the commandments of God because he wants to see God's will done on earth as it is in heaven. In heaven the will of God will become the will of man, and man will not conceive of the commandments of God as rigorous or harsh. In keeping the commandments here on earth, he is preparing himself for that future state of perfection in glory.

Finally, obedience to the law is an integral part of the believer's salvation; that is, salvation in its present tense.[6] When men are saved, it is from sin to holiness. But how is holiness brought about? It is effected by conformity to the law of God. Because of regeneration the believer delights in the law of God and obeys it spontaneously, having been liberated from the power of sin.

The refutation of that position will follow with the setting forth of the premillennial view of law and grace. But it should be stated here—and it is of the utmost importance—that we have never seen a proper or adequate exegesis of the third chapter of 2 Corinthians by any who maintain that the law is binding upon the believer for his walk under grace. It is either omitted altogether, as in the case of Masselink[7] and others, or it receives such a treatment as causes one to wonder whether these men themselves are not at times struck by the manifest forced character of their explanations and interpretations.

Probably the greatest contrast in the Word of God is that which exists between law and grace, yet it is one that is least understood and most often confused, as evidenced by the discussion given above. The principles of law and grace are mutually destructive; it is impossible for them to exist together. For "if by grace, then is it no more of works: otherwise grace is no more grace. But if it be of works, then is it no more grace: otherwise work is no more work" (Rom. 11:6). To mix those two principles is to dull the keen, hard edge of the law and to destroy the blessed and glorious liberty of grace. Against such the apostle Paul pronounced twice the anathema to be found in the first chapter of the epistle to the Galatians (vv. 8-9). The extremely solemn nature of that anathema is more readily evident when it is remembered that it has never been revoked, but stands today as irrevocable a warning as when the apostle penned it. It behooves the believer, then, to study well those two principles that he may the better give each its proper place. There are several distinctions between law and grace that must now be considered.

According to the unmistakable testimony of Scripture, the Law—by which is meant the Mosaic system of statutes, ordinances, and commandments—had a definite beginning in point of time and also a definite termination. Grace as exhibited today likewise had its inception at a specific time and will be displayed until a specifically predicted time. Many are of the opinion, and amillennialists are among them, that the Law has always existed. It has not. Law, as a principle contained in a system of works, has existed from the day that God commanded Adam to refrain from eating of the fruit of the tree in the midst of the garden. But the Law, designated as the Mosaic code, came into being with Moses (Rom. 5:13-15). The Scripture states: "For the law was given by Moses, but grace and truth came by Jesus Christ" (John 1:17). Of course, that verse does not imply that law never existed before Moses, any more than it implies that grace and truth were not in the world before the manifestation in the flesh of the blessed eternal God the Son.

The Law of the Jewish commonwealth did begin with Moses, and the specific display of grace and truth as seen in the New Testament did come by Jesus Christ. The Law as an active force has ceased to exist, because the death of Christ fulfilled all the requirements of the Law. "For Christ is the end of the law for righteousness to every one that believeth" (Rom. 10:4). Paul writes in Galatians that the Law "was added because of transgressions, till the seed should come to whom the promise was made" (Gal. 3:19). The seed is explained to us when Scripture states: "Now to Abraham and his seed were the promises made. He said not, And to seeds, as of many; but as of one, And to thy seed, which is Christ" (Gal. 3:16). The termination of the Law, then, occurred with the death of Christ on Calvary.

Grace in its fullest aspects began to be manifested when the Law was done away. (The reign of the Law in the kingdom age has been treated in the analysis of the premillennial view.) The epistle to Titus affirms, "The grace of God that bringeth salvation hath appeared to all men" (Titus 2:11). The grace that came by Jesus Christ and now offers salvation to all—"For there is no difference between the Jew and the Greek: for the same Lord over all is rich unto all that call upon Him" (Rom. 10:12)—that grace, I say, will terminate at the catching away of the Body of Christ to be ever with the Lord. The distinction between law and grace is of primary importance.

Law and grace are to be distinguished in regard to the respective groups to which each addresses itself. The Law was addressed and given to one people and only one—Israel. Moses asked Israel: "And what nation is there so great, that hath statutes and judgments to righteous as all this law, which I set before you this day?" (Deut. 4:8). He specified further: "This is the law which Moses set before the children of Israel: These are the testimonies, and the statutes, and the judgments, which Moses spake unto the children of Israel after they came forth out of Egypt" (Deut. 4:44-45). The Lord Jesus in His upper room discourse said: "But this cometh to pass, that the word might be fulfilled that is written in their law" (John 15:25). Paul, in enumerating the advantages of Israel before Christ's earthly ministry, declared that to them belonged the adoption, the glory, the covenants, the giving of the law, the service of God, the promises, the fathers, and Christ after the flesh (Rom. 9:4-5).

In spite of those clear and unequivocal statements of Scripture there are those who insist the law was meant for all mankind. To whom, now, is grace offered? Paul revealed that "the grace of God that bringeth salvation hath appeared to all men" (Titus 2:11). Because God has concluded all "under sin" and because all have come short of the glory of God, the grace of God is manifested to all and is appropriated for all time by "him which believeth in Jesus" (Rom. 3:9, 23, 26). All are under the same divine judicial sentence, and the remedy offered is universal in its application. How different here are the principles of law and grace.

Law stands in contradistinction to grace in respect to its requirements. The former, ministering to those of the old creation, the natural man, is limited in its adaptation to its subjects. Those requirements must first be met before the blessings of God can be received. It is "do and live" and "do and be" (Lev. 18:5). In complying with the requirements as best the natural man can in his most limited ability or disability, he is seeking to gain acceptance with God. In the Mosaic system it is: "Thou shalt not avenge, nor bear any grudge against the children of thy people, but thou shalt love thy neighbour as thyself: I am the Lord" (Lev. 19:18). In grace, however, where the requirements are such because one has been accepted of God, the teachings are superhuman requirements. Grace says: "Live and do," and, "Be to do." In the epistles to the Romans, the Ephesians, and the Colossians, the Spirit first tells us what God has done for the believer, then He declares what he is to do (Rom. 12:1 ff.; Eph. 4:1 ff.; Col. 3:1 ff.). In grace the requirements are never to be met in the sense of paying a debt or an already due obligation. The standard of the requirements in the Law was the whole Mosaic legal system; in grace the standard is no less than "a perfect man, unto the measure of the stature of the fulness of Christ" (Eph. 4:13).

Christ said: "A new commandment I give unto you, That ye love one another; as I have loved you, that ye also love one another" (John 13:34). Paul exhorted believers to walk with all lowliness and meekness, with longsuffering, forbearing one another in love (Eph. 4:2; Col. 3:13). The Spirit of God further revealed through Paul that believers are to reckon themselves dead indeed to sin, but alive unto God through Jesus Christ our Lord (Rom. 6:11). They are to yield themselves unto God as those that are alive from the dead, and their members as instruments of righteousness to God (Rom. 6:13). They are to cleanse themselves from all filthiness of the flesh and spirit, perfecting holiness in the fear of God (2 Cor. 7:1). They are to walk in the Spirit and not fulfill the lusts of the flesh (Gal. 5:16). Through the Spirit they are to mortify the deeds of the body and live (Rom. 8:13). Believers are to recognize that they who are Christ's have crucified the flesh with its affections and lusts (Gal. 5:24). They are to put off concerning the former conversation the old man, which is corrupt according to the deceitful lusts (Eph. 4:22), and being renewed in the spirit of their minds, to put on the new man, which after God is created in righteousness and true holiness (Eph. 4:23-24). Christians must live soberly, righteously, and godly, in this present world, looking for that blessed hope, and the glorious appearing of the great God and our Savior Jesus Christ (Tit. 2:12-13).

Less than those requirements could not be asked of those who have been constituted sons of God, citizens of heaven, those seated in the heavenlies with Christ. In its requirements the Law commands; grace exhorts. Failure to comply with the enactments of the Law brings punishment (Heb. 10:28); in grace failure robs of joy and abounding peace, and stunts spiritual growth. Is it possible to find two principles that differ so decidedly in their essential characteristics?

But that is not all. Law is unlike grace in the enablement that is offered to those who are under it. Although the requirements under Law do not equal those under grace, there is no divine enablement in keeping the Law. One can search for even the slightest hint of divine enablement in all of the 613 laws of Exodus, Leviticus, Numbers, and Deuteronomy, and one will not find it (cf. Gal. 3:11, 12; esp. 3:21). On the other hand, although the requirements in grace are far above those under the Law, abundant enablement is provided. The indwelling Holy Spirit is He "which worketh in you both to will and to do of His good pleasure" (Phil. 2:13). When the one under grace is walking by means of the Spirit, He empowers unto every good word and work (2 Thess. 2:16-17). For instance, if the believer is to love his brother in Christ even as Christ loved him, then he has the enablement to do it, "because the love of God is shed abroad in our hearts by the Holy Ghost which is given unto us" (Rom. 5:5).

The basis of the Law is a covenant of works; that of grace is a covenant of grace. Human merit is the foundation stone of the Law; the merit of Christ is the foundation stone of grace. The Law spoke on this wise: "And all these blessings shall come on thee, and overtake thee, if thou shalt hearken unto the voice of the LORD thy God" (Deut. 28:2); "but it shall come to pass, if thou wilt not hearken unto the voice of the LORD thy God, to observe to do all his commandments and his statutes which I command thee this day; that all these curses shall come upon thee and overtake thee" (v. 15). A covenant of works is grounded in what the flesh can do; a covenant of grace is based upon faith in what God has done and is willing to do.

When the children of Israel were at the foot of Mount Sinai, they were told how graciously God had dealt with them. He had borne them on eagles' wings and had brought them unto Himself (Exod. 19:3-4). Yet when they were told of the Law, which would require them to acquire merit before God, they confidently asserted that they would do all that the Lord had spoken (v. 8). That confidence in the flesh is seen again after the Law had been given, at which time they repeated that whatever the Lord had spoken to Moses they would perform (Exod. 24:3, 7). Paul told believers under grace, "We are the circumcision, which worship God in the Spirit, and rejoice in Christ Jesus, and have no confidence in the flesh" (Phil. 3:3). The reason is not far to seek, for what the Law could not do because of the weakness of the flesh, God sent His own Son in the likeness of sinful flesh to condemn sin in the flesh, so that the righteousness of the Law might be fulfilled in us who walk not after the flesh, but after the Spirit (Rom. 8:3-4).

Perhaps one of the greatest distinctions between the principles of law and grace is that in respect to the purpose of each. Many Jews, Gentiles, and even Christians believe that the Law was given by God that man might come to God and be accepted by Him. Righteousness, they maintain, was the inevitable, not to say intended, outcome of the diligent keeping of the Law by conforming to all of its manifold precepts and injunctions. To tell such people that the purpose of the Law is altogether foreign to their conception of it is to brand oneself as an antinomian with the professed desire of abolishing all law, even moral law.

But what does Scripture say? Paul told us by the Spirit that whatever things the Law says, it says to them who are under the Law, so that every mouth may be stopped, and all the world may become guilty before God (Rom. 3:19). Again he wrote: "Moreover the law entered, that the offense might abound" (Rom. 5:20). Yet again he declared: "Wherefore then serveth the law? It was added because of transgressions, till the seed should come to whom the promise was made" (Gal. 3:19). The Law was our schoolmaster to Christ, so that we might be justified by faith (Gal. 3:24). The Law, therefore, was introduced to show man his utter lack of merit before God and the impossibility of gaining any by reliance on his own strength. It was added to give sin the added character of transgression against the Law of God.

So many writers fail to see that while the Law itself, coming from God and partaking of His nature, is "holy and the commandment holy, and just, and good" (Rom. 7:12), that it cannot render man holy and just and good. The Law did not show carnal and natural man his good nature (which he does not have), but his sinful and corrupt nature. Nor need we deceive ourselves into thinking that the Law made anything perfect, for the Law made nothing perfect, but the bringing in of a better hope did (Heb. 7:19; 10:1). Furthermore, what the Law could not do is just as important as what it did. The apostle testified that by the deeds of the Law, no flesh shall be justified in the sight of God, for by the Law is the knowledge of sin (Rom. 3:20). That view of the Law is the clear and normal one set forth by the Scriptures. The passages bearing on the subject could be multiplied, but the ones cited above will suffice.

But what is the purpose of grace? The full purpose of grace is that by the death of the Lord Jesus Christ all the redeemed by faith might be brought into glory, so that in the ages to come He might show the exceeding riches of His grace in His kindness toward us through Christ Jesus (Eph. 2:4-8). Until that time, by grace through faith God has purposed to save those who believe in the finished work of Christ. It is further the avowed purpose of grace to teach that, denying ungodliness and worldly lusts, believers should live soberly, righteously, and godly in this present world, as they look for the blessed hope and glorious appearing of the great God and our Savior, the Lord Jesus Christ (Titus 2:12-13).

There is yet another contrast between law and grace which should be drawn. It views the respective results of the operation of those principles upon the individual. Law brings death; grace gives life, for the letter kills, but the Spirit gives life (2 Cor. 3:6). The one is the ministration of death; the other, the ministration of the Spirit. The former is the ministration of condemnation; the latter, the ministration of righteousness (2 Cor. 3:7-9). That is nowhere so well portrayed as in the events occurring at the giving of the Law and those at the descent of the Holy Spirit on Pentecost. Of the former it is written that there fell of the people of Israel that day about three thousand men (Exod. 32:28). Of the latter it is stated that the same day there were added to the Body of Christ about three thousand souls (Acts 2:41). In spite of all the positive and definite distinctions between the principles of law and grace, amillennialists hopelessly mix and confuse them. No wonder, then, that those two systems, the amillennial and premillennial, differ in their interpretation of the whole Bible.

Premillennialism and amillennialism, as already shown, appear poles apart on the subject of law and grace. That stems directly from the overall covenant of grace theory of amillennialists. The theologian Berkhof dislikes the dispensational distinctions, because to him they are quite arbitrary. In the matter of that which is arbitrary it would be difficult to find more arbitrary distinctions than those he finds in the dual aspect of the covenant of grace,[8] which is far from clear or conclusive. In commenting on the dispensations, he holds:

The fourth is designated the dispensation of promise and is supposed to terminate with the giving of the law, but Paul says that the law did not disannul the promise, and that this was still in effect in his own day (Rom. 4:13-17; Gal. 3:15-29). The so-called dispensation of the law is replete with glorious promises, and the so-called dispensation of grace did not abrogate the law as a rule of life. Grace offers escape from the law only as a condition of salvation—as it is in the covenant of works—from the curse of the law, and from the law as an extraneous power.[9]

Certain observations are in order here. First of all, the age of promise did terminate as a test with the giving of the Law, for there is no evidence that the administration of promise conditions, as with the patriarchs, went on into the Mosaic period. The Law itself did not disannul the promise because that promise was to find its highest expression in the fulfillment of redemption (see Gal. 3:8). In a real sense the age of grace is related to the Abrahamic Covenant as Galatians shows, as well as the figure of the olive tree in Romans 11. But to state that the Law did not disannul the promise is not tantamount to declaring that the Law was in the age of promise, or that conditions of life and testing of the age of promise were carried over into the age of law.

Second, to hold that the dispensation of Law is full of glorious promises does not minimize one whit the fact that the Law is a ministration of condemnation and death (2 Cor. 3:7, 9). That certainly is not in keeping with the testing of man under conditions of promise.

Third, to maintain that the dispensation of grace did not abrogate the Law as a rule of life is to misunderstand completely the force of the argument in the entire epistle to the Galatians. Those addressed were believers in the churches of Galatia; they were not trying to be saved by the Law but seeking to live under it. Paul anathematizes such a course of action (Gal. 1:8-9; 5:12).

Finally, if grace offers release from the Law only as a condition of salvation, what is to be done with the forceful argument throughout Romans 7? Paul is proving that the believer, who has not been able to be saved by Law, cannot live an acceptable life before God by seeking to keep the Law in his saved condition (cf. Col. 2:6-7).

Hamilton, along with other amillennialists, finds fault with Scofield's statement that Israel *rashly* accepted the Law in place of the covenant of promise.[10] Whatever word is employed, is it not true that Israel promised wholehearted obedience to a proposed covenant before hearing the terms of it (see Exod. 19:8)? Is it not true also that gracious conditions were their lot before that time, as attested by the statement in Exodus 19:4? The acquiescence of the people to the covenant in Exodus 24:3 is different, for they had heard the features of the covenant by that time; but it reveals the same confidence in the flesh. Hamilton contends against the reinstitution of the Law for Israel after the age of grace in the Tribulation period and subsequent to it, as held by premillennialists. But is it not passing strange that such zeal should be manifest on that point, when amillennialists place the believer under law as a rule of life during this age of grace? He misunderstands Scofield on the matter of the basis of salvation in the age of law and the age of grace.

> Now this teaching that under the law men did righteously and so *became* righteous, while under grace they are *declared* to be righteous for the sake of Christ's righteousness which is clothed upon them, raises the question at once as to how the Old Testament saints were saved. The notes of Dr. Scofield would necessitate declaring that they were saved by keeping the law. Fortunately Dr. Scofield is not consistent on this point for he elsewhere declares that grace is the only way of salvation. However, the position taken sets the dispensation of law squarely over against the dispensation of grace, and so contradicts one of the central teachings of the Bible.[11]

It should be pointed out that Scofield nowhere teaches that under law men did righteously and became righteous. They had no spiritual life to keep the Law (Gal. 3:21), and the Law brought them not justification, but condemnation (Rom. 3:19). Furthermore, only one way of salvation is ever taught by dispensational millenarians. Finally, if the dispensational position sets the age of law over against the age of grace, it is exactly what Paul does in Romans 11:6 and 2 Corinthians 3. No central teaching of the Bible is contradicted, for none based on Scripture proof is involved. Revealing further his misunderstanding of the position on law, Hamilton charges those who say believers are now under grace and not under law with the claim that "we need not trouble ourselves with the ten commandments!"[12] That is both inaccurate and misleading, giving the impression that dispensationalists are antinomian. What does Hamilton do with Romans 10:4 and Romans 13:8-10? All that the Law could ever require by way of righteousness is fulfilled in us by the Holy Spirit. See Romans 8:1-4. How do legalistic amillennialists explain that passage?

But the confusion is not ended. Hamilton tells us, "It is perfectly true that we are not under law but grace [but that is what amillennialists deny]. No one would claim that we are today saved by keeping the law perfectly. That does not mean, however, that we are free today from the demands of the law, or that it is not our life rule or guide."[13] Paul was speaking to believers in his warning in Galatians 5:1. Moreover, Hamilton makes no difference between what Christ calls His commandments and the commandments of Moses. Surely, no one will presume to claim they are the same.

Homer Payne has the adequate answer to the claim that believers are under law for their rule of life. He points to the Council of Jerusalem of Acts 15, where the very matter in dispute was not "whether the Law is a means of merit for lost sinners, which even amillennialists disallow, but whether it is a requirement of life after salvation by faith. This last is taught by amillennialism and logically so as they reject dispensational distinctions."[14] If they note Galatians 3:23-25, they cannot avoid the conclusion that the age of law is placed in contradistinction to the age of grace. Paul is contending that law is not the rule of life for the believer now, the very opposite from the view taken by amillennialists. "This is a serious dilemma and perhaps accounts for the earnest if ineffectual efforts of Berkhof and Wyngaarden to make mere interpretation of the Law the scapegoat in their reference to the crucial passages concerned."[15] Moreover, let it be considered that apart from Romans 3, the New Testament passages disallowing the force of the Law now, were directed not to unbelievers seeking to be saved by that means, but to believers who sought this means as a rule of life.[16]

Nondispensationalists strongly attack dispensationalists for making the Sermon on the Mount irrelevant to believers today, hence lost to them. Ryrie pointedly asks them:

> Why is the Sermon on the Mount made the focus of the attack? Nobody ever criticizes dispensationalism for teaching that the dietary regulations of the Mosaic law [as well as those governing the celebration of the feasts and the wearing of certain apparel] have no application to the Christian. The Sermon on the Mount, however, is different. It contains the Golden Rule, the Lord's Prayer, and other favorite passages. To suggest even that its direct revelation to the Christian is open to question inevitably involves people's emotions before their doctrine. Of course the dietary laws are just as much inspired Scripture as the Sermon on the Mount—a fact which emotions easily overlook.[17]

Both dispensationalists and antidispensationalists, in all honesty, have to make certain allowances or "adjustments" in interpreting the sermon. Says Ryrie:

> This is the dilemma every interpreter faces. If literal, it cannot be for today; if for today, it cannot be literal. And this is not a dilemma that faces only dispensationalists. The point is perfectly plain: Whatever the dispensational interpreter may do to the Sermon, it might not be as bad as the nondispensationalist's adjusting and spiritualizing. Indeed, it can be said that even the nondispensationalist does not apply the Sermon fully today, even though he tries to apply it directly.[18]

Dispensationalists actually teach that: (1) the primary goal of the sermon is the Messianic kingdom; and (2) as with all Scripture the sermon has application to believers of this age. Chafer, though accused of robbing the believer today of the blessing of the sermon, assigns the sermon to the kingdom, then asserts: "A secondary application to the church means that lessons and principles may be drawn from it."[19] Ryrie ably concludes the discussion:

> This is the heart of the dispensationalist's interpretation of the Sermon. . . . At least it does justice to literal interpretation, and the consis-

tency of one's hermeneutical principle is far more important than the defense of one's theological system. It in no way disregards the importance of the ethical teachings of the Sermon for today, and it gives proper recognition to the ultimate purpose of the Sermon.[20]

Finally, as for truth for the church, the teachings of the Lord Jesus on the way of salvation, the Holy Spirit, the church itself, prayer in Christ's name, and the rapture are not found once.

As a corollary to the whole problem of the sermon is the Lord's Prayer. Nondispensationalists believe it is the model prayer for disciples of Christ for all time. When confronted with Matthew 6:12 and the difficulty of reconciling it with general New Testament teaching, various attempts, which are forced and strained, are resorted to solve the problem. An adequate statement is this:

> The problem raised by the conditional nature of this petition for forgiveness may be explained as follows: In the fully developed doctrine of Christian salvation there are two areas of divine forgiveness. The first area is that of the forgiveness that comes to the sinner at the time of justification, and deals with the guilt of his sins in a total sense (Eph. 1:7). To h s forgiveness there is attached but one condition, i.e., to receive it once for all by faith in Christ (Rom. 4:5-8). The second area of forgiveness covers the relation of the divine Father to those who have become His children and deals specifically with the matter of fellowship whenever it is broken by sin. To obtain such forgiveness we must confess and forsake the sin (1 Jn. 1:9; cp. Ps. 66:18 and Prov. 28:13). The forgiveness mentioned here in v. 12 belongs in this second area, because it occurs in a prayer given to disciples of Christ (5:2) who could call upon God as their Father (6:9, 26). The ultimate motive for forgiving our debtors is based upon the grace of God, and appears later in the progress of revelation (Eph. 4:32; Col. 3:13).[21]

Apparently, Ladd was motivated to a new study of the question of the kingdom by the claim made by dispensationalists relative to the Sermon on the Mount. He contends, "It is immediately obvious that a system which takes this greatest portion of Jesus' teaching away from the Christian in its direct application must receive a penetrating scrutiny."[22] It is in place to ask why John 13 to 17 was not taken into account here. It is surely a larger portion than the Sermon on the Mount, and it does apply directly to the believer. It is almost half again as long as the Sermon on the Mount. But does Ladd really believe all the portions of the gospel are for believers now primarily? What is to be made of the great prophetic discourse in Matthew 24 and 25? Will that be made to apply today directly and primarily?

Consider Matthew 5 to 7 and ask whether 5:22 is applicable, in the primary sense, mind you, today. If so, how can one reconcile it with other New Testament truth? If all in the gospel is primarily for us, then why not heed the command of the Lord Jesus in Luke 24:49 or in Matthew 24:20? The truth of the matter is that the gospels are far from being as simple of interpretation as amillennialists and antidispensationalists would have us believe. Why? Because they treat three important ages: the law age before the death of Christ, the then-coming age, or the age of grace, which is now (where John 13-17 applies directly), and the kingdom age in the future.

Ladd rightly notes that the Sermon on the Mount nowhere indicates how God's righteousness is to be obtained,[23] but asks, "If a man does not know how to forgive his fellow men their trivial offenses against him, how can he make any just claim that he had been forgiven the immeasurable debt of his sin against God?"[24] But that is not what the text states. It does not declare that in the measure in which you exhibit forgiveness to others, you manifest your realization of the much greater debt God has forgiven you. The passage under consideration is a prayer of entreaty that sets up a proportion, or basis, of forgiveness: as the one, so the other. Dispensationalists believe in manifesting forgiveness too, let it be noted, but they go to Ephesians 4:32 for the scriptural exhortation. Too many read Ephesians 4:32 into Matthew 6:12, and that without warrant.

Dispensationalists also recognize that believers are blessed with all spiritual blessings in Christ, so they are able, after giving due consideration to primary application, to receive blessing and enrichment from any part of the Bible, let alone the gospels. One does not have to arm himself to exterminate the Canaanites, as Israel was commanded to do by the Lord, but he can learn from those portions of the Word how much God hates sin anywhere, and His condign punishment upon it. P. B. Fitzwater has summarized the situation well: "This so-called Sermon on the Mount is the royal proclamation, or the setting forth of the laws which shall prevail when Christ shall reign as King. The Sermon on the Mount is strictly kingdom and not Church truth. However, the principles of righteousness set forth are of perpetual and universal application."[25]

Allis finds that the "difference between the law and the promise was not one of kind but of degree."[26] But it is difficult to see how diametrically opposite principles can be spoken of as differing only in degree. What is to be made of John 1:17; Romans 10:5 ff.; the epistle to the Galatians with its contrasts; and 2 Corinthians 3? He would be horrified if dispensationalists taught two ways of salvation, yet he states: "The law is a declaration of the will of God for man's *salvation.*"[27] What, then, is to be the interpretation of Galatians 2:21 and 3:21? The Law was most assuredly *not* for salvation (see Romans 5:20).

Almost without cessation, dispensationalists have been charged with teaching salvation by works in certain ages and salvation by grace in others. Because that is a very damaging and serious charge, dispensationalists have repeatedly pointed out the falsity of the charge of dual or multiple ways of salvation. It appears that some antidispensationalists prefer to set up straw men in order to achieve a hollow or worthless victory. In spite of the clarity of James 4:6, which reveals degrees of grace in one dispensation, the antagonists will not permit dispensationalists to speak of more or less grace in different dispensations. The conclusion is inescapable: nondispensationalists equate dispensations with various ways of salvation.[28]

It appears that covenantists are so occupied with showing that dispensationalists are heretical with regard to the vital way of salvation that they have masterfully covered up their own statements, which reveal their own position as unbiblical in that area. Here is a statement of Allis: "The Law is a declaration of the will of God for man's salvation." In spite of Hebrews 10:4, he claims Old Testament sacrifices were efficacious.[29]

Two indisputable dispensationalists make their doctrinal stance eminently clear. Chafer asserts: "The law was never given as a means of salvation or justification."[30] Scofield, who is supposedly quite culpable here, declares: "Law neither justifies a sinner nor sanctifies a believer."[31] Antidispensationalists appear incapable of reconciling dispensational statements of one method of salvation with differentiation between law and grace.[32] One is reminded of the potent question: "Who is this that darkens counsel by words without knowledge?" (Job 38:2, NASB; also 42:3).

How could Allis make such declarations? He does so on the basis of his contention that the Law also is a declaration of the all-embracing covenant of grace.[33] Is it realized now the serious conclusions to which covenantism leads? It combines, blends, and fuses features that are kept distinct in the Scriptures. The keen edge of the Law is blunted and dulled, and the glory and riches of grace are beclouded and bedimmed. For Allis and all amillennialists, the Law must be of perpetual obligation, as binding now as it has ever been or ever will be.[34] Second Corinthians 3 makes plain that the Law was done away as to obligation for anyone now. Why is it that amillennialists in their discussion of the Law do not mention 2 Corinthians 3 or John 1:17? It is not surprising that Allis soon sees the Lord's Prayer as not legal. He criticizes Scofield for maintaining it is.[35] He explains the passage thus: those who have been forgiven much, must also be ready to forgive. He is reading Ephesians 4:32 into the passage. The prayer does not read: "Forgive us our debts since we have forgiven and do forgive our debtors."

No clearer exponent of grace has graced this generation than Chafer. He saw clearly the vital distinctions between the law age and the grace age. He notes,

> Though almost every intrinsic value contained in the law system is carried forward and incorporated into the present grace system, it still remains true that the law as an ad interim system did come to its end and a new divine economy superseded it. No more decisive language could be em-

ployed on this point than is used in John 1:17; Romans 6:14; 7:2-6; 10:4; 2 Corinthians 3:6-13; Galatians 3:23-25; 5:18. These Scriptures should not be slighted, as they too often are, by those who would impose the law system upon the heavenly people.[36]

Men do not enhance the true unity of Scripture by attempting to fuse two contrary principles into one system. "The differences exist already in Scripture; the dispensationalist does not invent them."[37] How can one reconcile on the amillennialist principle what the Lord stated concerning entering heaven maimed and halt (Matt. 18:8-9) and the words in Philippians 3:20-21, or the threat of hellfire after the Lord has stated that His own shall never perish (John 10:28-29)?[38]

If one terms this age the dispensation of grace, it appears to many to be a denial of grace in any other age. Yet another matter that mystifies antidispensationalists is this: When dispensationalists make such demarcation between law and grace (on the basis of John 1:17 and Romans 11:6), do they intend to teach that there was no grace in the age of law? No, they mean no such thing. Ever since Adam sinned, it has been God's grace that has saved man, regardless of how miserably he failed under any age test (1 Pet. 1:19-21). It is a case where after Calvary the sluice gates of God's grace were opened widest (cf. Rom. 3:21-26; Eph. 2:4-9). Grace was not absent in the law age, but it was not the dominating principle in God's dealing with men. Instances of displays of grace in the age of law are these: (1) God's dealings with Israel in the wilderness of Sinai after the giving of the Law, even though chastisements abounded; (2) His choice of them as His nation at all (Deut. 7:14-16); (3) His bestowal of the gracious Davidic Covenant (2 Sam. 7); (4) His grant of the unconditional New Covenant (Jer. 31:31 ff.); and (5) His continued presence with them (Exod. 33:12-16).[39]

In conclusion, Ryrie has discerningly touched the heart of the issue:

These displays of grace under the law did not lessen the exacting demands of that law. The law did not cease to be law simply because God was gracious during that economy. Neither does this display of grace during that period lessen the proper antithesis between the Mosaic economy and the economy introduced by Christ. . . . No system of theology can ignore either emphasis, contradictory as they might seem, even in the name of theological logic.[40] [Let it be understood that] whatever God has done in behalf of man in any age, being based on the death of Christ, is a manifestation of grace; but the present, unforeseen age is unique in this that its divine purpose is, to a distinguishing degree, the supreme demonstration of God's grace. Had this distinction been observed, a number of misunderstandings regarding dispensational truth would have been obviated. Because it is believed that this age is peculiarly one of divine favor does not militate against the belief that God's grace is abundantly exercised in all other ages.[41]

When Allis asks whether Chafer teaches his students not to pray the Lord's Prayer, the latter rightly questions whether Allis teaches his students to pray the prayer of Matthew 24:20.[42] It was inevitable that the all-important death and resurrection of Christ should have age-changing effects. Chafer asks, "After a new order is established through the death and resurrection of Christ, men like Nicodemus, the Apostles, and Saul of Tarsus were saved by a new birth, not because they were utter failures in Judaism, but because a new and vastly different relation to God was provided. Why should Saul who before the law was blameless need to be saved at all?"[43]

Those and other equally pertinent questions are explicable only on the basis of a change in God's dispensational dealings with man. But, again, that is not to state that the believer now is lawless or antinomian. "Much that is vital in the law system is restated and incorporated in the principles which instruct the believer in his manner of life under grace, but this fact does not place the Christian under law. It is probable that certain features of the law which governed the thirteen colonies under English authority were incorporated in and adapted to the legal system which afterwards became the law of the United States, but that fact would not be sufficient ground for the claim that the United States is now under the rule of England."[44]

In no realm of theology is it more important the expositor of Scripture be clear than in that which relates to the vital distinctions between law and grace. The dispensational premillennial position alone harmonizes all the statements of Scripture; the covenantal, amillennial viewpoint confuses the issues and leaves wholly untouched large areas of Scripture.

Notes

[1]W. Masselink, *Why Thousand Years?* pp. 145-46.
[2]Ibid. C. I. Scofield, *The New Scofield Reference Bible,* fn. 2, p. 94 on Exodus 19:2 is illuminating concerning the events at Sinai. "It is exceedingly important to observe that: (1) the Lord reminded the people that hitherto they had been the objects of His free grace; (2) the Law is not here proposed as a means of salvation but as a means by which Israel, already redeemed as a nation, might through obedience fulfill her proper destiny as a people for God's possession, an holy nation, and a kingdom of priests; and (3) the Law was not imposed until it had been proposed and voluntarily accepted."
[3]Ibid., pp. 148-52.
[4]Ibid., pp. 155-57.
[5]Ibid., pp. 137-38.

[6]Ibid., pp. 160-61.

[7]Ibid., pp. 155-62.

[8]L. Berkhof, *Systematic Theology*, pp. 284-89.

[9]Ibid., p. 291.

[10]F. E. Hamilton, *The Basis of Millennial Faith*, p. 28. See fn. 2 above.

[11]Ibid. See Scofield, *New Scofield Reference Bible*, p. 1124, fn. 1 on 1:17.

[12]Ibid., p. 29.

[13]Ibid.

[14]H. L. Payne, *Amillennial Theology as a System*, p. 57.

[15]Ibid., pp. 153-54.

[16]Ibid., p. 223.

[17]C. C. Ryrie, *Dispensationalism Today*, p. 106.

[18]Ibid., pp. 106-7.

[19]L. S. Chafer, *Systematic Theology*, 5:97. Even the much maligned Scofield Reference Bible states: "In this sermon our Lord reaffirms the Mosaic law of the O.T. theocratic kingdom as the governing code in His coming kingdom on earth (5:17), and declares that the attitude of men toward this law will determine their place in the kingdom (5:19). . . . Although the law, as expressed in the Sermon on the Mount, cannot save sinners (Rom. 3:20), and the redeemed of the present age are not under law (Rom. 6:14), nevertheless both the Mosaic law and the Sermon on the Mount are a part of Holy Scripture which is inspired by God and therefore 'profitable for doctrine, for reproof, for correction, for instruction in righteousness' (2 Tim. 3:16) for the redeemed of all ages" (Scofield, *New Scofield Reference Bible*, p. 997, fn. 4 at 5:3).

[20]Ryrie, *Dispensationalism Today*, p. 108.

[21]Scofield, *New Scofield Reference Bible*, pp. 1000-1001, fn. 4 at 6:12.

[22]G. E. Ladd, *Crucial Questions About the Kingdom of God*, p. 106.

[23]Ibid., p. 127.

[24]Ibid.

[25]P. B. Fitzwater, *Christian Theology*, p. 535.

[26]O. T. Allis, *Prophecy and the Church*, p. 37.

[27]Ibid., p. 39.

[28]Ryrie, *Dispensationalism Today*, pp. 110-12.

[29]Allis, p. 39.

[30]L. S. Chafer, *Grace*, p. 113.

[31]Scofield, *Scofield Reference Bible*, p. 1245.

[32]Ryrie, *Dispensationalism Today*, p. 115.

[33]Allis, p. 40.

[34]Ibid., p. 41.

[35]Ibid., p. 46.

[36]L. S. Chafer, *Dispensationalism*, p. 48.

[37]Ibid., p. 51.
[38]Ibid., p. 62.
[39]Ryrie, *Dispensationalism Today*, pp. 116-20.
[40]Ibid., p. 120.
[41]Ibid., pp. 70-71.
[42]Chafer, *Dispensationalism*, p. 103.
[43]Ibid., p. 92.
[44]Ibid., p. 95.

15
Israel and the Church

If amillennialists and premillennialists differ widely in their understanding of law and grace, there exists no more concord in their conceptions of Israel and the church. It has already been noted in the discussion on the covenant of grace that amillennialists connect the people of God throughout all dispensations, making them all the church of Christ.

Kuyper holds that Israel was always a group in the Old Testament within the national Israel, who obeyed the Lord and were well-pleasing to Him. Of course, in the Old Testament the true Israel was recruited from among the Jews, but in the New Testament Israel is formed mostly from among the Gentiles with a small minority from among the Jews. Furthermore, he maintains that Israel is a typical people wherein all is symbolical, even as rebirth is symbolized by circumcision. That body reveals the spiritual content of the covenant of grace.[1] Although the symbolical name Israel is applied to the church, Israel is not to be found among the Jews but in the church, which has only a small portion from among the Jews. Masselink insists that because, in the Old Testament, church and State are together, to belong to the nation included membership in the Old Testament church.[2]

The contradiction between those two amillennialists is evident on the surface: One makes the church only a select group in Israel in the Old Testament, whereas the other conceives of the church and Israel as coextensive. All amillennialists, however, find fault with the position that the premillennialists give to the Jew. It is said that the preeminence of the Jew in the premillennial system is easily understood, since the whole doctrine of chiliasm is an outgrowth of pre-Christian Jewish writings. Much refutation is not necessary to answer that argument, for premillennialists merely recognize that if God speaks about a certain people through two-thirds to three-fourths of His revelation and promises them certain blessings, which were noted in the survey of the premillennial view of the kingdom in the Old Testament, that He means for them to have just that much prominence. Millennialists do not find it their duty to instruct the Word as to the eminence it should or should not give to any nation.

In giving the premillennial position on Israel and the church, one, first of all, must define the term "Israel." The word is used in Scripture in several ways. It was first given to Jacob on that memorable night when he wrestled with God and prevailed (Gen. 32:28). Scriptures use the term when speaking of all the descendants of Jacob or the twelve tribes (Judg. 20:1). That is more particularly true of the time prior to the division of the Solomonic kingdom. With the breaking off of the ten tribes from Rehoboam, the term is applied to them as the kingdom of Israel (1 Kings 12:19; 2 Kings 1:1; Hos. 1:1). Finally, it is the designation of those believers in Christ who are the natural descendants of Abraham (Rom. 9:6). Here we must make a distinction. It is proper to speak of believing Jews and believing Gentiles as Abraham's spiritual seed (so Paul designates them in Galatians 3:8, 9), but spiritual Israelites are believing Jews only.

The difficulty in many cases begins with the misinterpretation of Romans 9:6 and Galatians 6:16. Upon examining Romans 9 one can easily see that when Paul declares, "For they are not all Israel, which are of Israel," he is not speaking of a distinction between Israel and the church or between Gentile Christians and Jewish unbelievers. He is rather distinguishing between those in the nation Israel who are unbelievers, Abraham's natural seed, and those of Israel who are believers, the spiritual seed of Abraham. The Gentiles or the church are here nowhere in view.

In Galatians 6:16 the apostle concludes his message: "And as many as walk according to this rule, peace be on them, and mercy, and upon the Israel of God." William Sanday and Arthur C. Headlam are of the opinion that Paul uses the term here metaphorically of Christians.[3] But C. J. Ellicott in commenting on the passage doubts whether that terminology could be applied to Christians in general.[4] In contradistinction to all that the apostle has said denouncing the Judaizers, he uses the term here of those who were once Israelites after the flesh, but are now the Israel of God or the spiritual children of Abraham, who would not oppose the apostle's glorious message of grace which he had brought to the Galatian believers. The Scriptures never use the term Israel to refer to any but the natural descendants of Jacob.[5]

Because premillennialists differentiate between Israel and the church, it is not to be thought that they do not see the similarities between the two groups. Those can merely be mentioned in passing. Both have covenant relations with God. Both are related to God by blood redemption that is centered in the Lord Jesus Christ. Both are witnesses for God to the world. Both are of the seed of Abraham. Both are to be glorified. Both are called to a walk of separation. Both have one shepherd. Both have common doctrines. Both are called the elect of God. Both are dearly beloved of God. Both are vitally related to God as illustrated by the figure of marriage. Both are the recipients of eternal life.

But it is the poorest of logic to contend that because two groups have several points in common they are identically the same. As a matter of fact, Israel and the church have more differences between them than they have similarities. Chafer has well pointed out, besides the similarities mentioned above, some twenty-two contrasts between Israel and the church.[6] Reference will be made to them all, with emphasis on several in particular. Israel had a physical birth; the church has a spiritual birth in addition to a physical birth. The headship of the nation Israel resides in Abraham, that of the church in the Lord Jesus Christ. Israel is related to all the covenants of God that were made after the call of Abraham; the church is related to the Abrahamic and New only. God's dealings with Israel have been individually and nationally; with the church He deals only individually. Israel is to be found in both the Old and New Testaments; the church is found only in the New.

As far as Christ's ministry was concerned, He claimed to come to the lost sheep of the house of Israel; when the church is in view the Lord commands to go to all creatures. As to the death of Christ, Israel is nationally guilty and will yet be saved by His sacrifice; the church is now redeemed to God by that death. For Israel, Christ is spoken of as the Messiah, Immanuel, and King; He is the Head, Bridegroom, and Lord of the church. Israel is spoken of as the son of God through national covenant relationship; the members of the church are sons of God by individual and personal regeneration. The Spirit of God came upon some in Israel; He takes up a permanent abode in every member of the Body of Christ.

At the end of the ministry of Christ on earth, He gave two farewell addresses. The one on the Mount of Olives concerned Israel and looked to the completion of the Jewish age; the other in the upper room concerned the church and looked upon the cross as an accomplished fact (cf. Matt. 24, 25; Mark 13; Luke 21 with John 14-17). To Israel He promised that He would return in power and glory to set up the kingdom; the church has His word that He will come again to receive her to Himself that where He is, there she may be also. Israel is spoken of as the servant of the Lord. The church of Christ is in Christ in a most vital relationship as His Body and Bride. As to the kingdom reign, the nation Israel will be subjects of the King; the church, His Bride, will reign with Him as coreigners. Israel had a priesthood; the church is a priesthood. Israel is revealed as the wife of Jehovah, now untrue but later to be restored; the church is seen in the Scriptures as the Bride of Christ. In the New Jerusalem, which is not synonymous with heaven, Israel will be seen as the spirits of just men made perfect, whereas the church will appear as the church of the firstborn. Do not those differences show that the church and Israel are not the same body of people?

But consider now a few other differences. In Genesis 22:17 God had promised Abraham a seed as the stars of the heaven and as the sand that is upon the seashore, speaking of an earthly and a heavenly seed. The church is that heavenly seed and Israel is the earthly seed. Israel's promises, hopes, and blessings are all related to the earth; those of the church are heavenly. That is well illustrated by the book of Joshua and the epistle to the Ephesians. In the first, the goal is possession of the land of Palestine with all the blessings attendant upon such an occupation in obedience to God. In the second, the sphere is heavenly, the warfare is heavenly, and the blessings are all spiritual in Christ Jesus in the heavenlies. Failure to discern God's earthly and heavenly purposes has been the cause of much of false Bible teaching. The consummation of God's purposes for Israel will be realized when Israel, as a converted nation, will dwell in the land of Palestine under the rule of the Son of David on the Davidic throne in Jerusalem, with blessings flowing out to all the nations of the earth.

God's purpose in the church is that through the substitutionary death of the Lord Jesus Christ, He might bring many sons into glory, so that in the ages to come He might show the exceeding riches of His grace in His kindness toward us through Christ Jesus. Are not those purposes wholly divergent from one another? The vital point of contact between them is that they are both dependent upon the Lord Jesus Christ for their complete and final fulfillment.[7]

All is contrast between Israel and the church as far as nationality is concerned. In the definition of Israel above it was shown that the nation is composed of all the natural descendants of Abraham through Jacob. As noted, it is a physical birth that entitles the individual to his standing in the nation. With the church, however, the situation is decidedly otherwise. In the first place, she is composed of members from all the nations of the earth. In the second place, the individual is entitled to his position by virtue of a spiritual or new birth. Need there be confusion when the Scriptures are so clear and explicit in those particulars?

The church and Israel did not come into existence at the same time nor are they coterminous upon the earth. Israel had its beginning from the call of Abram from Ur of the Chaldees and will be found on the earth in all ages. The church, however, had its inception at Pentecost, when the Holy Spirit came to abide with believers after having baptized them into the Body of Christ. Her pilgrimage on earth will be terminated by the rapture. The distinction is clear: Israel in all dispensations from that of promise, the church in the dispensation of grace only.

Israel was governed (and will be in the millennial age) by a principle wholly foreign to that which is in force in the church age. Israel was under the Mosaic system, which expected one to "do and live" and "do and be," as indicated in the discussion on law and grace. It afforded no divine enablement, but could only pronounce finally: "Cursed be he that confirmeth not all the words of this law to do them" (Deut. 27:26). It was a system founded upon a principle of works and was dependent upon the energy of the flesh for its accomplishment. The principle governing the church is that of grace. It is rooted in the covenant of grace and looks to God for its execution. It expects one to "live and do" and "be and do." First, the individual is constituted a son of God, then he is asked to do with the enablement of the Holy Spirit those things that are worthy of the vocation wherewith he is called. The apostle Paul through the Spirit definitely stated what things are required of the believer. They are as high above the law requirements as heaven is above the earth. Is it possible, then, to find two such groups as Israel and the church, whose governing principles differ so decidedly in their essential characteristics, yet are so often confused?

As already indicated, the greatest diversity possible exists between the two views. The material is indeed voluminous, and at times the argument becomes involved; therefore, there is the greater need to adhere strictly and rigidly to scriptural concepts and terminology.

Since Allis's work is specifically on that theme, his contribution will be treated first. It will not be possible to take up each point in the entire book, but the purpose will be to face the main issues contained in it. It is somewhat surprising to find that at the outset Allis defines the Jewish problem as consisting of these elements: Israel's (1) rejection of the Messiah; (2) scattering among the nations; (3) continuance in unbelief; and (4) persistence in regarding herself as a "peculiar people" who will rule the earth at the coming of the Messiah.[8] That is a mixture of elements that do not belong together: the first three features are valid, but the last has absolutely nothing to do with the question.

A similar mingling of things that differ is found when he questions whether the church is to offer the Jew salvation or help him to obtain the kingdom. As to the first there is the clear word in Romans 10:12-13, and as to the second there is the equally lucid declaration in Romans 11:25-27 and Isaiah 60. But the heart of the question is reached in these words: "If the Church is a mystery first revealed to the apostle Paul, it cannot be predicted in the prophecies of Isaiah; and if these are taken literally it is not foretold in them."[9] It will be the task of Allis to prove that the church is not a mystery first revealed to Paul, and to that end he expends much labor as will be seen. Once more he defines the issue that faces him: "Does the Christian Church fulfill, or does it interrupt the fulfillment of the Old Testament predictions concerning Israel? Is the Church age a mystery period unknown to the prophets, or did they foresee and predict it? This is the vital issue which confronts every student of Dispensationalism."[10] It confronts every student of the Word of God as well and must be faced sooner or later.

He begins the treatment of the subject proper by a consideration of the word "mystery." He quotes Colossians 2:2; 4:3; Ephesians 1:9; 6:19; 2 Thessalonians 2:7; and 1 Timothy 3:9, 16, and concludes that a mystery does not imply necessarily that a matter was entirely unknown (note the qualifying wording). It could still be a mystery for him if known, but not fully known.[11] That is invalid if there is no further evidence to substantiate such a claim. Indeed, he admits in speaking of the words, "not made known unto the sons of men," in Ephesians 3:5, "This declaration taken by itself would seem to imply that it was absolutely new."[12] But he has no intention of taking those words by themselves, for his aim is to give his own definition of a mystery as that which was not completely unveiled in the Old Testament but was completely hidden from the carnally-minded.[13] He has no solid foundation for so construing the wording of the passage in Ephesians 3. But he maintains that the absolute statement is changed into a relative statement by the words "as it has now been revealed," (NASB, RSV) which "definitely deny that such was the case and as definitely assert that it was previously known, only not with the same clearness and fullness."[14] That is an attempt to evade the full force of the words, but it will not hold. It is not a matter of whether the mystery was somewhat revealed in the Old Testament, only to be revealed fully in the New Testament in the words of Paul, but that it was not revealed or known at all in the Old Testament, necessitating a new and clear revelation in the New Testament.

What was the necessity for such a new revelation? Since the Old Testament prophets saw the first and second comings of Christ telescoped together as in Isaiah 61:1-3 and did not foretell the church age, they knew only of those Old Testament conditions in which Gentiles shared blessings with covenant Jews on the basis of becoming proselytes, as with Ruth, and foretold of the millennial age when Jew and Gentile would be in blessing together in the kingdom of Messiah. But they never knew of nor foretold a status of affairs where Jew and Gentile would be fellow heirs, fellow members, and fellow partakers as in the Body of Christ in this age. For that scriptural and valid reason God had to make the new revelation through Paul. Further proof will be forthcoming. The words "as it has now been revealed" cannot be twisted into making the statement relative, because one is not dependent upon Ephesians 3 alone for the definition of the mystery. Consider Romans 16:25-26 where there are no qualifying words, and to which Paul has reference when he says in Ephesians 3:3, "As I wrote before in a few words."

Allis claims to find in the Old Testament, in germ form in the Abrahamic covenant, "complete equality" between Jews and Gentiles. That is intended to fortify his contention that the church is not a new revelation. He maintains, "Clearly, the equality of Gentile with Jew was predicted in the Old Testament."[15] He advances no proof from Scripture, apart from the reference to the Abrahamic covenant, that such was the case. If the mystery was known in the Old Testament, it should be easy to show where it is stated as based (as it must be) on the death and resurrection of the Savior. Psalm 22 notes that a generation will serve Him, whereas Isaiah 53 only indicates that He will see His seed. But neither passage nor any other in the Old Testament even remotely mentions a distinctive body like the church. The error of the amillennialists is that they take every Old Testament reference to a coming redemption in which Jew and Gentile will share, as tantamount to a prophecy of the church. That is an invalid conclusion and a non sequitur. Passage after passage does foretell salvation for Jew and Gentile alike, but there is no intimation that those redeemed segments of the human family combine to be fellow heirs, fellow members, and fellow partakers in the Body of Christ of this age. Moreover, neither Allis nor any other amillennialists can explain why, when entrance into the Body of Christ is by the baptism of the Holy Spirit (1 Cor. 12:13), there is no reference to the baptism of the Holy Spirit in any book of the Old Testament. Nor is there such a mention in the Tribulation period nor the Millennium.

The next step in Allis's argument is to deal with the word "hid." He points out the obvious that a thing hidden is not nonexistent, but he goes on to contend that it does not mean the existence is unknown, but only inaccessible.[16] It is true that the parables of our Lord were hidden from His disciples (Luke 18:34), and the gospel is hidden to the lost (2 Cor. 4:3), but that is a far cry from the concept of "hid in God." He concludes, "Consequently, it is natural to infer that Paul's knowledge of the mystery which he had received by 'revelation' (Eph. 3:4) was not nearly so much the revelation of new truth as what is meant by the words, 'Then opened he their understanding that they might understand the Scriptures' (Luke 24:45)."[17] That type of argument is inadmissible for this reason: when Christ was risen, He directed the understanding of His disciples to the Old Testament Scriptures long known among them, but only improperly or dimly understood. He needed only to illumine their minds concerning what Moses and the prophets and the writings had spoken; He did not introduce new revelation to them. He charged them rather with folly (Luke 24:25) for their unbelief in all that the prophets had already revealed. To the Pharisees and others, when His person and mission were not comprehended, He needed only to say: "Search the Scriptures, for in them ye think ye have eternal life: and they are they which testify of me" (John 5:39). Why? Because those things had been revealed in the Old Testament. They were neither hidden in the Old Testament nor hidden in God. But our Lord never said nor did Paul, "Search the Scriptures for in them you will find the truth of the church." That which was embedded in Scripture could be searched out; that which was hidden in God, in His mind, in His plan, in His counsels, needed not searching out but an initial revealing or disclosure—and that was precisely and clearly presented by Paul.

Allis builds upon the very conclusion he has not proved to indicate "the danger of taking Paul's first statement as complete," then dilates on the supposition that Paul is trying to guard against the very doctrine the dispensationalists insist on most emphatically.[18] His inconclusive exceptions to the plain force of the passage by means of forced exegesis do not alter the case; in most unmistakable terms Paul is stating that he is revealing that which was not made known hitherto.

When it comes to the question of whether Israel will return to their own land, he states, "It is significant that practically all the texts upon which the claim is based that the Jews are to return to their own land and enjoy special privileges, are taken from the Old Testament. Even more significant is the fact that while Paul devotes a considerable part of Romans (chapters ix-xi) to the discussion of the future of the Jews, he has nothing to say about their restoration to their own land or of their enjoying special rights and privileges."[19]

Several observations are in point here. First of all, one is at a loss to see why the restoration of Israel to her own land is invalidated, because almost all the texts are from the Old Testament. Is the Old Testament less inspired than the New? Is not the chief emphasis in the Old Testament Israel and her relationship to the Lord? What would be gained by added mention of the same promises in the New Testament? Is the Old Testament the place where are found the prophecies relative to the coming and death of Christ as well? Are those predictions invalidated, because they are found in the Old Testament? That is strange reasoning for one who has studied the Old Testament.

Second, surely Allis has overlooked the very clear passage in Romans 11:26-27 when he can declare that Paul has "nothing to say" on the restoration of Israel to her own land. Zion is clearly found in the passage (not to be spiritualized away), and the restoration of the nation is presupposed, if they are there delivered and saved by the returning Messiah. His note later on Romans 11:26 claims it is "decidedly precarious" to take Romans 11:26 as though Paul were speaking of the very thing Allis claims Paul omits.[20] The conclusion is, "He might well have expressed himself much more plainly here where such a statement would be most appropriate and pertinent." That is reasoning in a vicious circle. He claims that, if Israel were to be restored to the land in the end time, Paul would have mentioned it in Romans 9-11; when Romans 11:26 is adduced in support, he contends that it is precarious to make it say that very thing (though surely a literal coming of the Lord is spoken of and a literal conversion also in the passage before us). Then he finds fault that, if Paul did mean what the premillennialists claim, "he might well have expressed himself much more plainly." Paul has made it abundantly clear, and one would as leave defend a lion as defend him. After the foregoing discussion one is not quite prepared for the position that "this does not necessitate the inference that Israel will not return to and possess the land of Canaan. . . . This much however may be said. By ignoring this subject as completely as they do, the writers of the New Testament indicate at the very least its relative unimportance."[21] But he cannot have the argument both ways.

Another argument proposed against the doctrine of the mystery of the church is stated thus: "The attempt to make Paul the exclusive recipient and custodian of what is called 'church truth' has another serious consequence. It tends to make the apostle to the Gentiles an apostle to the Gentiles exclusively."[22] That is a non sequitur, and injects that which is irrelevant to the discussion. Why is his contention invalid here? It has no point, because, although Paul indicated in Romans 11 that he magnified his office as apostle to the Gentiles, he prefaced all his remarks on Israel with the expression of his unbounded love and passion for them in Romans 9:1-5. Furthermore, Peter was an apostle to the circumcision, but he ministered in the home of Cornelius, in Samaria, and elsewhere as he found opportunity. How is any of that related to the call of the apostle Paul? If the God who called him to the apostleship entrusted him with the revelation of church truth, in what way would that serve to hamper his ministry elsewhere?

To find fault with dispensationalists for not treating Ephesians 3:5, especially the words "as it has now been revealed," is to conjure up a straw man.[23] The reason Allis takes so much time on that passage is that dispensationalists have been using it through the years to show the new revelation of the mystery of the church. Witness the commentaries of the premillennialists. On the other hand, it will be revealing to ascertain, as some of us have, how few amillennialists even touch upon the subject of the revelation of the church. Most content themselves with the usual pronouncement that Israel of the Old Testament is the church of the New Testament. Let it be said clearly that, after Allis has diluted the content of the revelation in Ephesians 3, one is inclined to wonder what the revelation really is.

Allis introduces the figure of the olive tree of Romans 11:17-24, as do other amillennialists, to show the relation that supposedly exists between the New Testament church and the Old Testament economy. The error into which Allis falls is that "the tree represents the true Israel."[24] As will be shown more fully later from S. Wilkinson, the phrase "the true Israel" is nonbiblical. The tree represents the root of Abrahamic blessing, with a reference to Genesis 12:3 (especially the last clause, "all the families of the earth"). There is failure to realize that all can partake of the blessings of the Abrahamic covenant in salvation through Christ, the Seed of Abraham, yet not necessarily belong to the New Testament church. If Allis feels that dispensationalists have ignored the passage in Romans 11, he should consider their commentaries on Romans 9-11, and especially the extended discussion on that very theme in John Wilkinson's *Israel, My Glory*. It is a classic, and unanswerable.

Allis's difficulty in discussing Isaiah 55, as in the case of Daniel 9, is that whenever he finds a reference to the work of Christ in redemption in the Old Testament prophets (and there are admittedly a number of such references), he immediately injects an ambiguity by stating that by so much the prophet is definitely predicting the church age.[25] That is the point to be proved.

After numerous attempts to find the church in the prophets and the Psalms, Allis informs his readers that a contrary position robs the church of its "exceeding precious promises contained in the Old Testament which she is fully entitled to claim and possess."[26] He is using language borrowed from the premillennialist, for the exact reverse is the actual situation. Moreover, his fallacy arises from the fact that he views the age of the church as the consummation of all the ages of God's redemptive plan, and does not see the coming age of vindication of which Christ spoke repeatedly and even extendedly (see Matt. 24-25) in the gospels. Take the important example of Matthew 19:28. That verse is not even treated in the entire length of his work.

When he refers to Acts 15:13, Allis states, "It is perhaps the best passage in the New Testament for testing the correctness of the Dispensational method of interpreting Scripture."[27] It is the purpose of Allis to attempt to prove that James's quotation of the Amos passage contradicts the premillennial contention that the Old Testament does not speak of the church age. He is aware of the interpretation of Scofield that there is given here an outline of the purpose of God for this age and the beginning of the next. For Allis that would have no relevance to the question under debate. But he is aware that there is relevance, for he states Darby's position, which is correct: James's quotation indicates an analogy between the conversion of the Gentiles during this age and the ingathering of the Gentiles in the kingdom age.[28] That also must be rejected because James could have stated it more clearly, if that had been his intention. Who is to be a judge of that in the last analysis? When one comes to Allis's interpretation, he finds that the passage speaks of the resurrection and ascension of Christ and His session at the right hand of God, exercising His sovereign power in a manner far beyond anything David could have dreamed of.[29] In other words, Christ in His place at the right hand of God has more than restored the lost fortunes of the Davidic dynasty, and that is all that is meant by Amos' prophecy. But Allis explains nothing of the reason the prophecy is couched in such terms as "tabernacle of David" nor of the meaning of the words "as the days of old." Nor can the words, "I will return and build," be pressed into signifying that Christ will "build again" in relation to the church age and the ingathering of Gentiles in that period.[30] And what is the force of the "again" in his interpretation? Why should words be rendered meaningless by a departure from the grammatico-historical principle? Before long it is learned that the "hope of Israel" in Acts 28:20 really means the hope of the world, both Jew and Gentile? Do you see what has been done? He has arbitrarily shifted the expression from "hope of Israel" to make it mean "hope of the church." That cannot and will not be allowed. That is not the method of sober biblical interpretation.

When the Jewish remnant is considered, due emphasis cannot be allowed that theme for it would be "a long step in the direction of Judaizing the Bible."[31] Is our salvation Judaized because Christ came as a Jew born of a Jewish virgin? Since one cannot afford to Judaize large portions of the Bible, the 144,000 of Revelation 7 must be saints of the church. But since when are church saints designated after tribal distinctions, and Old Testament tribes as well? Their testimony presents a problem, too, for Allis contends: "Viewing human history as a whole, we may say that God has never left Himself without a witness. . . . Yet, shortly after this unparalleled event [he refers to the rapture] and within an incredibly short time (less than seven years), 144,000 Jews and an innumerable multitude of non-Jews will be saved. Is this probable? We do not say, Is it possible? . . . The least that can be said is that it is quite contrary to the analogy of Scripture."[32] He himself has stated the very reason there is no other analogy in Scripture—because it is *unparalleled.* Is there wisdom in seeking the probable or possible parallel of an "unparalleled event"?

That Allis's position on Israel and the church is the normative one for amillennialists can be seen from the writings of other amillennialists. Hamilton holds that Paul repeatedly claims that Christians are the true Israel,[33] and by virtue of that they are heirs of the promises of God to Abraham.[34] He is not altogether clear on the premillennial position, for he insists that the Old Testament promises of blessings are to be accorded, according to the premillennial view, to the nation Israel regardless of their faith in Christ. Needless to say, no part of the Word of God promises anyone anything apart from faith.[35] However, when he speaks of Romans 11:26 he informs his readers: "Notice that it is the *salvation* of the Jewish race, not its restoration to national prosperity under the Messianic King that is here promised. . . . The context makes it perfectly plain that the only way of salvation is through believing in Christ as Saviour (verse 23), and that salvation is to take place in a racial way for all Jews who are then living, when the total number of the elect Gentiles is complete at the close of this dispensation."[36]

A national conversion of Israel is not a tenet in the amillennial scheme of prophetic events. The amillennialist G. L. Murray conforms to the usual view, holding that when Israel rejected Christ, they ceased to be Israel, so that that designation now refers to all believers in the Lord Jesus Christ.[37] For Berkhof the true Israel (note that recurring phrase in amillennial presentations) is found in the New Testament church of Jesus Christ,[38] and the Israel of God in Galatians 6:16 has reference to all New Testament believers.[39] He must admit that on the latter point there are such commentators as Eadie, Ellicott, Zahn, and Burton who are not in agreement with his viewpoint. His work on systematic theology was written (1946) before the establishment of the state of Israel, so it is not difficult to see, on the basis of amillennial principles, how he has erred in claiming: "It is very doubtful, however, whether the Scripture warrants the expectation that Israel will finally be re-established as a nation and will as a nation turn to the Lord. Some Old Testament prophecies seem to predict this, but these should be read in the light of the New Testament."[40] Time has effectively laid his argument to rest. So much of the difficulty arises from amillennial failure to see that God has an elect people in the Old Testament and an elect people in the New Testament. That clarifies the great prophetic discourse in Matthew 24-25; the elect there are those of Judea, the Jews.

Kromminga, with his attempt to reconcile premillennialism with covenant doctrine, objects to the concept of an earthly people and a heavenly people as a modern idea.[41] It needs to be remembered that there are some who claim that the principle of the Reformation was also a modern idea. The paramount question must be: is it found in the Word of God? Spiritual Israel is defined by him as consisting of all believing Gentiles and all believing Israelites,[42] and "true Christians" are the spiritual seed of Abraham.[43] When he comes to Revelation 12, he interprets the woman as representing both the Old Testament church and the New Testament church. It is an untenable premillennialism that is tacked on to covenantism; there are too many inner tensions in the situation.

Suffice it to say, all premillennialists of consistent view hold that Israel and the church are two different entities. Even the liberal C. H. Toy holds that there is a future for national Israel indicated in the Scriptures. He is quoted as an unprejudiced witness in the matter at hand. He notes,

> In point of fact, the prophets announced the complete restoration of the Israelitish nationality, with political power and glory, with religious leadership and general pre-eminence over the other nations. The idea of religious re-creation was always prominent, but it was never dissociated from the expectation of political regeneration. The nation was to be exemplary in obedience to the divine law; and by its enlightenment, its holiness, and its suffering, was to lead foreign nations to the truth, and be their recognized head.[44]

On behalf of the premillennial position, W. M. Smith has done a service in clarifying the historical situation. He writes,

> It is true that this doctrine of a future blessedness for Israel as distinct from the Church was revived in the nineteenth century, but that it was *new* is not correct. Even three hundred years ago, in this country, a president of Harvard University, Increase Mather, was writing books defending the doctrine of the return of the Jews to Palestine according to a prophetic program and a particular place for those Jews.[45]

Hospers has shown that one must not carry analogies to unwarranted limits. It is one thing to realize that the sacrifices of the Old Testament ceased because they were fulfilled in the cross of Christ. But that does not warrant us in assuming at the same time that Israel is discontinued because of the church.[46] He points out correctly that when one finds the expression "seed of Abraham" in the New Testament, "good logic and rhetoric must regard the designation 'seed of Abraham' as applied to Gentile believers, as tropical."[47] Does Israel ever equal the church? He answers, "It is enough to say that the Old Testament recognizes the incoming Gentiles into the number of God's elect. But this is not equivalent to saying that Israel equals the Church. The national Israel remains the regular Covenant people of God."[48]

It is well to consider the amillennial argument based on Ephesians 2:12-14. That passage is supposed to teach that believers now occupy the commonwealth of Israel, so that the church is Israel. The passage beginning with verse 11 pictures the difference between Israel and the Gentiles before the coming of Christ. Verse 12 especially dilates upon the fact that Gentiles as such did not share in the blessings of Israel. One of the expressions indicates that they "were alienated from the commonwealth of Israel." The amillennial position is that, since believing Gentiles have been made nigh by the blood of Christ, they have by so much become members of the commonwealth of Israel. But the passage does not state that at all. The commonwealth of Israel has reference to their national economy with special reference to God's covenant dealings with them. Gentile believers now do not enter that commonwealth, nor do they become Israelites. They are rather termed "fellow-citizens with the saints, and of the household of God." That is not the commonwealth of Israel. It denotes citizenship of a heavenly character and a place of new birth in the household of God. One must beware of intrusions of a third element that is unproved.

In the matter of the Israel of God of Galatians 6:16, R. J. Reid has the testimony of Scripture with him when he equates them with believing Jews, or those whom Paul calls Jews "inwardly" in Romans 2:28.[49] Bengel is worthy of quotation here when he holds: *"The Israel of God is in antithesis to the circumcision* (the Jews). The Israel of God are believers of the circumcision, or Jewish nation (Phil. 3:3). The meaning of the apostle, which is by no means Jewish, has seized on an expression inconsistent with the idiom of the people; for the Hebrews do not say, *Israel of God;* nor do they even use the proper name in the construct state."[50]

Probably as clear writers on the question of Israel as can be found in the literature of our day are John Wilkinson and his son, Samuel Wilkinson. Engaged for years in the work of evangelization of Israel, they carefully studied through the years the biblical basis for the hope of Israel. John Wilkinson contends that the very wording of Galatians 6:16, coming to the Israel of God after praying for blessing on believing Gentiles, effectively eliminates any reference to believing Gentiles at all. The passage does not teach that Gentiles are ever called Israel.[51] He says, "We believe there is not one single instance in the Word of God, Old Testament or New, in which the term Israel can legitimately be applied to any but the natural descendants of Jacob."[52] Why is it that the New Testament calls all believers the "seed of Abraham"? His answer is forceful and discerning:

All believers in Christ are thus by the authority of Scripture Abraham's spiritual seed. But this does not imply that believers of Gentile origin are *spiritual Israelites*. One does not *include* the other; one *excludes* the other. No one but a converted natural Israelite is properly and scripturally a spiritual Israelite. The very fact that I, a believing Gentile, am a child of Abraham by faith, is the very reason why I am not a spiritual Israelite. Israel was a name given by God to only one man, Jacob, whose children were children of Israel, and whose descendants were and are designated Israelites. The term Israelites legitimately applies to all the descendants of Jacob, and to none others. Are not believing Gentiles spiritual Israelites? No, certainly not. Why not, if they are children of Abraham? Are not the terms 'spiritual seed of Abraham' and 'spiritual Israelites' one and the same as to their meaning? They are not the same thing in themselves, though they both apply equally to all truly converted natural Israelites, they being spiritual Israelites and spiritual seed of Abraham also. Why are not believing Gentiles spiritual Israelites? Because Israel was a term applied to Jacob *after* he was circumcised, and is never applied to any but Jacob's circumcised descendants. Abraham became the father of believers—circumcised and uncircumcised; so that blessings flowing out of this covenant might reach all nations, whilst blessings affecting Israelites as such, would be confined to the elect nation. This teaching will become perfectly clear by a careful study of Romans iv and Galatians iii.[53]

No one is at liberty to interchange words used with precision in Scripture, as Wilkinson has shown. An analogous case is this: One may correctly call Mary the mother of our Lord, but not the mother of God, as Romanists do.

When Samuel Wilkinson comments on Romans 2:28 and 9:6, he does not make the error of many by injecting believing Gentiles here; the apostle is distinguishing in Israel those who are worthy of the name because of faith, and those who have no such claim because they are related to Abraham only as a natural posterity.[54] National Israel, though temporarily set aside, is still Israel,[55] and when the New Testament indicates that the church is made up of believing Jews and believing Gentiles, it does not by so much warrant the conclusion that the entities from which those two remnants come are thereby obliterated. There are now three divisions of the human race instead of two: namely, the Jew, the Gentile, and the church of God (1 Cor. 10:32).[56] He argues cogently the positive proof that the church cannot fulfill the promises to Israel. When the promises to Israel are studied carefully, it will be immediately seen that "it is the necessity, in order to the full realization of the said promises, of a *two-stage* repatriation of the twelve-tribed people of Israel to the territory that was made over to them by spontaneous grant, long before the Sinaitic Covenant of Law was drafted, signed or sealed . . . the first stage, partial and in unbelief, the second stage, complete, final and in exulting and assured faith."[57] Samuel Wilkinson shows that the term "true Israel" is both inaccurate and unscriptural,[58] and places his finger on the source of the difficulty with regard to Israel. He claims, "The whole confusion arises from making partial and temporary deprivation of blessing to mean final and full repudiation."[59] Yet the very purpose of Romans 11 is to stress that the fall of Israel is neither full, final, nor fatal.

A. Pieters has written an entire volume on the theme of the seed of Abraham; his purpose is to determine their identity.[60] He begins his investigations from the standpoint of covenant theology, and it is seen to permeate every position taken. It did not require faith alone to qualify for membership in the Abrahamic covenant; children of members and slaves also automatically became members by birth or purchase.[61] Membership in the covenant society was not of itself permanent; it could be lost and was lost.[62] He declares, "Although etymologically and at first it denoted descent by blood, it soon acquired a technical meaning that was quite independent of such descent. When our Lord said to a group of Jews: 'I know that ye are Abraham's seed' (John 8:37), He had no idea of affirming that the persons before Him were descended by blood from the patriarch. He meant only that they were members of the covenant group."[63] There is no evidence beyond his own statement that the words acquired a new technical meaning; that is arbitrary in the extreme. The assurance with which he approaches the meaning of our Lord in the matter is not at all warranted. He is trying to divorce the seed of Abraham idea from the national concept altogether. He has not yet explained why, in the first provision of the Abrahamic covenant, God promised to make of Abraham "a great nation." That does not tally at all with Pieters's covenant group idea. For him God never made any promises to the Jewish nation[64] but just to "the continuing covenanted community," whatever that may imply.

Arguing in that vein, it is not long before Pieters denies that those whom we call Jews today are descended from Abraham.[65] This author has never encountered that argument in an orthodox writer, but often among liberals who deny the validity of any of God's literal promises to anybody. He quotes no scriptural basis for any of those broad generalizations. What would he make of Jeremiah 30:11 and scores of other passages that are lucid in their pronouncements? They are not in parabolic nor allegorical form. By now one should be prepared for some new definition of the term "seed of Abraham," and one is not disappointed. He contends, "The expression 'Seed of Abraham,' in biblical usage, denotes that visible community, the members of which stand in relation to God through the Abrahamic Covenant, and thus are heirs to the Abrahamic promise. Note that this is a visible community, i.e., a company of men, women and children in families, including believers and unbelievers alike, so long as they remain within the circle of the covenant. . . . It is not a company of the elect, but a social group, recognizable as such by the world at large."[66] Pieters does not restrict spiritual promises to a nation as such but is satisfied to assign them to a new category, which includes believers and unbelievers, mind you, which he calls a social group.

The church, according to him, is "the New Covenant Israel,"[67] and God has only one redeemed and holy people, which is the Christian church. That is an oversimplification of the matter without the requisite Scripture authority. The seed of Abraham is equated with the New Covenant Israel, which in turn is equated with the Christian church.[68] And in all that, the seed of Abraham is supposed to comprise unbelievers also; that is surely using the term in a manner divorced from the Scriptures. To add another feature, the claim is made that there is a "spiritual Israel," which is identical with the elect, the invisible church.[69] Once an interpreter begins to multiply phrases and concepts without biblical foundation, there is difficulty in knowing where to stop. The Bible never speaks of a "spiritual Israel."

When Pieters summarizes his position, he maintains:

> We are stating a historical fact, clearly contained in the sacred records [which he does not quote], that in or about the spring of the year A.D. 30, the mass of those who then called themselves Israelites ceased to be such for prophetic and covenant purposes, having forfeited their citizenship in the commonwealth of Israel by refusing to accept the Messiah, and that after this event all the privileges of the Abrahamic Covenant and all the promises of God belonged to the believing remnant, and to them only; which remnant was therefore and thereafter the true Israel and Judah, the Seed of Abraham, the Christian church. Thus the promise was fulfilled strictly and definitely to the designated parties.[70]

In other words, with the rejection of Christ by the Jews, God declared Himself through with the Jews.[71] The insurmountable difficulty with that position is that it does not square with passages like Romans 11:1. One must take his stand with Paul that God has not cast off His people from their covenant relationship, even after the crucifixion, though many others may discard them. But Pieters knows his views on Israel run counter to passages in the New Testament, so he informs his readers: "This argument is not invalidated by the fact that elsewhere the apostle speaks of his unbelieving countrymen also as 'Israel.' In a time of transition such a double use of the word was unavoidable."[72] By that admission he gives way the falsity of his own position.

But so determined is he to find all in the church and nothing in the literal

Israel now, that when he comes to discuss Romans 3:1-2, and the reference is to Jew, and not Israel, he makes the trustees of the "oracles of God," which are the New Testament writings, the Christian church. And even if the Old Testament Scriptures are meant, he argues, then the church is still the one who holds the trusteeship.[73] That is an amazing interpretation of Scripture. It is well known who preserved the Scriptures before there was a Christian church and have done so to this very hour. They cannot be accused of not guarding the Scriptures because they have substituted their Talmud. On the same premise the church, in spite of its many translations to which he points, has substituted its creeds of the church, which evidently have not always enlightened the eyes of the adherents.

In order to be thoroughgoingly consistent, he cannot allow any of the privileges of Romans 9:4 to apply to the Israel of the Old Testament. Every feature must be made to apply to the visible church. The adoption is made individual when it is national (compare Exod. 4:22 with Gal. 4:4-5); the glory is equated with that of Romans 8:18 instead of the Shekinah glory which is referred to; the being made nigh of Ephesians 2:13 does not make the visible church the heir of the covenants with Israel (which are national), the service is not the present-day worship of Romans 12:1, but the Levitical ministrations.[74] He uses an alchemy of his own to transmute all into his theory, which is arbitrary throughout.

One has been afforded thus far a number of exegetical surprises, but the greatest is yet to come. Pieters writes,

> God does not always have His way in His own world, which is the world's deepest tragedy. So it was in the matter of the Jews. God willed that after the institution of the New Covenant, there should no longer be any Jewish people in the world—yet here they are! That is a fact—a very sad fact, brought about by their wicked rebellion against God; but is it not monstrous to hold that by reason of this wickedness the said undesired and undesirable group are now heirs to the many and exceedingly precious promises of God? Shall we be accused of anti-Semitism, because we speak thus of the Jews? We have not spoken so harshly as the Apostle Paul, who knew them intimately and loved them passionately.[75]

That is the strongest statement of anti-Semitism this writer has found in any Christian work.

Several observations are in order. First, Pieters sets up grave doubts in the minds of his readers when he can entangle God in such a hopeless maze as he indicates in his first sentence. Second, the reason the existence of the Jews is such "a very sad fact" to him is that it completely upsets his views on Israel and the church. According to him, since the church is heir to all that was Israel's, there is no reason for the Jews or Israel to exist now. But somehow (see Jeremiah 31:35-37) they persist, and that is a fact very uncomfortable, to say the least, for his theories born of his covenantism. History has given the lie to his views. Third, he is oblivious of the fact that the visible church, too, is a failure in her testimony for Christ. See Revelation 2 and 3, as well as the epistles of Paul. Finally, can Pieters honestly place himself on a level with Paul in attitude toward Israel and speak the sentiments of Romans 9:3? Paul was not anti-Semitic and he showed it. All others who wish to fill the same category must give some evidence of the same.

If God is through with the Jew,[76] it is in point to inquire whether Paul ceased to be a Jew after his conversion (Acts 21:39). Was he still an Israelite (Rom. 11:1)? Was he still a Hebrew (Phil. 3:5)? Nothing is gained by offering ideas supported with little or no exegesis of pivotal passages of Scripture, and then when exegesis is submitted, to give it the most forced turn.

Israel is Israel, and the church is the church. God has given us large bodies of truth in the Old Testament and in the New Testament concerning them. There is no good reason for confusing them, mingling them, or equating them. Let no one rob Israel, hoping thereby to enrich the church, but at the same time impoverishing both Israel and the church.

Notes

[1]A. Kuyper, *Chiliasm or the Doctrine of Premillennialism,* pp. 7, 19, 24.

[2]W. Masselink, *Why Thousand Years?,* p. 32.

[3]W. Sanday, "The Epistle to the Galatians," in C. J. Ellicott, ed., *Commentary on the Whole Bible,* 7:463. Ladd proceeds more cautiously. "Paul avoids call-ing the church Israel, unless it be in Galatians 6:16, but this is a much disputed verse" (Clouse, *The Meaning of the Millennium,* p. 25). It may be pointed out that that verse is the Waterloo of those who would identify Israel and the church, as will be shown more fully later in this chapter.

[4]C. J. Ellicott, *The Epistle to the Galatians,* p. 154.

[5]See the adequate note on the discussion in NSRB, p. 1223, fn. 1 on Romans 9:6.

[6]L. S. Chafer, *Systematic Theology,* 4:47-53 (expanded to 24 contrasts).

[7]It is difficult to discern the thinking behind such a statement as: "While the New Testament clearly affirms the salvation of literal Israel, it does not give any details about the day of salvation" (Ladd in Clouse, p. 28). The problem often arises because of a confusion of "the times of the Gentiles" (Luke 21:24, a political phrase) and "the fulness of the Gentiles" (Rom. 11:25-27, a soteriological phrase), but the context of the Romans passage states lucidly both the time, place, and participants of that great day. Furthermore, details are forthcoming in abundance in Jeremiah 23:5-8;

Ezekiel 36:24-29; 37:22-23, 27-28; and especially Zechariah 12:10—13:1.

[8]O. T. Allis, *Prophecy and the Church*, p. vii.

[9]Ibid., p. 24.

[10]Ibid., p. 55.

[11]Ibid., p. 90.

[12]Ibid., p. 91.

[13]Ibid., p. 92.

[14]Ibid., pp. 94-95.

[15]Ibid., p. 95.

[16]Ibid., p. 96.

[17]Ibid., pp. 96-97.

[18]Ibid., p. 97.

[19]Ibid., pp. 99-100.

[20]Ibid., p. 305.

[21]Ibid., p. 101.

[22]Ibid., pp. 104-5.

[23]Ibid., p. 107.

[24]Ibid., p. 109.

[25]Ibid., pp. 129-130. Ladd is willing only to state concerning the 144,000: "... God's people ... they are sealed and thus delivered from the wrath" (G. E. Ladd, *A Commentary on the Revelation of John*, p. 112). Later he comments on Rev. 12:1: "This heavenly woman is mother both of Messiah and of the actual church on earth ... it is easier to understand the woman in a somewhat broader sense as the *ideal* [italics his] Zion, the heavenly representative of the people of God" (ibid., p. 167).

[26]Ibid., p. 133.

[27]Ibid., p. 145.

[28]Ibid., p. 148.

[29]Ibid.

[30]Ibid., p. 149.

[31]Ibid., p. 219.

[32]Ibid., pp. 225-26. Gundry also assumes the amillennial interpretation of the identity of the 144,000 of Rev. 7. R. H. Gundry, *The Church and the Tribulation*, p. 80, also pp. 23-24.

[33]F. E. Hamilton, *The Basis of Millennial Faith*, p. 55.

[34]Ibid., p. 56.

[35]Ibid., p. 38.

[36]Ibid., pp. 52-53.

[37]G. L. Murray, *Millennial Studies: A Search For Truth*, p. 31.

[38]L. Berkhof, *The Kingdom of God*, p. 161.

[39]Ibid., p. 162.

[40]L. Berkhof, *Systematic Theology*, p. 699.

[41]D. H. Kromminga, *The Millennium in the Church*, p. 57.

[42]D. H. Kromminga, *The Millennium*, p. 57.

[43]Ibid., p. 60. It borders on the tragi-comedy to witness the nondispensational amillennialist Hoekema and the nondispensational premillennialist Ladd in agreement thus (Hoekema's comment on Ladd): "I agree that the church is often spoken of in the New Testament as spiritual Israel [not once] and that the basic dispensational principle of an absolute distinction between Israel and the church, involving two distinct purposes of God and two distinct peoples of God, has no biblical warrant [see above Part One, chap. 3]. I concur wholeheartedly with what is said about the present spiritual reign of Christ and about the present reality of the kingdom of God" (Clouse, p. 55).

[44]C. H. Toy, *Quotations in the New Testament*, p. xxvi.

[45]W. M. Smith, "Israel and the Church in Prophecy," p. 957.

[46]G. H. Hospers, *The Principle of Spiritualization in Hermeneutics*, p. 19. After admitting that he is a nondispensationalist because he does not distinguish between Israel and the church throughout the divine program, Ladd declares: "I do not see how it is possible to avoid the conclusion that the New Testament applies Old Testament prophecies to the New Testament church and in so doing identifies the church as spiritual Israel" (Clouse, pp. 20, 23). Further, "The prophecies of Hosea are fulfilled in the Christian church. If this is a 'spiritualizing hermeneutic,' so be it" (ibid., p. 24). That is strange language, to say the least, for an avowed premillennialist. Notice the reasoning: "If Abraham is the father of a spiritual people, and if all believers are sons of Abraham, his offspring, then it follows that they are Israel, spiritually speaking" (ibid.). Does it follow, and where is that stated? John Wilkinson has effectively demolished that type of reasoning, which is without basis in Scripture.

[47]Hospers, p. 30.

[48]Ibid., p. 31.

[49]R. J. Reid, *Amillennialism*, pp. 10, 12, 32.

[50]J. A. Bengel, *Gnomon of the New Testament*, 4:58; also H. L. Payne, *Amillennialism as a System*, p. 118.

[51]J. Wilkinson, *Israel, My Glory*, p. 20.

[52]Ibid., p. 21.

[53]Ibid., pp. 17-18.

[54]S. H. Wilkinson, *The Israel Promises and Their Fulfillment*, p. 23.

[55]Ibid., p. 59.

[56]Ibid., pp. 107-8.

[57]Ibid., p. 120.

[58]Ibid., pp. 125-26, 144.
[59]Ibid., p. 170.
[60]A. Pieters, *The Seed of Abraham*, p. 13.
[61]Ibid., p. 16.
[62]Ibid., p. 18.
[63]Ibid., p. 19.
[64]Ibid.
[65]Ibid., p. 20.
[66]Ibid., pp. 20-21.
[67]Ibid., p. 65.
[68]Ibid., pp. 66-67.
[69]Ibid., p. 67.
[70]Ibid., p. 76.
[71]Ibid., p. 125.
[72]Ibid., p. 90.
[73]Ibid., p. 95.
[74]Ibid., pp. 95-97.
[75]Ibid., p. 123.
[76]Ibid., p. 125.

16

The Church and the Kingdom

In the discussion of the amillennial conception of the kingdom in the Old and New Testaments, it was pointed out that the amillennial view holds that the New Testament teaches that the kingdom is spiritual rather than earthly and is partly realized now rather than all future. Vos believes that, although Christ made the kingdom a present reality, He still spoke of it as future in harmony with His first and original prophetic usage of the kingdom.[1]

Mains believes that premillennialism slights the present spiritual order in maintaining that Christ's reign will be effectively established on earth only after His glorious return. For them, he alleges, the present age of the church is but a twilight preparation as compared with the glory that shall come to the world in the millennial age. He admits that the Jews of old always thought of the Messianic reign as being realized upon the earth itself. That it would be a heavenly and spiritual kingdom apart from the earth never suggested itself to Israel. He does not explain that strange phenomenon.[2]

Kuyper holds that the expectation of an earthly kingdom received its death-blow when worldwide gospel preaching was commanded by the Lord Jesus.[3] Masselink, however, is an amillennialist who deals with the subject with some degree of fulness. He begins by showing the supposed error of the Scofield Bible in distinguishing between the kingdom and the church. He conceives of the error of the premillenarians as having its roots in the postponement or abeyance theory.[4] The chiliasts, he alleges, understand that Christ spoke of His kingdom as being present or "at hand," and they must make those passages mean something else. Their preconceived notions that the kingdom is future and earthly drive them to some sort of harmonization between a future material kingdom and the passages that speak of the kingdom as present. That is accomplished by the postponement theory. For himself the church is the kingdom as prophesied in the Old Testament prophets, although it does have, to his way of thinking, a future aspect also.

His objections to the theory of the postponement of the kingdom are several. They will be answered later in presenting the premillennial conception of the church and the kingdom.

His first criticism of the abeyance theory is that the Messianic kingdom is not dependent upon the Jews for its establishment. Neither Christ nor John the Baptist gave the impression that the setting up of the kingdom depended upon the attitude of the Jews. In fact, Christ never foretold that His kingdom depended upon His second coming, but rather said that it would be taken from the Jews to be given to the Gentiles, "a nation bringing forth the fruits thereof."

Second, it denies apparently the design of Christ's coming. The Scriptures never reveal that Christ came to set up an earthly kingdom. He came rather to seek and to save that which was lost, to minister rather than to be ministered unto, and to save a world of sinners.

Third, it is manifest from the teaching of the Word that Christ's kingdom could only be set up through His suffering. The only way to the throne was the way of the cross and suffering.

Fourth, the abeyance theory makes the cross uncertain.[5] The question is asked as to what would have become of the death and resurrection of Christ had the Jews accepted the alleged offer of the kingdom. Premillennialists, according to him, make the whole glorious truth of the substitutionary death of the Son of God dependent upon the timely refusal of the Jews to receive the kingdom offered by the King. That is the greatest objection to the postponement theory.

But there are other criticisms of the view. Furthermore, the infallibility of Christ is at stake, for either Christ was right or He was mistaken when He spoke of His kingdom as present. The only intelligent interpretation of the phrase "at hand" is that the kingdom was then ready to be realized and actualized. Did Jesus have to change His mind about the kingdom and its establishment? The whole postponement theory, he insists, involves the teachings of the Lord in contradiction, for He ever spoke of it as present.

The postponement theory, or heresy as it has been called on one occasion, denies the unity of the church. It rejects the tenet that the church is the true Israel of God. It finds no continuity or organic unity of God's revelation linking the Israel of the Old Testament with the church of the New. Moreover, the denial of the unity of the church involves a refusal to believe that the middle wall of partition has been broken down between Jew and Gentile. The chiliast is said to teach two ways of salvation, one for the Jew and one for the Gentile. The Jew of the Old Testament economy was saved in a manner different from that whereby the New Testament believer is redeemed to God. The manifestation of God's wrath in the millennial kingdom is to take the place of the preaching of the gospel.

Finally, the postponement theory is criticized because it disregards historical testimony. The Christian church has always held that Israel is the church. The view had adherents among the faithful of the apostolic age, among the church Fathers, and among the Reformers of the sixteenth century. It is impossible that the church should have been allowed to proceed for so many centuries in error when the Holy Spirit is present in her midst.

A consideration of the premillennial position of the church and the kingdom reveals one of the reasons for the great divergence of results that inevitably follows from an adherence to either view. The two views differ here as much as they do anywhere. The premillenarian distinguishes between the kingdom of God, the kingdom of heaven, and the church. Those terms have been purposely stated in that order, for they should logically be dealt with in that succession. By the kingdom of God chiliasts understand the all-inclusive rule of God the Father, God the Son, and God the Holy Spirit over the entire universe, particularly with regard to all moral intelligences everywhere and at all times. The kingdom of heaven is the earthly sphere of the kingdom of God and is visible and outward. The church is a part of the kingdom of heaven in its mystery form, as was pointed out in the discussion of Matthew 13. One cannot do better here than to quote the distinctions made by Scofield in his Reference Bible:

> The kingdom of God is to be distinguished from the kingdom of heaven ... in five respects: (1) The kingdom of God is universal, including all moral intelligences willingly subject to the will of God, whether angels, the Church or saints of past or future dispensations (Lk. 13:28, 29; Heb. 12:22, 23); while the kingdom of heaven is Messianic, mediatorial, and Davidic, and has for its object the establishment of the kingdom of God in the earth (... I Cor. 15:24, 25). (2) The kingdom of God is entered only by the new birth (John 3:3, 5-7); the kingdom of heaven, during this age, is the sphere of a profession which may be real or false (Mt. 13:3, note; 25:1, 11, 12). (3) Since the kingdom of heaven is the earthly sphere of the universal kingdom of God, the two have almost all things in common. For this reason many parables and other teachings are spoken of the kingdom of heaven in Matthew, and of the kingdom of God in Mark and Luke. It is the omissions which are significant. The parables of the wheat and tares, and of the net (Mt. 13:24-30, 36-43, 47-50) are not spoken of the kingdom of God. In that kingdom there are neither tares nor bad fish. But the parable of the leaven (Mt. 13:33) is spoken of the kingdom of God also, for, alas, even the true doctrines of the kingdom are leavened with the errors of which the Pharisees, Sadducees, and the Herodians were the representatives ... (4) The kingdom of God "comes not with outward show" (Lk. 17:20), but is chiefly that which is inward and spiritual (Rom. 14:17); while the kingdom of heaven is organic, and is to be manifested in glory on the earth ... (5) The kingdom of heaven merges into the king-

dom of God when Christ, having "put all enemies under His feet," "shall have delivered up the kingdom to God, even the Father" (I Cor. 15:24-28).[6]

Because two things have points of similarity does not make them identical. Because a state has trees, city government, state government, police enforcement of laws, and a number of things in common with the United States as a whole, does not warrant us in concluding that the United States and that state are identical. And yet the same line of logic is followed by amillennialists who insist on making no differentiation between the kingdom of heaven, the kingdom of Christ, the church, or the kingdom of God. Those distinctions are vital and must be made to harmonize the Word of God.

Many considerations cause the premillennialists to deny that the kingdom is fulfilled in the church of this age. First of all, the phrase "at hand" does not mean "immediately near." Immediateness and imminency are not synonymous terms. When Paul spoke of the night as far spent, and the day at hand, he did not mean it was immediately near (Rom. 13:12). Nor was that what Peter meant to convey when he declared that the end of all things is at hand (1 Pet. 4:7). So the argument of Masselink that Christ's kingdom is present because of that phrase does not commend itself to our thinking.

Furthermore, when the people thought that the kingdom of God should immediately appear, because He was near Jerusalem, He revealed to them in the parable of the nobleman going into a far country that the kingdom was future, after a lapse of a long period of time (Luke 19:11-15). Moreover, the premillennialists are open to proof that will demonstrate that all the Old Testament prophets depicted of the kingdom age and its characteristics is fulfilled in the church. In a day when the minds of men are occupied with thoughts of war, as they have been for years, how can anyone logically reconcile that with what Isaiah, or Jeremiah, or Ezekiel foretold of the reign of peace on the earth during the kingdom age? Where is the renovated earth? Since when is Satan bound, no longer to tempt men? Those and many other questions could be propounded to show the utter impossibility of identifying the church with the kingdom.

Ottman points out succinctly that if the posterity of David in the present dispersion, with the kingdom of the house of David gone, and the throne done away with, and displaced by a spiritual kingdom over which Christ rules from the throne where He is now seated, can be reasonably taken as a fulfillment of God's covenant with David, then words have indeed lost their meaning and the Bible must be from henceforth an insoluble riddle.[7] Much has been made, in fact, of the session of Christ in heaven as mentioned by Peter in Acts and the other apostles, the attempt being made to show that that proves Christ's present reign. It is overlooked, alas, that He sits not on His own throne, as He shall in the kingdom, but He Himself declares (Rev. 3:21) that He is seated on His blessed Father's throne. But premillennialists have not exhausted their reasons for believing that the church is not the kingdom.

The gospel of the kingdom is national, whereas the gospel of grace is individual. There is no room to confuse the two. The kingdom and all that pertains to it are earthly; the church is heavenly. J. H. Todd makes the claim that any student tracing through the epistles to find the references there to the kingdom, will discover that of the seventeen passages dealing with the kingdom, there are only three (Rom. 14:17; 1 Cor. 4:20; Col. 1:13) that can be taken to apply to the present time. All the rest refer to the future.[8] H. Lummis brought out what appears a most important argument for the distinction of the church and the kingdom. He claimed that one cannot expect a more absolute separation between these two ideas than that which is made in the New Testament by the terminology employed in describing each.[9]

When the Lord Jesus Christ spoke of the origin of His church, He used the word *oikodomeo* in the following construction: *oikodomeso mou ten ekklesian.* That word is found twenty-four times in the New Testament but is never joined with the word that is used about ninety times in the gospels alone in such expressions as "the kingdom of heaven" and "the kingdom of God." The word used in the Septuagint of Daniel for the establishment of the kingdom is *anastesai,* to set up or raise up. Finally, N. West maintains most reasonably that the kingdom cannot be located between the first advent and the second advent of the Lord, because during that period Israel will be nationally cut off, and the Millennium will begin with a national resurrection of Israel, according to the prophecy of Ezekiel 37; furthermore, in the period between the advents the Gentile colossus will still be standing, whereas the kingdom age begins with the utter and complete destruction of the colossus, according to the prophecy of Daniel 2. Let that suffice to show that the kingdom is not the church.[10]

But what shall be said of the objections of Masselink to the truth which he calls the postponement, or abeyance, heresy?[11] They are answered in order.

First, it is denied by him that the establishment of the Messianic kingdom was dependent upon the Jews. If that is so, why, then, did the Lord Jesus come preaching to Israel that the kingdom of heaven was at hand (Matt. 4:17, 23)? Why did He command the disciples to preach, not to the Gentiles or even the half-Jews, or Samaritans, but rather to the lost sheep of the house of Israel (Matt. 10:5-7)? It is also passing strange that when He was approached by the woman of Canaan for help, He said He was not sent but unto the lost sheep of the house of Israel (Matt. 15:21-28). When He offered Himself as King, it was to Israel that He did so (Matt. 21:1-11). Then again, when Paul spoke of the ministry of Christ, he made clear that it was a ministry to the circumcision for the truth of God to confirm the promises made unto the fathers (Rom. 15:8). All the promises to David concerning the coming kingdom revealed that the son of David was to rule over regathered Israel. From the human standpoint, then, the establishment of the Messianic kingdom is dependent upon the Jews, as Peter bore out so well in Acts 3:19-21 (cf. also Matt. 23:39).

Second, the premillennial postponement theory is supposed to deny the glorious design of Christ's coming, because it holds that Christ came to set up an earthly kingdom. The millenarians do not maintain that the only purpose of God's coming was to set up the kingdom. He came to offer the kingdom to Israel, to reveal the Father, to put away sins, to destroy the works of Satan, to leave His followers an example, to provide a foundation for the church, and to prepare for the second advent—all to glorify God. That He did purpose to set up an earthly kingdom is evident from the content of His message and that of His disciples, as has been shown at length in the discussion of the premillennial view. If Christ did not mean to set up an earthly kingdom, then His triumphal entry into Jerusalem is inexplicable. If the Lord Jesus never intended to establish an earthly kingdom, why did He not set the disciples right from the very start when they began to dispute about preeminence in the coming kingdom? One could multiply questions, but consider the next objection.

Third, it is maintained that the kingdom is realized through suffering. The chiliasts do not deny this. All the blessing in the world in all ages is directly traceable to the death of Christ. Indeed, the kingdom is to be realized through suffering. So the Old Testament prophets understood the messages of God and His purposes. There is no objection, real and sustainable, in that against the millennial view. That was God's purpose, and He so realized it.

Fourth, it is claimed—and this is closely allied to the former question, or argument—that the abeyance theory makes the cross uncertain, because if the Jews had accepted the kingdom, what would have happened to the death and resurrection of Christ? In the first place, the Jews did not accept Christ, which makes the objection nothing more than a supposable case. Also, the case is analogous to the events at Kadesh-Barnea. Did not the Lord know that Israel would not enter the land in that generation? Yet He offered them all the opportunity of doing so. Furthermore, the offer of the gospel in this age comes under the same category. All know well enough, and all the more does God know, that everyone in this age is not to be saved. Nevertheless, the command is to preach the blessed gospel to all people. It is the same old question of the sovereignty of God and the responsibility of man. The cross, it is true, was in the determinate counsel and foreknowledge of God, but it was executed when men with wicked hands took and crucified the matchless and adorable Son of God. Finally, there is a possibility that had the Jews as a nation accepted Christ as their King, that in the setting up of the kingdom some traitor from the nation, suppose he was sponsored by the Roman authorities, would have delivered Him up to be crucified. So the case is not an insoluble one. God had provided Himself with a Lamb from the foundation of the world.

The fifth objection is that the postponement theory militates against the infallibility of Jesus, who, if He knew the kingdom was not at hand and present, should not have said so. If He did not know it, then He was mistaken. It has been pointed out that "at hand" does not imply immediately following, but only conveys the idea of imminence. Furthermore, the Lord conditioned the establishment of the kingdom on national repentance, which was not forthcoming from Israel. He also knew that Israel would reject Him, for He claimed to come to seek and to save the lost. Christ was just as infallible in offering the kingdom to Israel as at hand, as was God the Father in setting the land of Canaan before Israel to go in and possess it.

In the sixth place, the postponement of the kingdom is said to destroy the unity of the church, that in the Old and New Testaments. This work has already dealt with that question in the preceding chapter. Furthermore, the premillennial conception of the kingdom postponement is charged with teaching two ways of salvation. How that can honestly be gleaned from the millennial view, it is hard, even impossible, to see. But the charge is made. It is said that the middle wall of partition has been broken down between Jew and Gentile, which means that the church is the same in the Old and New Testaments (Eph. 2:14-18). Surely amillennial scholars should be able to discern from a diligent study of the Scriptures that when Paul speaks of the breaking down of the middle wall of partition, he is speaking of the church in the New Testament made up of believing Jews and Gentiles. Where does he mention Old Testament saints at all? Nowhere in the church are they to be found. All premillennialists believe God has one way of saving both Jew and Gentile; namely, through the vicarious and substitutionary death of the Son of God to satisfy the demands of a holy and righteous God who from His very nature hates with a perfect hatred all that the Word reveals as sin. Paul's argument in Romans 4:1 ff. seeks to make clear that God has always justified guilty sinners by faith. Their faith has been counted unto them for righteousness. To be saved by faith is not synonymous in the Scriptures with being a member of the church. There have been saved people before the church age, and there will be saved people after the church age has closed, that will not be reckoned as a constituent part of the church. How much confusion there is from a wrong conception of the nature, origin, purpose, and constituency of the church! That objection is a most serious charge against the millennial view and wholly unfounded.

Finally, amillennialists accuse the abeyance theory of disregarding historical testimony. Earlier in this discussion it was shown that the early church, as admitted by scholars and patristic experts, was premillennial. Apart from that, there have been throughout the ages of the history of professing Christendom, numbers of believers that have held the premillennial position. Furthermore, the historic argument never proves anything of itself. It must be supported by other considerations. Recapitulating the arguments thus far, then, it has been shown that the church cannot possibly be the covenanted and promised kingdom of David, all the theorizing and objections of the amillennialists to the contrary notwithstanding.

As has already been seen, the church was in the Old Testament neither by way of manifestation nor by way of prediction. Homer Payne has stated it well:

> The nature of the church is what is basic in the mystery and Paul does expressly say that the church as a body is 'new' (Eph. 2:15). This is the Achilles' heel in Allis' theory. It is not an inference of dispensationalism but the plain word of Scripture that the church as such *is* a 'new man.' It is not Israel made over. It is not the Messianic Kingdom with spiritual alterations. It is not Zion. It is categorically declared to be a *new* thing which may not be disallowed by the interpretation of qualifying clauses.[12]

Ladd puts it in this fashion:

> If it had been possible to gather the great prophets of the kingdom in a conference and ask them questions about the present church age, it is likely that there would have resulted more differences of opinion that now exist concerning the future millennial kingdom [note in this connection the force of 1 Peter 1:10, 11, a passage which is referred to once by Allis without any explanation], for the Holy Spirit had not revealed to the Old Testament prophets the events which should transpire between the two advents of Christ. So true is this that some students are unable to find the church in the Old Testament, except in type.[13]

But if the church is not in the Old Testament in manifestation or prediction, the same does not hold for the Messianic kingdom. The Messianic kingdom, though not manifested in the Old Testament economy, was amply prophesied there. Amillennialists, who find that Israel and the church are the same, are desirous of equating the church with the Messianic kingdom in greater or lesser degree. Vos is an able spokesman for the amillennial position, and, besides his work on theology, has written a book on the kingdom and the church. In speaking of the phrase "the kingdom of God," he states: "As to the former phrase, this is used already by John as something familiar to his hearers; it is not, however, a phrase of O.T. coinage; while the idea occurs in the O.T., the finished phrase is not there as yet. Probably it is of Jewish provenience; exactly how old it is we cannot tell."[14] Two important features issue from that statement which will be useful for later discussion. John was using a phrase familiar to his hearers, and the exact origin of the terminology is not certain as to time. The kingdom Christ announced "is that Kingdom which lay in the future to the O.T. perspective."[15] With that, premillennialists can agree. But it is not long before Vos takes the position common to many that there was a difference between Jesus' concept of the kingdom and that of the Jews. He holds:

> The kingdom remained to the Jews in its essence particularistic; pros-

elytism did not do away with the fact that pagans, in order to partake of its benefits, would previously have to become Jews through circumcision. The Kingdom-hope of the Jews was also politically-nationalistically colored, whereas in the teaching of Jesus its tendency was in the direction of universalism. Finally, there was a considerable mixture of sensualism in the Jewish eschatology. Here the discrimination is more difficult to make. It mainly consists in this, that what to the Jews was a species of literal sensualism, was to Jesus an exemplification of His parabolic frame of mind, which makes the heavenly enjoyments, while retaining their full realism, yet processes of a higher, spiritualized world, in which even the body will have its place and part.[16]

Several observations should be made to that involved statement. (1) Vos does not explain why the Jewish conception of the kingdom was so politically and nationalistically inclined. (2) It is not made clear why Jesus reversed their concept and on what basis. (3) One cannot go along with survivals of Gnosticism in the amillennial view, which make them discountenance all that is material, as though directly antithetical to the spiritual and moral. (4) The type of accommodation he suggests for Jesus under the term "His parabolic frame of mind" is not acceptable. Moreover, what does Vos do with the "literal sensualism" of Matthew 19:28 and Luke 22:28-30? Is that to be laid to the account of the "parabolic frame of mind"? (5) On what ground is one justified in injecting "heavenly enjoyments" here at all? (6) Spiritualization in Scripture is indefensible even when employed in the interests of "a higher, spiritualized world."

There will be a treatment at some length of the two phrases, "kingdom of God" and "kingdom of heaven," but Vos's position is characteristic of many amillennialists and nondispensationalists. He makes them the same. He contends, "The question arises what this—to us, somewhat mysterious—term 'Kingdom of Heaven' signifies . . . it attaches itself to the Jewish custom of using the word 'Heaven,' together with other substitute terms, in place of the name of God, because the latter had in its various forms become an object of increasing avoidance. 'Heaven' thus simply meant 'God' by a roundabout manner of speaking."[17] It must be remarked that it is striking the way in which amillennialists can dismiss all that the Jews conceived of the kingdom that Christ did not accept, but claim He conformed nonetheless to their superstitious avoidance of the use of the name of God. Where is the proof that He was governing Himself by their concepts here, when He did not on the larger question of the nature of the kingdom? Vos's view of the kingdom is that Christ Himself by His labors began the work of the kingdom on earth, then His followers continue that "Kingdom-producing labor" throughout the ages of the history of the church on earth, at which time by a world-changing catastrophe God will usher in "the eschatological Kingdom-state."[18] That is the familiar amillennial order of the kingdom of grace becoming the kingdom of glory. He complains that the premillennialists keep the church and the kingdom apart,[19] whereas he adduces Matthew 16:18-20 to show that the church and the kingdom are not separate institutions, but "in principle one."[20] To be sure, Christ and His work are essential for both the church and the kingdom, but that is a far cry from making them identical.

In his specific work on the subject of this chapter, Vos rightly begins with the assertion that the message of Christ on the kingdom presupposes His taking the Old Testament as the basis for all His work.[21] Whether it surprises some or not, he holds that Christ never spoke of the kingdom of God as having previous existence; it was something new, something to be realized.[22] As far as the hope of the kingdom of God is concerned, it is made equivalent to the Messianic hope of Israel.[23] Then without Scripture proof Vos maintains that Christ had to protest against the popular Jewish misconception of the kingdom that was intended to bring Israel both preeminence and glory.[24] Quite inadequate is his explanation of the use of "kingdom of heaven" in Matthew. He holds:

> In Mark and Luke 'the kingdom of heaven' is not found. This raises the question, which of these two versions more literally reproduces the usage of Jesus Himself. In all probability Matthew's does, since no good reason can be assigned, why he should have substituted 'the kingdom of heaven,' whilst a sufficient plausible reason for the opposite procedure on the part of Mark and Luke can be found, in the fact, that, writing for Gentile readers, they might think such a typically Jewish phrase, as 'the kingdom of heaven' less intelligible than the plain 'kingdom of God.' Of course, in holding this, we need not imply that in each individual case, where the first Evangelist has 'kingdom of heaven,' this phrase was actually employed by Jesus. All we mean to affirm is the general proposition that Jesus used both phrases, and that insofar Matthew has preserved for us an item of information no longer obtainable from the other two Synoptical Gospels.[25]

As will be seen later, the explanation is in another direction. It is not true that when Jesus referred to the kingdom of heaven, He had in mind the kingdom of God.[26] Vos has more evidence with him when he maintains, "Although the phrase 'kingdom of heaven' is not found in the Old Testament, the word 'heaven' appears there already in significant association with the idea of the future kingdom."[27] The basis for the concept is indeed in the Old Testament.

Vos acknowledges:

> It must be admitted that the Old Testament does not distinguish between several stages or phrases in the fulfillment of the promises regarding the kingdom, but looks upon its coming as an undivided whole. John the

Baptist also seems to have still occupied this Old Testament standpoint. This, however, was due to the peculiar character of the prophecy in general, in which there is a certain lack of perspective, a vision of things separated in time on one plane.[28]

Moreover, it can be shown that the New Testament also presents more than one phase of the kingdom.[29] Christ's work on earth is supposed to have been "a provisional stage of realization of the kingdom,"[30] but in what sense that is true, the reader is not told. Even less convincing is Vos's interpretation of the mystery parables. He maintains, "What else could so suitably have been designated by Jesus 'a mystery' in comparison with the Jewish expectations than the truth that the kingdom comes gradually, imperceptibly, spiritually?" He is using the term "mystery" in a way not warranted from New Testament usage.

Vos notes that there was a change in the teaching of our Lord, but his reason given does not do justice to the elements involved. He contends, "Thus in condescension to Israel he took up the thread of revelation where the Old Testament had left it, to give a new and richer development to it soon after in his epoch-making parabolic deliverances."[31] If Israel was in such error on her views of the kingdom, it is impossible that Christ should change the tenor of His message "in condescension to Israel." It does not conform to the New Testament portrait of Christ. But Vos does have a point in showing the unhappy character of some of the amillennial terminology. He states, "It should be observed that our Lord's teaching relates to two aspects of the same kingdom, not to two separate kingdoms. The ancient theological distinction between a kingdom of grace and a kingdom of glory is infelicitous for this reason."[32]

Apparently contradicting a former position that Christ taught out of regard for the views of Israel, Vos informs us:

> A tendency exists with some writers, especially of the class who insist that Jesus had no other than the eschatological conception of the kingdom, to identify the view ascribed to Him with the current Jewish expectations. This would involve, that he was not only mistaken in regard to the time of the kingdom's appearance, but also held an inherently false idea regarding its nature, not having entirely outgrown the limitations of His age and environment on this point.[33]

Those words sound strangely similar to those that issue from liberal sources. What Christ is supposed to have done is to have borrowed not much more than the name of the kingdom from Judaism, then to have heightened it and ennobled it by extracting from it the political, the national, and the sensual (by which is meant the material).[34] When all those elements are subtracted from the Old Testament expectation of the kingdom, there is little, if any, affinity between the predicted kingdom and the one in realization portrayed by amillennialists and those who reject the Old Testament testimony. The point of contact is one only, and that is the name. It takes more faith to believe that interpretation than it does to believe the premillennial view.

But Vos has not eliminated all the difficulties. He may talk of the sensualistic elements in the Jewish view of the kingdom, but he finds Christ speaking of eating, drinking, reclining at table, inheriting the earth, and much more, in connection with the kingdom. There is always the evasive refuge of spiritualization, and to that he resorts, but with a word of caution: "On the other hand, we must remember that it is possible to go too far in the spiritualizing interpretation of this class of utterances. We may not dissolve everything into purely inward processes and mental states, as modern theologians do when they say that heaven and hell are in the hearts of men."[35] Read that last sentence again and see if this discussion has been too drastic in its characterization of his method of interpretation. Have we not indicated the same limit to which his course will lead? It is to the land of no return in interpretation. The parallel he draws is valid: If the amillennialists claim strenuously that the kingdom is only in the hearts of men, why not heaven and hell also?

At last Vos is willing to admit:

> It is easy to speak disparagingly of the gross realistic expectations of the Jews, but those who do so often attack under the pretense of a refined spiritualism the very essence of biblical supernaturalism. After all deductions are made, it must be maintained that the Jews could not have cherished this vigorous realism, had they not been supernaturalists at heart, trained in that great school of supernaturalism, the Old Testament. In this matter Jesus was in full agreement with their position.[36]

Heartiest agreement is accorded that statement of Vos; but at the same time one is at a loss to see how he can reconcile that position with all that he has declared thus far. One cannot have the argument both ways. When he comments on Matthew 16:18 and 18:17, his position is not at all like that of Allis. He writes, "The first on the other hand deals with the church for the express purpose of introducing it as something new, of describing its character and defining its relation to the kingdom."[37] If the church is something new, and it is, then it was not in existence nor foretold in the Old Testament. Further proof is presented when commenting on Matthew 16:21: "Plainly then in his mind there was a connection between the results of his suffering and the origin of the church."[38] That is valid and susceptible of Scripture proof, but it demolishes the view that holds there could be a church before the cross of Christ. Ephesians 1:19-23 is far too clear on that point. It took the death, the burial, the resurrection, and the ascension of Christ to the right hand of the Father, before there could be a church.

Though he has previously argued the connection between the church and the kingdom on the basis of the Matthew 16 passage, Vos states: "It would not be impossible, of course, to give a plausible interpretation of this connection on the view, that the church and the kingdom are separate things."³⁹ But one cannot allow him (on the basis of Matt. 13:41) to equate the "kingdom of the Son of man" with the "church of Jesus," as he attempts to do, solely on the basis that both phrases treat of a kingdom which is a body of men under the Messiah as ruler.⁴⁰ Then one could have the equation that, because a lion is an animal and a tiger is an animal, therefore a lion is a tiger. No one is at liberty so to commingle expressions that have so many features of a diverse nature. The explanation as to how the kingdom becomes the church cannot be substantiated.⁴¹ The strong language used for the coming of the kingdom dare not be softened to fit into a newly made picture of the church, and Vos tries with difficulty to oversimplify, but cannot escape the resort of spiritualization to give the argument some semblance of plausibility.

Berkhof points out at the outset of his treatment of the kingdom that the Reformers hardly gave special attention to the subject or developed an adequate idea.⁴² That may account in some measure for the great diversity of views among students of the subject. He gives the various opinions on the kingdom of God thus:

> We learn that it is simply the reign of God in human life and human affairs, but also that it is a community that recognizes the will of God as the law of its life; that it is purely an ideal, hovering far above the actual life of the world, but also that it is a present reality with some concrete embodiment; that it is identical with the Church or with the Christian State, but also that it is simply the perfect social order, the utopia of the Socialist, or the millennial kingdom of peace and happiness.⁴³

Manifestly, there is great difference of opinion, and all the views cannot be correct. The theme is truly a complex one,⁴⁴ but it is certainly not beyond human comprehension. When Christ began His preaching of the kingdom, He sounded a familiar note, for the prophets of Israel had pointed forward to a kingdom of righteousness and peace. Thus far one can agree with Berkhof, but when he insists that Jesus took the kingdom concept and "enlarged and transformed and spiritualized it,"⁴⁵ he cannot be followed. How Christ could do all that is claimed, and yet not change the fundamental character, is difficult to see. No wonder His view of the kingdom ceased to be that of the Jews.⁴⁶ It is claimed that Christ gave no definition of the kingdom of God, but included in the comprehensive idea are a number of essential elements.⁴⁷ Those elements are said to be the abstract and concrete meanings of the word kingdom.

The kingdom comprehends a present and gradually developing idea, as well as a future hope, according to Berkhof.⁴⁸ It is conceded with reference to the apostles that "because they looked upon the Church as a visible manifestation of the Kingdom, it does not seem strange that, while they mention the Church more than a hundred times, they are comparatively silent about the present Kingdom, and reserve the name, 'Kingdom of God,' primarily for its future glorious manifestation."[49] Although there may be desired a fuller elaboration of his first statement, he is correct in his judgment of the comparative silence on the present kingdom, and that in opposition to those who make so much of what they like to term the spiritual phase, or content, of the kingdom. For Berkhof there is no real difference between the present and the future kingdom.[50] A shift, however, has come in these times emphasizing the eschatological aspect of the kingdom, and that apart from premillenarians. The eschatological school of New Testament criticism has rescued the concept from complete submergence in the present scene.[51]

There are points of agreement between the eschatologist and the premillennialist. Both maintain (1) Christ's concept of the kingdom was the same as that of His contemporaries; (2) their view was determined by Old Testament prophecy; (3) Jesus did not spiritualize the idea of the kingdom and establish the kingdom while on earth; (4) in His ministry the realization of the kingdom was dependent on the repentance of the Jews; and (5) Christ never stated that the kingdom was a present reality.[52] Berkhof correctly defines the premillennial concept of the kingdom,[53] concluding: "The coming Kingdom then will be the theocracy restored, in which Jesus Christ, the great Son of David, will rule as God's representative."[54] Because he favors a spiritualized kingdom, he finds fault with the view that would make the kingdom a political kingdom after the analogy of the kingdoms in Daniel 2.[55] He does not explain, however, why the Old Testament itself placed the kingdom of the Messiah in juxtaposition with the four universal kingdoms preceding it. He is also in error when he claims: "Premillenarians are compelled by the logic of their system to deny the present existence of the Kingdom of God."[56] Premillennialists claim that the Messianic Kingdom is not now in existence, but they do recognize the mystery form of the kingdom (a provisional arrangement not seen in the Old Testament, but revealed in Matthew 13); and furthermore, they believe all believers are immediately admitted to the kingdom of God (John 3:3), which is not an identical concept, as we shall show later.

Taking the normal amillennial position, Allis contends: "The kingdom announced by John and by Jesus was primarily and essentially a moral and spiritual kingdom. It was to be prepared for by repentance."[57] True, the kingdom Christ and John announced was to be a moral and spiritual kingdom with spiritual requirements, but that is not tantamount to holding that the kingdom concept was spiritualized. Allis believes that if Christ had come to set up the kind of kingdom the Jews expected, He would not and could not have replied to Pilate in the words of John 18:36.[58] That is to misunderstand "not of this world" as though it meant "not in this world."

The expression is explained by our Lord Himself when He states that kingdoms of this world, of this world system, are inaugurated and sustained by physical force and warfare. His will be in this world but not of that origination.

Never forget that a literal kingdom can have and must have spirituality. Because Christ rules, it will be a spiritual kingdom. It is blasphemous to suppose that He would have part in anything not spiritual, but that is not maintaining that the kingdom is to be spiritualized into meaning the church and the rule of God in the hearts of men, without reference to the fulfillment of the Davidic Covenant. But Allis recognizes that the Davidic promise must be here somewhere, and includes it thus: "While in a sense Jewish and Davidic, the kingdom which Jesus announced was also to be world-wide."[59] That statement is inadequate, for it leaves unexplained the sense in which the kingdom Christ announced was both Jewish and Davidic. On such vital points ambiguity might have been avoided, because they touch the core of the contention.

Ladd is convinced that anyone studying the gospels for the first time would not make a distinction between the kingdom of God and the kingdom of heaven;[60] but that cannot be normative for that important subject. Though he equates the kingdom of heaven with the kingdom of God, he still wants a future aspect of the kingdom of heaven,[61] and that in a "future literal earthly aspect of the kingdom of God before the final consummation."[62] Unfortunately, the amillennialists will not allow him to have the kingdom in their manner for the first advent, and then a premillennial and earthly kingdom for the second advent. Premillennialists also are not convinced of the validity of this two-way argument. Furthermore, if he makes the terms "kingdom of heaven" and "kingdom of God" synonymous, he has the same difficulty that he poses for the dispensationalist in Matthew 19:23, and for Matthew 18:3-4 as well.[63]

He cannot be revealing an adequate acquaintance with the dispensational literature on the distinction between the "kingdom of heaven" phrase and the "kingdom of God," when he maintains, "Although it is not usually clearly stated, this distinction is to be deduced from the Old Testament background."[64] It is the Old Testament background that he has already bypassed from the outset of his work. He states, "Practically all modern critical scholarship recognizes that the difference between the two phrases is one of language only."[65] That is true, but it can also be truthfully said that the same scholarship denies the verbal, plenary inspiration of the Scriptures. That is not the valid criterion for New Testament doctrine. The premillennialist and fundamentalist, whether dispensational or not, will have to content himself with being in the minority. Modern critical scholarship cares little, if at all, about any literal kingdom, when it has already discarded the great doctrines of grace of the Scriptures.

No argument can be based on the assumption that the gospels are translations from the Aramaic.[66] Though Torrey of Yale and others have amassed much material on the problem, it is still an unproved theory. The people of the Lord's day were bilingual, and their thought patterns were colored by Old

Testament truth. The matter cannot be settled with finality, but there are evidences that the gospels are not translations.

Ladd contends that the kingdom of God is primarily a soteriological idea, the rule of God in the redeemed life.[67] That idea is seemingly interchangeable in the gospel records.[68] Instead of explaining why only Matthew used "the kingdom of heaven," he asks why Matthew used the kingdom of God idea four times.[69] Not to anticipate the later discussion, it can be affirmed that the phrases are not "equivalent to salvation."[70] When men are invited to receive the grace of God in salvation today, they are not urged, "Repent ye, for the kingdom of heaven is at hand." Oversimplification can be an enemy of the truth, as is abundantly attested by the attempts of Job's friends to find a solution to his problem.[71] Ladd is convinced that the exegetical difficulties for the dispensationalist in Matthew 19:23 are insurmountable.[72] But he has failed to realize that the realm of professing Christendom includes the real as well as the false; there are wheat and good fish, as well as tares and bad fish. Professing does not convey only the idea of the false and the unreal. And one does not speak of "the kingdom of God in mystery form,"[73] but the kingdom of heaven in mystery form on the basis of Matthew 13. The matter of the leaven in Luke 13:21 will be treated presently.

More than once it is declared that Christ spoke Aramaic to the Jews,[74] then there follows a lengthy discussion on the nuances of the word *basileia, eggiken,* and *ephthasen.*[75] It is readily admitted that the word *basileia,* as well as the Hebrew *malkhuth,* has an abstract as well as a concrete meaning. There must be supporting arguments to take one of those meanings over against the other. Can it be proved that the words had identical connotations in the Greek as in the Aramaic, in the Greek mind as in the Jewish mind? It is well known from a study of the Old Testament that the Semitic frame of mind emphasizes the concrete rather than the abstract. For that reason the Old Testament is couched in Semitic languages. It would have been more than ludicrous to an Old Testament saint, to say nothing of the Jew today, to speak of a kingdom of the Messiah and mean by that only a spiritual state or condition by means of repentance, such as was called forth by the preaching of the prophets. For the Semitic mind, a kingdom is primarily a realm, then the authority exercised therein.

The amillennialist is consistent in expecting a spiritual kingdom now and in the future; Ladd, however, has a spiritual kingdom now and a literal, earthly one in the future on the basis of the same body of evidence. He must posit a future kingdom, for he rightly notes: "It is quite true that the Old Testament prophecies look forward primarily to the earthly aspect of the kingdom."[76] It is not stated what other aspect of the kingdom they were justified in anticipating, when "basing their interpretation upon such prophecies, the Jewish people expect a kingdom of an outward, political, earthly sort."[77] Before the fulfillment of the prophecies, one must insist, it was impossible for them to know all the ramifications of the plan of God for this age, which was not yet revealed. Is one justified in judging Israel for not knowing the relationships of prophetic truth, when the prophets themselves did not know the relative times of the death and reign of the Messiah? The fault of Israel is that of all unbelievers: They did not believe all God had said (Luke 24:25-26).

Our Lord declared in so many words that, if they had been taught of the Father, they would have come to Him (John 6:45). Is one to understand that the reason Simeon, Anna, Mary of Bethany, and others believed in the Messiah was that they understood in what connotation the Lord used the word *basileia* or *malkhuth?* Or the ramifications of *eggiken* and *ephthasen?* Their views, like that of the apostle Peter, called for an earthly kingdom then; but when the repentance of Israel was not forthcoming for its establishment, then their genuine faith in their Messiah and Savior helped them over every difficulty. That is clear today with converts from Judaism. When once their hearts are convinced of the genuineness of the claims of Jesus as their Messiah, and they realize their need of salvation from sin, they are prepared to own Him as Deity, though they may not have thought of Him and His claim in that light before.

That premillennialists, who make a distinction between the kingdom of heaven and the kingdom of God, have foundation for their position is made clear by Chafer. Too many equate the kingdom of heaven with the kingdom of God, so that they can make them tantamount to the church, which is supposed to fulfill all Old Testament prophecies. For such expositors the logical sequence to a spiritual kingdom now is the heavenly kingdom of the future. Their fallacy is pointed out:

> No attempt is made by these expositors to explain why the term *kingdom of heaven* is used by Matthew only, nor do they seem to recognize the fact that the real difference between that which these designations represent is to be discovered in connection with the instances where they are not and cannot be used interchangeably rather than in the instances where they are interchangeable. Certain features are common to both the kingdom of heaven and the kingdom of God, and in such instances the interchange of the terms is justified. Closer attention will reveal that the kingdom of heaven is always earthly while the kingdom of God is as wide as the universe and includes as much of earthly things as are germane to it. Likewise, the kingdom of heaven is entered by a righteousness exceeding the righteousness of the scribes and Pharisees (Matt. 5:20), while the kingdom of God is entered by a new birth (John 3:1-16). So, again, the kingdom of heaven answers the hope of Israel and the Gentiles, while the kingdom of God answers the eternal and all-inclusive purpose of God. To be more explicit: Matthew 5:20 declares the condition upon which a Jew

might hope to enter the kingdom of heaven. Matthew 8:12; 24:50-51; 25:28-30 indicate that children of the kingdom of heaven are to be cast out. Neither of these truths could apply to the kingdom of God. Again, the parables of the wheat and the tares, Matthew 13:24-30, 36-43, and the parable of the good and bad fish, Matthew 13:47-50, are spoken only of the kingdom of heaven.[78]

Chafer asks whether the amillennialist has led men to salvation in the crucified and risen Savior by asking them to repent for the kingdom of heaven is at hand.[79] Too, that type of preaching was to be accompanied by certain designated miracles as a seal; have they been evidenced? What elements are found in the church that differentiate it from the kingdom? To that Chafer answers,

> The essential elements of a grace administration—faith as the sole basis of acceptance with God, unmerited acceptance through the perfect standing in Christ, the present possession of eternal life, an absolute security from all condemnation, and the enabling power of the indwelling Spirit—are not found in the kingdom administration. On the other hand, it is declared to be the fulfilling of 'the law and the prophets' (Matt. 5:17, 18; 7:12), and is seen to be an extension of the Mosaic Law into realms of merit-seeking which blast and wither as the Mosaic system could never do (Matt. 5:20-48). These kingdom injunctions, though suited to the conditions that will then obtain, could perfect no one as men in Christ are now perfected, nor are they adapted as a rule of life for those already complete in Christ Jesus.[80]

Before the conclusion of this portion of the chapter, it is in point to consider the extended treatment of E. Miller on the subject of the kingdom of God and the kingdom of heaven. He correctly defines the kingdom of heaven as representing God's work to reestablish His will on a rebellious earth, whereas the kingdom of God is universal in scope, comprehending the heavens and farthest reaches of the universe, going beyond the bounds of the kingdom of heaven.[81] While God is now building the kingdom of heaven in mystery form, Satan is injecting the counterfeit, so that the angels at the end of the age will have to make the separation. It must be kept in mind that the kingdom of heaven includes a mixture of the good and bad.[82] Those who contend on the basis of Matthew 5:20 and 18:3, for an identity of the kingdoms on the basis of the conditions for entrance, need to be reminded that those who are true and genuine in the kingdom of heaven can by virtue of their genuine faith be admitted into the kingdom of God. But it is stated of the kingdom of heaven—and it cannot be similarly held for the kingdom of God—that it includes tares as well as wheat, bad fish as well as good, foolish virgins as well as wise.[83]

The kingdom of God, universal in scope and outreach, was begun in beauty, harmony, and obedience in the Garden of Eden before the Fall, and in the heavenly realms also before the creation of the universe. Satan began the revolt in heaven, and man on earth followed on in that rebellion against the kingdom of God.[84] In the Old Testament we find prophesied a kingdom wherein God's will will be recognized and carried out. See 2 Samuel 7:7-16, Isaiah 9:6-7, and Jeremiah 23:5-6 among many others.

Coming to the New Testament, one is introduced before long to a form of that kingdom not foreseen in the Old Testament.[85] Miller maintains rightly, "The mystery form of the Kingdom of Heaven is developed exclusively in the Gospel of Matthew. It is in this Gospel alone that we find the expression *the Kingdom of Heaven*. Matthew's is the great dispensational Gospel, for here the Holy Spirit is pleased to disregard chronological order that dispensational order may be paramount."[86]

It is safe to say that John the Baptist, who proclaimed the kingdom of heaven at hand, knew nothing of the mystery form of that kingdom, for it was not revealed by our Lord Jesus until after the death of John. What John preached was the kingdom predicted by the Old Testament prophets.[87] It had earth in view, and probably got its name from the "God of heaven" of Daniel's prophecy (Dan. 2:28, 44). That is a title used by God when He is disowned on earth, as He was in Israel when Ezekiel saw the Shekinah glory depart (Ezek. 11:22, 23). God's purpose is to realize His will on earth as it is in heaven.[88]

Miller divides the subject in this manner: the prophetic form of the kingdom covered by the Old Testament, the mystery form, which is found between the two advents of the Lord, and the final form, or the kingdom in manifestation, realized in the millennial reign of Christ.[89] When the kingdom was announced as at hand, Israel alone was in view; when the kingdom is in its mystery form, the Jew is set aside nationally, and Gentiles are admitted on the same basis of faith with individual Jews.[90] The kingdom in mystery form comprehends the mystery that is the church. Those who contend that dispensational premillennialists hold to no present spiritual phase of the kingdom (see Col. 1:13), reveal that they do not understand that position relative to the kingdom of heaven in mystery form. After the birth of the King, the event next in order, according to the prophets, was to be the kingdom.[91] But that was conditioned upon national repentance, which was not accorded the lowly Messiah. When the kingdom is realized in its final manifestation, the antecedent condition of its establishment then will still be the repentance of Israel. See Matthew 23:39 and Acts 3:18-21.[92]

During the time that the kingdom is in mystery form, the church, which is the Body of Christ, is in process of formation. The church could not be revealed until the work upon which it is based, the death of Christ, was an accomplished fact in the purpose of God.[93] It should be remarked here that amillennialists accuse premillennialists of predicating a kingdom without the cross in the New Testament, when they claim the existence of the church in the Old Testament without the cross. The mystery was revealed when the rejection of Christ by Israel was evident.

The claim that the kingdom of heaven is identical with the kingdom of God, as has been seen, is based on the fact that certain parables, applied by Matthew to the kingdom of heaven, are made relevant to the kingdom of God in other gospels. That could not be so unless the two were identical, they assert.[94] Miller shows that the greatest and clearest difference between the kingdom of God and the kingdom of heaven is the topographical; they cover spheres that are not identical. The kingdom of heaven occupies itself with the earthly sphere for the realization of the will of God on earth as it is in heaven. It does not engage itself with matters of the heavens or the universe. The kingdom of God is more comprehensive and includes the heavens and the universe. To be sure, the kingdom of heaven has much that falls within the scope of the kingdom of God; but there is also much in the kingdom of heaven of the character of evil, which is not "generically in the Kingdom of God."[95] Because Satan counterfeits the real and sows tares where the good master has sown wheat, evil is present in the kingdom of heaven. Christendom has a portion within it that is only profession and not possession.

What of the parables common to both kingdoms? Miller's answer is to the point when he states:

> The question may well be asked, how can we explain the fact that Matthew applies the parables of the *mustard seed* and of the *leaven* to the Kingdom of Heaven while Luke applies them to the Kingdom of God. These are the two parables which describe the external and the internal development of the Kingdom of Heaven—the external growth into a monstrosity and the parallel internal development of evil. Because the spheres of the two kingdoms overlap it is not strange that these parables are applied to both kingdoms. However, there is no attempt made to apply the parables of the *wheat and tares* or the *dragnet* [or he could have added that of the wise and foolish virgins] to the Kingdom of God.
>
> The explanation of this apparent difficulty may be simply illustrated by using our own country as an example. The expression the *United States of America* includes not only the forty-eight states in continental America, but includes all its territories and possessions as well. Now, let us suppose that a rebellion should break out in an outlying possession such as Alaska. A news commentator from this country in reporting the news might say that there is a rebellion in Alaska, whereas another commentator, perhaps from Russia, in reporting the same news might say that there is a rebellion in the United States of America. [Compare the several uses of the word "Yankee."] Both reports are true, only the one localizes the report to a specific place in the country, while the other generalizes it to the country

where it belongs. Likewise the Holy Spirit in dealing with dispensational truth in Matthew's Gospel localizes the conditions to the earthly sphere by using the term *Kingdom of Heaven,* but in Luke He is not concerned with dispensational truth and therefore uses the general term in the sense that the Kingdom of Heaven is in the universal sphere of the kingdom of God.[96]

An even more serious difficulty is said to exist for the view that distinguishes between the two kingdoms. In John 3:3 it is indicated that the new birth is basic to entrance into the kingdom of God, whereas in Matthew 18:3 it is stated that conversion is the prerequisite for entrance into the kingdom of heaven. The position is taken by many students of the gospels that what John indicated by the new birth is what Matthew had in mind by conversion. Thus the conditions for entrance into both kingdoms would be the same, and the logical conclusion would be that the kingdoms are identical also. But not all is similarity in those passages; the differences are determining. Miller puts it splendidly:

The subject of John 3:3 is singular while that in Matthew 18:3 is plural. John's message is to the individual; Matthew's is to plurality of individuals—the people of Israel collectively. The new birth is an individual matter; it is never applied in a collective sense to a people. The *new birth* is the work of God through the regeneration of the Holy Spirit apart from the volition of man. *Conversion,* on the other hand, as used by Matthew means 'to change or turn from one belief or course to another,' 'to change from one state to another,' and may be accomplished by the volition of man. Matthew's language very aptly applies to Israel as a nation; she must turn from or change her course or belief before she can be established in her own land under the rulership of her Messiah. Other points of dissimilarity may also be pointed out, but enough has been said to show that Matthew's passage very fittingly applies to Israel, showing the absolute necessity for her to change her course before she can enter into the Kingdom of Heaven, which will be set up in Manifestation by the coming again of Her Messiah. While the passage in John applies to the individual—whether Jew or Gentile—showing the absolute necessity of the new birth—the receiving of a new life—before he can enter into the Kingdom of God."[97]

No, the church is not the kingdom, and the kingdom of God is not equivalent to the kingdom of heaven, if all the Scripture data are taken into account.

Next in the discussion of the church and the kingdom is the question of the postponement of the kingdom. That plank in the dispensational premillennial view has come in for much criticism and attack in recent years. It is clearly set forth in the notes of the Scofield Reference Bible, but of late it has been singled out for special attack. Murray states, "The truth is that instead of offering the Jews an earthly kingdom, the Jews offered the kingdom to Jesus."[98] Fitzwater has stated the premillennial viewpoint with clarity: "When the Church has been caught up, removed from the earth, then will be resumed the kingdom message begun by John the Baptist when he cried, 'Repent ye: for the kingdom of heaven is at hand' (Matthew 3:2). . . . When John's voice was stilled, Christ took it up, and when Christ was rejected and crucified, the kingdom passed into abeyance—the nobleman went into a far country to receive for himself a kingdom and to return."[99]

Homer Payne answers those who cannot reconcile the postponement of the kingdom with a spiritual phase of the kingdom. He maintains:

> The thing which most amillennialists fail to grasp is that *the literalist does accept the inward and spiritual nature of the kingdom.* In fact the only reason for the postponement of the kingdom at the first advent according to the literalist, was the refusal of the Jews as a nation to accept the spiritual requirements of the kingdom. These were repentance and regeneration by faith in God. It is right here that . . . amillennialists set up a straw man and tear him down, asserting that the literalist holds a materialistic and grossly carnal conception of the kingdom.[100]

A typical charge against the postponement view is that it does away with the necessity of the cross. Allis states first, "The necessity of the Cross was present in the mind of Jesus from the very beginning of His ministry. Both John and Jesus declared this definitely and emphatically."[101] One should be willing to go even further, on the basis of Scripture, and state that the necessity of the cross was present in Christ's thinking from eternity. To hold that Christ offered the kingdom to Israel as at hand, is equal, it is maintained, to saying, "It made the Cross unnecessary by implying that the glorious kingdom of Messiah could be set up immediately. It left no room for the Cross since Messiah's kingdom was to be without end."[102]

In the offer of Peter in Acts 3 the amillennial argument that the offer of the kingdom bypasses the cross is laid to rest summarily. Thank God, the cross was a glorious historical fact by that time, and the kingdom offer was still valid. God was prepared to accomplish exactly what He promised them through Peter that day, but Israel was no more ready at that time than during the earthly ministry of the Son of God.

Another unwarranted conclusion of Allis is, "The Church required the Cross while the kingdom did not, that the gospel of the kingdom did not include the Cross, while the gospel of the grace of God did include it."[103] There is no Scripture to support that claim. But after much repetition of the same charge, Allis concludes: "Dispensationalists do not reject the Cross or minimize its importance: they glory in it."[104] It would be apropos to ask Allis whether in the light of Leviticus 18:5 (which states that, if a man did the statutes of the Lord, he should live in them) and Deuteronomy 30:11-14 (which declares they are not inaccessible, but rather nigh), he would assume that by the keeping of the law God had intended to render the cross unnecessary or meant to leave no room for the cross.

Chafer, always a true evangelist at heart, will not abide the charge that premillennialists render unnecessary the cross by their view on the postponement of the kingdom. Against the amillennialists who make the claim he writes:

> These men are Calvinists, yet they are disturbed over the seeming conflict between divine sovereignty and human will. If the ground of their objection to the 'postponement theory' stands, then there was no assurance that there would be a Jewish nation until Abraham made his decision to obey God; there was no certainty that Christ would be born until Mary gave her consent; there was 'no assurance that Christ would die until Pilate so ordered. In the light of two determining facts, namely, (a) that Jehovah's Lamb was in the redeeming purpose slain from the foundation of the world and (b) that had Adam *not* sinned there could have been no need of a redeemer, why did Jehovah tell Adam not to sin? And what would have become of the redemptive purpose had Adam obeyed God?[105]

Chafer cogently asks, if no kingdom was offered Israel, why Israel did not shout that they would not believe on the Savior for their salvation, but rather cried, "We will not have this man to reign over us."[106] His position, and that of all premillennialists, is, "The death of Christ is neither incidental, accidental, nor fortuitous. It is the central truth of the Bible and the central fact of the universe. It was also in the purpose of God that Christ's death should be accomplished by Israel as their act of rejecting their King. It is also true that they did not and could not reject what was not first offered to them."[107] And again, "All God has ever done or will do for sinful men is wrought on the sole basis of Christ's death."[108]

Berkhof twice asserts that the "so-called postponement theory" is a necessary link in the premillennial system, though he finds it is void of scriptural basis.[109] The reason he believes it is without basis is because he cannot find that Christ offered any literal, earthly kingdom.[110] The answer is clear: he finds no offer of the Old Testament kingdom, because he has spiritualized it into a present reality in the hearts of believers, and that in accepted amillennial fashion. When he calls the postponement view "a comparatively recent fiction,"[111] it is evident he has not considered the work of G. N. H. Peters dating from nearly a century ago. Contrary to the claim of Berkhof, the premillennial view does not imply a denial of the present existence of the kingdom, but it is in mystery form.[112] The existence of the kingdom in mystery form empties his arguments of their force so completely that he calls the interpretation a "subterfuge."[113] He would like the early and later teaching of Christ to be considered without break, and that would mean that Christ spoke only of the same kingdom throughout.[114] But is it not clear that He never had to explain the kingdom of heaven to the disciples, but He did explain at great length (Matthew 13) the meaning of the mystery parables? It is stated that the people did not understand and their hearts were hardened in unbelief regarding the mystery parables. There was a change in message, and He was careful to explain it to the believing.

It will not do to find fault with the condition of Israel's repentance as necessary to the establishment of the kingdom. What, then, is the force of Matthew 23:39? Something is certainly being conditioned on the repentance of Israel. See also Hosea 5:15. And it is not discerning to claim that the postponement view makes the mission of Christ a failure.[115] Is that to be our interpretation of John 1:10-11? When Berkhof asks what would have become of the cross if Christ had succeeded in setting up the kingdom, he is entering into the realm of speculative theology.[116] But there is a possible answer. It is conceivable that, had Israel as a nation accepted the offered kingdom by national repentance and regeneration by faith, the cross could still have been a historical reality through the conniving of the vicious traitor Judas, even in the very act of the establishment of the kingdom; he could still have betrayed Christ to the Roman powers. But such questions are like asking what happens if one of the nonelect of earth should accept Christ as Savior.

Thiessen has pointed out clearly that the parable in Luke 19:11-27 shows, perhaps more clearly than any other, that there was to be a postponement of the kingdom.[117] He contends, "Surely Jesus never rebuked anyone for expecting such a kingdom. When the mother of the sons of Zebedee requested of Christ that her sons might sit, the one on His right hand and the other on His left, in His kingdom . . . she and her sons certainly meant the earthly kingdom. It would seem that here, if ever, our Lord would have corrected their 'erroneous' views of the kingdom, if there were any to correct; but He did not do so. All that He criticized in them was their selfish ambition. . . . There is not one word [nor in Acts 1:6] of reproof or correction as to their expectation of an earthly kingdom."[118] There was understanding rather than misunderstanding on the subject. And Luke 19:11-27 is not the only passage on the postponement. Years ago Professor J. G. Princell divided the twenty-one kingdom parables into five groups. They comprise the major prophetic element in the gospels. The five parables that concern the postponement of the kingdom and the waiting for it are: Luke 12:36-40; Luke 12:42-48; Luke 19:11-27; Luke 21:29-33; and Mark 13:34-37.

Ladd, though a premillennialist, has joined forces with the amillennialists in attacking the postponement of the kingdom. The reader is met at the outset with the unusual procedure of discussing the concept of the kingdom without treating the Old Testament evidence. That is contrary to inductive logic. That serious weakness, already pointed out in the preface by Smith, plagues the entire discussion throughout the work. It is building an edifice without a foundation. But there is purpose in it also: If the Old Testament material be ignored, then the New Testament material can be handled in a way that does not embarrass it by comparison with the Old Testament testimony. Christ Himself never hesitated to measure His life and mission by the Old Testament (John 5). Why should the kingdom be different? A number of Ladd's positions have been treated in other places in this work, so the discussion will confine itself to specific points on the postponement alone. In all fairness he must admit that the adherents of the postponement view do teach "that the kingdom of God is a present reality in the lives of God's people."[119]

Premillennialists are not the only ones who hold that Christ offered the Jews the kind of earthly kingdom they expected. Schweitzer, though a well-known critic, holds the same.[120] But Ladd claims, "This is not necessarily true. Jesus may very well have transcended the views of his contemporaries."[121] Without indicating it to them? That sounds like the argument that liberals use when they discuss whether Jesus believed in the Mosaic authorship of the Pentateuch. It can be dangerous. Besides, it places an unknown quantity in place of a well-defined and known one. Furthermore, Peters has rightly shown that such deprecation of the Jewish ideas of the kingdom came first from the infidels Strauss, Bauer, Renan, and others.[122]

Furthermore, it is maintained that "Jesus did not offer to the Jews the earthly kingdom *anymore than he offered himself to them as their glorious earthly King.* Here we may take our stand on firm ground."[123] The ground will be seen to be not so firm, when one considers the reason for the so-called triumphal entry. Why such a presentation of Himself to His people, if He were not offering Himself to them as King? There is no explanation, moreover, for the beginning of the gospel according to Matthew with the designation of Christ as the son of David, nor for the conclusion of the gospel accounts where the accusation, which God would not allow to be altered, proclaimed Him as King of the Jews.

Ladd's explanation of the reason for the postponement view is not valid. He writes, "This theory has been vigorously espoused because of the effort on the part of non-millenarians to interpret the kingdom *entirely* as a present spiritual reality, without any future earthly manifestation. However, such a theory is not necessary and it is beset by grave difficulties."[124] Wholly apart from the position of the amillenarians, premillennialists hold to a postponement view, because the literal kingdom offered by Christ to Israel on the basis of repentance was not received. Thus the kingdom was postponed, as is clear from the postponement parables in the gospels.

The reason Israel did not accept Him was not because of their misunderstanding of the kind of kingdom He offered, but because they were unwilling to repent and believe (John 5:40). Too, in the case of the disciples who did accept Him, why were they still disputing as to who would have the positions of honor in His kingdom? Why do they still ask about the restoration of the kingdom to Israel in Acts 1? Evidently their views of the kingdom did not hinder their acceptance of Christ as Savior. The fact of the matter is that they who accepted Him had the same view of the kingdom as the multitude who refused and rejected Him. Has one forgotten Peter's rebuke of our Lord in Matthew 16? If they were in such error about the kingdom, why did Christ continue His predictions in the vein of Matthew 19:28?

Those are all embarrassing features to those who oppose the postponement of the kingdom because of Israel's allegedly erroneous views on the kind of kingdom. Our Lord corrected Peter on the subject of the necessity of the cross, then why not on the nature of the kingdom they were expecting?

A serious charge against all who hold that "Jesus offered to Israel the same kingdom which he now offers to both Jew and Gentile,"[125] thus making it equivalent to an offer of salvation, is that such a position destroys the uniqueness of the ministry of Christ to Israel. If He was preaching a message similar to that of the prophets and nothing more, then there is great loss in the uniqueness of His ministry. But His ministry was glorious in that, though He called them to repentance and faith, He also made it clear that thereby they could have Him as their long-awaited Davidic King and the millennial reign as well.

Ladd admits that Christ was King, for he maintains, "Jesus did not present Himself to Israel as the Davidic king, *as Israel interpreted that kingship.* He was the King, indeed. Matthew makes this as clear as can be. But he came not on a throne of glory, but 'meek, riding upon an ass' (Zech. 9:9)."[126] The triumphal entry is a difficult hurdle for those who oppose the postponement of the kingdom. It is said that Christ did offer Himself as King, but in a way other than they were expecting Him, or could have expected Him. A kingdom of some kind is offered, yet it must not be the prophesied Davidic kingdom. Why did Christ speak of Himself as Son of Man, if He were not presenting Himself as Davidic king? See Matthew 19:28. But the matter of the triumphal entry must be explained, and Ladd attempts it in this way: "It is difficult to see how Jesus could have offered to Israel the earthly Davidic kingdom *without the glorious Davidic king* who was to reign in that kingdom. The very fact that he did not come as the glorious King, but as the humble Saviour, should be adequate evidence by itself to prove that his offer of the kingdom was not the outward, earthly kingdom, but one which corresponded to the form in which the King himself came to men."[127]

We submit that though He came in lowly garb, Christ was the glorious Davidic King. Why did He come in the manner prescribed for the King by Zechariah? Could that not be confused in the minds of the people as a literal offer of a literal kingdom and thus to be avoided at all costs? That was one episode that should have been omitted, for it embarrasses beyond endurance the opposition to the postponement position. It was not, "Thy Saviour cometh unto thee," but, "Thy King cometh unto thee." When Christ presented Himself to men as Savior, His method is indicated in the encounters with Nicodemus, the woman of Samaria, Mary Magdalene, and others. He never presented an offer of salvation, as understood by amillennialists and their followers, riding upon an ass. And more, what message did Jesus preach while riding on the ass? Did He offer salvation as is done today? He preached nothing and expected His riding into the city to speak for itself as the fulfillment of prophecy. When the Pharisees wanted to still the crowd who were shouting, for their *King*, mind you, Christ would not permit it (Luke 19:40). The case is too clear to need further elaboration. At this late hour it will not do to claim, "Nothing was postponed."[128]

As a final argument, Ladd sees an analogy to his view of the kingdom. Since there are two comings of Christ, there may also be two manifestations of the kingdom, one spiritual and one earthly.[129] The difficulty here is that the Old Testament clearly enough confirms the two advents in more than one passage, but that same Old Testament (whose testimony was by-passed by him from the beginning) does not indicate the kingdom of the Messiah in two senses. It predicts one type of kingdom, which will be set up finally at the second advent.

In one of his most recent works Ladd attempts to supply the lack of treatment in studies on the teachings of Jesus and the kingdom of God, of "the dynamic concept of the rule of God as the integrating center for Jesus' message and mission."[130] He claims that evangelical Christians have been so concerned with the eschatological futuristic phases of the kingdom of God that they have lost sight of the relevance of it for present Christian life. (But compare the treatment above of Matthew 13 and Colossians 1:13 among other passages.) His declared aim is not to minimize the future aspect of the Kingdom.[131] He believes that the concentrated study on the subject of the kingdom of God for the past few decades justifies the pronouncement by a recent survey of New Testament research that there has resulted "the discovery of the true meaning of the Kingdom of God."[132] Regardless of that optimistic appraisal, there is much ground to be possessed yet in view of the lack of consensus among liberal scholars of the primary aim and mission of Christ's first advent. That is all the more patent when Ladd states: "Although the burden of Jesus' message was the Kingdom of God, he nowhere defined it."[133]

The heart of Ladd's thesis is found in these statements:

> The centrality of this abstract or dynamic character of the Kingdom of God is illustrated by the fact that the Hebrew word *malkuth* [not the only Hebrew word for "kingdom" in the Old Testament] bears primarily the dynamic [a term of his own coinage] rather than the concrete meaning, and refers first to a reign, dominion, or rule and only secondarily to the

realm over which a reign is exercised. Even when *malkuth* is used of human kingdoms, the primary reference is to the rule or reign of a king.[134] When he mentions the concrete sense, he does so in a footnote: "We must also recognize that *malkuth* can be used to designate the realm over which a king reigns. See, e.g., 2 Chron. 20:30; Esther 3:6; Dan. 9:1; 11:9; Jer. 10:7. This fact will be important in the analysis of the New Testament concept."[135]

In refutation of his position the reader is referred to the discussion earlier in this volume. Certain additional observations are in order. If the concrete concept (realm) is not primary, how is it that both the Abrahamic and Davidic covenants emphasize the realm aspect? As early as Genesis 12:7 (and by a special appearing of the Lord to Abraham) the land is mentioned. Where else would his multiplied progeny exist (v. 2)? Where would redemption's program, which would enfold in its blessings all the nations of the earth, be executed, if not in the land, even Jerusalem? If realm is not paramount, then how does one explain the wording of 2 Samuel 7? Notice the details, for they are the heart of the matter. Verse 10 states "I will appoint a place for my people, Israel, and will plant them, that they may dwell in a place of their own, and move no more." Place is stressed twice (cf. Amos 9:14-15, esp. v. 15). Note verse 12 with "descendants" and "kingdom"; verse 13 with "throne [not abstract rule] of his kingdom"; verse 16 with "your house and your kingdom"; and "your throne." Observe further that in Psalm 110, for example, where rule is mentioned (v. 2), it is "out of Zion," a realm, and in verse 6 where judgment of the nations is indicated, it is "many countries." How can those concrete concepts be transmuted by hermeneutical alchemy into abstract ones? Why do they need to be?

Again, the insightful McClain meets the issue squarely and adequately. In commenting on Ladd's dual-kingdom position, he maintains: "In opposition to this theory it should be said that, while the Bible does make a clear distinction between the Universal Kingdom which is everlasting and the Mediatorial Kingdom which is limited in both location and time, neither the Old Testament prophets nor our Lord knew anything about two Mediatorial Kingdoms, the one "spiritual" and the other "earthly."[136] In a footnote he adds: "What Dr. Ladd seems to be doing is to abstract two elements or aspects from the *one* [italics his] Mediatorial Kingdom and make of them two kingdoms to be established respectively at two separate times on earth, and occupying two separate ages."[137] That dichotomy is analogous to the rabbinical concept of two Messiahs instead of one in two comings (cf. Zech. 12:10 ff.). One cannot have it both ways. What is yielded to the amillennial position for the first advent cannot be retrieved for the premillennial view for the second advent.

Ladd continues, "The Kingdom will be achieved in history by historical events which will see the rise of a Davidic king who will rule over a restored

Israel, bringing peace to all the earth. This truly Hebraic prophetic hope is historical, earthly, and nationalistic in that the messianic salvation is accomplished through Israel."[138] Then again he affirms, "Although the Old Testament hope may be characterized as an eschatological hope, it also remains an earthly hope. The biblical idea of redemption always includes the earth. . . . The Old Testament nowhere holds forth the hope of a bodiless, nonmaterial, purely 'spiritual' redemption as did Greek thought."[139] It could not have been more correctly stated, but it is not an integral part of an abstract concept of the kingdom for the first coming.

Ladd himself admits difficulty with the basic elements of his view. "If the Kingdom of God by definition is the rule of God, we can understand how God can manifest his rule in the person and mission of Jesus and again at the end of the age. But if the Kingdom by definition is the eschatological order, it is difficult to understand how the Kingdom itself can be both present and future."[140] It can be readily demonstrated that the dilemma is of his own making, as indicated repeatedly above. Yet he states, "There should . . . be no philological or logical reason why the Kingdom of God may not be conceived of both as the reign of God and as the realm in which his reign is experienced."[141] Why should it be so difficult to realize that the use of "reign" or "rule" as a dominant consideration for kingdom allows ground for the amillennial view, which will not and cannot agree to "realm" in Revelation 20 and other eschatological passages.

Briefly, two further observations need to be touched on here. As with covenant amillennialists, Ladd holds to a dual hermeneutic. He regards the church "the new people of God," as replacing Israel.[142] In one of his concluding remarks he states, "The church, as has often been said, is a people who live 'between the times,' " a remark which sounds like the "parenthesis" concept so maligned by all nondispensationalists, premillennial, postmillennial, and amillennial.[143]

The discussion of this chapter must not be closed without considering even briefly the valuable testimony of Peters on this important theme. That remarkable writer gives an extended section of his work to the offer of the kingdom, then shows clearly that Christ never corrected the ideas of the Jews on the kingdom. Because of their unbelief He indicated the kingdom was not immediately to appear.[144] He manifests the source of the contention that the Jewish idea of the kingdom could not be Christ's. Some men who denounce the "Jewishness" of the idea of the kingdom offer at the first advent, defend it vehemently for the second advent.[145] Peters rightly shows that to call the kingdom God's reign in the heart is to substitute the means to the kingdom for the kingdom itself.[146] One must understand the postponement to know the true nature and purpose of this dispensation, and without the Old Testament the kingdom cannot be understood.[147] Peters has done a splendid work in treating the many ramifications of the subject throughout his three volumes. In conclusion, Israel is not the church, and the church is not the kingdom of Old Testament prophecy. That kingdom, offered and rejected by Israel, is postponed for future complete, literal fulfillment. Such a view is falsely accused of bypassing or minimizing the cross, but that charge is unsubstantiated. Daniel 9:26 alone connects the cross with the postponement of the kingdom. "Cut off" surely signifies the death of the Messiah. "Have nothing" must mean that He does not get the kingdom. Note the gender of "his own" in John 1:11. It cannot mean only a spiritual kingdom in the hearts of men, for in that sense He did have numerous disciples even in His earthly ministry. The King was rejected and His kingdom postponed for the second advent until realization in the millennial reign.

Notes

[1]G. Vos, *The Teaching of Jesus Concerning the Kingdom of God and the Church,* pp. 38-65, esp. pp. 58-61.

[2]G. P. Mains, *Premillennialism: Non-scriptural, Non-historic, Non-scientific, Non-philosophical,* p. 122.

[3]A. Kuyper, *Chiliasm or the Doctrine of Premillennialism,* p. 7.

[4]W. Masselink, *Why Thousand Years?,* p. 119-21.

[5]Ibid., pp. 121-25.

[6]C. I. Scofield, *The Scofield Reference Bible,* p. 1003. See also C. I. Scofield, *The New Scofield Reference Bible,* p. 1002.

[7]F. C. Ottman, *Imperialism and Christ,* pp. 304-5; cf. also his *God's Oath,* pp. 4-7.

[8]J. H. Todd, *Principles of Interpretation,* p. 53.

[9]H. Lummis, "The Kingdom in the Church," in N. West, ed., *Premillennial Essays of the Prophetic Conference,* pp. 191-96.

[10]N. West, *The Thousand Years in Both Testaments,* p. 27.

[11]W. Masselink, pp. 152-54.

[12]H. L. Payne, *Amillennial Theology as a System,* p. 199.

[13]G. E. Ladd, *Crucial Questions About the Kingdom of God,* p. 96.

[14]G. Vos, *Biblical Theology,* p. 398. Cf. also G. Vos, *The Kingdom and the Church.*

[15]Ibid., p. 399.

[16]Ibid., p. 400.

[17]Ibid., p. 402-3.

[18]Ibid., p. 404.

[19]Ibid., p. 426.

[20]Ibid., p. 427.

[21]Vos, *The Kingdom and the Church,* p. 14.

[22]Ibid., p. 15.

[23]Ibid., p. 18.

[24]Ibid., pp. 19-20. Something of a shift in position may be discerned when Ladd maintains: "We cannot find warrant in the Scripture for the idea that Jesus is Lord of the church while the king of Israel. We do not find in Scripture the idea that Jesus begins his Messianic reign at his parousia and that his kingship belongs primarily to the millennium. We find on the contrary that the millennial reign of Christ will be the manifestation in history of the lordship and sovereignty which is his already" (Clouse, *The Meaning of the Millennium,* p. 32). Caution is needed not to attempt a blending of premillennial and amillennial positions. They are logical opposites.

[25]Ibid., p. 24.

[26]Ibid., p. 25. The amillennialist Hughes is not so certain in these matters as Vos is. He quotes Acts 15:15-18 as proof, mark you, that the Old Testament prophets foretold the church age. He takes "the rebuilding of David's house to be accomplished in God's building of his church. . . ." Such conclusions without proper exegetical foundations are of doubtful value. He adds, "If there is a difference between the 'kingdom' and the 'church,' the apostles and evangelists of the New Testament seem to have been unaware of it" (P. E. Hughes, *Interpreting Prophecy,* p. 107). How does he conclude that the writers had no knowledge of a difference between the kingdom and the church? Why not treat Ephesians 2 and 3:1-10 exegetically to build on Scripture and not on an ipse dixit?

[27]Ibid., p. 26.

[28]Ibid., p. 30.

[29]Ibid.

[30]Ibid., p. 31.

[31]Ibid., p. 39.

[32]Ibid.

[33]Ibid., p. 41.

[34]Ibid., p. 42.

[35]Ibid., p. 43.

[36]Ibid., p. 44.

[37]Ibid., p. 77.

[38]Ibid., p. 80.

[39]Ibid.

[40]Ibid., p. 82.

[41]Ibid., p. 83.

[42]L. Berkhof, *The Kingdom of God,* preface.

[43]Ibid., p. 11.

[44]Ibid., p. 12.

[45]Ibid., p. 13.
[46]See G. L. Murray, *Millennial Studies: A Search for Truth*, p. 70.
[47]L. Berkhof, *The Kingdom of God.*
[48]Ibid., p. 18.
[49]Ibid., p. 19, fn. 5.
[50]Ibid.
[51]Ibid., p. 87.
[52]Ibid., pp. 87-88.
[53]Ibid., pp. 139-40.
[54]Ibid., p. 141.
[55]Ibid.
[56]Ibid., p. 166.
[57]O. T. Allis, *Prophecy and the Church*, p. 70.
[58]Ibid., p. 71.
[59]Ibid.
[60]G. E. Ladd, *Crucial Questions*, p. 107.
[61]Ibid., p. 108.
[62]Ibid., fn. 32.
[63]Ibid., p. 108.
[64]Ibid., p. 111.
[65]Ibid., p. 122.
[66]Ibid.
[67]Ibid., p. 83.
[68]Ibid., p. 107.
[69]Ibid., p. 108.
[70]Ibid.
[71]Ibid., p. 124.
[72]Ibid., pp. 109-10.
[73]Ibid., p. 111.
[74]Ibid., p. 123.
[75]Ibid., p. 124.
[76]Ibid., pp. 127-28.
[77]Ibid.
[78]L. S. Chafer, *Dispensationalism*, pp. 64-65.
[79]Ibid., p. 85.
[80]Ibid., p. 50.
[81]E. Miller, *The Kingdom of God and the Kingdom of Heaven*, p. 8.
[82]Ibid.
[83]Ibid., pp. 8-9.
[84]Ibid., pp. 13-22.
[85]Ibid., p. 41.
[86]Ibid.

[87]Ibid., p. 42.

[88]Ibid., p. 43.

[89]Ibid.

[90]Ibid., p. 44.

[91]Ibid., p. 45.

[92]Ibid., p. 48.

[93]Ibid., p. 57.

[94]Ibid., p. 60.

[95]Ibid., pp. 60-61.

[96]Ibid., pp. 62-63.

[97]Ibid., pp. 63-64.

[98]Murray, p. 69.

[99]P. B. Fitzwater, *Christian Theology*, p. 522.

[100]H. L. Payne, pp. 120-21.

[101]Allis, p. 72.

[102]Ibid., p. 230.

[103]Ibid., p. 231.

[104]Ibid., p. 234.

[105]Chafer, *Dispensationalism*, p. 26.

[106]Ibid., p. 28.

[107]Ibid., p. 29.

[108]Ibid., p. 70; for his further comments on the subject, see his *Systematic Theology*, 5:340-49, especially pp. 347-49.

[109]L. Berkhof, *Systematic Theology*, p. 713, and Berkhof, *The Kingdom of God*, p. 151.

[110]Berkhof, *Systematic Theology*, p. 714.

[111]Ibid.

[112]Berkhof, *The Kingdom of God*, p. 152.

[113]Ibid., p. 167. McClain calls for a clear distinction in phraseology: "The parables of this chapter [Matt. 13], it is said carelessly by some, describe the kingdom of heaven as now existing in 'mystery form' during the Church age. Now it is true that these parables present certain *conditions* related to the Kingdom which are contemporaneous with the present age. But nowhere in Matthew 13 is the establishment of the Kingdom placed within this age" (A. J. McClain, *The Greatness of the Kingdom*, p. 441). The establishment is put at the end of the age (cf. vv. 39-49 with vv. 41-43).

[114]Ibid., p. 168.

[115]Ibid., p. 169.

[116]Ibid., p. 170.

[117]H. C. Thiessen, "The Parable of the Nobleman and the Earthly Kingdom," p. 180.

[118]Ibid., pp. 182-83.

[119]Ladd, *Crucial Questions,* p. 50, fn. 18.
[120]Ibid., p. 70.
[121]Ibid.
[122]G. N. H. Peters, *The Theocratic Kingdom,* 1:433.
[123]Ladd, *Crucial Questions,* p. 113.
[124]Ibid.
[125]Ibid., p. 124.
[126]Ibid., p. 114.
[127]Ibid., p. 117.
[128]Ibid., p. 131.
[129]Ibid.
[130]G. E. Ladd, *The Presence of the Future: The Eschatology of Biblical Realism,* p. xi. The first edition of this work was entitled *Jesus and the Kingdom.*
[131]Ibid.
[132]Ibid., p. 3.
[133]Ibid., p. 45.
[134]Ibid., pp. 46-47.
[135]Ibid., fn. p. 47.
[136]McClain, p. 275.
[137]Ibid., fn. 7.
[138]Ibid., p. 53.
[139]Ibid., p. 59. He rightly states: "There is no Greek dualism or Gnosticism in the Old Testament hope" (ibid., p. 63).
[140]Ibid., pp. 128-29.
[141]Ibid., p. 195. At the same time he is on solid ground in his claim: "We have no proof that the early church equated the Kingdom with the church" (p. 202, fn. 20), and again: ". . . the New Testament does not equate believers with the Kingdom" (p. 263).
[142]Ibid., pp. 222, 249-50.
[143]Ibid., p. 338.
[144]Peters, *The Theocratic Kingdom,* 1:379-85, especially on Luke 19:11-27.
[145]Ibid., 1:412-23; 433-44.
[146]Ibid., 1:577-81; 585-86.
[147]Ibid., 1:590-91.

17

The Rapture and the Revelation

Amillennialists and some nondispensational premillennialists, with a few posttribulational dispensationalists, are at one in seeing no distinction between the coming of Christ for His saints and His coming with His saints, commonly spoken of as the rapture and the revelation. J. T. Mueller maintains that the coming of Christ is referred to by various descriptive terms, as the apocalpyse, epiphany, parousia, day of God, Day of the Lord, day of the Lord Jesus, day of the Lord Jesus Christ, that day, the last day, the great day, the day of redemption, the day of wrath, the Day of Judgment, and the day of revelation.[1]

H. A. A. Kennedy, another amillennialist, finds it hard to distinguish between what Christ says of the parousia and what he calls the coming of the kingdom of God.[2] Hiemenga has the premillennial view somewhat confused in his attempted refutation of its position. He notes that the premillennialists expect the Lord to come back for His church in the rapture. After the period of the Great Tribulation, they expect Him to come back to earth to establish an earthly kingdom in Jerusalem and to reign over the nation Israel for a thousand years. After the thousand years, Satan is to be loosed for a short time, and then the Lord will come to judgment. Therefore, he concludes the premillennialists really expect three second comings, whereas the amillennialists believe there will be but one second coming.[3]

Millenarians are said to distinguish between the rapture, the revelation, and the parousia. The first precedes the second by seven years, and the second anticipates the third by a thousand years. That presentation of the premillennial view is not strictly correct, as will be shown in a later discussion. Vos finds it most difficult to distinguish the events linked with the parousia, and believes that the problem is such a complicated one as not to be ripe for solution at the present time. He is confident, however, that the parousia coincides with the resurrection and the ushering in of the future aeon.[4]

On the other hand, premillennialists distinguish between the coming of the Lord for His saints and His coming with His saints. Some speak of the rapture and the revelation as two events in the second advent, or as two phases or aspects of the second coming. Such designations are erroneous, as will be seen later. Upon what basis or ground do the premillennialists make any distinction at all between the rapture and the revelation? Many do so from the Greek words *parousia* and *apokalupsis,* making the former refer to the rapture and the latter to the revelation. Do the passages bear that statement out? We think not. Moulton and Geden in their exhaustive concordance of the Greek New Testament give three words which are translated in English by the word "coming."[5] They are *apokalupsis, epiphaneia,* and *parousia.* The first is found eighteen times in the New Testament; the second occurs six times; and the third is used twenty-four times, as many times as the first two words combined. A perusal of all the passages wherein those words are found reveals some interesting facts.

For instance, the word *apokalupsis* is used in five different senses. In Luke 2:32 the evident meaning is to lighten, in the sense or usage of a verb, denoting the purpose of the coming of Christ without, in all probability, any eschatological significance whatever. The reference in Romans 2:5 seems to point to the judgment of the Great White Throne. The usages in Romans 16:25; 1 Corinthians 14:6, 26; 2 Corinthians 12:1, 7; Galatians 1:12; 2:2; Ephesians 1:17; 3:3 are all without eschatological import and refer to disclosures of truth. Of the remaining references, four undoubtedly speak of the coming of Christ for His saints, the rapture. They are Romans 8:19; 1 Corinthians 1:7; 1 Peter 1:7, 13. The last three have reference to the coming of Christ with His saints, the revelation. They are 2 Thessalonians 1:7; 1 Peter 4:13; and Revelation 1:1. As a matter of fact, then, the word *apokalupsis,* which is taken to mean the revelation of Christ, is used more times to speak of the rapture. How does it fare with the other words?

The word *epiphaneia* has three meanings. In 2 Timothy 1:10 it unquestionably refers to the first advent of the Lord Jesus and is without eschatological significance. Of the remaining five times, it is used four times (1 Tim. 6:14; 2 Tim. 4:1, 8; Titus 2:13) of the rapture and one (2 Thess. 2:8) of the revelation. So no argument either way can be based on that word.

The word *parousia* is used in three senses at least. Sometimes it means merely any coming or presence. In that sense it is used of Stephanus, Fortunatus, and Achaicus in 1 Corinthians 16:17; of Titus in 2 Corinthians 7:6-7; of Paul in 2 Corinthians 10:10; Philippians 1:26 and 2:12; of the man of sin in 2 Thessalonians 2:9 (eschatologically important); and of the day of God in 2 Peter 3:12 (also of eschatological significance). The remaining sixteen references speak of both the rapture and the revelation. The rapture is found in ten instances (1 Cor. 15:23; 1 Thess. 2:19; 4:15; 5:23; 2 Thess. 2:1; James 5:7-8; 2 Pet. 1:16; 3:4; and 1 John 2:28). The revelation is referred to in Matthew 24:3, 27, 37, 39; 1 Thessalonians 3:13; and 2 Thessalonians 2:8. *Parousia,* then, although it is used more times of the rapture when it has an eschatological import, yet is not so employed exclusively. It is concluded, then, that the distinction between the coming of Christ for His saints and with His saints is not to be gleaned from a study of the Greek words themselves.

The differentiation between the rapture and the revelation is made clear rather by a comparative study of the Scriptures on the coming of the Lord Jesus Christ. When that is done, there are several interesting differences to be found in the passages that speak of the return of the Lord from heaven. There are some fourteen distinctions discernible between the coming of the Lord for His own and the return with His saints.

(1) The rapture is spoken of in the Scriptures as a mystery. In the two extended passages on that truth in 1 Corinthians 15 and 1 Thessalonians 4, the coming of Christ for His saints is treated as that which was never known by or revealed to Old Testament prophets. But the visible and glorious coming of the Messiah to earth is a subject upon which much is to be found both in the Old Testament and the New. It is certainly a vital distinction that definitely separates the two events. (2) The coming of the Lord Jesus for His own will not be seen by the world, whereas His visible appearing will be seen by all when He comes in power and great glory with His holy angels. (3) At the first event believers will be judged at the judgment seat of Christ for rewards for satisfactory service, whereas at the second advent the nations will be judged as to their fitness to enter into the millennial kingdom of the son of David. (4) Christ will appear to the church as Bridegroom, Lord, and Head; to Israel in the revelation He will come as King, Messiah, and Immanuel. (5) The rapture hope is centered in the fact that the Lord is at hand; with regard to the visible return of the Lord, the central thought is that the kingdom is at hand. (6) When the church is caught up to be with Christ, creation will remain unchanged; when the revelation takes place all creation will be delivered from the bondage of corruption. (7) The first event has no relation whatever to the nations; the second event sees their judgment. The remaining distinctions are just as clear. In the rapture the church will be removed from the earth; in the revelation she will be returning with Christ. At the first event Israel will be unaffected; in the second she will have all her covenants fulfilled. Evil will not come into view when Christ takes His own to Himself; when He comes with them, evil will be ended, Satan will be judged, and the beast and the false prophet will be destroyed. In the first event there will be no signs to mark its approach, and it is a timeless event; in the second event there will be signs that precede its approach, and it will have a specific time and place in the prophetic scheme of the Scriptures. One is spoken of as the "Day of Christ" and the other is referred to as the "Day of the Lord." In the former, Christ will come as the "Morning Star"; in the latter, He will appear as the "Sun of Righteousness" who brings healing in His wings. Finally, at the rapture Christ will come into the air and will not set foot on earth; at the revelation His feet will stand once again on the Mount of Olives, which is before Jerusalem on the east. Surely,

then, premillennialists are warranted in distinguishing between the rapture, which is solely church truth, and the revelation, which concerns all the earth also.

For the amillennialist the second advent is one indivisible event; the premillennialist distinguishes between the rapture for the church and the revelation, which is the visible appearance of Christ to the earth. Between those termini comes Israel's unfinished age, the seventieth week of Daniel's reckoning (Dan. 9:27). As has been set forth earlier in the body of this work, the church will be raptured before Daniel's last week, the Tribulation period, begins. All those features have been under steady fire from various sources in recent years.

That the pretribulation rapture of the church is not a novel view, but rather an early view, has been shown by Thiessen. He cites as basis for his position the *Shepherd of Hermas,* Book 1, Fourth, chapter 2 (ante-Nicene Fathers), which reads: "Go, therefore, and tell the elect of the Lord His mighty deeds, and say to them that this beast is a type of the great tribulation that is coming. If then ye prepare yourselves, and repent with all your heart, and turn to the Lord, it will be possible for you to escape it, if your heart be free and spotless in serving the Lord blamelessly."[6] That event is restricted to the church. There are no prophecies that relate Israel to the rapture.[7] The phrase "in Christ" in 1 Thessalonians 4:16 has the same soteriological concept that it has in Ephesians and throughout the New Testament; it refers to believers of the church age.

Hamilton has misunderstood the premillennial position when he claims that premillennialists hold to a second and third coming, because they differentiate between the rapture and the revelation.[8] Would he speak also of two ascensions of our Lord after His resurrection—one on the day of the resurrection (John 20:17) and the other forty days later from Olivet (Acts 1:9)? Were those not two stages in the same redemption event? So it is with the rapture and the revelation. They have different peoples and objectives in view.

Hamilton expresses concern that the Holy Spirit should be absent from the earth during the Great Tribulation.[9] For some that makes conversion and salvation impossible during the Tribulation period.[10] There is failure here to realize, when speaking of the Three Persons of the Godhead, where one of the Trinity may be residentially or potentially by reason of His omnipresence. Christ is residentially at the right hand of the Father (Psalm 110:1 and the epistle to the Hebrews), but He dwells in believing hearts by faith (John 14:23). The Holy Spirit can be residentially in heaven during the Great Tribulation, and yet regenerate souls as He did in Old Testament times. After all, the Tribulation is the end of the Jewish age, an incidental proof that the church is not on earth at that time.

How much confusion can result from a misunderstanding of the dispensations is evident when Hamilton wonders why the rapture is not mentioned in the Olivet Discourse in Matthew 24.[11] Since that is Israel's age depicted in its last stages, and the church is the only body related to the rapture, it would be confusing to have the rapture in Matthew 24. The church is not in Matthew 24 because the church is not in the Tribulation period described there (Matt. 24:21). Amillennialists practically to a man feel compelled to take the "brethren" of Matthew 25:40 to mean saints of the church. No one will deny that the term is repeatedly used of believers of the church age, but the word is not restricted to them. Hamilton must concede that Peter, Stephen, and Paul in public address speak of even unbelieving Jews as "brethren."[12] Those in view are the earthly brethren of our Lord after the flesh, as Paul spoke of them with regard to himself in Romans 9:1-5.

Will Hamilton find the rapture of the church in 1 Thessalonians 4:13-18? For him it is only another instance where the supposed error of the premillennialists is evident. He declares, "Most premillennialists, however, declare that the words, 'the dead in Christ shall rise first,' is a contrast, not between the dead believers and the living believers, but between the dead believers and dead unbelievers! We submit, however, that such an interpretation is an arbitrary wresting of the text."[13] It must be declared that the statement concerning "most premillennialists" is not true, and he cites not one authority for it. Because the passage is church truth, the apostle is indicating that dead believers will not be separated from living believers in the coming of Christ for His own.

Hamilton contends 1 Thessalonians 5 is directly against the pretribulation view, because the passage assumes the Day of the Lord will be the same for believers and unbelievers. For him the argument is conclusive because "the day of the Lord is the day of rapture."[14] That reveals a confusion of scriptural terms: the Day of the Lord (of which the Tribulation is a part) is definitely not the day of the rapture, which precedes it. Paul is stating the very opposite of that which Hamilton claims. He is telling believers that they know about the Tribulation, but it will not overtake them. They will not be overwhelmed by it. Note the difference in the pronouns: *"ye* have no need"; *"yourselves* know"; "When *they* are saying"; "cometh upon *them*" and *"they* shall in no wise escape." It is crystal clear that Paul has placed believers in the first category, not to be touched by the calamities (the "ye"), and the unbelievers in the second division, which is to know judgment (the "they"). That significant alternation between "ye" and "they" runs through the passage. It is a telling portion in proof of the position that the church will not pass through the Tribulation.

In treating 2 Thessalonians 1:7-10 Hamilton joins the time of the judgment with the glorification of the Lord in His saints. The passage is supposed to mean that the judgment occurs at the time of the coming, the glorification, and the marveling.[15] The answer is simple. Christ will not only be glorified in His saints when He comes for them (1 Thess. 4), but when He comes with them as well (2 Thess. 1). The fact that Christ will be glorified does not warrant one to say that is the glorious coming in the revelation. It is a mixing of terms without justification. Now, one would surely be justified in understanding that 2 Thessalonians 2:1-10 was written to show the church of Thessalonica that the Tribulation could not transpire until the rapture took place; but Hamilton again confuses the comings and makes "the manifestation of his coming" stand for the coming of Christ at the times specified in verse 1.[16] The rapture is indicated in the departure of the Holy Spirit in verse 7, whereas verse 8 speaks of the revelation in judgment upon the evil participants of the last days, the man of sin and his confederates.

Finally, the passage in Revelation 16:14-16 is adduced to show that the pretribulation view is in error, for here is a warning to believers amidst unbelievers when believers should not be on earth at all.[17] There are believers on earth, the remnant in Israel, but they are not saints of the church age. For amillennialists the words "saints," "brethren," and "elect" must always have the same interpretation, regardless of the context, and that reference is to the church. It can evidently not be said too often that God has two elect people: Israel (Deut. 14:2) and the church (Eph. 1:4).

At no point is a compromising premillennialism more at sea than in this discussion. Kromminga reveals such a dilemma, for he also speaks of "the third coming of Christ."[18] He asks, "After all, to mention what appears to be the greatest of the recent innovations [recall the witness of the *Shepherd of Hermas*], does it really matter so much, whether the saints will be raptured before the great tribulation or pass through it?"[19] It matters so much that, if the church does go through the Tribulation, the hope of the believer is bedimmed, the church age is confused with the law age, and the book of the Revelation is lost in unrelieved confusion. Those points are pivotal and not peripheral, and they are not ours to barter away so easily. It is the amillennial contention that, deprived of the Revelation 20 passage, premillennialism becomes a nonentity. It always pays the opposition to whittle away at the points of difference and to minimize them to the greatest extent, the more easily to suggest their abandonment altogether. But what is spoken of here is a whole system of biblical interpretation, well integrated and fitted together. Injury to *any* part sensibly affects the whole. Thus the rapture contains within it issues of surpassing importance.

Kromminga does have difficulty in finding the church in the book of Revelation. No wonder; it is not there from chapter 4 through the book until chapter 19.[20] Since he does not keep Israel and the church distinct, he finally finds the church in some strange places. Actually, most of the instances he cites relate to the Jewish remnant of the Great Tribulation, the saints of the Most High of Daniel 7. The final admission is made that "we do not see the Church directly in her historical manifestation."[21] And she is not, not because she is lost beneath the cloud of tribulations, but because she has already been raptured to glory in the presence of the Bridegroom.

The pretribulation coming of Christ for His own is not feasible for Berkhof, because the elect of Matthew 24:29-31 are gathered together *"immediately after the great tribulation."*[22] According to his understanding it should have occurred before the time of trial. Again the difficulty stems from not recognizing that the elect of the passage are Israel of the last days, and not the church. Is that not discernible from the references to "the abomination of desolation . . . in the holy place"; "them that are in Judaea"; "on a sabbath"? They have nothing to do with the church in the past, in the present, or in the future, in time or in eternity.

Berkhof denies the imminence of the return of the Lord,[23] but he avoids mentioning what "several important events must occur" before that event. When he gives his own view of the coming, it may mean His advent in spiritual power at Pentecost or the destruction of Jerusalem.[24] If that is true, is it not interesting that the New Testament, written after the first event, and a large part of it after the second mentioned event, should still speak of that coming as lying in the future?

He will not permit that the Tribulation, with its reversal to Old Testament conditions and the absence of the indwelling Holy Spirit, yet witnesses a greater effectiveness than the proclamation of the gospel of God's grace.[25] It is not the interpreter's office to indicate what shall be the purpose of God in the gospel in any age; it is not a question of the power of the gospel. Will one cavil with God because Jonah, a disobedient prophet at that, was used to bring Nineveh to God, whereas the grand and glorious Isaiah served only to harden his own people by his message (Isaiah 6)? Calvinists, of all people, should be the last to find fault with the purpose and sovereign will of God.

Allis devotes an important chapter of his work to a discussion of the coming of the Lord. He concedes, "Belief in a still future spiritual millennium does undoubtedly tend to weaken the Christian's expectancy of the coming, by referring it to a remote future."[26] Anything that dims the hope of the believer is harmful. He calls the "any moment doctrine" the second great plank in the platform of dispensationalism.[27] It may be pointed out that the "any moment" stems from the phrase "in a moment" of 1 Corinthians 15:52 and is eminently biblical. He denies as invalid the argument that, if the coming of the Lord is not imminent, men will not be vigilant to watch for Him.[28] But actually and practically has it not worked out precisely in that way? Those who have expected the coming of the Lord at any time have generally and demonstrably been influenced by it in their life and service for Christ. That is incontrovertible and a matter of record. Take the case of the evangelists of the past one hundred years as an example. Is it not true that, when the Roman Church set aside the truth of the imminent coming of the Lord, she allowed herself an earthly position and privileges not called for in the Word? Do not the parables on the coming in the gospels (the same principle for His coming for the saints as with His saints) reveal that when the servants felt the coming of their Lord was a long way off, their actions were detrimentally affected thereby? In practically the same context Allis admits the strong appeal of the doctrine of the imminent return of the Lord.[29]

The reason he assigns for the strong appeal of the "any moment rapture doctrine" is personal profit and a desire to escape both trials here and the ushering into the presence of the Lord by death.[30] Let it be firmly stated here that many who have held the doctrine of the imminent return have suffered more for the cause of Christ at home and on the foreign field than those who make such charges, which are common among midtribulationists and post-tribulationists. The basic difficulty lies in the fact that those men will not allow Matthew 24:21 to stand in its full and natural meaning; they must water it down to refer to almost any trial of the believer when on earth. That is invalid and will not pass muster.

Adhering to a view that often oversimplifies, thus eliminating so many elements that differ, Allis is unable to see any distinction between the rapture and the revelation.[31] He inquires why Paul, James, and John did not distinguish between them. Their language is not confusing, as he claims, but the case is that both the Old and the New Testaments use words for "coming" in a variety of different senses, so the context must be determining. An Old Testament context must be studied carefully to discern whether the sacred writer is speaking of the first advent or the second. It also must be realized that the coming for the saints is "mystery" truth, as stated in 1 Corinthians and 1 Thessalonians.

In another section of his work, Allis treats the second advent parenthesis and pretribulationism. He finds fault with the premillennial view because Matthew 24 is silent about the church,[32] but it must be realized that the passage cannot speak of the church when it deals with Daniel's seventieth week, where the church is not found. One cannot treat the first sixty-nine weeks of Daniel 9 literally and the last week spiritually. It is no argument that, if the elect of Matthew 24 mean the Jewish remnant of the future, then Matthew uses the word in a different sense from Paul who uses it of church saints.[33] That should occasion no surprise, because there is warrant. Paul uses the word "law" in Romans 2 and 3 in at least three different senses. Any writer is permitted to use a word in two different senses, provided that the meaning is not obscured. See Zechariah 10:3, where the same Hebrew word *(paqadh)* is used in two diametrically opposite meanings in the same verse, being translated "punish" and "visit." Paul and James speak of justification in different senses. Why should that occasion confusion?

Allis will allow the "we" of 1 Thessalonians 4:15 to represent Christians at the coming of Christ in the rapture, but he will not permit the "you" and "ye" of Matthew 24 to represent the godly remnant in the end of the Jewish age. The reason given is that those disciples were shortly to be part of the church at Pentecost, hence could not be representative of the Jewish remnant.[34] That is notably weak for two reasons: (1) Those disciples at the time our Lord spoke to them were *not* part of the church; and (2) all agree that the apostles lived in a transitional period from the law age to the age of grace. Surely Peter's message given him in Matthew 10, as he preached it according to the express charge of Christ, was vastly different from his message in Acts 10 in the home of Cornelius, again in the leading of the Lord.

Much time is spent on a treatment of Revelation 4-19, and the request is made for a discussion of the rapture at chapter 4.[35] The emphasis in the book of Revelation is not primarily on the church in heaven, but on the events on the earth. The bulk of the book is occupied with judgment that will fall on a godless world. No one can dictate to the Holy Spirit in the matter of where He will reveal the truth of the rapture. Consider the number of books in the New Testament, and then consider in how many of them there is mention of the truth of the rapture. It cannot be emphasized too strongly that we interpret truth where we find it, not where we should like to have it.

One is somewhat surprised to find that Allis thinks it intolerable for dispensationalists to speak of an Old Testament figure ("elder"), which is Jewish, as representing the New Testament church.[36] What about the New Testament use of the word "elders," and what of Presbyterian elders? Are they not in order? He considers the possibility that the 24 elders are not the church at all,[37] but their song in 5:9-10 points them out as redeemed of the church from all nations.

Allis dismisses the biblical bases of pretribulationism, which are the nature of the blessed hope and the nature of the Great Tribulation as a time of God's punishment. It is done "at once."[38] If refutation could have been given, that was the place to do so. His comment on Revelation 7 is, "This is one of the most emphatic statements of the comprehensive, world-wide mission of the Christian Church to be found anywhere in Scripture."[39]

First of all, when is the church seen divided under tribal distinctions? Second, their redemption is related to the blood of the Lamb, just as that of Adam and Eve, or Abel, or anyone else in the history of man, but that does not put them in the Body of Christ. Furthermore, he cannot arbitrarily disregard the statement that they have come out of "the great tribulation [lit., the tribulation, the great one]," which he repeatedly interprets as the great trials of the church throughout her history in the world. Fourth, if the 144,000 are symbolic of the church, why is there need to represent the same group again and in a different manner in the same chapter? Last, and this is conclusive, how is it that John the apostle, a member of the Body of Christ, when asked by one of the elders who they were, indicated his ignorance of their identity? Did he not know the church?

In the final analysis, the reason for the opposition comes to the fore: Allis laments that the glorious picture that could belong to the church (by misapplication of Scripture) is given to a Jewish remnant instead. That should occasion no end of surprise. A believer should rejoice that souls are won to Christ, regardless of the agency, but it is a tragedy ("one of the tragic results" of premillennial and dispensational teaching) to his way of thinking, if it is the Jews who do so, instead of the church.[40] Was it a tragedy that the church had its origin and first impetus from Jews? This is a rather late hour to bemoan the tragedy of God's use of Jewish heralds to preach any message of His blessed chosing.

Reese has written a work that deals with the theme of this chapter. It is actually an attack on the Darby position relative to the pretribulation rapture and related events. He comes to grips with the issue in the first chapter, which is whether the old premillenarians were right in holding to a single and unified coming of Christ before the Millennium, or those who believe there is to be a rapture followed by a revelation. He maintains, "The fundamental point in our inquiry concerns the relation of the Rapture of the risen and transfigured saints to the Day of the Lord: does the one precede the other by a period of several years."[41] He is wrong in claiming there are only three undisputed passages in the Bible on the rapture. He omits 1 Corinthians 15:50-58; Philippians 3:20-21; and 1 Thessalonians 1:9-10. He begins his investigation with a discussion of the resurrection of Old Testament saints with the purpose of inquiring into the time of that resurrection. Soon he comes to the crux of the matter: "Living Israel is restored, and the sleeping saints are brought to life, at the beginning of the Messianic Reign, not some years or decades before, as the new theories require."[42]

We admit that to be true, because we do not place Old Testament saints in the rapture, as some dispensational premillennialists do, as is clear from the previous discussion in this volume. "In Christ," it is maintained, refers only to New Testament believers. The resurrection of Old Testament saints is cared for by Daniel 12:1-3 and is presupposed in Revelation 20:1-6. Kelly and Darby deny that Isaiah 26 deals with a physical resurrection [43] (and some deny it in Daniel 12), but such is not the view of this writer. Our position, then, refutes Reese's, for it does not lump the resurrection of Old Testament saints (which comes before the visible appearance of Christ) with that of New Testament saints, which is antecedent to the former by a seven-year period. But Reese is combining separate entities when he synchronizes the time of John 6:39-54 with the time of Daniel 12:1-3. His only proof is his own statement to that effect.[44] He cannot logically object to stages in the first resurrection, for they are indicated plainly in 1 Corinthians 15: "each man in his order." The admission is made later that "the last day" of the John passages could refer "to the last period of God's dealings with men in time."[45]

But while one cannot agree to include Old Testament saints in the rapture, for they are excluded in 1 Thessalonians 4, neither can one accept the placing of the resurrection of New Testament saints and all the faithful dead at the time of the inauguration of the Messianic kingdom.[46] Reese refuses to sever the resurrection of Old Testament saints from that of New Testament saints because it serves his thesis. He has overlooked one vital feature: If 1 Corinthians 15:50-54 reveals exactly what the Old Testament did concerning the resurrection of saints (and all saints are grouped together by him), why then does Paul begin the passage by calling the revelation a "mystery"? That he does not, and cannot, explain. It was not known to the Old Testament, because the church was not known to the Old Testament. There can be no church until there is a crucified, buried, risen, ascended Head seated in heaven at the right hand of God, Head over all things to the church, which is His Body.

When Reese comes to 1 Thessalonians 4:13-18, the reader is frankly disappointed when he claims: "The singular thing is that beyond the elementary fact of its occurring at the Advent, the passage *in itself* furnishes no evidence whatever upon the point [that is, on the time of the resurrection]."[47] He would find it singular because it is not speaking of the resurrection of Old Testament saints, and here he cannot rely on an Old Testament quotation as in 1 Corinthians 15 (where, it is true, the apostle is quoting Isaiah 25 for purposes of illustration of the *principle* rather than for purposes of designating the *time* of the resurrection). He concludes that there is nothing in 1 Thessalonians 4 against his posttribulation rapture view. But his argument collapses the moment it is realized that the resurrection of New Testament saints comes at the rapture and that of the Old Testament saints after the Tribulation and before the revelation. Because of one weakness Reese would like to claim the victory. He writes, "The whole Darbyist case collapses, therefore, before their admission that I Thess. iv includes the raising of the O.T. saints."[48] In all fairness he should recognize that other dispensationalists do not hold that view. He is making that one point carry too much weight. When it serves his purpose, Reese can make the elders of Revelation 4 represent angelic beings, quoting Bullinger.[49] The elect of Matthew 24 are, to be sure, the Christians of every land, a view that disregards any geographical notes in the text.[50] On his own basis he rules our "forever" the pretribulation rapture.[51]

In summarizing the position of the book, Reese never adequately treats Daniel 9:24-27. An excursus of a few pages is insufficient (pp. 30-33). He mistakes the restrainer of 2 Thessalonians 2 for the Roman Empire. The use of the neuter and the masculine, as John does for the Holy Spirit in his gospel, reveals that the restrainer is the Holy Spirit. And His ministry is in keeping

] 295 [

with His character. He loses track of the argument on the rapture, solely because some claim it will be secret. Does that touch the heart of the problem he is discussing? It is thus concluded that there will be a rapture for the church, which may occur at any moment, to be followed by the seven-year period of the Great Tribulation, which will be brought to a close by the visible coming to earth of the Lord Jesus Christ (Revelation 19).

Because terminology is of the essence in this discussion, it is vital to the matter to preserve proper distinctions. Ladd, however, in his argument against the two aspects of Christ's coming—the rapture and the revelation—claims there is "a single, glorious event."[52] To maintain his position he must unwarrantedly identify the day of Christ (Phil. 1:6, 10; 2:16) with the Day of the Lord (2 Thess. 2:2, 8), although he recognizes that the first is a day of blessing and anticipation for believers, whereas the second is a terrifying day of judgment. He argues, "The identity of the day of the Lord and the day of Christ is further substantiated by the conflation of those two phrases. God will confirm His people unto the end that they may be unreprovable 'in the *day* of our *Lord* Jesus Christ' (1 Cor. 1:8; italics his). The day of Jesus Christ and the day of the Lord are one and the same day, the day of Christian expectation."[53]

Upon what basis is such a conflation obtained? It has already been shown upon what hermeneutical grounds a distinction between the rapture and the revelation can be and must be sustained. With the clear force of biblical prophetic testimony at hand it is remarkable that Ladd should ask: "Where does the Word of God assert that the day of Christ is to be distinguished from the day of the Lord?"[54] It would be easy to reply by asking where Joel and Zephaniah speak of the Day of the Lord and mean thereby the day of Christ as well, to say nothing of New Testament usage.[55]

In spite of the fact that it is well known that the terminology of New Testament eschatology, specifically, *parousia, epiphaneia,* and *apokalupsis,* is used in different senses, the New Testament scholar Ladd disregards the evidence that has been already set forth in this volume, when he declares: "The Revelation is continually made the object of our hope; the Rapture must therefore occur at the Revelation of Christ. The Scripture nowhere asserts that there is a Rapture which will take place before the Revelation."[56] What does he make of John 14:1-3, 1 Corinthians 15:50-58, or 1 Thessalonians 4:13-18? Where does he place them in his eschatological scheme of events? Furthermore, where does the Scripture join the rapture and the revelation in one passage? The burden of proof is upon Ladd when this writer has shown more than a dozen distinctions between the two events.

Ladd claims that pretribulationists place the judgment of believers for reward between the rapture and the revelation, whereas according to him that judgment is at the epiphany, which is identical with the revelation at the termination of the Tribulation period. But the words indicated do not convey the meanings he assigns them in their respective contexts.[57] His final word here is, "We can only conclude that the distinction between the Rapture of the Church and the Revelation is an inference which is nowhere asserted by the Word of God and not required by the terminology relating to the return of Christ."[58] What is wrong with inferential logic when based upon clear statements of the Word?

Although Ladd decries the use of inference in the arguments of others, he is ready to employ assumption in his own.

> The natural assumption is that the Rapture of the Church and the Resurrection of the dead in Christ will take place at His glorious coming. The burden of proof rests on those who teach that this is not the proper order of events. We *know* Christ is coming at the end of the Tribulation. We *know* the living saints are to be caught up to be with Christ when He comes. We *know* the dead will be raised at His coming. The Word of God is clear on these points [italics his].[59]

Notice, first of all, four uses of "come" and "coming" without indicating any differentiation between the distinct appearances of Christ to the church or to Israel and the world. Strictly speaking, the term "coming" should be employed for the first advent (to Israel and the world) and the second advent (to the same entities). The Lord's return for His Bride (only mentioned in the New Testament) should technically be designated the rapture, resting on the wording of 1 Thessalonians 4:17 ("caught up" answers to the Latin *rapio,* whence rapture, the verb being so employed in the Latin Vulgate). It will thus be readily seen that "coming" alone is not precise to convey the specific sense of a passage. However, that constitutes no problem to posttribulationists or amillennialists who lump both events into one transaction.

Second, Ladd's first statement is in serious error. The rapture and the resurrection of the dead in Christ are identical in time (cf. 1 Cor. 15:52, where the timeless factor is clear as well as the two companies of saints: "corruptible" and "mortal"; also, 1 Thess. 4:16, where the groups of believers are "those who are asleep" and "we who are alive"). Nothing is said to precede them in God's eschatological chronology. However, that event is never indicated as taking place "at His glorious coming" or the revelation. Why are the more than a dozen differences between those two events not confronted instead of being disregarded? Why bypass them and cry for the burden of proof to rest upon those who see distinctions in those things that differ? The Scripture order of events is simple and demonstrable: (1) Christ raptures His Bride (not at the end of the Tribulation but before it, as already demonstrated in this volume more than once); (2) the Tribulation as the wrath of God is poured out on earth's unbelievers; (3) Christ returns to earth with His already resurrected and translated saints. That is the simple, uncomplicated, unconfused chronology of the Word of God, which was taught practically all writers of prophetic literature today. Even Ladd must admit that the program here enunciated is straightforward: "This interpretation possesses a deceptive simplicity."[60]

Ladd suggests that if pretribulationism were correct, it should appear in certain passages where it does not. For example, he claims that Matthew 24:31 and 1 Thessalonians 4:16 have "elements of striking similarity," which he does not specify. He believes that the Olivet Discourse is speaking of the rapture because he has already confused the age which the discourse treats. For his posttribulation view he must have the rapture in the Olivet Discourse to place the church in the Tribulation. The example the Lord Jesus gave of Noah's days (Matt. 24:37-39) cannot refer to the rapture where believers are caught up for blessing, whereas Noah's contemporaries were swept away in judgment. All is contrast of the clearest type.[61] In discussing 2 Thessalonians 2 he claims that the rapture does not precede the events spoken of there because he has ruled it out in his interpretation of verse 7. At the same time he has to admit that the rapture in "1 Thessalonians 4 says nothing about the Tribulation."[62] The valid reason is that the church will not be there. Because he holds the church will be in the Tribulation period, he has to maintain that there is no pretribulation rapture in Revelation 8-16. That is so for two substantial reasons: (1) the church has been raptured before chapter 8 and before a single seal judgment has taken place (see above in the discussion of the twenty-four elders of chapters 4 and 5), and (2) the church is not on earth in chapters 8-16 to be raptured at that time.[63]

Throughout his discussions Ladd persists in asking for one passage of Scripture to give the chronology of the end time events that would prove a pretribulation rapture. Not once does he admit there is no such passage that confirms his posttribulation rapture. No man can dictate the revelation of truth. When he comes to the treatment of 1 Thessalonians 4:14-17, he admits: "Only one passage in the Word of God describes the Rapture by name."[64] He then states: *"Nothing is said about what happens immediately after the meeting* [italics his]. It is just as possible, and, as we shall show later on, even suggested by the word used for the 'meeting,' that after this meeting, Jesus continues His descent to the earth, but now accompanied by His saints."[65] What, then, was the purpose of momentarily catching them away to midair? Obviously, Ladd—and this he has in common with other antidispensational posttribulationists—thus accomplishes a fusion of the rapture (a coming for the saints) with the revelation (a coming with the saints). It is a futile attempt to make the passage bear a weight never intended in the simple language employed. Besides, where is the time needed for events to transpire in heaven, for example, believers' judgment for rewards and the marriage of the Lamb and His Bride, between the rapture and the revelation?

Does the reader consider that the arguments thus far may be too strong or overdrawn? Then note this: "There is no ground whatsoever to assume that there must be a *considerable* interval of time between the Rapture and Christ's coming with His Church. They may be two aspects of a single indivisible event" (italics added).[66] It is strange that some declared premillennialists have in recent years come to amillennial positions in those areas. Moreover, because the lock washer of the pretribulation rapture is removed, other verified positions of premillennialism are questioned or denied.

Ladd maintains that pretribulationists divide the resurrection of the dead into three parts: (1) the first resurrection (Rev. 20:4-5)—"the resurrection of all the saints, which will occur at the coming of Christ *for* [italics his] His Church at the beginning of the Great Tribulation; (2) the resurrection of the tribulation martyrs at the end of the Tribulation; and (3) the second resurrection at the end of the millennium (Rev. 20:12-15)."[67] He fails to see the stages of the first resurrection in the explicit passages of 1 Corinthians 15:24-28 and Daniel 12:1-2. Yet he declares: *"The two stages of the first resurrection should be as clear as the fact of the two resurrections* [italics his]."[68] As a matter of fact, Revelation 20:4-5 exactly sets forth more than one group in the first resurrection before the Millennium.

All recognize that 1 Thessalonians 5:9 is a pivotal text, which clearly supports pretribulationism, but Ladd understands the passage thus:

> We hasten here to agree that the Church which Christ has redeemed by His precious blood will never experience the wrath of God. If the question of the Rapture and the Tribulation is to be settled on this issue alone, the only alternative is a pretribulation rapture, for the Church will never suffer God's wrath. However, this admission does not lead to pretribulationism for the verse in question says nothing about either the Rapture or the Tribulation. All it asserts is that the Church will not fall under God's wrath. The wrath in question may not refer to the Tribulation at all, but to God's wrath in the final judgment (Rom. 2:5). However, if it does include the Great Tribulation, the verse neither asserts nor suggests that the Church will be *removed* [italics his] from the world; it is only promised deliverance.[69]

The text itself says, "For God has not destined us for wrath, but for obtaining salvation through our Lord Jesus Christ" (NASB). First, the passage indicates the overruling purpose of God for the church. Second, it states that the aim of God for believers is salvation through the Lord Jesus. Third, the themes are limited in no sense whatever; they are general and comprehensive. Fourth, there is no mention or hint of specifics as rapture or Tribulation. Fifth, for a posttribulationist to claim that the church will never undergo God's wrath and yet hold that the church will go through the Great Tribulation, is an oddity of interpretation of great proportions. What is the Tribulation if not the very time of God's wrath? Read carefully Revelation 6:16 and 15:1, 7 and 16:1, 19. Who is authorized to make those verses mean other than their plain, comprehensible sense? Sixth, how can Romans 2:5 in any logical manner modify the meaning of 1 Thessalonians 5:9? The contexts are totally different, and the ones addressed are entirely separate—unbelievers in Romans and saved in 1 Thessalonians. Seventh, how is it possible for the church not to be removed from the world and yet be promised deliverance? You cannot have it both ways. To say that 1 Thessalonians 5:9 states nothing about the rapture is beside the point. Why should it mention anything beyond its lucid disclosure?

In order to bring this portion of the discussion on the rapture and the revelation to a close, it will be well to consider Ladd's treatment of the vital witness of the book of Revelation. The reader will recall how often one single passage has been called for that will state that the church will be kept from the Tribulation. There is such a verse, which is clear and free of ambiguity, and it is Revelation 3:10: "Because you have kept the word of My perseverance, I also will keep you from the hour of testing, that hour which is about to come upon the whole world, to test those who dwell upon the earth" (NASB). Those who are addressed are believers. They have been faithful to the Lord in their walk. The promise of God is unmistakable to keep them from the hour of Tribulation that will overtake the world. Those singled out for judgment are clearly unbelievers who have dwelt (Greek, "settled down," a condition the opposite of the pilgrim character of the church, 1 Pet. 2:11) upon the earth.

What is Ladd's interpretation of that significant verse? He says, "This verse appears at first sight to teach a pretribulation rapture." He adds, "The language of this verse, taken by itself, could be interpreted to teach complete escape from the coming hour of Tribulation." He readily admits that the Greek preposition is *ek*, "out of." Then he concludes, "This language, however, neither asserts nor demands the idea of bodily removal from the midst of the coming trial."[70] He prefers, in spite of the simple meaning of the common preposition *ek*, to believe that the church will be insulated, as it were, from the trials of the Tribulation while she passes through it. Why was not the well known preposition *dia* ("through") used in the passage? What reader of Scripture could have understood the verse in that arbitrary and strained meaning?

But Ladd continues, stating that there is no rapture in Revelation 4.[71] He argues that, even if the elders represent the church, there is "no idea of a previous rapture."[72] Whether he calls it rapture or by any other name, there was a transference of the church from earth (and the dead saints from their graves) to heaven. He will not even allow that the crowns (*stephanoi*) of the elders signify rewards, but only rule. Is not rule or sovereignty a reward for the saints of this age? The best he can do with the elders is to posit a probability that they are angels. Where in Scripture are angels ever reckoned according to human time limitations? Where are they ever recipients of rewards? Where are angels ever involved with "the prayers of the saints" (5:9)? Where do angels sing a redemption song for themselves or, more probably, for others?

After conceding that "church" occurs nineteen times in chapters 1-3, and it must be added never again in the book for she is seen only as the wife of the Lamb (19:7; 21:9) and the bride (22:17), he errs grievously in seeking to avoid the implications of these facts: "One very important fact they [pretribulationists] do not recognize: the marriage feast does not occur until after the return of Christ in glory."[73] The Scripture is very specific that it is first in 19:7-10 (the marriage supper of the Lamb), then 19:11-19 (the coming of the Lord Jesus in glory). Why reverse those events?

After much discussion on watching and waiting for Christ's coming, it is admitted: "With the exception of one passage, the author will grant that the Scripture nowhere explicitly states that the Church will go through the Great Tribulation. . . . Nor does the Word explicitly place the Rapture at the end of the Tribulation."[74]

It is extremely unfortunate that in a work free of animus there should appear at the close an unsubstantiated accusation that pretribulationism "sacrifices one of the main motives for worldwide missions, viz., hastening the attainment of the Blessed Hope. The pretribulation doctrine as it is usually taught robs the Church of one of the most dynamic incentives for worldwide evangelization."[75] That is untrue! Because pretribulationists assign Matthew 24:14 and Revelation 7:1-8 to the Jewish remnant at the end of Israel's age, they are accused of robbing the church of motive for worldwide missions and one of the most potent incentives for worldwide evangelization. In all clarity it is in place here to refer all posttribulationists to the incentives and motives indicated in Matthew 28:18-20 (Mark 16:9-20), Luke 24:44-48, and John 20:21.

The challenge is issued here to check missionary personnel and evangelists to discover whether pretribulation doctrine has robbed them of either motive or incentive in their exemplary ministries. Ladd—and other posttribulationists are equally culpable here—takes umbrage that the church, indwelt by the Holy Spirit, should fail to do in two thousand years what a Jewish remnant will accomplish in seven years. First, it is not a matter of the power of the gospel in any age, but the purpose of God in the gospel. Second, will not the Jewish remnant also be indwelt by the Holy Spirit? Third, did not Jewish believers in the church accomplish in a short time (Col. 1:6) what the church has not duplicated since? Finally, sadly enough, is not the final record of the church on earth one of failure (cf. the church of Laodicea in Rev. 3 and Paul's epistles with Peter's and John's), just as Israel was a failure in her mission before the beginning of the times of the Gentiles? Why cavil at whomever it pleases God to use in any age to accomplish His glorious purpose among men? Let God be praised that it is done!

The posttribulationist Barton Payne oversimplifies the issue of the rapture and even minimizes its importance as he declares:

But despite the volumes that have been written, and the regrettably bitter discussion that has occurred relative to it, the rapture is specifically mentioned just this once [reference to 1 Thess. 4:17] in all of Scripture. This fact alone should behoove Christian believers to caution, about elevating the interpretation of a doctrine of such minor biblical emphasis into a veritable touchstone of evangelical fellowship.[76]

If the doctrine of the rapture is such a minor emphasis in the Bible, how is it that so many volumes have been written on it? Why was there compulsion to add another work on such a minimal matter? Bitter discussion is an exercise that is not limited to either side of the issue. Is 1 Thessalonians 4:17 the only specific mention of the rapture? Among others, what of John 14:1-3 and 1 Corinthians 15:50-58? If Payne is seeking the actual word to justify importance, where is the word "Trinity" found in the Hebrew, Aramaic, Greek, and English texts, or in any other language? How can anyone find fault with magnifying the doctrine of the believer's hope, in view of the fact that it centers in the Lord Jesus Christ?

How is it possible to adduce Isaiah 25:6-11 in the matter of the time of the hope of the church in the light of the plain words of our Lord in Matthew 16:18? One is not surprised that according to Payne, Matthew 24 speaks not of Israel, but the church: "But, apart from Darbyist presuppositions, a less likely possibility would be hard to discover"; and on the basis of Matthew 21:43 he confidently maintains ". . . any nation, in fact, *except* [italics his] Israel. . . ."[77] He declares that no valid exegesis will yield any other subject of the Olivet discourse than the church. His unusually broad and restrictive comments relative to Israel reveal that he has not kept abreast of such incisive discussions as that of McClain on Matthew 21:43 treated above. Also, valid exegesis requires more than a ready ipse dixit. For instance, in Matthew 24, whose age is spoken of (v. 3)? An abomination of desolation is in whose holy place (v. 15)? When does the church observe the Sabbath (v. 20)? What does the church have to do with Judaea or its mountains (v. 16)? Is the church included in "all the tribes of the earth" (v. 30)? If so, why is she mourning? Is she the elect to be gathered by angelic agency "from the four winds, from one end of heaven to the other" (v. 31)? Is she designated as "this generation" (v. 34)? Can that exegesis be called "valid" that overlooks so many vital details?

In discussing the meaning of John 14:1-3, he writes, "The interpretation that seems the most plausible contextually is that *at a believer's death* [italics his], 'I come and will receive you unto myself' in glory."[78] That exegesis seems to bypass the obvious in order to maintain the dubious. It is strange that posttribulationists never assign a reason why believers must experience the Tribulation.

Moreover, many of them go to extreme lengths to nullify passages that teach pretribulationism in order to maintain their claim that there is not a single passage in the Bible that teaches the doctrine. Two examples should suffice.

On Revelation 3:10 Barton Payne explains: "For it is the being harmed by the hour, not the being in the hour, against which the Philadelphian church is promised protection."[79]

Knowing the importance of Revelation 4 for any view of the Tribulation, he believes the elders (4:4) could well be angels, since elders are "literally 'older ones.' " Where does Scripture ever assign age, let alone other human specifics, to angels? Why are they crowned? In what sense can they sing of redemption? As seen above, they represent the church in heaven, a catastrophic refutation for all posttribulationists (as well as midtribulationists and "partial rapturists"). As to the church not being found after chapter 3, he says "but this in itself proves little."[80] How much does it prove? If so little, he could attempt a minimal rebuttal, which he does not. He decides that "In fact, the greatest single objection to dispensational pretribulationism is that the Bible simply does not teach it."[81] If so, why so much trouble to refute it?

Knowing full well that one of the strongest arguments against posttribulationism is the surrender of the doctrine of imminence, Barton Payne accuses the opposition of that very practice. He declares, "Dispensationalism has therefore been consistently guilty of denying the church's hope in the imminence of Christ's appearing."[82] He offers no proof for the accusation. He levels the same charge against "the modern posttribulational movement."

One reading of Payne's work will demonstrate how he seeks to cancel the position of Reese, Ladd, and more recent posttribulationists.[83] He supports his view by first showing how certain events (e.g., the death of Peter, John 21) have already been fulfilled, so they constitute no difficulty for imminence. He claims dispensationalists are embarrassed in their position on the imminence because of their "hypothetical pretribulation rapture," which according to him requires some chronological sequence in events in 1 Corinthians 15:50-58 and 1 Thessalonians 4:13-18.[84] His lack of clear distinctions between the rapture and the revelation add to the confusion, as well as an unawareness that the elements of the rapture occur simultaneously (especially, 1 Cor. 15:52 and 1 Thess. 4:16-17). He lays the "errors" of pretribulationism and "reacting" [vs. Darby] posttribulationism to their adherence to a "rigorous futurism."[85] Then in the longest chapter in the book (chap. 4, pp. 104-59) he treats antecedents to the imminent appearing under three classifications: (1) potentially present antecedents, (2) future antecedents, and (3) alleged (actually past) antecedents.

Early in the discussion that follows, Barton Payne indulges in language reminiscent of Reese. Against pretribulationists and reacting (according to him) posttribulationists he exclaims: " 'A plague on both your houses!' one is tempted to cry. 'Need I admit this dilemma and choose between one of these two harsh alternatives?' In light of the scriptural conclusions reached in the two preceding chapters, the evangelical not only need not, he must not!"[86] In the discussion that follows, he proposes a synthesis of the three methods of prophetic interpretation: historical, futurist, and past (or preterite). [87] What results is actually a past-tribulationism. Specifically, events clearly predictive are relegated to a past fulfillment in order to maintain imminence for Christ's appearing. For example, even Daniel 9:24-27 is given a preterist significance only, extending in application no further than A.D.70.[88] That results in a forced exegesis and a truly emasculated eschatology, when even the book of Revelation, except for some nine verses, is assigned to the realm of the past.[89] First, how is it that the book is called a prophecy (1:3)? Is it not an apocalypse (1:1)? Is 1:19 not indicative of its three natural, successive divisions? Does not the book unfold three series of septenary judgments? What more is needed to show that that is the time of unparalleled agony for the unsaved?

Not to prolong the discussion, certain features may, nevertheless, be pointed out. He employs double fulfillment, then decries it.[90] He admits after so long a discussion that he cannot tell the duration of the Great Tribulation.[91] He makes the notations of time in Daniel 12 refer to Antiochus's anti-Jewish persecutions; he understands Daniel 7:25 and 12 thus: "[It] could be anything from three and a half days to seven and a half decades; and it seems best to say simply that we will know the tribulation is over when we see the Lord coming in glory."[92] To what limits Payne's strange preterite identifications can lead can readily be seen thus: "Christ has promised that He will return some time; and, after all, an unusually apt candidate for the Antichrist is Nikita Khrushchev right today!"[93]

Apart from an attempt to give a reason why the church should experience the Great Tribulation (resting it wholly on Romans 5:3), he does not break new ground from the well-known posttribulation arguments.[94] His novel approach is in his "classical" posttribulationism, which turns out to be pasttribulationism: "For the great tribulation, as classically defined, is potentially present, and perhaps almost finished. . . ."[95] That type of interpretation demands a tremendous amount of allegorizing of the judgments of the Revelation.

When Payne moves away from interpretation of given passages, he quotes for the most part unknown men in their attacks against dispensationalism, saying it promotes by superficial modern methods of evangelism a generation of soft Christians, sponsors antinomian fundamentalism, and cuts the nerve of missionary endeavor, especially among the Jewish people.[96] When Payne mentions "a high proportion of posttribulational writers," who have been or are active foreign missionaries, he goes on to name five. How many times more are there of pretribulational, dispensational missionaries? Where are the posttribulational missionary societies, Bible conferences, Bible institutes and colleges, and reference Bibles? How many of the five Auca martyrs were of pretribulational persuasion? The largest missionary organization for the evangelization of the Jews throughout the world has been consistently dispensational, pretribulational, and premillennial throughout its existence. Payne has to admit: "Darbyism as a movement has been in the forefront of world missionary activity; and many of the leading men of God of the past 100 years have been of pretribulational persuasion."[97]

When L. J. Wood comes to his treatment of the rapture, he wisely spends time in characterizing the Tribulation period in its distinctive features.[98] Then he presents implied evidences that the church will not go through the Tribulation.[99] Next, he marshals the evidence for the imminence of the return of Christ for His own.[100] Here he correctly points out that there will be no warning before the rapture, differing with posttribulationists who postulate a preparation signal of seven years.[101] At the very least, the cessation of sacrifice in Jerusalem (Dan. 9:27) will be a sufficiently clear warning of three and one half years in order to be forearmed.[102] When posttribulationists adduce New Testament passages to indicate an interval before the rapture, they deduce therefrom the possibility, if not probability, of a lapse of Tribulation time even today. Wood's refutation is valid when he indicates that the details under discussion are all general in nature, requiring no specific time length for fulfillment. He argues, "Because these items are intangible[103] as far as their duration is concerned, no one then living could tell when they were sufficiently complete so as to permit the Second Coming. Or, put differently, no one then living could tell from them that Jesus could not come at any given moment . . . it is true that so long as Peter lived, Jesus could not come . . . who knew how long it would be before Peter would die? . . . It could occur at any time. . . . Peter was no longer young when Jesus spoke these words, for He used the phrase: 'When thou *wast* [italics his] young.' "[104]

Closely related to the rapture and the revelation is the vital doctrine of resurrection. According to the pretribulationist view there are two stages or aspects to the resurrection of the righteous: one before the Tribulation and one after it; the first at the rapture and the second at the revelation.

Posttribulationists, who are not amillennialists, hold to one resurrection, that following the Tribulation, with another resurrection after the kingdom age.[105] Posttribulationists, as Wood rightly shows, stress Revelation 20:4-6 most in the doctrine of the resurrection. Their argument is that, if that is the first resurrection (and after the Tribulation), how could there be one seven years before that before the Tribulation? Posttribulationists in common with amillennialists overlook the fact of stages in the first resurrection (cf. 1 Cor. 15:22-24).[106] It is well to recognize that there is more than one entity even in the second death (cf. Rev. 19:20—the beast and the false prophet; 20:14 also includes more than one element). It is unnecessary and even detrimental to sound doctrine to restrict the scope of the first resurrection.[107]

Walvoord, who has written most recently on the themes under considera-

] 305 [

tion and especially in refutation of Gundry's work, discerningly points out the significance of the whole question in the realm of theology. He states: "It becomes evident that pretribulationism is more than a dispute between those who place the rapture before and after the tribulation. It is actually the key to an eschatological system. It plays a determinative role in establishing principles of interpretation which, if carried through consistently, lead to the pretribulational and premillennial interpretation."[108]

Most, if not all, posttribulationists lean heavily on the historic argument that the early church Fathers were posttribulational, though premillennial. It is not realized, however, that they do not follow the posttribulational scheme and program of the Fathers.[109] Their difficulty is evident: how to explain the predicted events that precede the second coming, whether past or present. Furthermore, "Pretribulationists have often pointed out that if every living saint is raptured at the time of the second coming this would, in itself, separate all saints from unsaved people and would leave none to populate the millennial earth."[110] Probably the greatest obstacles in the way of a posttribulational rapture are John 14:1-3, 1 Corinthians 15:50-58, and 1 Thessalonians, passages in which the rapture is predicted but not a word is said of anything remotely resembling the Tribulation. There is not a single rapture passage that warns of an impending Tribulation for the church.[111]

As stated in the beginning of this volume, the hermeneutical principle is the controlling factor in all facets of the questions relating to eschatology, as well as the other divisions of theology. One is not surprised, then, to find that posttribulationists, as is true of amillennialists, confuse Israel and the church. They hold either that the nation Israel has been displaced by the church or Israel merges with the church to constitute what they call "the community of the redeemed" or, more often, "the people of God." In a related matter, Gundry's view is that, because there was a transition from Israel to the church over a period of time (in Acts), there must be a similar transition between church and the Millennium.[112] That is an inference without proof: the rapture is nowhere equated with the force of the finished work of Christ on Calvary. Besides, in Acts there was no time element to be reckoned with (apart from the fifty days until Pentecost), but Israel's interrupted age (between Daniel's sixty-ninth and seventieth week) has already gone on for so many centuries. How and why must it be prolonged? Where is it stated that the church (not just certain redeemed ones) is in the Tribulation?[113] That posttribulationists disagree radically among themselves should occasion no surprise, because they are not in agreement on how literally or figuratively they are to interpret prophetic portions.[114]

What may be equally serious is that many posttribulationists are in confusion on the very nature of the Tribulation. Few, if any, state explicitly the horrendous nature of the Tribulation; they inject distinctions without a difference as their arguments on "the wrath of God" versus the "wrath of man"; many resort to unusually convoluted reasoning in trying to explain the meaning of Revelation 3:10, their veritable Waterloo, as to whether the keeping is out of or through the hour of trial, and whether it is from the events of the hour or just the hour itself![115] It is a matter of fact, and it is a desolating argument, that the church is never used in any passage on the Tribulation.[116] When posttribulationists claim that pretribulationism as held today (an argument equally telling against them) does not date from the Fathers, it is strange that they do not realize that the doctrine of imminence—central to pretribulationism and lost in mid- and posttribulationism—is clearly attested among the early Fathers.[117] No matter how much it may be argued to the contrary, the church is robbed of her blessed hope if the Tribulation precedes it.[118] The saints of the church will not be kept through the Tribulation, but removed from it. Only 144,000 of Israel are sealed to be protected from the ultimate horrors of that time; even the two witnesses of Revelation 11 will be martyred once their ministry is accomplished.[119]

Walvoord is eminently correct in holding: "The evident trend among scholars who have forsaken pretribulationism for posttribulationism is that in many cases they also abandon premillennialism."[120] Hence there is relevance for this treatment in a work on premillennialism versus amillennialism.

Notes

[1]J. T. Mueller, "Parousia," ISBE, 4:2249-50.
[2]H. A. A. Kennedy, *St. Paul's Conception of the Last Things*, pp. 175, 282.
[3]J. J. Hiemenga, *The Second Coming of Christ and What About a Millennium?*
[4]G. Vos, "Eschatology of the New Testament," ISBE, 2:981-86.
[5]W.F. Moulton and A. S. Geden, *A Concordance of the Greek Testament*, pp. 93, 374, 764.
[6]H. C. Thiessen, *Introductory Lectures in Systematic Theology*, p. 476.
[7]H. L. Payne, *Amillennial Theology as a System*, p. 232.
[8]F. E. Hamilton, *The Basis of Amillennial Faith*, p. 24.
[9]Ibid., pp. 25-26.
[10]G. L. Murray, *Millennial Studies: A Search for Truth*, p. 141, and D. H. Kromminga, *The Millennium*, p. 67.
[11]Hamilton, p. 69.
[12]Ibid., p. 79.
[13]Ibid., p. 101.
[14]Ibid., p. 102.
[15]Ibid., p. 103.
[16]Ibid., p. 105.
[17]Ibid., p. 117.

[18]D. H. Kromminga, *The Millennium in the Church*, p. 246.
[19]Ibid., p. 266.
[20]Ibid., p. 337.
[21]Ibid.
[22]L. Berkhof, *Systematic Theology*, p. 696.
[23]Ibid.
[24]Ibid., p. 696.
[25]Ibid.
[26]O. T. Allis, *Prophecy and the Church*, p. 167.
[27]Ibid., p. 698.
[28]Ibid., p. 167.
[29]Ibid., p. 169.
[30]Ibid.
[31]Ibid., p. 170.
[32]Ibid., p. 171 *et passim*.
[33]Ibid., p. 184.
[34]Ibid., p. 193.
[35]Ibid., p. 194.
[36]Ibid.
[37]Ibid., p. 198.
[38]Ibid., p. 200.
[39]Ibid., p. 206.
[40]Ibid., p. 216.
[41]A. Reese, *The Approaching Advent of Christ*, p. 34.
[42]Ibid.
[43]J. N. Darby, *Synopsis of the Books of the Bible*, 2:330.
[44]Reese, pp. 35-36.
[45]Ibid., p. 53.
[46]Ibid., p. 55.
[47]Ibid., p. 63.
[48]Ibid., p. 67.
[49]Ibid., p. 68.
[50]Ibid., p. 91.
[51]Ibid., pp. 124, 133, 207.
[52]G. E. Ladd, *The Blessed Hope*, p. 62. There is an interesting and strange parallel here to Israel, who, on the basis of the clear testimony of the Old Testament, have held continuously to only one coming of the Messiah.
[53]Ibid., pp. 92-93.
[54]Ibid., p. 93.
[55]See C. I. Scofield, *The New Scofield Reference Bible*, p. 1233, fn. on 1:8.
[56]Ladd, *The Blessed Hope*, p. 67.

[57]Ibid., p. 68. He cites 1 Tim. 6:14 and 2 Tim. 4:8, where the rapture alone is in view. His final proof presented is Titus 2:13-14. Is not the church present in both events when Christ comes for her, then with her?

[58]Ibid., p. 69.

[59]Ibid., p. 71.

[60]Ibid., p. 90. He makes the "saints" in 1 Thess. 3:13 mean "holy angels," an obvious evasion. He finally chooses the position that in 1 Thess. 4:14 the coming for the saints is the same as the coming with the saints, thus emptying the plain sense of all meaning.

[61]Ibid., pp. 72-73.

[62]Ibid., pp. 73-74.

[63]Ibid., p. 75.

[64]Ibid., p. 77.

[65]Ibid., p. 78.

[66]Ibid., p. 91.

[67]Ibid., p. 81.

[68]Ibid.

[69]Ibid., p. 84.

[70]Ibid., pp. 85-86.

[71]Ibid., p. 96. He inaccurately states that pretribulationists find no rapture in the gospels (p. 113). They assuredly find it in John 14:1-3.

[72]Ibid., pp. 96-97.

[73]Ibid., pp. 98-99, 165.

[74]Ibid.

[75]Ibid., pp. 146-47.

[76]J. B. Payne, *The Theology of the Older Testament*, pp. 48-49.

[77]Ibid., p. 55.

[78]Ibid., p. 74. In that text his interpretation is poles apart from that of R. Gundry *(The Church and the Tribulation)*, to say nothing of pre-tribulationists.

[79]Ibid., p. 78.

[80]Ibid., pp. 78-80.

[81]Ibid., p. 83.

[82]Ibid.

[83]Ibid., p. 85.

[84]Ibid., p. 91 ff.

[85]Ibid., p. 103.

[86]Ibid., p. 105.

[87]Ibid., pp. 105-6.

[88]Ibid., pp. 114-16.

[89]Ibid., p. 115. The passages that treat of the final persecution only are said to be 6:9-11; 7:14; 11:7-10; and 16:6.

[90]Ibid., p. 117.

[91]Ibid.

[92]Ibid., p. 119.

[93]Ibid., p. 121.

[94]Ibid., pp. 123, 133, 142-43.

[95]Ibid., p. 133.

[96]Ibid., pp. 165-67, 168.

[97]J. B. Payne, *The Imminent Appearing of Christ,* pp. 167-68.

[98]L. J. Wood, *Is the Rapture Next?* pp. 13-17.

[99]Ibid., pp. 20-26.

[100]Ibid., pp. 29-31.

[101]Ibid., p. 30.

[102]Ibid., pp. 32-33.

[103]They are found in John 15:20; 16:1-3; 14:12; Acts 1:4-8; 9:16; 20:23, 29; esp. John 21:18-19 (the death of Peter).

[104]Ibid., pp. 37-38.

[105]Ibid., p. 106.

[106]Ibid., pp. 106-12. Important passages that are relevant are Matt. 27:52-53 and Rev. 11:3-12, which indicate resurrection episodes apart from either the rapture or the revelation.

[107]Hebrews 9:7 mentions "once a year," but from Leviticus 16 it is unmistakable that the high priest's activity was not restricted to a solitary or unitary entrance. But he did enter on *one* day and *one* day only.

[108]J. F. Walvoord, *The Blessed Hope and the Tribulation,* p. 166.

[109]Ibid., pp. 24-33.

[110]Ibid., pp. 25, 52-53.

[111]Ibid., pp. 203-4, 106, 118.

[112]Gundry, pp. 12, 19, 21.

[113]Walvoord, *The Blessed Hope,* pp. 3, 4, 67, 86.

[114]Ibid., p. 37.

[115]Ibid., p. 35.

[116]Ibid., pp. 35, 50-51, 54, 103.

[117]Ibid., pp. 42, 45, 72.

[118]Ibid., pp. 104, 106.

[119]Ibid., p. 137.

[120]Ibid., p. 166.

18
Revelation 20 and the Millennium

To say at this stage of the discussion that the amillennialists and the premillennialists are irreconcilable in their respective interpretations of Revelation 20 and the Millennium would be to emphasize the obvious. The cause for the great difference of views between the two systems at this point is not directly traceable to Revelation 20 alone. All that has gone before in this study has laid the way. Perhaps here the contrast is the most evident, but that does not mean that it is the first place where amillennialists and premillennialists part company. In this particular phase of the subject, no more than in any other, can one allow himself to agree with a mediating position.

Milligan attempts such an inconsistency. Says he: "The thousand years are probably to be understood as literal, but if one prefers to believe otherwise he has a right to his own opinion. The particular length of time is not a matter of sufficient importance to justify a strife of words to no profit."[1] Here is evidence not only of a lack of appreciation of the issues involved—for in giving one thing away he makes room for the disposal of much more—but the statement is most inconsistent of Milligan, for he contends throughout his exposition of the book of Revelation for the literal interpretation, particularly with regard to the numbers of the book, drawing much in his interpretation from the numerology of the Revelation. But not all, nor the great majority, of premillennial expositors of the Scriptures take such a position. The ranks of the amillennialists as well as of the premillennialists are tightly drawn on the whole question of the interpretation of the twentieth chapter of the book of Revelation and the Millennium.

Consider now the position taken by the amillennialists. Mueller, in his treatment of the parousia, spends some time trying to prove that the kingdom of Christ is a present reality.[2] Afterward he notes that there is only one passage that at first seems to teach the contrary. That passage is Revelation 20:1-10. For him that passage can support the position of the millennialists only when it is interpreted with the barest literalness.

Such a procedure is claimed to be unwarrantable for several reasons. First, the passage is found in a book whose canonicity has been the cause of extended dissent. The answer here is that interpretation does not occupy itself with the question of canonicity. That belongs to the realm of biblical introduction. Second, the passage occurs in one of the most figurative books of the Bible. It is hard to see how that would militate against a consistent interpretation of the passage with the rest of the book of Revelation and the remainder of the Word. Third, it is said to constitute only an obscure part in a confessedly obscure book.

There are faults to be found with Mueller's statement. First, the part of Revelation 20:1-10 in the book of Revelation is only an obscure one when it is so treated by those who do not understand its true meaning. Interpretations of the passage, erroneous and groundless, render it obscure, but it is not so in itself. Furthermore, it must be stated emphatically that the book of Revelation is not an obscure book. On the contrary, the book is distinctly declared to be a revelation, an unveiling, a disclosure. It is also asserted that a literal interpretation contradicts what the Word uniformly teaches with regard to the nature of the resurrection body, which is said to be spiritual and not natural. That objection is not worthy of extended consideration, for it is without basis. Finally, Mueller finds that the passage does not speak of a millennial reign of Christ on earth and is not connected with the second coming of Christ (because the scene takes place in heaven) for the passage speaks only of souls.

That position is extremely weak and without scriptural foundation. The passage does speak of a millennial reign of Christ. No other reasonable interpretation can possibly be given to the plain words: "and they lived and reigned with Christ a thousand years" (v. 4). The millennial reign spoken of is to take place on earth. In Revelation 5:10 the redeemed and the four living ones sing a new song, which contains the words: "and we shall reign on the earth." Amos predicted that God would raise up the tabernacle of David and "build it as in the days of old" (Amos 9:11). In the days of old, if the Scriptures mean what they say, the tabernacle of David was on earth. Furthermore, when the seventh angel sounded the trumpet, the great voices in heaven declared anticipatively: "The kingdoms of this world [note that it is not in heaven, but of this world] are become the kingdoms of our Lord, and of his Christ; and he shall reign for ever and ever" (11:15). Third, the passage is directly connected with the second coming of Christ. The last verses of the nineteenth chapter record the coming to earth of the Lord Jesus Christ, so there is no necessity of mentioning the fact once more in the twentieth chapter. There is no flaw whatever in the chronology of John. And to maintain that the scene is a heavenly one because of the mention of souls is like building a house on quicksand. The whole question of the souls will be treated with the subject of the resurrection in the next chapter.

Kuyper, in trying to refute chiliasm, makes admissions that substantially give his position away. In commenting on the passage (Rev. 20:1-7), he notes:

Reading this passage as if it were a literal description would not only tend to a belief in the Millennium but would settle the question of chiliasm for all who might be in doubt concerning the same. . . . If we take it for granted now, that these thousand years are to be taken literally, that these thousand years are still in the future, and that this resurrection was meant to be a bodily resurrection, why then we may say, that at least as far as Revelation 20 is concerned, the question is settled. Then we must admit that Revelation 20:1-7 is a confession of chiliasm with all it contains.[3]

The point of further interest in his discussion is that he gives no good reason for not taking the passage literally. Surely the pretext of "the drapery of Oriental symbolism" cannot be applied to the passage at hand.

Hiemenga objects to finding a Millennium in Revelation 20, because nowhere else in the New Testament does he find any hint of the future establishment of a Jewish state on earth.[4] He never hears Christ, or Paul, or Peter, or John speak of such a glorious earthly kingdom to be set up for a period of a thousand years. Contrariwise, in the discourses of the Lord there is no room left for such a thousand-year period when He speaks of His return. In order to ascertain what the Scriptures say of the return of Christ, Hiemenga immediately leaves out of consideration the Old Testament, because the first coming of Christ was foremost in the minds of the Old Testament prophets.

It is a matter of common knowledge, admitted even by amillennialists, that the references to Christ's glorious return to earth far exceed those passages that speak of His coming in humility to suffer and die for sinful humanity. But Hiemenga proceeds, and in his progress he makes clear that nowhere in the whole Bible is there one word that Christ will come to reign over the Jewish nation for a thousand years. For him the Bible teaches exactly the opposite. So from one baseless statement to another Hiemenga goes to show that it is impossible to find the Millennium in the Bible. From such arguments the premillennial position has little to fear. It is easy to make sweeping statements. But where is the proof?

Vos admits that at first sight the passage Revelation 20:1-6 favors the doctrine of the millennial reign of Christ after the coming of Christ that is mentioned in chapter nineteen.[5] But he finds that historic sequence is a matter difficult to decide in the book of Revelation because of the principle of recapitulation; and the symbolical use of numbers, also, is to be taken into account. He therefore decides that the thousand years are synchronous with the other developments recorded earlier in the Revelation and describe the glorified state in the presence of Christ in heaven before the parousia of Christ. After commenting on the martyrs and the binding of Satan, he concludes that in a book so enigmatic as Revelation is, it would be most presumptuous to speak dogmatically. But, says he, because of the consistent and uniform absence of the whole concept of the Millennium in the eschatology of the

New Testament, the exegete ought to be doubly cautious before he asserts its presence here.

The same author, in treating the doctrine of the Millennium and Pauline eschatology, declares that Paul's conception of the present Christian state is so high that nothing less than the eternity to come could fittingly be its sequel. For the present state of the believer to be exchanged for one below the perfect heavenly life would be nothing short of an anticlimax.[6] Furthermore, throughout his soteriology and eschatology Paul causes us to believe that the present life of the believer is going on directly to the heavenly life, and for one to assume anything else would be harmful to the inner organism of Pauline eschatology. Such line of reasoning may sound plausible, but Christian doctrine is based in the first instance upon revelation and not reason. It is not for anyone to say what God will do next in the life of the believer, or what would serve as an anticlimax in that life. It is extremely difficult to see, moreover, how reigning with Christ in the Millennium would detract in the least from the believer's enjoyment of the eternal state in heaven.

Before examining the extended discussion by Masselink, it will be helpful to turn to one more witness on the amillennial side. Reference here is to the discussion of the Millennium and the Revelation by Warfield.[7] The reader will remember that he suggested that the meaning of the Revelation was best ascertained, not by verbal criticism, but by a "sympathetic imagination." Warfield is confident that there has been much less tendency-interpretation of Revelation 20 to support a previous theory, than there has been tendency-interpretation of the rest of the Word in corroboration of an idea derived from misconceptions of the teachings of the passage. Not only is the word *millennium* not to be found in the Scriptures, according to his way of thinking, but the thing itself is also unknown in the Word. In his interpretation of the passage he believes the apostle is giving a spectacle of utter peace. But it is such a thousand-year peace as is set about by war. One is not to think for a moment that the thousand-year peace is the so-called Millennium.

That idea is impossible, as can be seen from several considerations, but Warfield finds it necessary to give only one. The participants in it are spoken of as "souls." That cannot refer to disembodied souls that are to make up the church at the time of its highest development on earth. Neither can it be disembodied souls who are thought of as constituting the kingdom Christ intends to set up on earth. The vision must refer to the peace of those who have died in the Lord. The whole passage is merely an expansion of the text: "Blessed are the dead which die in the Lord, from henceforth" (Rev. 14:13). It is a picture of the intermediate state of the saints in heaven as they await the end. The thousand years represent the whole of this present dispensation.

When the passage speaks of the binding of Satan for a season (note his unusually forced exegesis), it really means he is bound with reference to a sphere. The literal binding of Satan never happens at all. What actually happens does so, not to Satan, but to the saints. If the passage appears to teach the contrary, Warfield asks the reader to lay that to the purposes of the symbolic picture. The saints are actually described as removed from the range of the attacks of Satan. But outside their sphere he is free; that is what is meant by the thousand years and the little season. The saints in heaven are free from Satan's onslaught for a thousand-year period of peace; the saints on earth are exposed to Satan's temptings and harassments for a little season. One could continue with a rather extended resumé of his position, but enough has been given to show, first, that he agrees with the other amillennialists only in denying the actuality of a literal millennial reign of Christ on earth, and second, that his position has nothing in it to commend itself. How well does it compare with the consistent and biblical presentation of the premillennial view of the doctrine of the Millennium?

Masselink, in that particular as in others, gives a most extended discussion of the amillennial view, as well as the best gathering up of the objections of the amillennialists to the millennial age.[8] In his preliminary remarks he attempts to make plain that the millennial doctrine is especially based upon Revelation 20, which is found in an obscure book. He claims it is a recognized fact that historic sequence is not to be sought for in the Revelation. He notes further that the student of the passage must bear in mind that nowhere else in the Bible is such a period mentioned outside of Revelation 20. With those precautions in mind, he claims, careful study will immediately reveal that the general features of premillennialism are entirely absent. Nothing is said of the return of the Jews to reconstruct an earthly kingdom, nor are the restoration of the Temple and the ceremonial laws and the rebuilding of Jerusalem to be found in the passage. Not a word is said of the preeminence of the Jew above Gentile Christians. The scene of the reign of the saints is not on earth but in heaven. The thrones seen are in heaven and not on earth, because the souls of the martyrs are seen in heaven. What the passage really teaches is the final and complete overthrow of Satan and depicts for us the blessedness of the intermediate state in the interadvental period.

He levels fifteen objections against the doctrine of the Millennium. Instead of setting forth those objections and then answering them later in a continued refutation, each objection will be answered in its place, as has been attempted briefly with the views previously noted in this chapter.

The first objection is that the premillennialists anticipate a period in which conversion is to be brought about by the sudden manifestation of God's power and anger. That is declared to be unscriptural, for there is only one way of salvation. The chiliast substitutes another way of salvation, it is charged, which is a decided departure from God's normal way of salvation. It is one that is different in kind than that which the apostles proclaimed and the Lord Jesus taught. In reply the premillennialists maintain that God has had and always will have but one way of salvation. There is only one name under heaven given among men whereby all must be saved. The Scriptures do reveal in Zechariah 12 that the spirit of grace and supplications will be poured out upon Israel when they look upon Him whom they have pierced. Israel will be saved in the same manner as the apostle Paul was saved—by a vision of the glorified Christ. Israel will be saved by faith in her crucified Messiah. Surely, then, there is no ground upon which Masselink can accuse the premillenarians of introducing a means of conversion other than the gospel.

His second objection is that the doctrine teaches a post-gospel salvation following Christ's coming, whereas the Scriptures reveal that this is the day of salvation. To be sure, the chiliasts teach that there will be men and women saved after the gospel dispensation, just as there were people saved before the gospel age. When Paul says this is the day of salvation, the day refers to the whole dispensation and means that anyone living in this age must be saved now or he will not be saved in a future dispensation. The Bible nowhere confines salvation to this age alone (otherwise neither could Abraham nor those in the Tribulation period be saved), but it does grant entrance into the Body of Christ through salvation in this age, which is the great point of difference in being saved in this age or in other ages. Men could be saved looking forward to the cross, just as there is salvation now in looking back to the cross, and as there will be in looking back to Calvary from a time subsequent to the church age.

A third objection is that the church is complete at Christ's coming. What has just been said answers that objection, too. The statement is valid insofar as it holds that the church will be complete when Christ returns, but, although no more will be added to the Body of Christ, many more will be added to the multitude of the redeemed of God. Again, it must be repeated, salvation in Scripture is not always synonymous with membership in the invisible church. That is the exalted privilege of this age and this age alone.

Another objection, closely connected to the previous ones, is made that there will be no means of grace for salvation after Christ comes back. Here Masselink reveals his sacramentarian tendencies. He holds that after the return of Christ there will be no more Lord's Supper, baptism, or the written Word. He gives no proof that the Word will end at the coming of Christ, for there is none. God's Word will be found on earth after the departure of the church for heaven. The Lord's Supper, he believes, will be gone, because it is ordained until He comes. Baptism was instituted until the consummation of the age that is synchronous with the return of Christ.

First of all, what assurance does he have that the ordinances cannot be administered by unbelieving ministers after the rapture of the church? And where in all the Word of God is salvation ever in the slightest degree said to be in any way dependent upon any ordinance? It is feared that Masselink himself approaches dangerously near a new way of salvation. As far as salvation after the coming of Christ is concerned, it will be brought about through the application of the Word by the Spirit to the hearts of individuals who have heard the message of God's witnesses. The ministry of the Spirit after the church age in the Tribulation period will approximate that of the Spirit in Old Testament times. In the millennial age, according to the prophecy of Joel, the Spirit will be poured out upon all flesh (2:28-32).

The next objection lodged against the premillennialists is a serious one, but one that cannot be sustained. It is claimed that the millennial view disparages the gospel, because it teaches conversion by a means foreign to the gospel, such as wrath, judgment, or a display of glory. Premillennialists assuredly do not disparage the gospel. It is true that Christ commissioned each believer to preach the gospel to every creature, but that does not automatically mean that everyone is to be saved. Premillennialists do not believe that the gospel has any less power than the amillennialists believe it has. It is the power of God unto salvation to everyone that believes, whether Jew or Gentile. But the burden of the proof rests on the amillennialist to show that it is the avowed purpose of God to save all in this age by the gospel. In other words, it is not a question of power, but a matter of purpose.

It is objected further that a great conflagration takes place at the coming of Christ, according to the prophecy of Peter. 2 Peter 3:10 speaks of the burning of the heavens and the earth and their displacement by the new heavens and new earth wherein dwelleth righteousness. It is impossible, so goes the objection, for all that to happen before the alleged Millennium. Premillennialists do not place this before the Millennium, but after it. So there is no room for objections here.

A seventh objection is that Christ's coming is commonly spoken of as "the end." In 1 Corinthians 15 the end is said to come after Christ has conquered death, which coincides with the resurrection of the saints. Then Christ will give the kingdom to the Father, and that would leave no interval between the resurrection and the end. That question will be dealt with in the next chapter on the resurrection.

Another objection related to the one just stated, is that this gospel dispensation is the last, so there can be no millennial age before the end. After the church age there is nothing more than the end. That is supposed to be substantiated from the use of "last days" in Acts 2:16-17; 1 Corinthians 10:11; Hebrews 1:1-2, and others. A careful study of those passages will reveal that what is meant is not the finality of all things. There are last days for Israel and last days for the church, a distinction which the amillennialists do not make.

Amillennialists believe they have an objection against the continued conversion after the second coming in the fact that the judgment of the world coincides with that coming. There will be no period of time after the coming of Christ for any to find Christ. In reply it can be briefly stated that the Bible nowhere speaks of a general judgment either before or after Christ's coming, or at Christ's coming. The whole question of judgment will be more fully treated in the last chapter of the comparison of the two systems.

But the objections have not ended yet. It is urged against the doctrine of the Millennium that Christ comes back to conquer the world and subdue His enemies over a long period of time extending over a thousand years. Surely, it is maintained, the conquest of Christ is already complete, for He now waits until it is complete. Everything will be restored at the coming of Christ. In answer to that objection, two questions are in order. If Christ does not return to subdue His enemies, then why is He seen in Revelation 19:11 coming on a white horse, at which time, so reads the Scripture, "in righteousness he doth judge and make war"? If Christ has vanquished every foe at the time of His return in glory, why does the Word note (19:15) that "he shall rule them with a rod of iron"?

A serious objection is found further with the chiliastic view, because it teaches the continuance of sin and death in the Millennium. According to amillennialists the coming of Christ puts down for all time both sin and death. There is one verse in the Old Testament that gives the refutation to the amillennial position, namely, Isaiah 65:20. The verse is in a context that shows it refers to the millennial age. It speaks of a child dying at the age of an hundred years, which means there will be death in the Millennium. It states further that a sinner a hundred years old shall be accursed, which reveals that there will be sin in the dispensation of righteousness.

An objection that is found in practically all amillennial discussions is that the condition of glorified saints is too exalted for an earthly Millennium. It is contended that, however glorious the Millennium may be, it could never reach the state of the eternal glory that is the portion of the godly at death. Saints in their glorified state must have surroundings commensurate with their position. They cannot, therefore, be conceived of as being brought back to a world of sin and sorrow. That would be in the nature of an anticlimax.

Of that objection several things need to be said. First, it is seeking to find a refutation of a revealed truth by something that appeals to reason. It is not man's prerogative to state what will be fitting or unfitting the saints in their glorified state. Second, the saints will reign with Christ in the millennial age. If it becomes Him to participate in an earthly Millennium, surely no servant of His will deem himself greater than his Lord. What is suitable for the Bridegroom will please the Bride also. Third, coreigning with Christ will not confine the church to the earth; she will still have free access to heaven.

The next objection of the amillennialist is akin to the one that has just occupied our attention. It is alleged that the supposed Millennium is inconsistent with Christ's state of exaltation. What will be an anticlimax for the saints, will surely be all the more sure for the Lord Himself. For Him to come back to a sinful earth for such a long time would be an unthinkably great step of humiliation after His present glorious exaltation. The chiliasts are accused of having too low an estimate of the exalted position of the saints and Christ when they can postulate a doctrine that involves bringing both the Lord and His saints back to a sinful environment. Besides, there will be a strange mixture of people with ordinary physical bodies and others with the resurrection bodies. To all that there is one conclusive reply: Christ Himself after His resurrection dwelt among sinful men for a period of forty days.

The fourteenth objection to the millennial age is that it discredits the finished work of Christ when it resumes the bloody sacrifice according to Ezekiel 40-48. Those sacrifices will serve as a memorial, looking back to Calvary as does the Lord's Supper now.

The final objection to the millennial age is that it expects a period of prosperity before the end of the world, when Christ in His eschatological discourses predicted woes, tribulations, and apostasy. There is a confusion here, to be sure, of what Christ said of the end of the Jewish age (the Tribulation period of Matt. 24, Mark 13, and Luke 21), with the end of the world, which takes place after the millennial reign, when the heavens and earth that now are will be replaced by a new heavens and a new earth.

It can be confidently stated, therefore, that the objections of the amillennialists are not valid. Their supposed proofs are not demonstrable. So many of their expositions of Revelation 20 and the Millennium take into account only the book of Revelation, when the chapter should be studied in the light of the whole Word as well. All the prophecies that were noted in the analysis of the premillennial view remain unchanged and steadfast until their actual fulfillment. No present spiritual kingdom or future eternal kingdom can take its place.

When Hughes comes to interpret Revelation 20, he readily admits it is a difficult passage, judging from the wide differences of view concerning its meaning. He believes amillennialism is inaccurately designated, because it does not relegate the thousand years of Revelation 20 to the nonexistent, but rather understands the number to have a symbolic value, interpreting "the millennium as virtually synonymous with this present age between the two comings of Christ, or, more precisely, between the coronation of the ascended Saviour and His return in glory. This position we believe to be most in accord with the perspective of the New Testament."[9]

It is not helpful to change terminology in midstream, nor does a double-pronged admission promote progress in discussion. He declares, "Actually, there is no indication in the passage before us that Christ's millennial reign is or will be an *earthly* reign. Nor, for that matter, does it state that it is a *heavenly* reign [italics his]. . . ."[10] Is the matter actually that ambivalent, a "much ado about nothing" affair? Few who have studied the subject in depth will be willing to go along with Hughes here.

One can judge immediately how close to Hughes's amillennial perspective is that of Ladd, who disallows dispensationalism with its consistent premillennialism. He asserts: "The thousand year period is no literal piece of history; it is a symbolic number coextensive with the history of the church on earth between the resurrection of Christ and his return. . . . The 'millennium' is the church age when martyred saints reign with Christ in heaven, awaiting the resurrection."[11] In view of that plain statement it is somewhat mystifying, if not downright contradictory, to affirm almost in the same breath: "A key issue in our understanding of the millennium is whether chapter 20 involves recapitulation, looking back from the end to the whole history of the church. In chapter 12, it is unmistakably clear that the passage looks back to the birth of Messiah. However, in the present passage, no such indication is to be found. On the contrary, chapters 18-20 appear to present a connected series of visions."[12]

Lest anyone wonder whether Ladd's position has been misunderstood or misrepresented, we quote him again: "We have argued above that Christ began his Messianic reign at his resurrection-ascension; but his present reign is invisible, unseen and unrecognized by the world, visible only to the eye of faith."[13] For clarity's sake alone it is a pity he does not employ the terminology of premillennialists instead of amillennialists. How is it possible on the basis of the data given, to have a first coming with a reign invisible, unseen, unrecognized by the world, visible only to the eye of faith, and a second coming with a kingdom visible, seen, recognized by the world, and visible to the eye of all?

The amillennialist Hoekema speaks for his position: "This living and reigning with Christ . . . shall continue throughout the thousand years—that is, throughout the entire gospel era, until Christ shall come again to raise the bodies of these believers from the grave. There is no indication in these verses that John is describing an earthly millennial reign. The scene . . . is set in heaven."[14] Surely, those in heaven should know where the reign is to be, and they clearly sing of the redeemed that "they will reign upon the earth" (Rev. 5:10, NASB). Unfortunately, that is not the only area where Hoekema has erred in the matter of the Millennium. He declares: "Amillennialists do not believe that the kingdom of God is primarily a Jewish kingdom which involves the literal restoration of the throne of David."[15]

First, it may surprise Hoekema, in view of his misunderstanding here of the premillennial position espoused in this work, to learn that premillenarians do not believe that the kingdom of God is primarily a Jewish kingdom. In the sense of God's universal rule over all created intelligences, it is obviously impossible to restrict the kingdom of God to the Jews. Moreover, in the sense of the realm of the redeemed (John 3:3, 5), it is equally clear that the kingdom cannot be limited to the Jews.

Second, Hoekema is in difficulty because, in common with amillennialists and nondispensationalists, he has confused the kingdom of God and the kingdom of heaven. The latter, found only in Matthew, is primarily a Jewish kingdom.

Third, any denial of a literal restoration of the Davidic throne flies in the face of Amos 9:11-15; Luke 1:32-33; and Acts 1:5-6. Why are those vital passages left untouched by amillennialists?

McClain, commenting on the common failing of the amillenarians, incisively states: "It indicates the ease with which antimillennialism slips into an attitude of antisupernaturalism in the physical realm. The Old Testament prophets were not hampered by any such dualistic prejudices. Recognizing the hand of God everywhere present in the processes of nature, they saw nothing incredible in the idea of a spiritual Kingdom where intrusions of supernatural power would become the rule instead of the exception."[16]

As great as are the divergences in interpretation of Revelation 20, the views as to the specific contribution of the chapter are equally diverse. McClain pertinently states it thus: "The unique contributions of Revelation 20 are at least two: first, a *chronology* of the coming Kingdom; and, second, a concise *outline* of constitutive events in their proper order, so clear that there should be no cause for misunderstanding."[17] That evaluation is a valid one, for it recognizes an orderly progression in the book of Revelation (1:19) as well as detailed events that cannot be slighted or minimized. He who sets aside much of the preliminary and preparatory evidences must come to an erroneous conclusion.

Ladd writes: "A millennial doctrine cannot be based on Old Testament prophecies but should be based on the New Testament alone. The only place in the Bible that speaks of an actual millennium is the passage in Revelation 20:1-6. Any millennial doctrine must be based upon the most natural exegesis of this passage."[18] That statement, to be commented on shortly, is followed by another, equally revealing. He informs his readers: "The strongest objection to millennialism is that this truth is found in only one passage of Scripture—Revelation 20. Nonmillenarians appeal to the argument of analogy, that difficult passages must be interpreted by clear passages. It is a fact that most of the New Testament writings say nothing about a millennium."[19]

First of all, Ladd is in serious error if he believes that any biblical doctrine of the Millennium can be established without the testimony of the Old Testament. Why should the Old Testament be eliminated by such an ipse dixit? Actually, he relinquishes much of the New Testament ground as well. That has been his Achilles' heel since first he ventured out on crucial questions of the kingdom (see above). To dismiss summarily the Old Testament evidence is a practice of amillenarians, no matter how stoutly Ladd may profess premillennialism.

What does one do with 2 Samuel 7 if the Old Testament is disregarded? What with passages like Isaiah 2, 9, 11, 35, 55, to mention only a minimal number? What of Jeremiah 23, 31, 33? What of Ezekiel 36 and 37 with 40-48? What does he do with Daniel 2 and 7? What with the overwhelming testimony of the so-called minor prophets, especially Amos 9, Micah 4, and Zechariah 14? And, in the name of all reason, how is Matthew's gospel to be interpreted without the millennial doctrine (see above Part Two)? In one sentence all the Old Testament evidence is set aside; in another all the New Testament witness is bypassed. That is unconscionable and cannot stand.

Second, to claim that the strongest objection to millennialism is that it is found in a single passage of Scripture is incredible. How many passages of Scripture are required before a doctrine can claim biblical ground? What Ladd, and all amillennialists, try to say is that the duration of the Millennium is stated in one passage. What of the crucial passage in 1 Corinthians 15:23-26, which demolishes completely their contention? Would they say Armageddon is found only in Revelation 16:12-16, because it is the only place where the war is named? Then what of Revelation 19:17-19?

No wonder amillennialist Hoekema is elated over his easy, but empty, victory: "I was happy to note Ladd's admission that this passage [he refers to Revelation 20] is the only place in the Bible which speaks of a millennium. . . . On this point, too, we are in agreement [he has already found an accord in their views that the church is spiritual Israel in the New Testament, and that the present spiritual reign of Christ is the dominant theme and fulfillment of Old Testament prediction]."[20] When Hoekema himself undertakes an exegesis of Revelation 20, it is evident how many presuppositions underlie his treatment. He claims, "If, then, one thinks of Revelation 20 as describing what follows chronologically after what is described in chapter 19, one would indeed conclude that the millennium of Revelation 20:1-6 will come after the return of Christ. As has been indicated above, however, chapters 20-22 comprise the last of the seven sections of the book of Revelation and therefore do not describe what follows the return of Christ. Rather, Revelation 20:1 takes us back once again to the beginning of the New Testament era."[21] Because he has committed himself to a series of recapitulations in the Revelation, Hoekema has latitude to rearrange the events of the book to fit his amillennial scheme, a procedure which, unfortunately, destroys the orderly progression of the book (cf. 1:19 and the detailed discussion above). On that point, however, Ladd parts company with Hoekema and correctly counters: "There is absolutely no hint of any recapitulation in chapter 20."[22]

By this time the reader will have become definitely aware of the many points of contrast between the premillennial approach to the Scriptures and that of the amillennialists. He will not be expecting that Revelation 20 will afford the first instance of diversity between the views. Yet it is repeated times without number that Revelation 20 is the only point of contention, the *locus classicus*, as it is called, of the premillennial system. There is no desire whatsoever to minimize the force of the passage; but it cannot be fairly made to bear the entire weight of the premillennial system. Nor does a denial of its literal character bear the whole weight of the amillennial view, as has been seen. The systems diverge in Genesis 1 and not in Revelation 20; in the latter chapter they reach their culmination and consummation.

Reid has stated it succinctly thus, "Regarding the Millennium, we may note that as 1 Thessalonians 4:13-18 is the only passage that describes *the manner* of the Rapture, so Revelation 20:2-7 is the only passage that reveals *the duration* of the earthly part of the kingdom, a kingdom which is the subject of numerous and varied descriptions in both Testaments."[23] D. Bosworth is just as frank in declaring that the "remark, that the passage which has given rise to the name, and which most directly and fully sets forth the Millennium, confessedly is Revelation 20:1-7, is doubtless correct so far as the precise time is concerned; but were not the main features clearly revealed in other scriptures, I confess I should look upon it with suspicion."[24] On the basis of Isaiah 24:21-23 he locates chronologically the millennial reign at the binding and imprisonment of Satan and his followers in the abyss.[25] On the basis of the accumulated evidence Thiessen states summarily, "Christ will be personally present on earth and sit on the throne of His father David."[26] That will exactly fulfill the Davidic covenant of 2 Samuel 7 and the confirmation of it by angelic visitation in Luke 1.

Some damaging admissions are made by amillennialists on that phase of the subject. Case admits that John's picture is couched in Jewish imagery and embodies the old prophetic concept of an earthly kingdom;[27] but his liberal outlook leaves only something that is suggestive and challenging out of all the material of the millennial hope.[28] Rutgers, on the other hand, in spite of his militant amillennialist attitude, concedes, "The *Apocalypse* XX:1-10 in reality contains nothing essential to the Pre scheme, save the symbolical number thousand."[29] The statement is valid except for the injection of the symbolism into the number *one thousand.*

A timely warning has been offered by Hospers, which might well be heeded in discussions of the Millennium. He submits that "the program of Chiliasm offers much that seems arbitrary. But this is the characteristic of absolute sovereignty, and in its construction we must be very careful not to explain the facts according to *our* ideas of propriety."[30] Amillennialists, who are mainly of Calvinistic persuasion, should appreciate his sentiment. A specific example is given.

Offense is often taken at Chiliasm because it gives the Jew such preeminence as if this trenches on the honor of believers. Granting this, who are we to say to God: What doest Thou? Least of any should the Calvinist take such offense. Who of us may complain of God because He did not bestow upon us the genius of a Kant? May some son of degraded parents accuse God because he was not born in a godly family? And why then should Gentiles imagine that there may not be a special function initiated by God with the Jews rather than with us? Let us fear to obtrude our sense of the fitness of things upon All-wise God. As the cross was an offense to the Jews, standing in the way of darling preconceptions, so Christians may seriously consider whether their aversion to the reinstatement of Israel does not arise from "high-mindedness." There is a deep reason for the "economy" (arrangement) of God by which Israel is first singled out, then rejected, and then again put forward.[31]

Among the preconceptions of amillennialists is their unduly low view of the character of the millennial reign of Christ. Hospers points that out in this manner:

> But why cannot our Lord's Millennial reign be another step in His exaltation? Is there anything unworthy about the idea of His reigning on the Throne of David, not with the present-day limitations of earthly kings, but in a way befitting the King of Kings? Why should not a Millennial reign round out in this world of sin the highest contact of the Redeemer with a fallen world, the last of its kind in preparation for the New Heaven and the New Earth, which will be a totally different order of things? The Amillenarian entertains an altogether too low an estimate of the Millennium.[32]

Murray, with other amillennialists, confuses the Millennium with the perfection of the eternal state, for the simple reason that he makes millennial descriptions speak of the eternal state.[33] Nor does he understand how the millennial reign can be possible in view of the eternal reign of Christ. Christ's reign on the throne forever is said to preclude its duration for a thousand years.[34] He does not realize that the millennial reign is extended beyond time (after its mediatorial phase is completed) into eternity. The solution is found clearly given in 1 Corinthians 15:24-28. It is simply not true, furthermore, that the millennial rule is a detraction from the glory of Christ.[35] It is a glorious step in his final and eternal exaltation with the Father and the Holy Spirit. No premillennialist seeks to rob Christ of an iota of His well-earned glory.

Berkhof gives a clear statement of the tenets of the amillennial view which he terms "purely negative."[36] But Berkhof draws unwarranted conclusions when he claims, "It [the amillennial view] has ever since been the view most widely accepted, is the only view that is either expressed or implied in the great historical Confessions of the Church, and has always been the prevalent view in reformed circles."[37] Democratic processes may be decided by the rule of the majority, but biblical interpretation is not susceptible of the same treatment. He has surely mistaken the premillennial position when he conceives that some "anticipate only a spiritual rule."[38] For him there are certain insuperable difficulties in the millennial view, which he states thus:

It is impossible to understand how a part of the old earth and of sinful humanity can exist alongside of a part of the new earth and of a humanity that is glorified. How can perfect saints in glorified bodies have communion with sinners in the flesh? How can glorified saints live in this sin-laden atmosphere and amid scenes of death and decay? How can the Lord of glory, the glorified Christ, establish His throne on earth as long as it has not yet been renewed. . . . How will sinners and saints in the flesh be able to stand in the presence of the glorified Christ?[39]

The most that can be said of such questions is that they partake of the method of the rationalist. Admittedly, the premillennial view calls for much that is supernatural, but does not the Bible give warrant for it?[40] The amillennialists fail here to realize: (1) that Christ in His glorified body dwelt among sinners for forty days after the resurrection, after having lived among them sinlessly for more than thirty years; (2) that they are confusing without foundation the millennial state with the absolute perfection of the eternal state; and (3) that saints and sinners live alongside one another today, sometimes in the closest bond of matrimony.

It is surprising that the theologian Berkhof should cling to the shopworn cliché that the Millennium is based solely on Revelation 20.[41] But that suits the amillennial purpose: If it be found in but one passage, then it may the more easily be deleted. But it is woven into the very warp and woof of Scripture and will not come out.

Premillennialists, furthermore, are accused of inconsistency in their literal interpretation of Revelation 20, because they make the chain of verse 1 figurative.[42] Let it be repeated that the literal interpretation, rightly called the natural interpretation, calls for the interpretation of figures as figures. But that is vastly different from the spiritualization that is resorted to by desperate amillennialists in their approach to the passage. Though Berkhof inveighs repeatedly against the so-called sensualistic and materialistic view of the Millennium, he writes of heaven: "We should not think of the joys of heaven, however, as exclusively spiritual. There will be something corresponding to the body. There will be recognition and social intercourse on an elevated plane."[43] That is surely allowing oneself what is denied to one's opponent. Yet one other matter troubles Berkhof, and it is the presence of sin and death in the Millennium,[44] but, strangely enough, he does not treat Isaiah 65:20.

Kromminga is not at all nonplused by the difficulty that forms an impasse for

Hamilton in Luke 20:35-36. He realizes it calls for "two distinct sets of saints."[45] However, he is unfair to the futurist interpretation of the Revelation. He maintains,

> In the case of all those who choose a futuristic interpretation of the Apocalypse this fact is quite plain. For, though it may be rather easy to demonstrate the apparent failure of all the other attempts to find a thoroughly satisfactory explanation of the book, and while without doubt an awareness of their failure has contributed largely to the vogue which the futuristic interpretation of the Apocalypse has nowadays, this does not guarantee that the futuristic explanation, whatever it is, will square with the coming events. In other words, the choice is in this case made without any chance at all of demonstrating the possibility of carrying through the interpretation of the visions of the book in harmony with the actual events. [It should be added here that he himself uses the continuous-historical and spiritual method, which leads to some strange conclusions.][46] Of course, there is by that same token also no danger that the interpretation will be disproven by the events while we wait for them; and this may be an attraction.[47]

That is quite unfair. His contention is that the futurist interpretation of the Revelation is so appealing because there is no way of checking on the interpretations, as they are placed in the future. If held to rigidly, that contention rules out all prophecy that is still future. Too, what of the eternal state and heaven? How can he prove that heaven is not just a figure? Again, he is wrong because some of the futurist interpretation of the Revelation has been eminently fulfilled, and in this day. Reference here is to the return of Israel and her establishment as a nation.

The weakness of amillennialism is pointed out and related to its principle of interpretation thus: "Amillenarians resent the implication that they deny the millennium of which Revelation 20 speaks so plainly. They also have a millennium of a kind, but they attach a symbolical significance to the thousand years and usually spread the so-called millennial period out over the whole of the Christian era. This feature ties Amillennialism to the spiritual approach. It cannot make its interpretation of the millennium good without the aid of a spiritualizing interpretation of the Apocalypse."[48]

But the premillennialist Kromminga does not hesitate to charge others of the same view with "judaizing chiliasm," because they understand the beloved city of Revelation 20 to be the Jerusalem of Palestine.[49] He does not state what city is meant according to his view. Moreover, is it accurate to claim, "It is plain, that the medieval spiritual conception of the millennium was predominantly ecclesiastical, and that the premillenarian conception of both the ancients and the moderns has all along been predominantly political. In this, both have been onesided"?[50] It is difficult to see how a kingdom that exalts righteousness and peace (Psalm 72) is predominantly political. It is literal and earthly, but it is spiritual and of God.

On the part of the saints there is ample need for the Millennium. Kromminga rightly states,

> Both Irenaeus and Tertullian had the idea that it was a matter of equity or propriety, that the saints should enjoy a kind of triumph in the same world in which they now suffer.... This explanation is virtually continued in the present-day Premillenarian conception of the millennium as primarily a reign of the resurrected saints with Christ over the nations that continue to people our earth during that period. It contrasts deeply and sharply with the postmillenarian conception which sees the primary importance and significance of the future millennium rather as connected with the human society which will then live and move here.[51]

And among those saints there must be those from Israel also. He admits there is some relevance of the Millennium for Israel,[52] though he does so cautiously. On the matter of procreation in the Millennium (contra Hamilton, as will be seen more fully later), he finds a possible fulfillment of Isaiah 65:17-25 in the reign of Christ.[53]

An admission is made by Allis, which, if consistently adhered to, would settle the entire controversy. He touches on Hosea 3:5; Amos 9:11; Jeremiah 17:19-27; 33:17-22; and Ezekiel 37:25, then maintains: "Many other prophecies might be mentioned. But these are sufficient to prove that these prophets foresaw a Davidic kingdom of the future that would follow the pattern of the kingdom of the past, aside from its failures, follies, and sins."[54] But again there is the erroneous equation of the Millennium with the eternal state, as he claims:

> Such a picture [without sin or suffering] of an ideal age raises only one serious difficulty. It is whether the Bible and especially the New Testament predicts or allows for such a period of blessedness before the eternal state is ushered in, or whether the picture given to us by Isaiah [chapter 11] is a description of that eternal state itself under earthly forms and images ... [amillennialists] deny that either in the Gospels or in the Epistles is there provision for such a millennium.[55]

The solution to the original erroneous position taken by him is certainly not a recourse to spiritualization. And the Millennium cannot be eliminated merely by identifying the Gog and Magog before the Millennium with the Gog and Magog after the Millennium. For amillennialists that would be desirable, for thereby they could squeeze out, as it were, the troublesome intervening Millennium.[56] The Gogs and Magogs are not the same at all: The definite location is given in Ezekiel 38 and 39, whereas Revelation 20 states clearly the universal character of that spasmodic, but ineffective uprising.

The character of the millennial reign never ceases to trouble amillennialists.

Allis writes, "In short, this millennial age will not differ essentially from our own as far as the basic facts of human life are concerned. Evil will be curbed, but not eradicated; its effects will be controlled, but not removed."[57]

Can it be fairly said that the millennial age will not differ essentially from our own when it is revealed that Satan will be bound, the earth renovated, and Christ will visibly rule on David's throne? That is to ask for the perfection of the eternal state, on the one hand, or to deny any real difference from the present age, on the other hand. Amillennialists are guilty of both. True to pattern, Allis objects to the essentially Jewish character of the Millennium,[58] but finally admits that church saints will reign also.[59] Finding fault with the subject matter of revelation is the method of the rationalist and ill becomes any Christian interpreter.

Allis argues the point of the sacrifices in Ezekiel 40-48. He contends, "The crux of the whole question is undoubtedly the restoration of the Levitical ritual of sacrifice. . . . Literally understood, this means the restoration of the Aaronic priesthood and of the Mosaic ritual of sacrifices essentially unchanged."[60] He realizes that premillennialists take the reinstitution of sacrifice as a memorial, but says: "This does not meet the situation at all."[61] Why is it inadequate to meet the situation? He counters:

> There is not the slightest hint in Ezekiel's description of these sacrifices that they will be simply memorial. They must be expiatory in exactly the same sense as the sacrifices described in Leviticus were expiatory. To take any other view of them is to surrender that principle of literal interpretation of prophecy which is fundamental to Dispensationalism and to admit that the Old Testament kingdom prophecies do not enter the New Testament "absolutely unchanged."[62]

Certain observations need to be made on that deliverance. First, if Allis calls for a hint that sacrifices will be simply memorial, he must be asked to point to the passage in the Old Testament where it is stated that the sacrifices of the Old Testament economy were pointing forward to Christ as Savior. Is there a passage that indicates, "This sacrifice means that coming Sacrifice"?

Second, it is amazing for an Old Testament scholar of undisputed Christian persuasion to claim that "the sacrifices in Leviticus were expiatory." The sacrifices in Leviticus were not expiatory, but anticipatory. So they were characterized by Scofield also, as Allis also admits by quoting Hebrews 10:4 on the very same page of his book.

Third, no confirmed premillennialist even thinks of surrendering the proved and tested principle of literal interpretation.

It is the practice of some writers, when writing on the matter of the Millennium, to wage a hot war; but when they arrive at the conclusion of their work, all is serene and peaceful. Hear Allis, "There are many things regarding the future which are by no means plain."[63] To that all agree, but it does not prevent the setting up of some kind of logical system of interpretation of the biblical data. But he concludes, "Whether there is to be such a millennium is a question which must be decided in the light of Scripture. It does not seem to involve any issue sufficiently serious [and that after he has spent a book trying to refute the opposite view] to warrant its being a divisive factor among those that are of the household of faith."[64]

Hamilton, though an amillennialist, admits it was possible to labor on the mission field in harmony with premillennialists.[65] He is more liberal than Murray, Rutgers, or Berkhof on the matter of the church's pronouncement on the millennial issue. He claims, "The historic position of the Christian Church has been that no official pronouncement should be made by the church as a church on the millennial issue, and that members were to be allowed to hold any view they desired."[66] As that is true, what becomes of the loud protestations of amillennialists that the creeds of the church affirm unequivocally the amillennial position? They cannot be proved. Having come to the amillennial view during seminary training, he is irenical in approach and states: "The church has almost universally refused to make such interpretations articles of the creeds of the various churches."[67] But it will not do for him to try to drive a wedge between so-called "historic premillennialists" and present premillennialists, unless he is prepared to classify himself as a thoroughgoing Augustinian amillenarian.[68]

He expresses a bit too much abhorrence at "all the blood and filth" of reinstituted sacrifices in the Millennium. Would it be more so than before the cross? Such statements sound dangerously close to what the liberals say of the pre-cross sacrifices. Too, it serves no good purpose to say the sacrifices "would seem to dishonor Christ and to approach dangerously close to blasphemy of His person."[69] The Lord's Supper is also a memorial. Does it dishonor Christ and "approach dangerously close to blasphemy of His person"? Christ is not dishonored, for just as sacrifices never took away sin even when pointing forward to the cross (Heb. 10:4), they will not in looking back to the cross.

Still amillennialists claim that premillennialists make little of the cross. They literally interpret the Word of God and hold that the cross has a memorial these centuries in the Lord's Supper and will have a memorial for a thousand years under the rule of Christ on earth. But Hamilton asks another question on the subject, one that is pointed and deserving of serious answer. He asks, "In the future state, even were there a millennium, what possible need could there be for a 'memorial,' either of Christ or His cross, with Christ present in person before the eyes of the believer?"[70] The answer is threefold. The church has had for over 1900 years a memorial of that sacrifice of Christ in the Lord's Supper; Israel as such has had none. It will be that memorial for them primarily. Second, if no sacrifices are needed where Christ is present, why were they permitted of God all through the earthly ministry of Christ? And, third, greater wonder still, why, after He had assuredly perfected our salvation forever on the cross, did God allow those sacrifices to go on until A.D. 70 when the Temple was destroyed?

But other features in Ezekiel 40-48 disturb Hamilton, and he declares:

> But most important of all these features [surely in his thought but not in the text of Ezekiel] of the ceremonial law, is the *requirement of circumcision* for those who are to enter the sanctuary. "No foreigner, uncircumcised in heart and *uncircumcised in flesh,* shall enter into my sanctuary, of any foreigners that are among the children of Israel."! (Ezek. 44:9). This would throw into the discard Paul's Epistle to the Galatians, for that was written specifically against those Judaizers who insisted that it was necessary to be circumcised as well as to believe in Christ for salvation. Just what would our premillennial friends suggest that circumcision would be a "memorial" of? Is it not plain that the principle of literal interpretation of *all* Old Testament prophecies is reduced to an absurdity by the mere contemplation of such a prospect during the alleged millennium?[71]

He has completely twisted the whole intent of the passage. All the prophet is saying is that the priests of that age, because of the prominence of Israel, would be of Israel. He certainly is not outlining the terms upon which salvation is received. But Hamilton, who is so concerned about the introduction of law into the Millennium on page 43, is the same writer who puts the believer today under the law (exactly what Paul is denouncing in Galatians—no law for the believer for justification nor for sanctification, other than being in-lawed to Christ) on pages 27 and 29 of his book. Strange anomaly! But how does he himself interpret that section of Ezekiel's prophecy? The reader is afforded an interpretation from an amillennialist on the theme. He holds, "These last chapters of Ezekiel must be intended to teach *spiritual truths under the symbolism of the temple and the restored nation!*"[72]

First, it should be pointed out that the liberal's explanation of the passage is exactly the same as Hamilton's. In the second place, why such an abundance of detail as in chapters 40-48 if the sole aim is to picture an ideal relationship between the Lord and His people? Is that true of 1 Kings 6 and 7 also, or was that a literal Temple? Is an event literal only because it has already happened? If so, what happens to all prophecy?

When the detailed exegesis of Revelation 20 is approached, it is found that the amillennialists are as far afield as they are on the broad context of the passage and its integration into the comprehensive eschatological program of the Scriptures. On the binding of Satan for a thousand years, Hughes comments: "This is better understood, within the perspective of the New Testament, as referring to the present 'times of the Gentiles' when the Devil is held under restraint as the Gospel is preached to all nations."[73] At first glance the reader may wonder whether Hughes has inadvertently omitted from consideration the important disclosure in 1 Peter 5:8 ("prowls about," NASB), but more follows. With equal confidence and optimism he holds, "No longer is Satan [in the church age] permitted to blind the nations with his deception."[74] Again, one may be inclined to question whether he has overlooked 2 Corinthians 4:1-4.

But when Hughes does cite 2 Corinthians 4:4 and 1 Peter 5:8, he states, "But his binding in relation to the nations is nonetheless real as the Gospel multiplies its conquests throughout the world."[75] From that statement one might be inclined to conclude that he has joined the ranks of the overoptimistic and now all but defunct camp of the postmillennialists. One cannot have Satan bound and loose at the same time; the logic of language will not permit it. In what sense is Satan, then, bound? In what way is he loose? To empty plain language of all meaning is self-defeating, confusing, and less than worthy of the tremendous theme under discussion. Hughes makes Matthew 12:24-32; 28:18-19; Mark 3:22-30; Luke 10:17-19; 11:21-22; John 12:31-32; Colossians 2:15; Hebrews 2:14-15; and Revelation 12:1-9 all to refer to the binding of Satan in Revelation 20:2-3.[76] Confidently, he concludes that, because Satan is already bound, "the millennium is not a future but a present reality."[77] And how, under such circumstances, is Isaiah 35:1 with a host of other passages to be understood?

Ladd takes a safe position on Revelation 20:1 in his statement: "It is an open question as to whether the binding of Satan in Rev. 20 is the same as that in Matt. 12 [vv. 28, 29] or is an eschatological event."[78] In the first place, Revelation 20 is an eschatological event. Second, it would appear that the contexts of the two passages are so diverse that the episodes cannot be identical.

The exegesis of the binding of Satan, as given by Hoekema, is so removed from factuality that it is tragic. He maintains, "We conclude, then, that the binding of Satan during the gospel age means that, first, he cannot prevent the spread of the gospel, and second, he cannot gather all the enemies of Christ together to attack the church."[79] He further states: "Throughout the gospel age in which we now live the influence of Satan, though certainly not annihilated, is so curtailed that he cannot prevent the spread of the gospel to the nations of the world."[80]

Those statements demand refutation. First, under God's sovereign permission Satan has all too successfully hindered the spread of the gospel in this age. Consider communist Russia, North Korea, Cuba, Vietnam, China, Rumania, East Germany, Albania, Yugoslavia, and countries of Africa, not to mention others. How free is the spread of the gospel in those lands? It is to be feared that Hoekema, in speaking of the enemies of Christ in their attacks against the church, has in mind the church in America, but such constitute a genuine but minor segment of the Body of Christ on earth. Second, how many enemies are needed to attack the church? Does Satan find he is bound only to a certain number and free as to the rest? Third, how is it that in his discussion Hoekema has failed to deal with vital passages like 2 Corinthians 4:14, 2 Timothy 2:26, 1 Peter 5:8, and 1 John 5:19, which have an immediate and profound relevance to the matter under discussion? How can one come to a logical, inductive conclusion after omitting so many vital and pertinent elements of the subject? Finally, by what exegetical process can Revelation 20:2 be constrained to speak of the gospel age at all? The immediate and broad contexts cry out against it.

Because the word *millennium* means a thousand years, amillennialists have labored long to explain it away as a troublesome element in the discussion. If that statement be considered too strong, note Hoekema:

> The book of Revelation is full of symbolic numbers. Obviously the number "thousand" which is used here must not be interpreted in a literal sense. Since the number ten signifies completeness, and since a thousand is ten to the third power, we may think of the expression "a thousand years" as standing for a complete period, a very long period of indetermi-nate length . . . we may conclude that this thousand-year period extends from Christ's first coming to just before his Second Coming.[81]

First and foremost, let it be stated clearly that if a number is used symbolically, the underlying literal force is discernible; for example, if the number *two* is symbolically employed, it is because two tables of stone at Mt. Sinai witnessed to God's holy requirements; two men, Moses and Joshua—and then Elijah and Elisha—witnessed to Israel of the will of God for them; the twelve were sent out two by two (Matt. 10), as were the seventy (Luke 10), to witness the gospel to Israel; two witnesses in Revelation bear out the same truth. *Four* is symbolic of the earth, because there are four points to the compass. *Six* is the number of man (Dan. 3:1 and Rev. 13:18), because he is made up of six parts—head, two arms, torso, and two legs. Ten does not signify completeness, but *seven* does. Notice the times *seven* is used in the book of Revelation: seven churches (1:4); seven Spirits (1:4); seven churches of Asia; seven lampstands; seven stars for the seven angels of the churches; three series of septenary judgments in the seals, trumpets, and bowls; and the seven benedictions, among others.

Second, to declare that "obviously" the number "thousand" is not to be taken literally, is a petitio principii, which will avail nothing.

Third, if numbers in the Revelation are to be taken symbolically, is that true of the seven churches in chapters 2 and 3? the seven messengers of the churches in the same chapters? the two witnesses of chapter 11? the 1,260 days of 11:3 and 12:6? the two beasts of chapter 13? The number *ten* signifies universality as in ten fingers, ten toes, Ten Commandments, and the ten men of Zechariah 8:23, as well as the ten horns of the fourth beast of Daniel 7 and the first beast of Revelation 13.

Fourth, explanation is needed as to how "ten to the third power" [a la Hodge/Warfield] can mean completeness and in the same time signify a "very long period of indeterminate length." The indeterminate length is needed to support the theory that the entire gospel age is in view. However, the Greek language knows better how to express "after a long time" (Matt. 25:19). To define it, as Hoekema does, makes a shambles of the number and of the period of time supposed to be indicated.

Finally, amillennialists repeatedly insist that the 1,000-years reference occurs once and only once in the Scriptures. The number occurs, not once, however, but in verses 2, 3, 4, 5, 6, and 7. The reference is in one chapter, but it appears six times in as many verses. Where does that type of phenomenon occur elsewhere in Scripture? Would it have been so consistently attacked if it had appeared in any other context? It is the veritable Waterloo of antichiliasm.

Another area of assault on the millenarian position centers on the common word "souls" (v. 4). It would seem unnecessary to state that the reference is to persons, not disembodied souls, but that also is not permitted to stand in the natural, obvious sense. Because of the mention of souls who had been beheaded, Hoekema claims, "We are confirmed in the conclusion that the locale of John's vision has now shifted to heaven . . . [so that] verses 1-3 describe what happens on earth during this time, and verses 4-6 depict what happens in heaven."[82] In all fairness, what is there in the wording of the passage that demands a shift from earth to heaven at verse 4? What is the natural meaning of "souls" in Acts 2:41 and 3:23?

Equally vexing for amillennialists is the mention in Revelation 20:4 of those who "came to life" (NASB) before they reigned with Christ for 1,000 years. The well-known nonmillenarian position is that the resurrection referred to here is a spiritual one, or regeneration, in verse 4; the resurrection mentioned later is said to be the general resurrection of all the dead, saved and unsaved (see next chapter of this work). McClain has penetrated and demolished that invalid argument thus: "In spite of all that has been written on the point, no one has ever produced a single indisputable instance in the New Testament where the Greek *anastasis* [resurrection] is ever applied to man's soul, or an instance where the new birth is ever called a 'resurrection.' "[83] Such evidence as that is incontrovertible.

However, Hughes, commenting on the subject of the first resurrection (Rev. 20:5), declares: "Scripture elsewhere contemplates *only one bodily resurrection* of the dead, which, because it involves the raising of all men, has customarily been known as the *general* resurrection" [italics his].[84] Incredibly, for confirmation he cites the Athanasian Creed. Splendid as that formula is, it must not be made the final court of appeal in biblical doctrine. When he does present Scripture, he refers to Daniel 12:2; John 5:28; Matthew 25:31; and Acts 24:15. Why does he not mention the pivotal passages in Luke 20:35 and Philippians 3:11, which specifically refer to an "out-resurrection from among dead ones"? Why does he not discuss even briefly the phases of the resurrection in 1 Corinthians 15:24-28 (see the treatment below in Part Four, chapter 19).

Hoekema, although he admits that "came to life" (20:4) can speak of a physical resurrection, is quick to ask,

> But is this "first resurrection" a physical resurrection—a raising of the body from the dead? Obviously not, since the raising of the body from the dead is mentioned later in the chapter as something distinct from what is described here (see vv. 11-13). Only if one believes in two bodily resurrections—one of believers at the beginning of the millennium and another of unbelievers after the millennium—will one be able to understand the *ezēsan* [Greek, "they came to life"] of verse 4 as referring to a bodily resurrection. Since the Scriptures elsewhere clearly teach only one bodily resurrection which will include both believers and unbelievers (see Jn. 5:28-29; Acts 24:15), what is described in the last clause of verse 4 must be something other than the physical or bodily resurrection which is yet to come.[85]

The matter under discussion is so vital to the issues of this volume that a proper and detailed refutation is called for. First, since Hoekema concedes that "came to life" (20:4) can designate a physical resurrection, why, then, does he question that it can mean such here? If the demands of the context pointed otherwise, there might be some ground for his question concerning the raising of the body from the dead. Is there such an exigency here? Assuredly not, for the apostle John is speaking of those who had been beheaded for their testimony. The verb itself, even in the English translation (which is faithful to the Greek original), indicates whether the reference is to man's material or immaterial part of his being. They were put to death physically, and they will come to life physically. The difficulty under which Hoekema is laboring is not in the text, but in the invalid presuppositions of his theological stance, because a first and second resurrection are totally foreign to his general resurrection of the amillennial camp. Besides, they logically lead to an interval that cannot be allowed in their denial of a millennial reign between the two resurrections.

Hoekema's use of "obviously not" comes as a bit jarring, because his reason for denial of a resurrection in verse 4 is the fact that a distinctly different resurrection is introduced in verses 11-13. That is precisely the teaching of premillennialism: There will be a first bodily resurrection unto life and a second bodily resurrection unto perdition. But the "something distinct" he mentions is an evasion of the obvious sense of the passage in order to eliminate

] 334 [

two bodily resurrections by postulating a first resurrection spiritually, whatever that could mean here, and a second, physical resurrection. The quotation of Alford above effectively lays to rest that oddity of exegesis. His position of one physical resurrection elsewhere he confirms, notice, by the choice of two Scriptures (John 5:28-29; Acts 24:15) where the contexts do not require a differentiation in resurrection, but only an emphasis of resurrection at all. Besides, why has he omitted from the discussion such determinative passages as Luke 20:35; Philippians 3:11; and 1 Corinthians 15:24-28, which clearly teach an out-resurrection from among the dead or distinct stages in resurrection? If 1 Corinthians 11:32 teaches that God will not judge His disobedient children with the world, and it does so teach, then how can anyone allow himself an interpretation of Scripture that postulates a general resurrection (a mingling of saved and unsaved) and a following general judgment (a confusing of redeemed and lost)? It is unscriptural and impossible (see chapter 20 for the matter of judgment).

Second, the "something other than the physical or bodily resurrection which is yet to come" is explained thus: "Though these believers have died, John sees them as alive, not in the bodily sense, but in the sense that they are enjoying life in heaven in fellowship with Christ."[86] When believers die, they can die in one realm only—the physical; when they come alive, they do so in one area only—the physical. Where does Scripture teach otherwise? If all is to be relegated to the sphere of the spiritual, in view of Ephesians 2:4-7 what need is there for a physical resurrection at all?

But Hoekema maintains,

As a matter of fact, even if *ezēsan* is interpreted to mean a bodily resurrection, the verse still does not describe the earthly millennium commonly held to by premillennialists. For on the basis of the common premillennial interpretation of Revelation 20:4, it is only *raised believers* [italics his] who are said to reign with Christ; nothing is said in this passage about a reign of Christ over people who have not died but are still living. The millennium of the premillennialists, however, is said to be primarily a reign of Christ over people who are still alive when Christ comes and over their descendants![87]

Two refutations are in order here. First, in the final sentence of Hoekema's statements he is either setting up a straw man or misunderstands the premillennial position. No premillennialists known to this writer, who has researched both the premillennial and amillennial literature for decades, hold that Christ will reign primarily over those who are still alive when He comes. According to 1 Corinthians 15:50-58; Philippians 3:20, 21; and 1 Thessalonians 4:13-18 (among others), the Bride of Christ who will reign with Christ will be constituted of translated and resurrected saints, the two companies now joined forever. Furthermore, the King and Queen will rule over people alive when

] 335 [

Christ comes (see Matt. 25:31-46), but there will also be some who have been resurrected from Israel (Dan. 12:1-2) and from the nations (Rev. 21:24).

Second, why should he require all elements of the premillennial view to be included in Revelation 20:4? Can he do such for the amillennial position? Why repeat truths already so fully presented in multiplied Old and New Testament passages? All truth is not found in one passage, even those doctrines of bibliology, theology proper, anthropology, angelology, hamartiology, Christology, soteriology, pneumatology, ecclesiology, or Israelology. Why, then, should the doctrine of the Millennium in eschatology be otherwise?

Before Hoekema has concluded, he believes another comment on the first resurrection is called for. He states:

> We must understand these words as describing not a bodily resurrection but rather the transition from physical death to life in heaven in Christ. This transition is here called a "resurrection"—an unusual use of the word, to be sure, but perfectly understandable against the background of the preceding context [proof?]. The expression "the first resurrection" implies that there will indeed be a "second resurrection" for these believing dead—the resurrection of the body which will take place when Christ returns at the end of the thousand-year period.[88]

The arguments here are almost incredible. It is admitted that the use of the word "resurrection" is unusual. It is possible in hermeneutics to allow such, if there are strong and unambiguous grounds for doing so. But he gives none whatever. Why is it not pointed out specifically what in the "background of the preceding context" compels one to understand such a unique usage (see Ladd's comments below).

Second, how can an amillennialist, who is a firm believer in a general (one) resurrection, suddenly propound a second resurrection, and that for the believing dead? The same words, it is claimed, are to be understood in two distinctly opposite manners in the same immediate context.[89] That position cannot stand.

Finally, Ladd deals the coup de grace from the solid ground of the Greek original. He correctly points out: "The verb [*ezésan*, 20:4-5]. . .is never in the New Testament used of life after death, *except in resurrection* [italics his]."[90] He further proves Hoekema's exegesis of 20:6 is in error: "The unbelieving dead . . . did not live or reign with Christ during this thousand year period."[91] However, the text actually reads: "The rest of the dead did not come to life until the thousand years were completed (NASB). Says Ladd, "A natural reading of the text clearly suggests that after the thousand years the rest of the dead did come to life."[92] The perils of a dual hermeneutic increase rapidly by compounding themselves.

When Hamilton tries to bring Luke 20:27-36 into conflict with Isaiah 65:20 on the premillennial interpretation of those passages, he notes the possible solution, but refuses it.[93] Is there, then, a desire to find a harmonization? And he gives no exegesis of the Isaiah passage himself, though the problem seems to burden him throughout his volume. He continues in another place, "It is a cardinal principle of premillennialism that there must be unbelieving nations present on the earth during the alleged millennium, ruled over by Christ with a rod of iron, because at the close of the millennium Satan is said to be loosed for a time to deceive the nations and to gather them to war against the saints . . . these nations are still rebellious at heart."[94]

His great concern is that if the wicked nations are purged out and sent into eternal fire at the beginning of the Millennium (if there is a Millennium), how could they gather to do battle against the saints after the Millennium? Let those points be taken in order. That the wicked nations will be purged out before the Millennium is sufficiently attested by the judgment of Matthew 25:31-46. That there are unbelieving ones during the Millennium who give only feigned obedience to the King is evidenced by Psalm 18:44; 66:3; and 81:15, where the original indicates they "lie." Now, when the natural force of Isaiah 65:20 is admitted with its indication of procreation in the Millennium, the picture is complete. The Millennium begins with only redeemed; those who have not experienced a resurrection (as the church and Old Testament saints) will live normal lives and bear children; they will not be born redeemed; and from among them will come the rebellious ones, the Gog and Magog of Revelation 20.

But Revelation 20 still haunts the amillennialist, so Hamilton inquires, "Is it not plain, therefore that there must be another explanation of the Rev. 20:7-9 passage about the deceit of the nations by Satan? The other explanation is of course that the whole passage refers to the time *before* Christ's Second Coming, when the Satan-deceived nations gather at the Battle of Armageddon."[95] It is only necessary to comment that not all his amillennialist protagonists will go along with him on that interpretation. And what is more important, what does he do with the coming spoken of in Revelation 19? After that unusually clear and vivid picture of the coming of Christ, it is wholly inadequate to speak of Revelation 20 as before the second coming of Christ.

Again, Hamilton tries to confine the premillennial view to certain passages; now it is the passages that speak of Christ's rule with a rod of iron. He claims they are "almost the very heart of the premillennial theory."[96] In Psalm 2:9 he substitutes "rule" for "break," but that leaves the "rod of iron" yet to be explained. He answers, "He shall act the part of a shepherd toward the nations with a rod of iron, as the vessels of the potter are broken to shivers." And comments, "That is, the Messiah, to protect His flock, the true people of God, from their enemies, will execute vengeance on the unbelieving nations who have been persecuting God's people."[97] Where do these enemies come from, if the wicked have been purged out before the Millennium?

Tendentious explanations frequent the passages of Hamilton's work. Here it can be illustrated with an important example. In discussing the vastly important 1 Corinthians 15:21-26 passage, he must admit the word "then" *(eita)* in 1 Corinthians 15:5 does call for "a slight interval of time."[98] The same is true of 1 Timothy 2:13 where the lapse of time is not indicated as to length. How can he say it is only a slight interval of time? If there is an interval admitted, his argument falls of its own weight. It might be well to treat of the analogous situation in Daniel 9:24-27 where an interval is made between the sixty-ninth week and the seventieth by the premillennialists. The interval is the church age as in Isaiah 61:1 ff. But the amillennialists fight such an interval, trying to make the seventy weeks conclude with the death of Christ. But the destruction of Jerusalem took place in A.D. 70, some forty years later, so the amillennialist has to admit the principle himself.

In treating the word "soul"[99] he notes that in 100 cases out of the 105 in the New Testament, it refers to the soul of man as distinct from his body. What about the other five references? He claims that the use of the word in Revelation 20 indicates that the first resurrection or new birth is spoken of and the reigning now of believers with Christ after their conversion. He does not explain why he injects the thought of a first resurrection for the new birth; it is true that the new birth is likened to a resurrection (Eph. 2:1), but it is not called "first." If it is first, then what is the second? It could only be first in relation to another resurrection or other resurrections of the same kind, or nature. When he treats the believers' reign now with Christ, they reign with Christ on earth after conversion and in heaven also.[100] Such is the view that may be called *ouranochiliasm.*

Reverting to the knotty problem of Isaiah 65:20 and Luke 20 (the explanation of which he has not ventured in the whole book), he contends, "The righteous cannot fall into sin and cannot bear children."[101] The first part of the statement is right and the second is wrong. Childbearing is not sinful, for it was commanded by God before the Fall. The solution to his problem is at hand, but he refuses it throughout the work.

As a rule an author reveals before the end of his work the animating force that has impelled him to a certain position or outlook. Hamilton maintains:

> One of the inexplicable questions that arises in the mind of a nonpremillennialist when one examines the theory of premillennialism which holds that the Jewish kingdom will be restored and be supreme during the alleged millennium, is why there should be so much enthusiasm on the part of a Gentile Christian [on the very next page he rejoices that in Christ there is neither Jew nor Gentile], for a theory which holds that the church will not be present on the earth during the alleged millennium? If, as they claim, the church will be up in the skies during that period while the Jews reign on earth, why should a Gentile believer today "bleed and die," for a

millennium in which he will have no direct or important concern?[102]

Hamilton appears to interpret Scripture on the basis of what glory can accrue to him ultimately, regardless of what it should mean actually, when properly interpreted. The truth is, of course, that the church will be in a position of surpassing glory during the millennial reign of the King, for she will be the Queen.

Not only is there great diversity of interpretation of individual passages on the Millennium between pre- and amillennialists, but there is no agreement on the function, necessity, and characteristics of the Messianic reign. Ladd declares, "In some way not disclosed in Scripture, the millennium is part of Christ's Messianic rule by which he puts all his enemies under his feet (1 Cor. 15:25). Another possible role of the millennium is that Christ's Messianic kingdom might be disclosed *in history*."[103] Most of his fellow-premillennialists would certainly state those elements with greater emphasis. Scripture does reveal how the Lord Jesus Christ will subjugate all His enemies with a "rod of iron" rule in the Millennium, which is His mediatorial reign to be followed by His rule with the Father and the Holy Spirit for all eternity (1 Cor. 15:24-28). Moreover, it is in the mediatorial, Messianic kingdom that all God's purposes and promises will be vindicated and realized in time and history.

Hoyt states succinctly the chief ingredients of the kingdom: "Nowhere in any formal sense does the New Testament expound the theology of the millennium. But men are made aware of the fact that there is a new order of revelation and control during the kingdom."[104]

Postmillennialist Boettner seems to find difficulties that do not trouble other nonmillennialists. He comments on the presence in the Millennium of mortals and immortals: "Such a mixed state of mortals and immortals, terrestrial and celestial, surely would be a monstrosity. . . . I wonder how anyone can take it seriously."[105] The wonder is, rather, how a Christian theologian, committed to the authority of the Scripture, can indulge himself in a judgment more suited to a rationalist, to say nothing of the presence of a not-too-latent gnosticism. The answer to his charge of "monstrosity" is available in these questions: How did the resurrected (immortal) Christ live for forty days in His post-resurrection ministry among His mortal disciples? how about resurrected Lazarus? what of Jairus' daughter? what will he do with the widow of Nain's son? And what of those raised by Elijah and Elisha, to say nothing of those in Matthew 27:51-53? How could so many instances have escaped the eye of the learned author?

When Hoekema comes to a discussion of Isaiah 11:6-9, he writes: "It can easily be understood that if a person believes in a future earthly millennium, he will see that millennium described in these verses. Such an interpretation is, however, by no means the only possible one."[106] What is his explanation of the Isaiah prophecy? He feels it speaks not of the Millennium, but of the new earth. That is a welcome departure from *ouranochiliasm* for an amillennialist, but if on earth, why not in the age when Messiah rules on earth? However, he does come back to the normative nonmillennial perspective when he states: *"As far as the thousand years of Revelation 20 are concerned, we are in the millennium now* [italics his]."[107] The situation in the discussion, then, is the same as at the beginning. What of Isaiah 2, 9, 35; Amos 9; Micah 4; Zechariah 14, and so many others?

McClain can be depended upon to come to the heart of the matter. He asserts: "Those today who are belligerently opposed to the idea of a literal Kingdom of Christ on earth are the scholars who either largely ignore the Old Testament or else dissolve in the acid of their 'spiritualization' those prophetic elements which are repugnant to them."[108] He says further: "As to the term 'carnal,' used so frequently by the objectors in an epithetical manner: if it can be applied properly to anything, certainly it would more fitly describe their alleged *present* [italics his] millennial 'reign' of the saints in church discipline than the premillennial view of the saints' future reign . . . if the term is to be used at all, it is of [the opposing view] of the saints' so-called present 'reign' in the church that deserves the term 'carnal.' "[109]

Ladd maintains his nonliteral kingdom for the first advent thus: "It is a spiritual reign in heaven which has already been inaugurated, and its primary purpose is to destroy Christ's spiritual enemies, the last of which is death."[110] The reader, after perusing the discussions thus far, will be able to decide as to the validity of his position. Why does Ladd diverge so clearly from other premillennialists? It is fairly and squarely attributable to his dictum: "A millennial doctrine cannot be based on Old Testament prophecies. . . ."[111] No man has the right so to confine an important biblical doctrine. The result is that so many of his deliverances parallel those of the amillennialists. He says, "I can find no trace of the idea of either an interim earthly kingdom or of a millennium in the Gospels."[112] At that juncture it would be enlightening to have his definition of "kingdom of heaven" in Matthew. But Hoyt has placed his finger on the difficulty and diagnosed it properly: "It is unfortunate that he cannot see that the Old Testament supplies the vast portion of material for putting the picture in full perspective."[113] Once and for all, it must be maintained that the materials for biblical theology must be sought for and gleaned from every part of the inspired, inerrant Word of God.

Try as they may, amillennialists cannot obliterate the obvious meaning of Revelation 20 to teach something other than a Millennium on earth. Their interpretative principles are strained to the breaking point in that chapter, and they break. Premillennialism is as valid in Revelation 20 as anywhere in the Bible.

Notes

[1]E. M. Milligan, *Is the Kingdom Age at Hand?* p. 323.

[2]J. T. Mueller, "Parousia," ISBE, 4:2251-2251A.

[3]A. Kuyper, *Chiliasm or the Doctrine of Premillennialism,* p. 9.

[4]J. J. Hiemenga, *The Second Coming of Christ And What About a Millennium?*

[5]G. Vos, "Eschatology of the New Testament," ISBE, 2:987.

[6]G. Vos, *The Pauline Eschatology,* pp. 235-36.

[7]B. B. Warfield, "The Millennium and the Apocalypse," pp. 599-617.

[8]W. Masselink, *Why Thousand Years?* pp. 194-208.

[9]P. E. Hughes, *Interpreting Prophecy,* pp. 97, 99-100.

[10]Ibid., p. 116.

[11]G. E. Ladd, *A Commentary on the Revelation of John,* p. 260.

[12]Ibid., p. 261.

[13]R. G. Clouse, ed., *The Meaning of the Millennium,* p. 39.

[14]Ibid., p. 169.

[15]Ibid., p. 177.

[16]A. J. McClain, *The Greatness of the Kingdom,* p. 235.

[17]Ibid., pp. 476-77.

[18]Clouse, p. 32.

[19]Ibid., p. 38. On the same page he states his view that 1 Cor. 15:23-26 "may refer to an interim kingdom if not a millennium.'

[20]Ibid., p. 55. In almost fifty years of study of the millennial issue, this writer has never read a knowledgeable premillennialist make such a postulate.

[21]Ibid., pp. 159-60.

[22]Ibid., p. 190.

[23]R. J. Reid, *Amillennialism,* p. 75.

[24]D. Bosworth, *The Millennium and Related Events,* p. 44.

[25]Ibid., p. 46.

[26]H. C. Thiessen, *Introductory Lectures in Systematic Theology,* p. 511.

[27]S. J. Case, *The Millennial Hope,* pp. 151-52.

[28]Ibid., p. 228.

[29]W. H. Rutgers, *Premillennialism in America,* p. 162.

[30]G. H. Hospers, "The Calvinistic Character of Pre-millennialism," p. 9.

[31]Ibid., p. 11.

[32]G. H. Hospers, *The Principle of Spiritualization in Hermeneutics,* p. 40.

[33]G. L. Murray, *Millennial Studies: A Search for Truth,* p. 46.

[34]Ibid., p. 66.

[35]Ibid., p. 92.

[36]L. Berkhof, *Systematic Theology,* p. 708; for an equally plain one from a

premillennialist, see D. H. Kromminga, *The Millennium in the Church,* pp. 297-98.

[37]Ibid., p. 708.

[38]Ibid., p. 712.

[39]Ibid., p. 715.

[40]See also the same position in L. Berkhof, *The Kingdom of God,* p. 176.

[41]Berkhof, *Systematic Theology,* p. 715.

[42]Ibid., pp. 715-16.

[43]Ibid., p. 737.

[44]Berkhof, *The Kingdom of God,* pp. 148-49.

[45]D. H. Kromminga, *The Millennium in the Church,* p. 60.

[46]Ibid., pp. 318 ff.

[47]Ibid., p. 297.

[48]Ibid., p. 298.

[49]Ibid., p. 305.

[50]Ibid., p. 349.

[51]D. H. Kromminga, *The Millennium,* p. 48.

[52]Ibid., p. 55.

[53]Ibid., pp. 60, 89, 104.

[54]O. T. Allis, *Prophecy and the Church,* p. 62.

[55]Ibid., p. 237.

[56]Ibid., p. 239.

[57]Ibid., p. 242.

[58]Ibid., pp. 242, 250-51, 260.

[59]Ibid., pp. 244-45.

[60]Ibid., p. 246.

[61]Ibid., p. 247.

[62]Ibid.

[63]Ibid., p. 261.

[64]Ibid.

[65]F. E. Hamilton, *The Basis of Millennial Faith,* preface.

[66]Ibid.

[67]Ibid., p. 18.

[68]Ibid., pp. 21-24.

[69]Ibid., p. 41.

[70]Ibid., p. 42.

[71]Ibid., p. 43.

[72]Ibid., p. 44.

[73]Hughes, p. 110.

[74]Ibid., p. 111.

[75]Ibid., p. 112.

[76]Ibid., pp. 113-15.

[77]Ibid., p. 116.
[78]Ladd, *A Commentary on the Revelation of John,* p. 260.
[79]Clouse, p. 162. He cites in support of his position Matt. 12:29; Luke 10:17-18; and John 12:31-32. Of the Lucan passage he admits: "These words, needless to say, must not be interpreted literally . . . in fact, a certain [how?] binding of Satan, a certain restriction of his power, had just taken place" (p. 163).
[80]Ibid., pp. 161, 164.
[81]Ibid.
[82]Ibid., p. 165. According to 2 Tim. 2:12 the obvious conclusion is that, as the suffering is on earth, so will the reigning be also.
[83]McClain, p. 488.
[84]Hughes, p. 119.
[85]Clouse, pp. 167-68.
[86]Ibid., p. 168.
[87]Ibid., p. 215, fn. 5.
[88]Ibid., pp. 170-71.
[89]Ibid., p. 171.
[90]Ibid., p. 190.
[91]Ibid., p. 191.
[92]Ibid., pp. 190-91.
[93]Ibid., p. 46.
[94]Ibid., p. 71.
[95]Ibid., p. 75.
[96]Ibid., p. 85.
[97]Ibid., p. 88.
[98]Ibid., p. 93.
[99]Ibid., pp. 131-32.
[100]Ibid., p. 132.
[101]Ibid., p. 135.
[102]Ibid., p. 139.
[103]Ibid., p. 39.
[104]Ibid., p. 45.
[105]Ibid., p. 49.
[106]Ibid., p. 174.
[107]Ibid., p. 181.
[108]Ibid., p. 496.
[109]Ibid., p. 503.
[110]Ibid., p. 30.
[111]Ibid., p. 32.
[112]Ibid., p. 38.
[113]Ibid., p. 44.

19

The Resurrection or the Resurrections

Amillennial and premillennial discussions make much of the question of resurrection, for it is of vast importance with regard to the doctrine of the Millennium. It would be worthwhile to spend a good deal of time on that point alone, but a lengthy discussion will not be attempted. It shall suffice for the purposes here to point out pivotal considerations and draw conclusions therefrom.

All amillennialists are agreed that there is but one general eschatological resurrection. Vos claims that the New Testament restricts the resurrection to a single epoch, and nowhere teaches a resurrection in two stages, one at the parousia, of saints and martyrs, and a second one at the end of the Millennium. He asserts, furthermore, that although pre-Christian Judaism had developed a theory of a Millennium, it had not held to a repeated resurrection, the whole resurrection being placed at the end.[1]

In another discussion on the Pauline eschatology, the same writer admits that a partial resurrection at the beginning of the Millennium and an all-comprehensive one at the end are by no means inherently contradictory.[2] He concedes that to postulate a general resurrection of believers and non-Christians would be to disrupt internally that resurrection; and as far as the general tenor of Pauline doctrine is concerned, he believes it must be admitted that the comprehensive interpretation is at a decided disadvantage. Although in another place he had declared that a repeated resurrection was not well established in pre-Christian Judaism, he finds himself constrained to note that the doctrine of comprehensive resurrection was not before or at the time of Paul an established doctrine of Judaism. In concluding his remarks, he states that the only explicit witness that amillennialists have for a comprehensive resurrection of wicked and righteous is to be found in Acts 24:15, which will be dealt with later.

Although Kuyper maintains that there is but one contemporaneous resurrection of both the just and the unjust,[3] and although Mains holds that all church creeds teach and have taught a simultaneous resurrection of the wicked with the righteous,[4] thus excluding a very foundation of premillennialism, Kennedy finds he cannot help but admit that the matter of a general resurrection is without the pale of Paul's thinking.[5] The resurrection of the unsaved must take place along different lines than that of believers, because the resurrection of the former does not follow the norm of the resurrection of the Lord Jesus Christ, whereas that of the latter is patterned after the glorious resurrection of the Savior.

Masselink's work lays five objections to a twofold resurrection.[6] First, he maintains that both the Old and New Testaments teach one resurrection. He quotes in support of that statement Isaiah 26:19 and Daniel 12:2, and cannot find a period of a thousand years between two resurrections, nor does he see any mention of two resurrections at all. In citing John 5:28-29 as the New Testament proof, he remarks that Christ placed the resurrection of the just and the wicked at the same hour.

His second objection to a twofold resurrection is that the resurrection of the dead is everywhere placed at "the end." It is said to take place at "the last day," and that means the end of time. In John 11 and three times in John 6, Christ speaks of the resurrection as connected with the last day, which excludes any other days or seasons after it, he insists. Hence it is the end of time.

A third objection is that Paul in Acts 24:15 mentions but one resurrection. He does not differentiate in his language between the resurrection of believers and unbelievers.

Fourth, the Scriptures reveal that the resurrection of the saints occurs at the day of judgment and in connection with it. The rejection of the ungodly is said to take place at the same time. There is absolutely no separation between them. In commenting on John 5:28-29, he claims it is hard to find a plainer statement of the "simultaneousness" of the resurrection of both groups than that one.

Finally, Christ's coming is called "the end," so that the inevitable conclusion is that the general resurrection and the judgment take place at the coming of Christ in glory.

The position of premillennialists is that there is a twofold resurrection, one of the just and one of the unjust. That is maintained as a result of the exegesis of the passages that speak of the resurrection. It is not possible here to deal with them all. In the discussion and exegesis of them the differences in interpretation between the amillennialists and the premillennialists will be presented. First of all, all premillenarians recognize, as do amillennialists, that the Scriptures speak of a spiritual resurrection. Paul is referring to that very thing when he writes the Ephesians that they have been raised up together and made to sit together in the heavenlies in Christ Jesus (Eph. 2:4-7). That takes place at regeneration. But the following discussion will deal only with those passages that have to do with physical resurrection.

Throughout the Old Testament mention is made of the fact of a future physical resurrection. It is in Daniel 12:2 that one finds the first mention of a twofold resurrection. There are some who find no reference in that verse to a physical resurrection, including A. C. Gaebelein, H. A. Ironside, and W. Kelly.[7] Those men believe that the national resurrection of Israel, spoken of in Ezekiel 37, is meant here. Fausset follows the view of S. P. Tregelles, which shall presently be considered.[8] The setting of the verse is most important. The prophet predicts in the first verse of the chapter a time of unprecedented trial and trouble for Israel, the Great Tribulation, which has already been studied at length. It is after that time of trouble that the physical resurrection is spoken of. The verse, then, speaks on the face of it of a resurrection of Old Testament saints, which leads one to believe that it is incorrect to find the resurrection of Old Testament saints in 1 Thessalonians 4. The reference there is undoubtedly to believers in the present dispensation only, those that are the "dead in Christ."

How, then, should Daniel 12:2 be interpreted? The translation of Tregelles is probably the closest to the original.[9] He renders the verse thus: "And many from among the sleepers of the dust of the earth shall awake; these shall be unto everlasting life; but those [the rest of the sleepers, those who do not awake at this time] shall be unto shame and everlasting contempt." That the resurrection is not general, but eclectic, is to be seen from the word *miyeshene,* from among those who sleep. The word *'elleh* translated "some" in both cases is never repeated in the Hebrew Old Testament in the sense of dealing distributively with a general class that has been formerly mentioned. Let that suffice to show that there are two resurrections spoken of. The verse does not reveal, and it should not be made to teach, exactly what period of time elapses between the resurrection of the first group and that of the second.

The evidence in the New Testament on the question of a twofold resurrection is much more full than that in the Old Testament. It will not be possible to deal with all the passages; those referred to will prove ample ground for the premillennial position. When the Sadducees propounded a question to the Lord Jesus one day concerning the woman who had seven husbands who left her no issue, the Lord answered: "But they which shall be accounted worthy to obtain that world, and the resurrection from the dead, neither marry, nor are given in marriage" (Luke 20:35). H.A.W. Meyer notes that verse reveals a resurrection, such as spoken of in Luke 14:14, which is to be differentiated from a resurrection in which the wicked participate.[10] Alford finds that the verse speaks of the first resurrection.[11] On the very surface of it, if all the dead are to be raised at one time, no one would have to be worthy to obtain a part in the resurrection, for all would have a part in it. Why, furthermore, the use of the phrase "from the dead"? If a general resurrection is taught in Scripture, the verse should have stated the resurrection of the dead. A. Plummer points out validly that the phrase *tes ek nekron* must be distinguished from the phrase *anastasis nekron*.[12] The latter is the more comprehensive and refers to a resurrection in which all the dead are raised. The former implies a resurrection in which some are raised and others are not. The former in a number of passages is used of Christ and the saints; in that connection it is equivalent to the resurrection of life. The other is the resurrection of condemnation spoken of in the Scriptures. Here, then, in Luke 20:35 is an additional proof that there is a twofold resurrection.

Another link in the chain of evidence is found in John 5:28-29. Amillennialists are most confident that those verses do teach a general resurrection. Study the passage carefully. It was after the Lord Jesus had healed the impotent man at the pool of Bethesda that He was accused of making Himself equal with God, when He declared God to be His Father in a peculiar sense. In reply to the accusations of the Jews, He explained the particulars in which He was equal to the Father. In connection with His power, He declared that the hour was coming and then was present when the dead would hear His voice and live. He continued: "For the hour is coming, in the which all that are in the graves shall hear his voice, And shall come forth; they that have done good, unto the resurrection of life; and they that have done evil, unto the resurrection of damnation [condemnation]" (John 5:28-29).

The use of the word "hour" has been deemed sufficient proof to amillennialists to conclude that the general resurrection is assuredly taught here. It should be noted, first of all, that a physical resurrection is spoken of, and not a spiritual resurrection. That is substantiated by the *en tois mnemeiosis,* in the graves." But what do premillennialists make of the word *hora?* S. H. Kellogg and W. E. Blackstone with many others maintain that it may refer to a long period of time.[13] The use of the same word in John 4:21-23 and in 5:25 shows that it can and does refer to an extended period of time. In the instances mentioned above, the "hour" has lasted throughout the present dispensation. Nor is that usage unknown throughout the New Testament. Paul uses the word "day" in 2 Corinthians 6:2 in the same manner. So the word "hour" does not militate in the least particular against the doctrine that there will be a first and a second resurrection, for, as Meyer has well pointed out, the word is capable of prophetic extension.[14]

According to the testimony of Vos, noted among amillennialists, the reference in Acts 24:15 explicitly speaks of one resurrection only.[15] The verse is found in Paul's message before Felix where he defends his position in the following words: "And have hope toward God, which they themselves also allow, that there shall be a resurrection of the dead, both of the just and unjust" (Acts 24:15). Meyer points out with others that the language here does not, in contradiction of the passages already studied, imply a general resurrection.[16] The language can legitimately be taken to mean a resurrection of the dead, one of the just and one of the unjust. For the passage to teach a general resurrection, all other passages on the same subject must be twisted and distorted to fit in with that one.

Probably more has been written on 1 Corinthians 15:21-28 in that connection than upon any other passage, because amillennialists as well as premillenarians realize that in that chapter there is the norm of the doctrine of the resurrection. Furthermore, the passage relates the resurrection directly to the kingdom. The setting of the passage is most important. The Corinthian church had among its number those who doubted the resurrection of believers. In order to prove that there is a resurrection of believers, Paul forged a three-linked argument, the logic of which is irresistible. First, he showed that there must be such a thing as a resurrection from the dead, otherwise it could not be said that Christ had risen from the dead. Then he pointed out that Christ must have risen, or there would be no basis for Christian faith and hope. Finally, he showed that on the basis of the resurrection of Christ, the resurrection of the saints is assured.

Beginning with verse 21, he noted that because death came by man, resurrection of the dead comes by man also. For as in Adam all die, so in Christ shall all be made alive. Every man shall have his respective order: Christ the firstfruits; afterward all believers; then the end. At that time Christ will deliver up the kingdom to God the Father, when He shall have subjected all rule and power to Himself. It must be remembered that Paul was speaking here of physical life and physical death only. Such is the force of the verb *zoopoietheson-tai.* The evident meaning of verse 22 is that all who are in Adam die, and all who are in Christ will be made alive. The *pantes* in each case is limited by the prepositional phrase that it modifies. The "all" is not the same in both cases, as some premillennialists hold. The phrase *en to Christo* has here its universal soteriological significance. A forced exegesis of the phrase is not necessary to prove the premillennial position. Some, on the other hand, have held that the phrase refers to professing Christendom. That view has no more to recommend it than has the view that all, saved and unsaved, are included.

In the next verses the apostle outlines the order of the resurrection. Every man is said to be in his own definite order, *en to idio tagmati.* The word *tagmati* is a military term and means "rank," "band," "troop," or "company." In the first is Christ; in the second are all those who are Christ's at His coming; in the third those who are not included in the previous bands. The interval between the first and second detachment is marked by the adverb *epeita,* which shows that the word does not imply immediate succession. This whole dispensation has already intervened since the firstfruits and the company that will rise at His coming. The explanation of Hodge that *tagma* here means only order of succession does not stand the test, according to Meyer and others.[17] After the resurrection of the second band, it is stated, comes the end. It cannot be maintained that the end is synchronous with the coming of Christ, as amillennialists would have us believe, for the adverb *eita* is capable of the same interpretation as the *epeita* noted above. There can be a long interval, and it will be shown later that there is, between the second and third contingents as there was between the first and second.

Robertson and Plummer do not commit themselves as to whether the coming is the end or not.[18] The context, according to F. Godet, does not allow *to telos* to refer to a resurrection at all. [19] It would have been, to his way of thinking, modified in some way by the apostle to bring out that thought, if that had been in the mind of the apostle Paul. Without modification it must refer, he claims, to the end of all things spoken of by the apostle Peter in 1 Peter 4:7. That is rather farfetched. The context is one that speaks of resurrection, and the end-resurrection is here in view, according to a number of commentators.

The apostle has shown that there are to be definite stages in the resurrection of the dead. First, Christ is the firstfruits; second, those who are Christ's at His coming; third, the end-resurrection of all unbelievers. What becomes of the Old Testament saints? There is no need to mention them, for their place has been noted in Daniel 12:2 as after the time of trouble that is to come upon Israel. But the apostle reveals when the end-resurrection takes place. It is when Christ has delivered up the kingdom to God the Father. It must be Christ's kingdom, covenanted and promised to His father David. There is a period, namely, the time of the kingdom, that elapses between the resurrection of believers and that of non-believers.

It is well to pause for a little while to note Philippians 3:11. In the passage Paul is recounting what he has given up for the Lord Jesus Christ at the time of his conversion. He reveals his purpose in the following words: "If by any means I might attain unto the resurrection of the dead." Paul is laying before the reader the thought that actuated him at the time of his acceptance of Christ. Vos thinks that Paul is viewing his own resurrection as dependent on his Christian life and service. He readily concedes himself that it is an unusual representation, but feels that no one has a right to maintain it impossible.[20]

It is impossible, because the Word nowhere makes the believer's resurrection contingent upon his life and testimony. The phrase *ei pos katanteso* is used when an end is proposed, but failure is possible. If there is but one resurrection for all, why would the apostle Paul contemplate missing it in his unsaved condition? That is impossible of explanation to anyone holding to a general resurrection.

What is the meaning, then, of the passage? Both Ellicott and Lightfoot[21] with many others refer the *eis ten exanastasin ten ek nekron* to the resurrection of the righteous, which is to be selective. The thought in the mind of Paul, then, at the time of his turning to God, was not that he might attain to the general resurrection in which all would participate, but that he might take part in the out-resurrection from among the dead, the resurrection of the just. The passage, therefore, teaches as clearly as any that there will be more than one general resurrection.

In bringing this portion of the discussion to a close, note Revelation 20:4-6. Here John reveals that he saw the martyrs of Christ raised and reigning with Him for a thousand years. The rest of the dead, however, did not live until the thousand years were finished. That is called the first resurrection; that is, of those that lived and reigned with Christ. Those who lived after the resurrection are said to be a part of the second resurrection. It is the common interpretation of amillennialists that the first resurrection is the spiritual resurrection that takes place at the regeneration of a sinner; the second resurrection is the general physical resurrection of all the dead of all time. If one is any judge at all, the amillennialist interpretation is at its poorest in its attempted and distorted explanation of that passage. But it is not the purpose to deal in lengthy detail with that passage. There is need merely to show that, instead of establishing the doctrine of the two resurrections as though it were nowhere else taught in the Bible, the passage serves only to confirm and corroborate all that has been seen in the study of previous passages.

In the first place, it should be pointed out that the martyred saints are not the only ones reigning with Christ. The passage reads: "And I saw thrones, and they sat upon them, and judgment was given unto them." That they are not the martyrs is clear from the separate mention of the latter in the clause following. Who are those that are sitting on the thrones? Reference is here made to the early stages of the first resurrection, the rearward of which is drawn up by the resurrected martyrs of the Tribulation period. In the vanguard, if Christ be omitted, are to be found the Old Testament saints who are resurrected after the Tribulation, and the New Testament saints who have received their glorified bodies at the coming of Christ for His own. Hiemenga is certain that the first resurrection is a spiritual resurrection, because only souls are spoken of. His contention carries no weight, because the Scriptures speak of a whole person by the word "soul."[22]

In Acts 2:41 the record is that "the same day there were added unto them about three thousand souls." Surely Luke is not speaking of disembodied souls (cf. also Acts 7:14; 1 Cor. 15:45; 1 Pet. 3:20; and others.) The inconsistency of the amillennialists is quite marked when they deny the first resurrection to be literal, where *zao*, "to live," and *anastasis nekron*, "resurrection," are both used twice, and yet maintain that verses 12 and 13 teach a literal resurrection, when neither of those terms is used there. Both resurrections must be literal, or both must be spiritual. When the verb *pepelikismenos*, "struck with an axe," is used, there is only one implication that is reasonable; namely, the death that followed was a literal and physical death. Other considerations to be kept in mind are that *ezesan* is never used in the New Testament of the disembodied state, and that *anastasis,* which is used fifty-two times, according to A. J. Gordon, never occurs in any other sense but the etymological one, with the single exception of Luke 2:34.[23]

N. West cites twenty-four authorities, a double jury, on the "first resurrection" of Revelation 20:5.[24] Several will be chosen. Bengel holds that the first resurrection is a corporeal one, because the dead became alive in that part in which they were dead, in their body.[25] Kliefoth maintains that the word "resurrection" certainly means a return to life by a bodily resurrection.[26] It is the same way in which Christ Himself stated that He lived again. Steffann contends that either both are literal resurrections or the Revelation reveals no resurrection of the dead at any time in the world's history.[27] Gill notes that the passage does not teach that they lived spiritually, for so they did before. The soul never dies.[28] The sense is that they lived again in their bodies, which were united to their souls. The discussion is concluded with a quotation from Alford.

> It will have been long ago anticipated by the readers of this Commentary, that I cannot consent to distort its words from their plain sense and chronological place in the prophecy, on account of any considerations of difficulty, or any risk of abuses which the doctrine of the millennium may bring with it. Those who lived next to the apostles, and the whole Church for 300 years, understood them in the plain literal sense: and it is a strange sight in these days to see expositors who are among the first in reverence of antiquity, complacently casting aside the most cogent instance of consensus which primitive antiquity presents. As regards the text itself, no legitimate treatment of it will extort what is known as the spiritual interpretation now in fashion. If, in a passage where two resurrections are mentioned, where certain *psuchai ezesan* at the first, and the rest of the *nekroi ezesan* only at the end of a specified period after that first—if in such a passage the first resurrection may be understood to mean spiritual rising with Christ, while the second means literal rising from the grave;—then, there is an end of all significance in language, and Scripture is wiped out as a definite testimony to any thing. If the first resurrection is spiritual, then so is the second, which I suppose none will be hardy enough to maintain: but if the second is literal, then so is the first, which in common with the whole primitive Church and many of the best modern expositors, I do maintain, and receive as an article of faith and hope.[29]

Dean Alford has without a doubt the weight of scholarship with him. To recapitulate, then, the exegesis of several pivotal passages has demonstrated that the teaching of Scripture is that there will be two resurrections. The passage in Revelation adds the important fact that the resurrections will be separated by the space of a thousand years, during which time Christ will reign over the earth with His saints in the covenanted kingdom of David.

The doctrine of two resurrections—one for the righteous and one for the wicked—is, as has been unequivocally demonstrated, one of the most basic tenets in the premillennial interpretation. It is equally vital to the amillennial position to adhere to a single resurrection. Again one is confronted with oversimplification that can be destructive of much truth, while it ignores large areas of truth at other times.

The departure from the original two-resurrection position can be traced to Augustine. Homer Payne states, "If the millennium was to be set aside the thousand year period between the first and second resurrection must be explained away. Thus the general resurrection doctrine developed. The acceptance of the doctrine of dual resurrection prior to Augustine is acknowledged even by Berkhof."[30] Departure from the norm in one realm of truth usually carries with it disastrous results in other areas.

Berkhof contents himself with sweeping statements when he comes to discuss the subject of the resurrection. He claims,

> There is no positive Scriptural foundation whatsoever for the Premillennial view of a double, or even a three- or four-fold resurrection, as their theory requires, nor for spreading the last judgment over a period of a thousand years by dividing it into three judgments. It is, to say the least, very dubious that the words, 'This is the first resurrection' in Revelation 20:5, refer to a physical resurrection. The context does not necessitate, nor even favor this view. What might seem to favor the theory of a double resurrection, is the fact that the apostles often speak of the resurrection of believers only, and do not refer to that of the wicked at all.[31]

By way of comment one should observe that there was a judgment carried out at Calvary. Thus there is at least one judgment not connected with eschatological times, and it is quite some time removed from the ones indicated in the future. Too, his belated admission that the apostles often treat the resurrection of believers only, needs to be carried to its logical conclusion. That the premillennialists do; the amillennialists cannot afford to without giving away their stand. His own view is expressed thus:

> According to Scripture the resurrection of the dead coincides with the parousia, with the revelation or day of the Lord, and with the end of the world, and will immediately precede the general and final judgment. It certainly does not favor the premillennial distinctions with respect to this doctrine. In several places it represents the resurrection of the righteous and that of the wicked as contemporaneous, Dan. 12:2; John 5:28, 29; Acts 24:15; Rev. 20:13-15.[32]

First of all, it is unscriptural to speak of "the end of the world," as Berkhof does repeatedly, for the simple reason that the phrase does not occur in the Bible. An end of an age is not the same as the end of the world. The end of this world, this inhabited globe, is recorded in 2 Peter 3, but Berkhof is not thinking of that apparently. Second, he does not treat exegetically the passages that he claims teach a single resurrection. The reader is aware already of the exegesis of those points in the earlier portion of this work. When Berkhof does treat a passage like Philippians 3:11 or the passages with the phrase *"ek ton nekron"* ("from the dead ones"), he finds fault with the premillennial interpretation that makes it a selective resurrection, though he must admit Lightfoot refers it to the resurrection of believers.[33] He prefers to understand it as raised from the state of the dead. If that be so, then why is the expression *never* found of the wicked dead?

Furthermore, Berkhof denies that "a better resurrection" in Hebrews 11:35, "the resurrection of life" in John 5:29, "the resurrection of the just" in Luke 14:14, and "the resurrection of the dead in Christ" in 1 Thessalonians 4:16 would lead one to conclude that there are two resurrections.[34] Not once does he refer to the troublesome Luke 20:35 in his discussion. There is an evasion in his statement: "These expressions seem to set that resurrection off as something apart. But these passages merely prove that the Bible distinguishes the resurrection of the righteous from that of the wicked and afford no proof whatsoever that there will be two resurrections, separated from each other by a period of a thousand years."[35] Theologian Berkhof will have to present more evidence, if he wishes others to arrive at the same conclusions as he. On occasion he characterizes the premillennial view as teaching "three resurrections," but he is more accurate when he speaks of "three stages of the resurrection."[36]

Revelation 20 cannot be avoided, so Berkhof notes the so-called obscurity of the book of Revelation when he comes to deny a double resurrection in that passage. He declares, "But the supposition that the writer is here speaking of a bodily resurrection is extremely dubious . . . the terms employed are not suggestive of a bodily resurrection. The seer does not speak of persons or bodies that were raised up, but of souls which 'lived' and 'reigned.' "[37] Luke in the book of Acts was surely not speaking of disembodied souls when he mentioned the salvation of 3,000 "souls" in Acts 2:41. He was referring to individuals, even as the expression today, "the poor soul," and the like are used. They could only live in the part in which they had died; namely, their bodies. He completely bypasses the testimony of Alford.

Murray presents some strange exegesis when he treats Philippians 3:11. He contends, "It can hardly be denied, therefore, that Paul's desire was to stand up and tower above the dead round about him (dead in trespasses and sins), and to be outstanding in consecration and spiritual power."[38] May that be classed as sober exegesis? Reese has difficulties of his own with his desire to telescope the rapture and the Revelation into one. In Revelation 20 he conceives the first resurrection as an undivided unit without any previous phase. He argues,

If such a prior resurrection [he refers to the rapture which is a stage in a resurrection, not an entire resurrection, as seen in 1 Corinthians 15] was known to John—as the theory presupposes—then how is it conceivable that he would call this resurrection the *first?* John ought to have written: 'this is the *second* resurrection; blessed and holy is he that hath part in the *second* resurrection.' But that he wrote *first* resurrection will be proof to all candid readers that he knew of none before it.[39]

His contention is not valid at all: the Scriptures do distinguish between phases of a resurrection, and more than one resurrection. There may be four seasons to a year, but that does not justify anyone in taking them to mean four years.

It is quite clear to Kromminga that Revelation 20:12-16 treats a resurrection scene and a judgment scene,[40] but he mixes passages that speak of resurrection with one that does not, when he pairs Matthew 24:31 with 1 Thessalonians 4:14-18 and 1 Corinthians 15:51-52. There is not a syllable nor hint of a resurrection in the first passage; the other two deal with the rapture of the saints.[41] Returning to Revelation 20:4-6 he shows clearly that "the unbelievers and reprobate are not mentioned as also resurrected not merely because Scripture does not throw the emphasis on the general resurrection but on the resurrection of the just, but for the very valid additional reason that the resurrection of the just and that of the unjust do not coincide in time but are separated by the intervening millennial reign of the saints with Christ."[42] That is true, for the Scriptures do not commingle such diverse elements as the resurrection of the just with the resurrection of the unjust. There is an unbearable inner tension between these two that is not allowed in Scripture.

In discussing 1 Corinthians 15 Hamilton thinks he gives the reason the wicked are not in view. He maintains, "The reason the judgment of the wicked is not specifically mentioned here is that he assumed the readers will know that Christ comes to judge all men, living and dead, righteous and wicked, and that the mention of the resurrection of the righteous involves in it the fact of the resurrection of the wicked at the same time, to be judged and sentenced to eternal punishment almost simultaneously."[43] Several comments are in order. First, Paul assumed no such thing as Hamilton assumes, and multiplied thousands of saints through the Christian era have not assumed it. Second, it cannot be too emphatically stated that the mention of the resurrection of the righteous does not carry with it the resurrection of the wicked at the same time. Finally, the matter of the judgment will be treated in the next chapter. Paul has some clear words on that subject in 1 Corinthians 11, where he speaks of God's chastening of believers that they might *not* be judged with the world.

On the matter of the resurrections in Revelation 20, Hamilton thinks he has definite proof that the first resurrection cannot be taken literally, because of the mention of the "second death," which is "a term which cannot possibly, by any stretch of the imagination, be called literal death."[44] Of course, it cannot be taken to be literal death, because the Holy Spirit carefully added the word "second" to the word "death," and, furthermore, that very passage explains that the second death is the lake of fire. When spiritual death is mentioned, it is known by the additional words, as in Ephesians 2:1, "dead in trespasses and sins." That is not physical death. But where in Revelation 20 does one find a syllable of a qualifying word or phrase to indicate that the resurrection is other than literal? An adjective is found that expresses order ("first"), because there is more than one resurrection. It is first, because there is a second resurrection. There is a second death, because there was a first (spiritual) death that issued (because Christ was not received as Savior) in the second death, which is eternal separation from God. One can be sure that, when the Holy Spirit wants a concept taken in other than the literal sense, He will use the qualifying word or words that make the idea intelligible.

There must be two resurrections from the plain statements of Scripture. The just and unjust will not be raised at the same time. Their destinies are not the same, and their resurrections are not. And those resurrections are divided by the millennial reign of Christ.

Notes

[1]G. Vos, "Eschatology of the New Testament," ISBE, 2:986.

[2]G. Vos, *The Pauline Eschatology*, pp. 215-16; cf. also pp. 215-25 and pp. 226-60 on chiliasm in Paul. It is interesting that P. E. Hughes sees nothing inherently discrepant between two logically exclusive views. After referring to 2 Cor. 5:1-4; 1 Cor. 15:42; Phil. 3:20, he says, "Yet even now, as they await this great and ultimate transformation, they are said to share in the first resurrection. Plainly, therefore, there is a resurrection that precedes the general resurrection" (*Interpreting Prophecy*, p. 120). He cannot have it both ways in his attempt to circumvent a Millennium between the resurrections. Moreover, he confuses the matter of resurrection by terminology pertinent to two different transactions. He places the second resurrection at "the moment of Christ's return at the end of this age" (for the believer). The fatal error of the whole work is that there are no hermeneutical guidelines by which prophecy is to be interpreted (ibid., p. 122).

[3]A. Kuyper, *Chiliasm or the Doctrine of Premillennialism*, p. 26.

[4]G. P. Mains, *Premillennialism: Non-Scriptural, Non-Historic, Non-Scientific, Non-Philosophical*, p. 48.

[5]H. A. A. Kennedy, *St. Paul's Conception of the Last Things*, pp. 249 fn. 1, 273, 275.

[6]W. Masselink, *Why Thousand Years*, pp. 186-94.

[7]A. C. Gaebelein, *The Prophet Daniel*, pp. 198-99; H. A. Ironside, *Lectures on Daniel*, p. 231; W. Kelly, *Notes on Daniel*, pp. 247-48.

[8]R. Jamieson, A. R. Fausset, and D. Brown, *A Commentary Critical, Experimental and Practical*, 4:454.

[9]S. P. Tregelles, *Remarks on the Prophetic Visions of the Book of Daniel*, pp. 162-65.

[10]H. A. W. Meyer, *Critical And Exegetical Handbook to the Gospels of Mark and Luke*, pp. 443, 522.

[11]H. Alford, *The Greek Testament*, 1:631.

[12]A. Plummer, *A Critical and Exegetical Commentary on the Gospel According to Luke*, pp. 359, 469.

[13]S. H. Kellogg, *Are Premillennialists Right?* p. 112; W. E. Blackstone, *Jesus Is Coming*, p. 57. Cf. also A. J. Gordon, *Behold He Cometh*, pp. 203, 208-9.

[14]H. A. W. Meyer, *Critical and Exegetical Hand-Book to First and Second Corinthians*, p. 546.

[15]Vos, *The Pauline Eschatology*, pp. 223-24.

[16]H. A. W. Meyer, *A Critical and Exegetical Handbook to the Acts of the Apostles*, p. 445.

[17]C. Hodge, *An Exposition of the First Epistle to the Corinthians*, p. 326. Cf. Meyer, *Critical and Exegetical Hand-Book to First and Second Corinthians*, pp. 355-56.

[18]A. Robertson and A. Plummer, *A Critical and Exegetical Commentary on the First Epistle of St. Paul to the Corinthians*, p. 354.

[19]F. Godet, *Commentary on St. Paul's First Epistle to the Corinthians*, pp. 357-58.

[20]Vos, *The Pauline Eschatology*, pp. 224,253-58.

[21]C. J. Ellicott, *A Critical and Grammatical Commentary on St. Paul's Epistles to the Philippians, Colossians, and to Philemon*, pp. 75-76; J. B. Lightfoot, *Saint Paul's Epistle to the Philippians*, p. 151.

[22]J. J. Hiemenga, *The Second Coming of Christ and What About a Millennium?*

[23]A. J. Gordon, pp. 202-3, 205.

[24]N. West, ed., *The Thousand Years in Both Testaments*, pp. 465-71.

[25]Ibid., p. 466.

[26]Ibid.

[27]Ibid.

[28]Ibid., p. 471.

[29]H. Alford, *The Greek Testament*, 1:631.

[30]H. L. Payne, *Amillennial Theology as a System*, p. 259.

[31]L. Berkhof, *Systematic Theology*, pp. 714-15.

[32]Ibid., p. 724.

[33]Ibid., p. 725.

[34]Ibid.

[35]Ibid.

[36]Ibid.

[37]Ibid., pp. 726-27.
[38]G. L. Murray, *Millennial Studies: A Search for Truth*, pp. 152-53.
[39]A. Reese, *The Approaching Advent of Christ*, p. 81.
[40]D. H. Kromminga, *The Millennium*, p. 80.
[41]Ibid., p. 81.
[42]Ibid., p. 84.
[43]F. E. Hamilton, *The Basis of Millennial Faith*, p. 95.
[44]Ibid., p. 121.

20

The Judgment or the Judgments

The setting forth of the respective views of the amillennialists and the premillennialists on the question of the resurrection is tantamount to demonstrating their relative positions on the matter of future general judgment of all the resurrected dead. On the eschatological horizon of the amillennial position three events, simultaneous and synchronous, stand out clearly and distinctly: the coming of Christ, the general resurrection, and the general judgment. According to those holding that view, judgment in the future is always linked with the coming of Christ; since there is but one coming in glory, the universal judgment takes place at that time.

Amillennialists must go to some extremes to make the different points of their view (which do not form a harmonious system) cohere. Murray, in commenting on John 5:24, declares: "Now the plain facts are that it is possible to come to judgment without coming to 'condemnation.' "[1] That view is not built on the basis of the original language. It is a violent disregarding of the meaning of the Greek. His statement makes the passage meaningless in the context. It goes far to destroy the gracious promise therein contained. Kromminga readily recognizes that there must be "a definite order in the judgment, since the believers cannot very well be imagined to exercise their function in judging Israel, the world, and angels before having themselves received their own judgment"[2] (see 1 Peter 4:17).

In treating the matter of the judgment, Hamilton lumps those spoken of in Matthew 25:31-46; 2 Thessalonians 1:7-10; and Revelation 20:11-15 together. He thinks they "would seem to indicate that all these judgments are at the same time."[3] Do we join the cross judgment of Satan (John 16:11) with the judgment in Revelation 20, just because the subject of the judgment is presented in both as Satan? Hamilton, however, is confident,

The only sane interpretation is the obvious one that all the judgments mentioned are the same judgment, when both the dead and the living are gathered before the great white throne after they have both been raised and raptured or, in the case of the wicked, gathered for judgment before the throne of Christ. After the general resurrection and the rapture of the righteous [are these separate?], the final judgment follows at once, and the eternal kingdom is set up.[4]

Joining together the righteous and the wicked at the Great White Throne judgment, where the issues have nothing to do with believers, will not stand the test of Scripture. Read carefully Revelation 20:11-15 and you will find no one who leaves the Great White Throne judgment for eternal life. All without exception go into the lake of fire. The book of life is produced to show they never trusted Christ and hence must be in the judgment of condemnation. Then the books of their deeds are brought forth to determine the degree of their eternal punishment. But no righteous are here whatsoever. The passage gives no justification for introducing them here.

Berkhof claims that from the very earliest times the doctrine of a final general judgment was related to that of the resurrection of the dead.[5] Dispensationalists may speak of judgment in the plural, but he claims the "Bible always speaks of a future judgment as a single event."[6] The reader can verify for himself that in each judgment the issues are distinctive and each judgment is well-integrated. We may take, for example, the judgment of the living nations in Matthew 25 with the judgment of believers in 2 Corinthians 5. What do those judgments have in common? Are not the subjects different? the bases different? the times different? and the results different? Indeed, they are. There is no general judgment taught in Scripture, as the amillennialists would have us believe.

Thus we have seen that the premillennial and amillennial views, beginning with a diverse principle of interpretation, differ radically and essentially, not merely peripherally, on the great truths of the Word of God. Only the premillennial system does justice to all the biblical data.

Premillennialists differentiate in the matter of judgment. They find four main eschatological judgments: that of believers, that of Israel, that of the nations, and that of the Great White Throne. In the discussion on the church under the analysis of the premillennial system it was stated that there are three divisions of the human race according to the clear testimony of Scripture; namely, the Jew, the Gentile, and the church. There is an eschatological judgment connected with each one of those three groups.

The first judgment we consider is that of believers. The discussion will follow five particulars: the subjects of the judgment, the time of the judgment, the place of the judgment, the basis of the judgment, and the result of the judgment. At the judgment of believers, only those who have come to God through the Lord Jesus Christ will be present. The time of the judgment will in all probability be at the rapture or shortly thereafter. The participants in that judgment will appear before the judgment seat of Christ, who is the Judge in all those judgments, for His Father has entrusted all judgment into His hands

(John 5:22). The basis of the judgment will be solely the works performed after the individual has been brought to God. All those works that have been accomplished through the empowering Spirit of God and through the motivation of the constraining love of Christ with the purpose of the glory of God will receive reward. The rest will be burned up. There will be works like gold, silver, and precious stones; others will be like wood, hay, and stubble. The result of the judgment will not affect in the least the standing of the believer in Christ; but he will either gain reward or suffer loss (cf. 1 Cor. 3:12-15). That judgment is never to be confused with any other. So often grace principles are compromised in the discussion of it. It is essential to keep its characteristic features well in mind.

There is to be a future judgment of Israel, besides that of the Great Tribulation, in which there will also be Gentiles and professing Christendom. The subjects of that judgment will be all Israel who will be living on the earth at the glorious appearing of the Lord Jesus. He will take them alone, for Israel shall not be numbered among the nations, from all the countries where they have been scattered, and will bring them into the wilderness of the peoples, where He will plead with them face to face (Ezek. 20:33-38). They will be judged as to whether they will truly turn to God and accept His King. The result will be a purging of the nation, with many entering into the land to enjoy the long-awaited kingdom of the Son of David.

The judgment of the nations is also clearly revealed in Scripture. In that judgment all the nations will be brought before the Lord Jesus when He returns in glory (cf. Matt. 25:31-46). He will sit on the throne of His glory. The nations will be judged as to their treatment of the Jewish remnant during the Tribulation period, which will be an indication of the general heart attitude of the individual toward God and His purposes. The outcome of the judgment will be the entrance of the sheep nations into the kingdom, later to be granted to enter into eternal life, while the goat nations will be denied participation in the kingdom and will go away into everlasting punishment.

The last judgment spoken of in the Word is that called the judgment of the Great White Throne (cf. Rev. 20:11-15). Its features are well-marked and distinct. The subjects of that judgment are all the unregenerate dead. It will take place after the thousand years of the millennial kingdom and will be preceded by the second resurrection. The assize will be held before the Great White Throne after heaven and earth have fled away. The subjects of the judgment will be judged as to the presence of their names in the book of life and according to their works. The outcome is that all, because their names are not written in the book of life, will be cast into the lake of fire to spend the eternal ages apart from the presence of the triune God and His holy saints.

Distinction should be made here between the judgment of the nations, mentioned in Matthew 25:31-46, and the judgment of the Great White

Throne, spoken of in Revelation 20:11-15. It is the common practice of amillennialists to identify those judgments as one. That is impossible for the following reasons. The first judgment is at the throne of His glory; the second is at the Great White Throne. The former takes place on earth (cf. Joel 3:1-2); in the latter, heaven and earth flee away. The one is before the millennial reign of Christ with His saints; the other is after the Millennium. The first concerns the nations; the second, all the dead. With reference to the judgment of the nations, there is no mention made of a resurrection; there is a resurrection before the judgment of the Great White Throne. In the former there are three classes seen: sheep nations, goat nations, and the Lord's brethren; in the latter there is but one class. No books are mentioned in the first; books are opened in the second. The issue in one is entrance or nonentrance into the kingdom; in the other, those not found in the book of life are cast into the lake of fire. In Matthew, the treatment of the Lord's brethren as an evidence of faith is the basis of judgment; in Revelation, it is faith in Christ and subsequent general conduct.

One word more need be said about the Great White Throne judgment before the close of this discussion. The book of life is brought forth to prove conclusively that those have never accepted God's way of salvation through faith in the finished work of the Lord Jesus Christ; all are unsaved. Why the need of the books, then, and the judgment according to works? The purpose here is to ascertain the degree of punishment. The standard in the one case demonstrates that the subject is worthy of eternal punishment; the measure in the second determines the degree of that punishment, conscious and eternal (cf. Luke 12:47-48). We conclude, therefore, that there is no such thing in the Word of God as a universal or general judgment.

Notes

[1]G. L. Murray, *Millennial Studies: A Search for Truth,* p. 171.
[2]D. H. Kromminga, *The Millennium,* p. 86.
[3]F. E. Hamilton, *The Basis of Millennial Faith,* p. 70.
[4]Ibid., p. 76.
[5]L. Berkhof, *Systematic Theology,* p. 728.
[6]Ibid., p. 730.

Part Five

Conclusion

Conclusion

The purpose of this study on the premillennial and amillennial systems of biblical interpretation has been to prove without a shadow of a doubt that the former is the only true biblical view and is the one that harmonizes the whole body of revealed truth. After preliminary considerations dealing with definition of terms and the importance of the study of eschatology, there were noted the fundamental canons of biblical interpretation, basic for the discussion. The analysis of the premillennial system followed, giving a detailed and connected presentation of the line of biblical evidence for the position. It was seen that the kingdom was an integral and important part of the Old Testament revelation. Its realization was the great hope of all Old Testament prophets and saints alike. There followed a setting forth of the fulfillment of the covenanted kingdom in the New Testament under the personal ministry of the King Himself, as well as the rejection and postponement of the proffered kingdom. The peculiar and significant place of the present dispensation in the whole plan of God for the kingdom was next examined in depth, followed by a study of the Tribulation period. The actual realization of the kingdom in its mediatorial aspect, which will merge into the eternal kingdom of the Father, concluded the presentation of the premillennial system.

In analyzing the amillennial view, the works of the chief and recognized amillennialists were employed to set forth their distinctive type of biblical interpretation. The covenant of grace was shown to be the binding element of the whole system, which stresses the progressive character of the revelation of God. The amillennial conception of the kingdom in the Old and New Testaments was next dealt with. In the comparison of the two systems, seven particulars were chosen upon which to contrast the two views: law and grace, Israel and the church, the church and the kingdom, the rapture and the revelation, the interpretation of Revelation 20 and the Millennium, the resurrection or the resurrections, and the judgment or the judgments. The attempt was made to show that there is hopeless confusion in the amillennial view on the question of law and grace; that there is an ungrounded mixture in the opposing view on the thoughts of the church and Israel; that the church and the kingdom are erroneously identified in the amillennial camp; that the rapture and the revelation are not distinguished in their writings; that their interpretation of Revelation 20 and the Millennium is inadequate, inconsistent, and indemonstrable; that the position of a universal resurrection was seen to be untenable; and that the contention that there is but one general judgment was also shown to be unsupported by the Scriptures.

The premillennial position is not only a possible one or a probable one, but it is the only one that does justice to all the facts and doctrines involved. The amillennial view can never be accepted as the biblical one, because it disregards too great a portion that it seeks to explain. It is well to conclude with the excellent statement from the pen of Ford C. Ottman:

> The denying of a king temporal and literal cannot do other than disparage the Word of God; the denying of a kingdom temporal and literal cannot do other than depreciate the glory of our Lord Jesus Christ, who, by the common consent of the prophets and of the apostles, was, according to the flesh, of the house and lineage of David, and who, as David's Heir, was to rule over the kingdom that should have no end.[1]

It is true that the attitude of the church is well-expressed in the words of the apostle John when he says: "Amen. Even so, come, Lord Jesus," but that does not imply in the least that the church cannot with joyful anticipation look forward to the time when she will reign with her Lord, who will be rightful King on the throne of His father David and will rule over the house of Jacob forever.

Notes

[1]F. C. Ottman, *Imperialism and Christ*, p. 305.

Bibliography

Albright, W. F. *From the Stone Age to Christianity*. Baltimore: Johns Hopkins, 1957.

Alexander, J. A. *Commentary on the Prophecies of Isaiah*. 2 vols. Edinburgh: Andrew Elliot, 1865.

Alford, H. *The Greek Testament*. 4 vols. London: Rivingtons, 1868.

Allis, O. T. *Prophecy and the Church*, Philadelphia: Presbyterian & Reformed, 1945

Angus, J., and Green, S. G. *The Cyclopedic Handbook to the Bible*, pp. 180-201, 233-48. New York: Revell, 1907.

Arndt, W. F., and Gingrich, F. W. *A Greek-English Lexicon of the New Testament*. 5th ed. Chicago: University of Chicago, 1960.

Bass, C. B. *Backgrounds to Dispensationalism: Its Historical Genesis and Ecclesiastical Implications*. Grand Rapids: Eerdmans, 1946.

Bear, J. E. "Dispensationalism and the Covenant of Grace." *Union Seminary Review*, July 1938.

Berkhof, L. *Systematic Theology*, pp. 262-301, 695-738. Grand Rapids: Eerdmans, 1946.

———. *The Kingdom of God*. Grand Rapids: Eerdmans, 1951.

Bengel, J. A. *Gnomon of the N.T.* 7 vols. 7th ed. Edinburgh: T & T Clark, 1873-77.

Biederwolf, W. E. *The Millennium Bible*. Chicago: W. P. Blessing, 1924.

Blackstone, W. E. *Jesus is Coming*. New York: Revell, 1980.

Boettner, L. *The Millennium*, Philadelphia: Presbyterian & Reformed, 1957.

Bosworth, D. *The Millennium and Related Events*. New York: Revell, 1889.

Brookes, J. H. *Till He Come*. Chicago: Gospel Publishing, 1891.

Case, S. J. *The Millennial Hope*. Chicago: University of Chicago, 1918.

Chafer, L. S. *Dispensationalism*. Dallas: Dallas Seminary, 1951.

———. *Must We Dismiss the Millennium?* Crescent City, Fla.: Biblical Testimony League, 1921.

———. Notes on Second Year Theology. Dallas Theological Seminary, 1933, n.p.

———. *Systematic Theology*. 8 vols. Dallas: Dallas Seminary, 1947.

————. *The Kingdom in History and Prophecy.* Chicago: Bible Institute Colportage Assoc., 1930.

Clouse, R. G., ed. *The Meaning of the Millennium.* Downers Grove, Ill.: Inter-Varsity, 1977.

Darby, J. N. *Synopsis of the Books of the Bible.* 5 vols. New York: Loizeaux, 1942.

Easton, B. S. "Resurrection." In *International Standard Bible Encyclopedia,* 4:2562-65. Chicago: Howard-Severance, 1930.

Ehlert, A. D. "A Bibliography of Dispensationalism." *Bibliotheca Sacra* 101:95-101, 199-209, 319-28, 447-60; 102:84-92, 207-19, 322-34, 455-67; 103:57-67.

Ellicott, C. J., ed. *Commentary on the Whole Bible.* 8 vols. Grand Rapids: Zondervan, 1954.

Erdman, C. R. "Parousia." In *International Standard Bible Encyclopedia,* 4:2251 B-F. Chicago: Howard-Severance, 1930.

————. *The Return of Christ.* New York: George H. Doran, 1922.

Fairbairn, P. *The Prophetic Prospects of the Jews.* Grand Rapids: Eerdmans, 1930.

Farrar, F. W. *History of Interpretation.* London: Macmillan, 1886.

Feinberg, C. L. "Mystery of Israel's Blindness." Master's thesis, Dallas Theological Seminary, 1933.

————. *The Prophecy of Ezekiel.* Chicago: Moody, 1978.

————. "The Sabbath and the Lord's Day." Graduate school thesis, Dallas Theological Seminary, 1932.

Fitzwater, P. B. *Christian Theology,* pp. 514-45. Grand Rapids: Eerdmans, 1948.

Gaebelein, A. C. *The Prophet Daniel.* 14th ed. New York: Our Hope, 1911.

Girdlestone, R. B. *The Grammar of Prophecy.* London: Eyre & Spottiswoode, 1901.

Godet, F. *Commentary on St. Paul's First Epistle to the Corinthians.* Vol 2. Edinburgh: T & T Clark, 1893.

Gordon, A. J. *Behold He Cometh (Ecce Venit).* 2nd ed. London: Thynne, 1934.

Graber, J. B. "Ultra-dispensationalism." Th. D. dissertation, Dallas Theological Seminary, 1949.

Gundry, R. H. *The Church and the Tribulation.* Grand Rapids: Zondervan, 1973.

Hamilton, F. E. *The Basis of Millennial Faith.* Grand Rapids: Eerdmans, 1942.

Harrison, N. B. *His Sure Return.* Chicago: Bible Institute Colportage Assoc., 1926.

Hebert, A. G. *The Throne of David.* London: Faber & Faber, 1946.

Hiemenga, J. J. *The Second Coming of Christ and What About A Millennium?* n.p., n.d.

Hodge, C. *An Exposition of the First Epistle to the Corinthians.* London: James Nisbet, 1868.

———. *Systematic Theology,* 3:837-67. New York: Scribner's, 1895.

Hospers, G. H. "The Calvinistic Character of Pre-Millennialism." G. H. Hospers, n.d.

———. *The Principle of Spiritualization in Hermeneutics.* G. H. Hospers, 1935.

Hughes, P. E. *Interpreting Prophecy.* Grand Rapids: Eerdmans, 1976.

Ironside, H. A. *Lectures on Daniel.* 2nd ed. New York: Loizeaux, 1920.

———. *Lectures on the Book of Revelation.* New York: Loizeaux, 1930.

Jamieson, R.; Fausset, A. R.; and Brown, D. *A Commentary Critical, Experimental and Practical on the Old and New Testaments.* 6 vols. Reprint. Grand Rapids: Eerdmans, 1948.

Kellogg, S. H. *Are Premillennialists Right?* New York: Revell, 1923 .

Kelly, W. *Notes on the Book of Daniel.* 7th ed. New York: Loizeaux, 1943.

Kennedy, H. A. *St. Paul's Conception of the Last Things.* London: Hodder & Stoughton, 1904.

Kromminga, D. H. *The Millennium.* Grand Rapids: Eerdmans, 1948.

———. *The Millennium in the Church.* Grand Rapids: Eerdmans, 1945.

Kuyper, A. *Chiliasm or the Doctrine of Premillennialism.* Grand Rapids: Zondervan, 1934.

Ladd, G. E. *A Commentary on the Revelation of John.* Grand Rapids: Eerdmans, 1972.

———. *Crucial Questions About the Kingdom of God.* Grand Rapids: Eerdmans, 1952.

———. *The Blessed Hope.* Grand Rapids: Eerdmans, 1956.

———. *The Presence of the Future: The Eschatology of Biblical Realism.* Grand Rapids: Eerdmans, 1974.

Larkin, C. *The Second Coming of Christ.* 8th ed. Philadelphia: Clarence Larkin, 1922.

Leathes, S. *Old Testament Prophecy,* pp. 275-91; 292-305. London: Hooder & Stoughton, 1880.

Lehman, C. K. *The Fulfillment of Prophecy.* Scottdale, Pa.: Mennonite Publishing House, 1950.

Liddell, H. G., and Scott, R. *A Greek-English Lexicon.* 2 vols. Oxford: Clarendon, 1948.

Lightfoot, J. B. *Saint Paul's Epistle to the Philippians.* London: Macmillan, 1883.

MacCorkle, D. B. "A Study of Amillennial Eschatology." Th.M. thesis, Dallas Theological Seminary, 1947.

Mains, G. P. *Premillennialism: Non-Scriptural, Non-Historic, Non-Scientific, Non-Philosophical.* New York: Abingdon, 1920.

Masselink, W. *Why Thousand Years?* Grand Rapids: Eerdmans, 1930.

M'Caig, A. "Christ as King." In *International Standard Bible Encyclopedia,* 3:1802-5. Chicago: Howard-Severance, 1930.

McClain, A. J. *The Greatness of the Kingdom.* Grand Rapids: Zondervan, 1959.

Meyer, H. A. W. *Critical and Exegetical Handbook to the Acts of the Apostles.* Edinburgh: T & T Clark, 1908.

———. *Critical and Exegetical Hand-Book to First and Second Corinthians.* New York: Funk & Wagnalls, 1884.

———. *Critical and Exegetical Hand-Book to the Gospel of John.* New York: Funk & Wagnalls, 1884.

———. *Critical and Exegetical Hand-Book to the Gospels of Mark and Luke.* New York: Funk & Wagnalls, 1884.

Miller, E. *The Kingdom of God and the Kingdom of Heaven.* Meadville, Pa.: E. Miller, 1950.

Milligan, E. M. *Is the Kingdom Age at Hand?* New York: George H. Doran, 1924.

Milman, H. H. *The History of Christianity.* 3 vols. in 2. New York: A. C. Armstrong, n.d.

Moorehead, W. G. "Millennium." In *International Standard Bible Encyclopedia,* 3:2052-54. Chicago: Howard-Severance, 1930.

Moulton, W. F., and Geden, A. S., eds. *Concordance to the Greek Testament.* 5th ed. rev. Edinburgh: T & T Clark, 1978.

Mueller, J. T. "Parousia." In *International Standard Bible Encyclopedia,* 4:2249-51 B. Chicago: Howard-Severance, 1930.

Murray, G. L. *Millennial Studies: A Search for Truth.* Grand Rapids: Baker, 1948.

Neander, A. *General History of the Christian Religion.* Translated by Joseph Torrey, 1:388, 620-44. Boston: Crocker & Brewster, 1856.

Orr, J. "Eschatology of the Old Testament." In *International Standard Bible Encyclopedia,* 2:972-79. Chicago: Howard-Severance, 1930.

———. *The Progress of Dogma.* Grand Rapids: Eerdmans, 1952. Ottman, F. C. *God's Oath.* New York: Our Hope, 1911.

———. *Imperialism and Christ.* New York: Our Hope, 1912.

Payne, H. L. "Amillennial Theology as a System." Th.D. dissertation, Dallas Theological Seminary, 1948.

Payne, J. B. *The Imminent Appearing of Christ.* Grand Rapids: Eerdmans, 1962.

———. *The Theology of the Older Testament.* Grand Rapids: Zondervan, 1962.

Peters, G. N. H. *The Theocratic Kingdom,* 1:47-67. New York: Funk & Wagnalls, 1884.

———. *The Theocratic Kingdom.* 3 vols. Grand Rapids: Kregel, 1952.

Pierson, A. T. *Stumbling Stones Removed from the Word of God.* London: Richard D. Dickinson, 1891.

Pieters, A. *A Candid Examination of the Scofield Bible*. Swengel, Pa.: Bible Truth Depot, 1938.

———. *The Seed of Abraham*. Grand Rapids: Eerdmans, 1950.

Plummer, A. *A Critical and Exegetical Commentary on the Gospel According to Luke*. Edinburgh: T & T Clark, 1896.

Putnam, C. E. *Non-Millennialism vs. Pre-Millennialism: Which Harmonizes the Word?* Chicago: Bible Institute Colportage Assoc., 1921.

Ramm, B. L. *Protestant Biblical Interpretation*. 1974 ed. Grand Rapids: Baker, 1974.

Reese, A. *The Approaching Advent of Christ*. London: Marshall, Morgan & Scott, n.d.

Reid, R. J. *Amillennialism*. New York: Loizeaux, 1943.

Robertson, A., and Plummer, A. *A Critical and Exegetical Commentary on the First Epistle of St. Paul to the Corinthians*. New York: Scribner's, 1929.

Rutgers, W. H. *Premillennialism in America*. Goes, Netherlands: Oosterbaan & Le Cointre, 1930.

Ryrie, C. C. *Dispensationalism Today*. Chicago: Moody, 1965.

———. "The Necessity of Dispensationalism" in J. F. Walvoord, ed., *Truth for Today*. Chicago: Moody, 1963.

Schodde, G. H. "Interpretation." In *International Standard Bible Encyclopedia*, 3:1489-90. Chicago: Howard-Severance, 1930.

Scofield, C. I., et al. *The Scofield Reference Bible*. New York: Oxford, 1917.

———. *The New Scofield Reference Bible*. New York: Oxford, 1967.

Shedd, W. G. T. *Dogmatic Theology*, 2:641-64. New York: Scribner's, 1891.

Silver, J. F. *The Lord's Return*. New York: Revell, 1914.

Smith, W. M. "Israel and the Church in Prophecy." *Sunday School Times*, 24 November 1945, p. 927; 1 December 1945, p. 957.

———. "The Prophetic Literature of Colonial America." *Bibliotheca Sacra* 100 (Jan.-Mar. 1943): 67-82.

Strong, A. H. *Systematic Theology*, pp. 566-84. New York: A. C. Armstrong, 1899.

Terry, M. S. *Biblical Hermeneutics*, pp. 101-8, 157-66, 288-303, 313-26, 356-89. New York: Methodist Book Concern, 1911.

Thayer, J. H. *A Greek-English Lexicon of the New Testament*. New York: American Book, 1889.

Thiessen, H. C. *Introductory Lectures in Systematic Theology*, pp. 469-513. Grand Rapids: Eerdmans, 1949.

———. Notes on the Dispensational Approach to the Bible. Dallas Theological Seminary, 1932.

———. "The Parable of the Nobleman and the Earthly Kingdom." *Bibliotheca Sacra* 91 (Apr.-June, 1934): 180-90.

Todd, J. H. *Principles of Interpretation.* Chicago: Bible Institute Colportage Assoc., 1923.

Toy, C. H. *Quotations in the New Testament.* New York: Scribner's, 1884.

Tregelles, S. P. *Remarks on the Prophetic Visions of the Book of Daniel.* London: Samuel Bagster, 1864.

Van Oosterzee, J. J. *Christian Dogmatics,* 2:577-82, 794-809. New York: Scribner's, n.d.

Vos, G. *Biblical Theology,* pp. 397-429. Grand Rapids: Eerdmans, 1948.

————. "Eschatology of the New Testament." In *International Standard Bible Encyclopedia,* 2:979-93. Chicago: Howard-Severance, 1930.

————. *The Pauline Eschatology.* Princeton: Geerhardus Vos, 1930.

————. "The Pauline Eschatology and Chiliasm." *Princeton Theological Review,* January 1911.

————. *The Teaching of Jesus Concerning the Kingdom and the Church.* Grand Rapids: Eerdmans, 1951.

Walton, I. *The Works of Richard Hooker.* 3 vols. Oxford: University Press, 1836.

Walvoord, J. F. *The Blessed Hope and the Tribulation.* Grand Rapids: Zondervan, 1976.

————. *The Millennial Kingdom.* Findlay, Ohio: Dunham, 1959.

————. *The Rapture Question.* Findlay, Ohio: Dunham, 1957.

————., ed., *Truth for Today.* Chicago: Moody, 1963.

Warfield, B. B. "The Millennium and the Apocalypse." *Princeton Theological Review* 2 (1904):599-617.

————. "The Millennium and the Revelation." In *Biblical Doctrines.* New York: Oxford, 1929.

West, N., ed. *Premillennial Essays of the Prophetic Conference in New York,* pp. 78-107, 174-203, 241-69, 405-28. Chicago: Revell, 1879.

————. *The Thousand Years in Both Testaments.* New York: Revell, 1889.

Wilkinson, J. *Israel, My Glory.* London: Mildmay Mission to the Jews, 1921.

Wilkinson, S. H. *The Israel Promises and Their Fulfillment.* London: John Bale, Sons, & Danielsson, 1936.

Wood, L. J. *Is the Rapture Next?* Grand Rapids: Zondervan, 1956.

Wyngaarden, M. J. *The Future of the Kingdom in Prophecy and Fulfillment.* Grand Rapids: Zondervan, 1934.

Moody Press, a ministry of the Moody Bible Institute, is designed for education, evangelization, and edification. If we may assist you in knowing more about Christ and the Christian life, please write us without obligation: Moody Press, % MLM, Chicago, Illinois 60610.